THE
NONPROFIT
WORLD

THE
NONPROFIT
WORLD

Civil Society and the
Rise of the Nonprofit Sector

John Casey

Kumarian Press

A Division of Lynne Rienner Publishers, Inc. • Boulder & London

Published in the United States of America in 2016 by
Kumarian Press
A division of Lynne Rienner Publishers, Inc.
1800 30th Street, Boulder, Colorado 80301
www.rienner.com

and in the United Kingdom by
Kumarian Press
A division of Lynne Rienner Publishers, Inc.
3 Henrietta Street, Covent Garden, London WC2E 8LU

Library of Congress Cataloging-in-Publication Data
A Cataloging-in-Publication record for this book
is available from the Library of Congress.

ISBN 978-1-56549-529-6 (hc : alk. paper)
ISBN 978-1-56549-530-2 (pb : alk. paper)

British Cataloguing in Publication Data
A Cataloguing in Publication record for this book
is available from the British Library.

Printed and bound in the United States of America

The paper used in this publication meets the requirements
of the American National Standard for Permanence of
Paper for Printed Library Materials Z39.48-1992.

5 4 3 2 1

To my parents, Stephen and Agi Casey.
They survived the Holocaust and Stalinism
and went as refugees to Australia.
The achievements of their children are testament
to their courage, perseverance, and love.

Contents

Tables and Figures

Tables

Figures

Acknowledgments

The genesis of this book was in a course on international non-profit organizations that I developed for the School of Public Affairs at Baruch College. The course was introduced in response to student demand and built on my own expertise in working with nonprofit organizations around the world. My first acknowledgment is to the many colleagues I have worked with who gave me input into the development of that course and who encouraged my interest in this field.

A special mention goes to Fred Lane, my first nonprofit management professor back in the 1980s and later a colleague and a friend. While I was writing this book, he sent a constant stream of relevant materials, feedback, and encouragement.

Earlier versions of sections of the book have appeared in papers and book chapters that I previously published. I would like to thank and acknowledge the work of my collaborators on those projects: Chapter 5 includes text published in John Casey, Bronwen Dalton, Rose Melville, and Jenny Onyx, "Strengthening Government-Nonprofit Relations: International Experiences with Compacts," *Voluntary Sector Review* 1, no. 1 (2010): 59–76. Chapter 5 also includes text published in John Casey, "Hybrid Discourses on Social Enterprise: Unpacking the Zeitgeist," in Thomas Lyons (ed.), *Social Entrepreneurship* (Praeger, 2013). Chapter 7 includes text published in John Casey, "Understanding Advocacy: A Primer on the Policy Making Role of Nonprofit Organizations," Working Paper Series, Center for Nonprofit Strategy and Management, Baruch College, New York, 2011. Chapter 8 includes text published in John Casey, "Cosmopolitan Leadership for International Collaborations," Special Edition: Symposium on Nonprofit Collaborations, *Journal of Leadership Studies* 7, no. 1 (2013): 70–75.

The structure of the book was inspired by my earlier book, *Policing the World: The Practice of International and Transnational Policing*. Although policing and nonprofits generally inhabit different policy and institutional realms, they are both becoming more globalized in surprisingly similar ways. Some of the general commentary in this book on the context of globalization is adapted from *Policing the World*.

I have worked directly with nonprofit organizations in a number of countries, but not in the full range of countries covered in this book; therefore, much of the content is based on secondary sources. I am indebted to the countless researchers, journalists, and practitioners who write about nonprofits in their own countries and those who have done comparative work.

A number of people read drafts at various stages and gave feedback. I would like to thank Karl Trautmann for the time he dedicated and his insightful criticisms. Colleagues at Baruch made significant contributions, in particular, Cristina Balboa, Susan Chambre, Iris Geva-May, Jack Krauskopf, and Michael Seltzer. Thanks also to Paul Ronalds and Jane Dilley.

Research assistance was provided during the project by graduate assistants at Baruch College, including Samantha Adolpe, Christina Jiménez, Magdalena Mazurek, Rohan Narine, and Heather Schultz.

Students in my classes at Baruch College provided information on the organizations in which they worked, insights into the dynamics of the nonprofit sector, and critiques of the manuscript. In particular, I would like to thank Maria Arengo for the information about the Mission Society, Manuel Castro for educating me about hometown associations, and Yang Song for her attention to an early version of the manuscript.

No book would be written without the support of the author's partner. In my case, a very patient Carol Dilley has given me more love and support than anyone could ask for. In the end, she even did an amazing job of editing the manuscript.

These people have all made the book better, but the responsibility for any weaknesses and mistakes is all mine.

—*John Casey*

1

The Nonprofit World

Almost every country in the world has witnessed a boom in its domestic nonprofit sector. In the early 1990s, Lester Salamon (1994) spoke about a global associational revolution, focusing primarily on the growth of nonprofits within each country and their increasing role in internal service delivery and policymaking. But a parallel international dimension to the revolution can also be found. The following examples illustrate the reach of the contemporary nonprofit sector.

• Accion was founded in 1961 by former law students from the United States as a grassroots development initiative in shantytowns in Venezuela. Currently, it is one of the premier microfinance organizations in the world. The microlending work was begun by Accion staff in Recife, Brazil, in 1971 as part of their efforts to support informal businesses and was subsequently extended throughout Latin America. In 1991, Accion established microlending programs in the United States in response to the growing income inequality and unemployment. New programs were established in Africa in 2000 and in Asia in 2005. Currently the US affiliate has an annual income of $20 million, which is used to support loan programs in the United States and around the world.

• In the mid-1990s, a policy officer at the Australia Council, the statutory body for arts funding and policy advice, became frustrated when she found that no single clearinghouse or organization existed to help in her comparative research on how other countries addressed cultural policy issues. The brainchild of her frustration was a proposal to start an international nonprofit association, headquartered in the Sydney offices of the Australia Council, which would bring together the lead arts and cultural agencies from around the world. From that proposal, a nonprofit organiza-

1

tion, the International Federation of Arts Councils and Cultural Agencies, was established in 2000. Currently, the organization has national members in seventy-four countries. In many countries the member agency is a government department (a ministry of culture or its equivalent) whereas in others it is a quasi-governmental or nongovernmental corporation (e.g., the US National Endowment for the Arts).

• Shack/Slum Dwellers International is a network of community-based organizations of the urban poor in thirty-three countries in Africa, Asia, and Latin America. It was launched in 1996 when federations of the urban poor in countries such as India and South Africa agreed that a global platform could help their local initiatives develop alternatives to evictions while also having an impact on the global agenda for urban development. In 1999, the organization became a formally registered entity with a secretariat in South Africa. The Urban Poor Fund International is a subsidiary of Shack/Slum Dwellers International, which provides capital to member national urban poor funds. In 2010, the fund provided $6.3 million for over 100 projects in sixteen countries.

• In June 2011, the Qatar Foundation became a major sponsor of FC Barcelona, the Spanish football club. The Qatar Foundation is a nonprofit organization started in 1995 by the then emir of that Gulf state and chaired by Sheikha Mozah bint Nasser Al Missned, the second of his three wives. Its goals are to serve the people of Qatar by supporting and operating programs in education, science and research, and community development and to promote international cultural and professional exchanges.

• The Friends of Danang is a volunteer group in Pittsburgh, Pennsylvania, that raises money for humanitarian projects in and around the city of Danang, Vietnam. It was launched on Veterans Day 1998, and most of the members are military veterans who fought in the US armed forces in the Vietnam War. An unincorporated association that raises some $50,000 annually, the Friends of Danang partners with more established organizations such as East Meets West, the Vietnam Children's Fund, and the Pittsburgh area Rotary Club to help build schools and medical clinics.

Michael O'Neill (2002) dubbed the United States the "Nonprofit Nation"; perhaps the time has now come to speak of the "Nonprofit World." The goal of this book is to help readers understand the full breadth and depth of a nonprofit world in which domestic and international nonprofits are increasingly influential in policymaking in the areas of economic justice, human rights, the environment, and criminal justice. They have become essential partners in the delivery of overseas aid and capacity-building programs, and they manage international collaborations between professionals in every industry as well as in a broad range of educational, cultural, and sports programs. As the scope of their work expands, nonprofits are faced with multiple organizational, political, and economic challenges.

Globalization and Nonprofits

Since the late 1980s, the world has experienced a new wave of globalization resulting from a combination of economic and political integration, the
widespread use of new communication technologies, and cheaper means of
transportation. Whether the current globalization is in fact unprecedented in
its level of economic integration and what its impact will ultimately be are
still widely debated. Even though the current era of globalization is
undoubtedly producing startling changes, one must keep in mind that
twenty-first-century societies and structures are firmly rooted in the globalization dynamics of the early to mid-1800s, the period in which growing
industrialization transformed work and social relations, and the newly
invented telegraph, railroads, and steamships meant that the mass of the
population could more easily communicate and travel across borders (see
Box 6.3). The focus of a recently published book about transnational perspectives on philanthropy is the creation of new institutional forms and "the
ease with which ideas cross national boundaries to influence decisions in
other countries" (Mendel 2011, 405). That quote suggests a twenty-first-
century dynamic, but in fact the author of the book is concerned with the
mid-1800s and the rise of philanthropy among urban elites in countries
such as Great Britain, Germany, and the United States. These countries
were among those to first witness both the wealth and the dislocation created by the Industrial Revolution.

Some authors claim that the new globalization signals the death knell
for countries as the primary political units; however, others note that countries, as political bodies, have survived earlier globalization processes and
continue to be the strongest entities. National authority may be under siege
from global market forces and supranational and multilateral structures, but
it has been simultaneously buttressed by the continued strength of national
identities, resistance to the loss of sovereignty, and the failure to produce
global institutions that can deliver the same effectiveness, decisiveness, and
accountability as national-level governments (Bislev 2004). Similarly, competing claims are being made regarding the economic costs and benefits of
globalization for nations, regions, and even individuals. Notwithstanding
such debates about the political and economic impact of an increasingly
connected world, it is evident that the current wave of globalization has
resulted in new cross-border flows and networks that are integrating not
only economies but also political and social cultures and producing complex relations of mutual interdependence. It is a more complex but also
more connected world. Those alive during the past century have witnessed
an explosion in population and in the number and size of organizations in
all sectors. At the same time, globalization, driven by new communications
technologies and swifter, cheaper transportation, has compressed time and

space. The governance of these new realities involves profound shifts in social and political equilibrium.

In many industrialized democracies, the expansion of the nonprofit sector has developed concurrently with pressures to reduce the size of the state and to pluralize service delivery. Globalization has facilitated the spread of market-based new public management and governance approaches to the provision of public goods and services, which have fostered the retrenchment of the state and the privatization of public goods and services, resulting in a surge of contracting to nonprofits (Alcock and Kendall 2011; Anheier and Kendall 2001; Osborne and McLaughlin 2002; Pestoff and Brandsen 2010; Salamon 2002a).

But however impressive the scope of the expansion and globalization of the nonprofit sector, it cannot match the scope and influence of governments, intergovernmental and multilateral institutions, or multinational business corporations. World Vision, one of the largest international humanitarian aid nonprofits, has global revenues of some $2.67 billion annually and 40,000 employees (see Chapter 6 for more information about the largest international nonprofits). In contrast, multinational corporate giants Walmart and ExxonMobil earn more than $400 billion each. Even the private security corporation G4S, formerly known as Group 4 Securicor, has annual revenues of more than $10 billion and more than 600,000 employees worldwide. Only a handful of nonprofits are in the same league as World Vision, but *Forbes* counts some 1,700 publicly traded for-profit corporations that generate annual global revenues greater than $2.5 billion (*Forbes* 2011), and hundreds more private companies and government corporations generate similar revenue. Thousands of governmental and intergovernmental instrumentalities also far eclipse the size and capacities of nonprofits. The City of New York, for example, has an annual operating budget of some $70 billion, the equivalent of the combined budgets of the twenty largest international humanitarian aid nonprofits.

Definitions

The key concepts in this book are analyzed in depth throughout the text, but in this introductory chapter some preliminary observations should be made about their usage.

Nonprofit, the term used to designate the organizations that are the focus of this book, is the most common term currently used in the United States, the largest marketplace for such organizations, and one of the most universally recognized terms in current international discourse on the sector. The choice to use the term *nonprofit* was made with full consciousness that other analogous terms are also widely used, and indeed preferred, in different countries. In Chapter 2, the parameters of the definition of *non-profit* and other common terms for these organizations and the sector are analyzed. *Nonprofit* and corresponding terms in other languages are almost universally recognized, and many other languages have simply borrowed the English word. In Italy, for example, the trading bank Banca Prossima (part of the Gruppo Intesa Sanpaolo) describes itself on its website as "*la banca dedicata esclusivamente al mondo nonprofit laico e religioso* [the bank dedicated exclusively to religious and secular nonprofits]." This description uses the English *nonprofit* even though the Italian translation *senza scopo di lucro* (without a profit purpose) is also widely used in Italy.

The single-word spelling *nonprofit* is favored ahead of the morphological alternatives of *non-profit* and *not-for-profit* primarily for stylistic reasons, so the hyphenated forms will be used only when applicable in direct quotes or in the names and titles of organizations and publications.

Public organization refers to an entity directly under the control of governments and to intergovernmental organizations, whereas a private organization is independent. The term *private* can cover both for-profit and nonprofit organizations, but common usage tends to associate the term primarily with for-profits, and it is generally used in that sense. The analysis in this book clearly demonstrates that the distinction can be blurred between public and private and between for-profit and nonprofit, and countless mixed and hybrid entities exist. But significant differences continue to be found in the logics and dynamics that characterize the public, for-profit, and nonprofit sectors, and the distinctions between them are a core element of the theoretical framework of this book.

Organization generally refers to an entity with its own separate legal personality, but the term is also occasionally used more informally to refer either to an unincorporated group of persons organized for a specific purpose or to a project or program that does not have its own formal legal identity as it is under the sponsorship of a larger organization. The definition of an organization at an international level is also complicated by the reality that what the public might perceive as a single unitary entity may in fact be a complex conglomerate or federation of interdependent, but legally separate, organizations. They may share the same global brand and work with common policies and intervention strategies but are structured as nominally independent in order to meet local legal requirements or to reinforce ownership by local stakeholders (see Chapter 6).

Sector refers to the grouping of individual nonprofits into a collective that is identified by the organizations themselves and by others as a distinct part of the economy and society. When used alone, *sector* refers to the entire array of nonprofits (i.e., the sector as a whole), whereas smaller segments of the nonprofit sector will be referred to by their interest areas (e.g., social services sector, education sector) or as a subsector, industry, or field (e.g., the health subsector, nonprofit housing industry, the community development field).

International and *global* are used to describe the scope, impact, and agency of nonprofit organizations that breach national borders. Other terms such as *transnational, supranational*, and *cross-border* also appear occasionally, particularly when authors and reports are being quoted. Despite attempts to parse such terms depending on the number of countries involved, or whether the relations are between or across nations, significant variations can be identified in how they are used by different authors in this field (Benessaieh 2011). Perhaps one could argue that an international activity does not attain the status of global until it can claim to be truly universal (yet another term to add to the mix), but in effect people speak of the global aspirations of organizations that have no illusions of operating in all countries or even on all continents. An alternative is the term *multinational*, yet here linguistic fashion intervenes as that term is more often associated with for-profit corporations, and the label *multinational corporation* is often used with a pejorative connotation that suggests rapaciousness. There is no etymological reason not to use the term *multinational nonprofits*, but to most readers such a term simply would not sound right. Generally, *international* is the preferred term, but the other terms will be used alone or in combination (i.e., *international* and *global*) if better suited for emphasis or if a better fit for the context. However, the terms *globalize* and *globalization* are preferred when focusing more on the processes of extending the scope of work into the global arena because of their more common usage, but the terms *internationalize, internationalization*, and *internationalism* will also occasionally appear.

Cosmopolitan is used in Chapter 8 to describe the leadership of nonprofits in the international arena. Chosen because it decouples the analysis of leadership from the context of nations or territories and focuses the analysis instead on the leaders' mind-sets instead of on the physical reach of their organizations, *cosmopolitan* is also a deliberate choice to help reclaim the positive meaning of a word that has a long and distinguished history but also a controversial one that serves to illustrate the potential perils of the use of any one term. During much of the twentieth century, particularly in the Nazi and communist eras in Europe and the Soviet Union, *cosmopolitan* was often a pejorative epithet used for those deemed disloyal to a nation or regime and beholden to foreign elements because of their ethnicity, religion, ideology, or worldview. Opponents were branded "cosmopolitan traitors," and the term was often used by anti-Semitic elements as a code word for "Jewish." Recently, however, *cosmopolitan* has been reclaimed as an affirmative descriptor for those who value diversity and are at ease working with different cultures and countries.

"Domestic" organizations and sectors, in contrast to "international" ones, operate primarily within national borders. *Domestic* is generally preferred to the other commonly used terms *indigenous* and *autochthonous* because these are often used to refer to native, precolonization populations. In many countries, the term *indigenous nonprofit* refers only to those organizations that serve the original native population.

Country is used to refer to a sovereign political territory bound by national borders. The term *state* can be used interchangeably with country, although it is avoided to minimize any confusion with a subnational state in a federal system such as the United States. Similarly, *nation* is generally avoided because it technically refers to a community of a common culture that is not necessarily bound by political borders. However, as many countries, even multicultural ones, also define themselves as a nation, that term occasionally slips in. Also the adjectival form *national* is preferred as no equivalent adjective exists for the noun *country*, and the equivalent adjective for *state*, *statal*, is not in common usage. Occasionally, the term *jurisdiction* is used if the emphasis is more on the legal nature of territory.

North and the *West* are used to refer to the wealthier industrialized democracies, while the global *South* refers to poorer, developing countries. These terms are used in this manner fully recognizing that they are both geographically inaccurate (I was brought up in Australia, an industrialized democracy located in the geographic South and East) and imprecise (whichever economic indicator is used as the dividing line, anomalies can always be identified above and below in terms of metrics such as the size of different countries' nonprofit sectors or their ranking in official development aid tables). However, they are broadly accepted vernacular and are useful shorthand. Other related terms will also be used occasionally throughout the book, such as *low-*, *middle-*, *and high-income* countries, the official designations used by the World Bank and other international institutions to classify economies, or *aid-donor* and *aid-recipient*, even though an increasing number of middle-income countries, such as Brazil and India, are both recipients and donors.

Almost every term identified in these previous paragraphs is contested, and the debates about definitions and demarcations will unfold throughout the book. An emblematic illustration of the possible confusion over core concepts in this book is the term *liberal*. In the United States, *liberal* is currently used, often in a pejorative sense, to define a progressive, left-of-center ideology. But classic liberalism promotes small government and independence from the state, beliefs more commonly associated with conservatives. In Australia, the Liberal Party is the more conservative of two major parties. A contemporary iteration, *neoliberal*, is often used to denote the resurgence of conservative desires to restrict and reduce government through the resurgence of the marketplace, but few conservatives self-identify using that term, and instead it is used mostly in a pejorative sense by commentators critical of that approach. To complicate matters even further, various qualified forms of liberalism appear in the literature to parse the possible ideological range: *laissez-faire liberalism* is used to describe classic liberalism in which the market assures freedom and justice, whereas *welfare liberalism* is used to describe support for a redistributive and more interventionist state.

Is Being Nonprofit Important?

For those interested in, and indeed obsessed with, nonprofits as objects of commentary and research, how other disciplinary contexts seemingly overlook or ignore them is often a revelation. Political science dissects the hollowing out of the state and the competing policy interests, sociology analyzes shifts in collective action and social movements, and the study of international relations explores the expanding role of nonstate actors, yet literature from those disciplines generally makes little or no reference to the organizational forms that operationalize those dynamics. The "nonprofitness" of organized interests, movements, and actors appears to be of little consequence.

In contrast, in this book I focus squarely on "being nonprofit." Yet one can fairly ask which framework should be used to examine any organization. Does it really matter, for example, that scouting, reputedly the largest youth educational movement in the world, with 30 million youth members in 165 countries, is organized through a network of national and international nonprofit organizations? The Geneva-based World Organization of the Scout Movement is described on its website as "an independent, worldwide, non-profit and non-partisan organization which serves the Scout Movement." Scouting has a rich and complex history as a global youth movement that began in the United Kingdom in the early part of the twentieth century, quickly spread around the world, and has been adapted with remarkable success to very different societies on all continents (Vallory 2012). Is its legal-institutional status of any consequence? Is the fact that scout groups are nonprofit just an anecdote, an incidental choice forced on them by the vagaries of the incorporation laws of different countries?

In most countries, nonprofits complete a two-step process to fully establish their legal identity. They first create a corporate structure from the array of possibilities available in their jurisdiction and then subsequently apply to the competent authorities to be registered for tax exemptions and other tax-related advantages, including the tax deductibility of donations bestowed on organizations providing public or social benefits. This description is deliberately vague, as wide variations can be found around the world in both the possible corporate structures and the competent authority for adjudicating the status of benefit organizations. In some countries, registering and obtaining the full tax advantages of nonprofit status are relatively easy and quick; however, in others, they are nigh unto impossible to achieve. In most cases such processes lump together a wide range of organizations. The legal UK corporate structure termed a "company limited by guarantee" includes social clubs, membership organizations, residential property management companies, sports associations, workers' cooperatives, social enterprises, and other nongovernmental organizations, not all of which are qualified to register with the Charity Commission as public benefit organizations (note that under current proposals, the company limited by guarantee will eventually be phased out and replaced by the "charitable incorporated organization").

Many scholars prefer not to treat such a kaleidoscope of organizations as a single class or genus; therefore, they treat nonprofitness as an incidental legal factoid instead of a core operating and analytical principle. I contend in this book, however, that being nonprofit is important. The fact that nonprofit is the organizational form of choice for certain movements, interests, and collective actions, and that this form has witnessed a dramatic growth since the 1970s, in essence competing with the public sector and market-based forms of organization for social and economic space and relevance, makes the institutional framework of nonprofit a key operating concept.

The example of scouting is emblematic of the issues involved. The official scouting movement is deliberately nongovernmental and nonprofit. Authoritarian regimes have appropriated the iconography and structure of scouting to create their own youth movements as extensions of the hegemonic party (e.g., the Nazi Hitler Youth, the Communist Young Pioneers), but these were never part of the World Organization of the Scout Movement because they did not meet the criteria of independence from the standing government. Similarly, commercial equivalents such as for-profit summer camps offer many of the same activities but do not achieve the local legitimacy or global status of the Scouts.

Some might argue that the fact of being a nonprofit is simply the administrative means that facilitate the desired ends, or it could just be the convenient form that follows the function. Perhaps some readers may feel that I focus too much on the micro- and mesolevel organizational dynamics of nonprofits, but without an understanding of the importance of the existence of the form and of the institutional choice to employ it, the broader picture is incomplete. I do not intend to overstate the role of nonprofits or to be their uncritical booster. I am unapologetic in my normative approach, seeking to strengthen the nonprofit sector (although not necessarily to

expand it) but also to hold it to a high standard of accountability and to analyze it with a critical eye. The nonprofit sector can be an effective deliverer
of responsive services, a clear voice for its constituencies, and a loyal partner to institutions from other sectors, but it can also be ineffective, stri-
dently unrepresentative, and manipulative.

Theoretical Frameworks

The centrality of nonprofitness and the focus on nonprofits as the primary
units of analysis in this book locate the analyses and commentary at the
intersection of two key middle-range theoretical frameworks through which
I seek to integrate contemporary empirical research with grand theories of
social dynamics.

First is a three-sector framework. The existence of a trichotomy of
three distinct societal domains, spheres, realms, or sectors permeates Western thinking, entrenched in academe by the separation between the disciplines of political science, economics, and sociology. In this book, the three
sectors are designated as public (government), for-profit (business), and
nonprofit, terms also commonly used within the three disciplines to distinguish between the three political, economic, and social domains. Even
though debates are long standing about the definitions and parameters of
the three sectors, the interplay between them is a core element of modern
social inquiry (e.g., the relations between economic and political outcomes
or between public goods and private goods). The sectors are distinct but
also linked and overlapping (Corry 2010), and the evolving relations
between them infuse the analyses in the book. Classical liberal theorists
emphasize the separation between public and private, whereas poststruc-
turalists focus on the continuities and cross influence, but I do not necessarily follow either school. The conceptualization of the nonprofit sector as the
"third sector" is examined in more depth in Chapter 2.

Second is the institutional framework, which focuses on the structures
and processes that continue to shape the dynamics of the nonprofit sector
and its relationships with the public and for-profit sectors (DiMaggio and
Powell 1983; Selznick 1996; S. R. Smith and Grønbjerg 2006). These structures and processes are "path dependent" in that they are the legacy of the
political, economic, and social histories of their polity, but the resulting
institutions are now also actors in their own right, pursuing their interests
and so determining the future direction of the relations. Since the beginning
of the global associational revolution in the 1970s, the market and civic
imperatives that characterized the early expansion of the nonprofit sector
have been largely institutionalized (Anheier 2014; Saidel 2011; Salamon
2006). Nonprofits are not simply passive inhabitants of societal spaces con-

ceded to them by other actors; instead, they actively operate to reconstruct the societies in which they operate and to redefine their roles and relationships. In this book, I focus on the evolving markers of institutionalization and on the logics that drive the resulting institutional arrangements. I highlight the role of nonprofits in socialization and the creation of collective identities as well as in persuasion and advocacy. Although the preceding may suggest a constructivist approach, the analysis of the work of nonprofits also reveals structuralist-realist elements as the nonprofits seek to exercise power over other actors. To reconstruct the societies they operate in, they employ a wide range of levers.

Occasionally in the book I include passing references to the signature concepts of key social theorists and philosophers whose works are commonly cited in the nonprofit and related social sciences literature. These theorists may not have first developed the concepts or coined the terms, but they are most closely identified with them in the context of the disciplinary debates surrounding nonprofits. Arguably, the theorists most commonly cited in the Western nonprofit canon are Pierre Bourdieu for social and cultural capital and habitus (patterns of action), Michel Foucault for discourse analysis and governmentality (the art of governing), Antonio Gramsci for civil society as a sphere of conflict that promotes or constrains activism, Jürgen Habermas for the public sphere and the role of deliberative democracy, and Max Weber for state authority and bureaucracy.

I have absolutely no pretensions of writing a book in the Foucaultian, Gramscian, or any other tradition. The theoretical terms are borrowed where appropriate to reflect their common usage by nonprofit scholars, but I do not parse the terms nor enter into debates about their interpretation or the merits of their application to the nonprofit sector. Some nonprofit scholars have produced reasoned analyses of the influences of these seminal thinkers (see, for example, the contributors to Edwards 2011a; Reinalda 2011), but most simply cite the concepts as shorthand descriptors for a range of sectoral and organizational dynamics. They are used in this latter sense in this book.

This Book

I seek to offer an analysis that situates the evolution of the nonprofit sector in the broader contexts of domestic and global public affairs while offering a critical analysis of the work of nonprofits that neither overstates their importance nor uncritically makes claims about their impact.

An extensive and growing literature can be found on the domestic nonprofit sectors of countries around the world and the differences between them. Literature also proliferates on the role of nonprofits in international affairs and on their impact in specific areas such as humanitarian aid or environmental issues. However, relatively little literature exists on the links between the parallel domains of domestic and international sectors. And much of the research and writing on international nonprofits tends to focus on a small subset of large prominent organizations working on hot-button global issues and ignores the work of thousands of smaller organizations and those that work in less high-profile areas such as setting safety standards, fostering international dialogues on hobbies, or fostering student exchanges. The purpose of this book is to help fill in some of the gaps by exploring the full contours of the global reach of nonprofits. By taking this broad perspective, I hope that readers will gain a better understanding of the policy implications of the growing role of nonprofits around the world and of the challenges facing the sector and individual organizations.

In the early chapters of the book, I focus on the comparative study of the nonprofit sectors around the globe by analyzing the different national environments in which contemporary nonprofits operate and the similarities and differences between them. I then shift the focus to the international dimensions of nonprofit work. In the final chapter, I speculate about the impact of future trends on the nonprofit sector around the world.

In detail, in Chapter 2, I analyze the growth of the nonprofit sector around the world and the nomenclature used in different countries. In Chapter 3, I examine the factors that have driven the growth of the nonprofit sector and analyze the determinants of the differences between national sectors in different countries. In Chapter 4, I introduce readers to the various comparative studies of nonprofit sectors around the world and examine the primary cultural frames that have emerged. In Chapter 5, I focus on the cross-national study of three key issues in the nonprofit sector. In Chapter 6, I examine the different dimensions of international nonprofit work, focusing on the increasing cross-border contacts and operations of formerly domestic nonprofits. In Chapter 7, I highlight those nonprofits created to work on international humanitarian aid and relief, to advocate on global issues, and to foster global communities. In Chapter 8, I explore the different management and leadership challenges faced by international nonprofits. And in Chapter 9, I examine the major trends that are having an impact on the future evolution of the nonprofit sector.

Throughout the book, I have included numerous boxes with short case studies and other practical examples of the operations of nonprofits, based on a variety of sources as well as on my personal experiences. When the source is a report, press article, or personal testimony, the adaptation attempts to stay faithful to the "voice" of the original.

This book reflects the linguistic, cultural, and institutional biases that are inherent in any attempt at researching and writing international reviews and comparative studies. I read English and Spanish, as well as some Catalan, French, Hungarian, and Italian and have worked with research assistants with knowledge of Haitian Creole, French, Nepali, Polish, and Tagalog, so the sources for the book are in all those languages. However, the book is still based overwhelmingly on English-language materials, particularly those published in the United States. The United States may not have the largest nonprofit sector in terms of number of organizations (that distinction goes to India), but it does have arguably the most globally influential sector and the most prolific publishing output based on a large community of academics and analysts who work in the United States or have been educated there.

The United States has regulatory and oversight systems that provide excellent access to current data about its nonprofit sector, which greatly facilitates research and writing about nonprofits. No other country can provide the depth of information about its nonprofit sector that is anywhere close to what is readily available to researchers and the public through US organizations such as the National Center for Charitable Statistics at the Urban Institute and GuideStar. Other English-speaking industrialized countries—Australia, Canada, the United Kingdom, and New Zealand—also have relatively large nonprofit sectors (see the cultural frames discussion in Chapters 3 and 4), relatively good access to data, and active academic research communities, and strong research communities can be found throughout Europe. In contrast, most other countries have sketchy data and few researchers, and the published research, particularly in English, is restricted to a few seminal tracts that quickly become outdated (see the section on international comparative studies in Chapter 4).

Evidence of the dominant role and profile of the United States abounds. In January 2012, the Swiss magazine *Global Journal* (2012) published its first list of the "Top 100" nonprofits around the world, one-third of which were from the United States (see more details in Chapter 6). The Foundation Center in New York recently published the first report from its working group, International Funding for Human Rights (Lawrence and Dobson 2013). The researchers worked with international partners to identify over 700 human rights funders worldwide, of which 93 percent were based in the United States, with 88 percent of the philanthropic funding coming from US organizations (note that 46 percent of the total philanthropic funds were spent internally in the United States and that in most European countries, government, not philanthropy, funds human rights efforts at home and abroad). Two funders, the Ford Foundation and the Open Society Foundations (see Box 3.7), both headquartered in New York, represented 25 percent of all philanthropic human rights funding.

The reality is that nonprofits from industrialized democracies dominate internationalization, whereas nonprofits in developing countries are generally seen as recipients of the largesse of wealthier countries. In this book, I have the pretention of providing a global perspective on the nonprofit sector, but the coverage of different continents and countries is uneven. The global aspirations of the book are mediated by the limitations of the data available and of the biases of US and other English-language authors who authored the bulk of the source materials. Just as US paradigms dominate global dialogues on the nonprofit sector (see discussion of the "American" model in Chapter 5), much of the analysis in the book uses the United States as the point of departure.

But perhaps the most difficult challenge of writing this book has been the temptation, or tendency, to fall back on generalizations. The immense diversity of the nonprofit sector is emphasized throughout this book. How is it possible then to make any declarations about the domestic or international nonprofit sectors when they might have to apply to organizations that include a multibillion-dollar hospital in an industrialized country, an international federation of aid and humanitarian agencies, a rural cooperative in a developing country, an international association of manufacturers of commercial products, a touring dance company, and a volunteer group of neighbors? Many times throughout this book, the reader will think, "But surely that does not apply to . . . ?" Chances are it might not. Or it just might. Some thirty years ago, Milton Esman and Norman Thomas Uphoff (1984) noted, in reference to local development organizations, that "almost anything one can say about [them] is true—or false—in at least some instance, somewhere" (54) and that statement could equally be applied to the nonprofit sector today. All efforts will be made throughout the book to specify the parameters of the applicability of the concepts and assertions.

2

The Rise of
the Nonprofit Sector

Collective social endeavors that do not seek direct personal gain
for individual participants are as old as human civilization itself, and few
chronicles can be found of even the most ancient societies that do not document voluntary religious, cultural, recreational, and charitable life. All
major contemporary religions promote as a central tenet of their teachings
some form of contribution to the work of faith-based organizations and to
the relief of the less fortunate. Throughout much of recorded history, assistance to the lower strata of societies has depended on the largesse of religious institutions or on the noblesse oblige of the wealthy, seeking to meet
their religious and civic responsibilities, to signal their status, or to placate
the masses.

The dialectics between the church and the secular state have been central
to the evolution of charitable works and voluntary organizations. In the early
1500s, Henry VIII of England, in his fight against papal authority, ended the
power of the Catholic Church and confiscated its property. Much of the charitable work transferred to the newly established Church of England parishes,
but private charities also assumed part of the burden. Subsequently, the English
Poor Laws of 1597 and 1601 and the Statute of Charitable Uses of 1601 sought
to rationalize and clarify the roles of the state, the Protestant Church, and private charitable donations. The preamble to the 1601 statute set out the first definition of charity in English law, which essentially remained unchanged for
400 years until the UK Charities Act of 2006.

As populations grew and more secular societies developed in modern
nation-states, networks of confraternities, mutual societies, guilds, humane
societies, and other collective and philanthropic endeavors emerged in the
eighteenth and nineteenth centuries to work alongside the eleemosynary

15

activities of faith-based organizations and the emerging government institutions to promote education, health, and culture and to assist those suffering the ravages of industrialization (Anheier 2014; Davies 2014; Edwards 2009; Fishman 2008; Hall 1992). These early private associations with a public purpose are the roots of what is now called the nonprofit sector. The social and political upheavals of the Industrial Revolution and the Enlightenment were the breeding grounds for such associations, and by the early to mid-1800s, with the evolution of laws regulating charitable activities, new legal structures for private corporations, and the emergence of contemporary taxation regimes, they began to exhibit many of the structural and organizational characteristics of contemporary nonprofits. Indigenous collective organizations have a long history in every country, but the rise of the new forms of association coincided with the peak of colonization, and so the European powers transmitted their emerging institutional templates around the world (see the extensive history documented in Davies 2014).

Some of the earlier organizations continue to operate today, albeit considerably modified. The New York City Mission Society celebrated its bicentenary in 2012. Founded in 1812 as the New York Religious Tract Society, the organization distributed Protestant literature to immigrant and poor New Yorkers but soon also provided relief in the form of food, clothing, and rent assistance. The New York Religious Tract Society later joined the evangelical city mission movement founded in Scotland by David Nasmith, who visited New York from 1830 to 1831 (although not until 1866 was the name formally changed to the New York City Mission and Tract Society and then shortened in 1913 to the New York City Mission Society). It continued to operate as a faith-based, but increasingly independent, relief and welfare organization throughout the nineteenth and twentieth centuries, introducing many service innovations and helping launch new projects and spin-off social service organizations. In the 1990s, the Mission Society formally ended all ties with the church and became a fully secular organization (but apparently, in an administrative oversight, maintained its tax status as a religious institution for a number of years). In 1988, the first world conference of city missions was hosted in Australia by the Sydney City Mission (now part of the rebranded Mission Australia). The 2012 world conference was held in Jinja, Uganda. Although many missions around the world have become avowedly secular, others continue to maintain their faith-based identity.

Similarly, the Society of St. Vincent de Paul was founded in Paris, France, in 1833 to serve impoverished people living in the slums. It soon expanded to other parts of France and abroad, with international affiliates established in Italy (1842), Belgium (1842), the United States (1846), and Australia (1854). A Catholic organization, St. Vincent de Paul has a "close relationship" with the church hierarchy, but it is formally autonomous. In some countries St. Vincent de Paul has sought to create a more clearly separate identity: the Australian affiliate recently rebranded its thrift stores as "Vinnies" (a common nickname in Australia for St. Vincent de Paul).

The examples of the city mission movement and the Society of St. Vincent de Paul demonstrate that an international dimension has long been a part of the nonprofit sector. Organizations such as the British and Foreign Anti-Slavery Society and the Aborigines' Protection Society, founded in the 1830s in Britain, and the International Committee of the Red Cross, founded in Switzerland in the 1860s, are early exemplars of global humanitarian aid and advocacy organizations (Davies 2014; Schechter 2010). The Red Cross continues as perhaps the best-known international humanitarian network (see Box 6.10 for why the Red Cross is described as a network and not an organization). The antislavery and aboriginal protection societies also continue today through their successor organization, Anti-Slavery International (see Box 2.1).

Box 2.1 Antislavery International

The Anti-Slavery Societies was the common name of two related British organizations—The Committee for the Abolition of the Slave Trade and The Society for the Mitigation and Gradual Abolition of Slavery Throughout the British Dominions. Both were established in the 1780s to fight against slavery in Britain and its colonies. When that objective was formally achieved with the emancipation of all slaves in British colonies in 1838, a successor organization was formed in 1839 to work for worldwide abolition. Its official name was The British and Foreign Anti-Slavery Society.

The Aborigines' Protection Society was founded by British Quakers and other abolitionists in 1837 to protect the health, well-being, and rights of the indigenous peoples subjected by the European colonial powers.

In 1909, the British and Foreign Anti-Slavery Society and the Aborigines' Protection Society merged to form the Anti-Slavery Society International. In the 1990s, the word *society* was dropped from the name and it became Anti-Slavery International. Headquartered in London, it campaigns against the persistence of various forms of slavery, including forced labor, child labor, and sex trafficking. The current annual budget of the organization is $3 million.

Source: See Anti-Slavery Society International, http://www.antislavery.org/english/what_we_do/antislavery_international_today/antislavery_international_pdf_documents.aspx.

Despite their long history, secular, independent nonprofit organizations were until recently relatively few in number and considered a somewhat marginal element in societies dominated by the marketplace, the state, or religious institutions. In more state-centric and authoritarian regimes, independent nonprofits were regarded with suspicion and hostility, and considerable resources were expended in restricting the freedom of association and curtailing any independent civic action outside the narrow confines of activities deemed allowable by the ruling regimes.

However, exponential growth has taken place in the activity and influence of nonprofits in almost every country in the world (Salamon 1994; Salamon and Anheier 1997). Nonprofits have become central to policymaking, the promotion of civic action, and the delivery of new quasi-public services. In addition to being more numerous, modern nonprofit organizations—perhaps better described as "postmodern" (Colás 2002)—are markedly more secular and nonpartisan in their affiliations, more universalist in their service delivery and policymaking aspirations, and more professionalized and commercialized in their operations than earlier iterations rooted in religious charity, political movements, or grassroots collective and voluntary action.

The narrative arc of the history of many individual historic nonprofit organizations can be seen as a metaphor for the whole sector: traditional roots have been severed, formerly all-voluntary activities have seen substantial growth and professionalization, and the formerly marginal has become mainstream. The modern nonprofit sector has been built on the foundations of centuries of collective endeavors and charitable work, but its current size, activities, and salience make it quantitatively and qualitatively distinct from what came before.

In the current climate of ascendancy of nonprofits, one can easily forget the vehemence with which the sector was suppressed or simply ignored through much of the twentieth century, even in democratic countries (see Ullman 1998 for a discussion of the marginalization of nonprofits in France until the 1980s). Now, nonprofits appear to be no longer the "poor cousins"; instead they are considered significant actors in the increasingly multilateral, diffused processes used for the design and delivery of public goods, along with other private and hybrid organizations, including for-profit firms and government-owned corporations. For the first time in the two centuries since they began to appear in their modern form, a worldwide political and social consensus appears to have developed—that secular, independent nonprofits are a desirable element of society and that their growth should be encouraged (Hall 1992). The Arab world is often cited as an exception to this consensus, yet the Islamic Development Bank (which covers the Arab world and other Islamic countries) has for many years emphasized the importance of partnerships with nonprofits in its development reports (Islamic Development Bank 2005).

In industrialized democratic countries with a longer history of independent associational life, the nonprofit sector has expanded and become a much more integral element in the development and delivery of public goods and services. In developing countries and those with authoritarian or single-party regimes, a nascent sector has more openly been pushing against previous constraints and opening up spaces of civic participation, often in concert with authorities that previously had spurned them, though some governments may continue to constrain them to a limited sphere of approved activities. In most countries, nonprofits have become a significant part of the national economic activity and all indications are that it is a growing sector in almost every country in the world (Salamon 2010). The work of a nonprofit entrepreneur in Iran is highlighted in Box 2.2.

The increase in the activity of nonprofits is in part a spontaneous phenomenon—the bottom-up growth in social action, activism, and civic participation. However, it is also the consequence of deliberate, top-down,

---

Box 2.2 A Female CEO of a Nonprofit in Iran

Saideh Ghods, an Iranian philanthropist and writer, is a nonprofit entrepreneur and chief executive officer (CEO) in a country that few commentators would immediately associate with an independent nonprofit sector and in a region that has few female executives. She has also created successful charitable links between countries whose leaders are in conflict.

In 1991, Ghods founded Mahak, a nonprofit focused on treating children with cancer, after she saw the shortcomings in the existing treatment systems when her own daughter was diagnosed with cancer. Mahak now has an annual turnover of $50 million and runs its own hospital and cancer prevention program. It works closely with the Iranian government but continues to be funded entirely from donations.

Working with the Iranian diaspora, Ghods also founded the International Society for Children with Cancer, a nonprofit registered in the United States that seeks to reduce the mortality rate of impoverished children suffering from cancer in developing countries. This organization was the first US nonprofit authorized by the State Department to send charitable funds to Iran.

Ghods also helped to establish the Breast Cancer Society of Iran and an environmental nonprofit, the Green Front of Iran.

Source: International Society for Children with Cancer, http://iscc-charity.org.

developmental policies by governments who see nonprofits as instruments for achieving their own objectives, by the for-profit business sector seeking to demonstrate its adherence to corporate social responsibilities, and by the growing nonprofit sector itself, which seeks to perpetuate and expand its activities. No single ideology has dominated the discussions in favor of expanding nonprofit activities. Conservatives consider them a key source of nongovernmental initiative for counterbalancing state power and introducing market forces into the delivery of public services. Progressives see them as the embodiment of grassroots activism that can help ensure that social services are effectively delivered to those most in need.

Paradoxically, the growth of the nonprofit sector has been characterized as resulting in both a diminution of government through cutbacks in agencies (i.e., smaller government departments due to outsourcing) and an expansion of government through the growth of third-party agents (i.e., more and larger nonprofits working at the behest and in service of governments). It is characterized as both the death knell for the welfare state and its salvation (Ullman 1998). Nonprofits give organizational form to sentiments such as the distrust of governmental institutions and the yearning for arenas for independent action, which neither the political right nor the left necessarily monopolize. As trust in the capacity of governments to deliver services and to create change wanes, nonprofits are seen to offer an alternative pathway for addressing societal challenges. In the aftermath of the 2008 global economic crisis, nonprofits have seen some peeling back of funding and fiscal privileges and increasing pressure to demonstrate their impact. However, nonprofits continue to play a central role in the different interpretations of governance and in future strategies for the delivery of public goods and services.

The nonprofit sector is immensely heterogeneous, spanning everything from large, multibillion-dollar, mainstream, professionalized institutions that function similar to for-profit firms and have close relations to governments and corporations, to small, hardscrabble, all-volunteer organizations providing services on shoestring budgets or pushing for systemic change from the fringe. Nonprofit organizations include BRAC (originally the Bangladesh Rural Advancement Committee; see Box 6.7), one of the world's largest nonprofits, which operates in fourteen countries and employs over 100,000 people, as well as local all-volunteer organizations seeking to improve their neighborhoods or provide social and recreational outlets to members, and small member-owned cooperatives providing local services.

Definitive global figures on the growth of the nonprofit sector are not available, as no single international repository of comprehensive statistics exists (see the discussion on the sources of international nonprofit data in Chapter 4), but many studies at national levels document the increases in numbers and salience within countries. Figure 2.1 shows the growth of registered nonprofits in the United States.

Figure 2.1 Registered Nonprofits in the United States

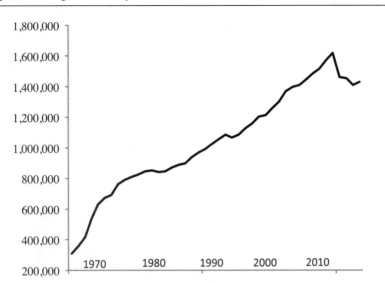

Source: National Center for Charitable Statistics 2014.
Note: Between 2010 and 2013 some 200,000 organizations (12 percent of the total) lost non-profit status because of a change in regulations. Deregistered organizations were either no longer active or were the local branches of national nonprofits.

As Figure 2.1 demonstrates, the growth may not be constant—in any country, spurts and contractions reflect the short-term impact of political transitions, economic cycles, and changing legislation or regulations—but the upward trend is the norm around the world. Table 2.1 gives examples of growth narratives from a number of countries and regions.

Despite a general consensus that the rise in prominence of nonprofits has been positive, they have not been universally welcomed or embraced, and many instances can be identified of considerable pushback against the growth of the sector. The report on African nonprofits by the International Center for Not-for-Profit Law (ICNL; 2014) cited in Table 2.1 also noted that, although some governments on that continent have developed enabling laws and regulations to support such organizations, others have enacted laws to severely restrict their operations (Salamon and Toepler 1997; see also Salamon 2002b). Some governments and elites may fear the rise of the nonprofits, as they constitute a potential threat to their hegemony, whereas other governments and elites promote a state-centric model of policymaking and service delivery that restricts the operational space afforded to nonprofits. A broad cross section of commentators of various persuasions are also skeptical that nonprofits can deliver what they promise or are critical of the outcomes of the operations.

Table 2.1 Growth Narratives

India

The number of [nonprofits] formed after 1990 has increased manifold, and the pattern of increase over the years is almost the same in all the States. There were only 144,000 societies registered till the year 1970, followed by 179,000 registrations in the period 1971 to 1980, 552,000 registrations in the period 1981 to 1990, 1,122,000 registrations in the period 1991 to 2000, and as many as 1,135,000 societies registered after 2000 (Government of India 2009).

South Korea

Since the June 1987 democracy uprising, activity in interest group politics has surged and [nonprofits] have become salient political actors that undertake public functions through private initiatives (H.-R. Kim 2003).

Sub-Saharan Africa

In the postindependence period, advocacy, development, and human rights organizations emerged across the continent. In addition, [nonprofits] increasingly played a critical role as service providers. Indeed, some commentators described their growth as an "explosion of associational life in Africa" (International Center for Not-for-Profit Law 2014).

Catalonia, Spain

The nonprofit sector has witnessed a long growth period over the past decades, which has resulted in a considerable increase in both their number and size, as well as in their social impact (TercerSector.net 2011).

Saudi Arabia

Saudi Arabian society has seen an unprecedented increase in demand for civic rights. As a result, many collaborative civil society initiatives have been undertaken to establish independent nonprofits working on public affairs issues. In response to these collaborative initiatives, the Saudi government enacted legislation that addresses the issue of registering and supervising these organizations (International Center for Not-for-Profit Law 2011a).

The greater prominence of nonprofits has also been accompanied by an increase in research and teaching about issues related to the sector (Mirabella et al. 2007; R. Taylor 2010). Individual courses on nonprofit management have been taught in various countries since the early 1900s, but the first full degree programs in nonprofit studies were not established until the early 1980s. However, since then, they have multiplied around the world. In 1971, the Association of Voluntary Action Scholars was founded in the United States (it subsequently became the Association for Research on Nonprofit Organizations and Voluntary Action), and similar national organizations of nonprofit scholars were founded in numerous countries around the world in the subsequent decades (D. H. Smith 2014). In 1978, a first international congress was held under the banner of the International Voluntary Action and Voluntary Associations Research Organization, which dissolved in 1983. Subsequently, in 1994, the new International Society for Third-Sector Research held its first congress to facilitate dialogues on research and teaching in this field on a global scale, and it continues as the primary international association. Currently, some 200 colleges and universities in the United States offer graduate degrees in nonprofit management (Mirabella 2014), and dozens more similar programs can be found in other countries. In Box 2.3 is profiled one of the many new education and research centers now being established around the world.

Box 2.3　ExCEL3 at Hong Kong University

In May 2012, Hong Kong University launched the interdisciplinary ExCEL3 project to build research and teaching capacity in the study of civil society and to help build sector capacity in Hong Kong. According to its website, "the project seeks to nurture innovation and entrepreneurship; to strengthen the leadership, management, governance, and organizational capacity of the third sector; and to build a platform that brings together philanthropists, foundations, and institutional investors with nongovernmental organizations, as well as the academic community." The project is sponsored by the Hong Kong Jockey Club.

Sources: ExCEL3, Excellence in Capacity-Building on Entrepreneurship and Leadership for the Third-Sector, and Hong Kong Jockey Club, http://www.socsc.hku.hk/ExCEL3/vision_and_misson/.

A Definition of Nonprofits

The most widely accepted definitions of nonprofit organizations and the nonprofit sector are based on a combination of structural and functional characteristics that describe the organizational forms they adopt and the activities they undertake. The Johns Hopkins Comparative Nonprofit Sector Project definition, later adopted by the United Nations for the purpose of creating comparable national surveys of nonprofits, uses the following five criteria for defining a nonprofit organization:

• Organized: It has some structure and regularity to its operations, including defined goals and activities, whether or not they are formally constituted or legally registered.

- Private: It is outside the structure of government, although it may receive financial support from the government and can carry out government contracts.
- Self-governing: It must control its own affairs in accordance with its own procedures.
- Not profit distributing: It does not exist to generate personal commercial gains, so any surpluses generated must be reinvested in the basic mission of the organization.
- Noncompulsory: Membership and contributions of time and money are voluntary and not required or enforced by law (Salamon and Anheier 1997; United Nations 2003).

A related approach is to focus on what makes nonprofits distinctive from organizations in other sectors. Nonprofits differ from government entities and for-profits because of their unique combination of production functions (they focus on public goods and benefits and not on profit maximization), governance structures (they are autonomous entities governed by members or boards of private citizens), revenue sources (they combine charitable donations, government grants and subsidies, and earned income), staffing (they include the significant contribution of volunteers), and their legal and tax treatment (most countries have specific legal forms for nonprofits, which confer a range of tax exemptions on the organizations and incentives on their donors) (Salamon 2010). As they are neither governmental nor for-profit, nonprofits have been seen as potentially combining the best of the other two sectors: the public interest, responsibility, and wide perspective of government, melded with the efficiency and knowledge of business (Etzioni 1973).

All of the characteristics ascribed to the sector have their own gray areas of definitional disputes. For example, the first criterion acknowledges that although all nonprofits are "organized," some nonprofits may not have formal incorporation or legal registration. However, it is not clear at what point unincorporated groups should be considered organizations and part of the sector, or how their contribution can be documented or measured. This distinction is a particular challenge in those societies where formal registration as a nonprofit can be difficult or expensive or may result in unwanted scrutiny by authoritarian regimes. In these situations, even the most organized groups do not register or may choose to present themselves as for-profit organizations. Even in industrialized democracies, the nonprofit sectors have vast informal components. In a 2010 report, the Australian Productivity Commission estimated that of 600,000 organizations in the nonprofit sector in that country (which has a population of 21 million), around 440,000 of them are small and unincorporated, with only 160,000 having incorporated structures (Australian Productivity Commission 2010).

Is an organization private and self-governing if it was founded under government initiative, has government representatives on its board of directors, receives the majority of its funds from government subsidies, or works under strict guidelines that determine its ambit of action? In many authoritarian countries, networks of nonprofits, created and officially sanctioned by the regime, are often dubbed GONGOs (government-organized nongovernment organizations) and, in international forums, represent the nonprofit sector in those countries. In democratic countries, governments also create or sponsor the creation of a range of instrumentalities that use nonprofit legal structures to deliver goods and services. In the United Kingdom, they are commonly referred to as QUANGOs (quasi–nongovernment organizations), and some commentators speak of manufactured organizations (Hodgson 2004). But even when organizations are formed independently, their heavy reliance on government patronage for both income and legitimacy engenders a complex debate on the meaning of independence. In 2011 in the United Kingdom, the Panel on the Independence of the Voluntary Sector, funded by nonprofit foundations, was created to analyze the debate and developed the Barometer of Independence covering "purpose, voice and action." The UK National Council for Independent Action, an advocacy group formed in 2008 to specifically counter government control of the sector, had already taken a position, claiming in an early submission to the panel that nonprofits had already lost their independence because they had been instrumentalized by successive governments and that organizations understand that their survival depends on their being fit for that purpose (Wiggins 2011). One of the first reports by the panel lends some credence to that view by concluding that many nonprofits that provide services through government contracts "are fearful of challenging government or local authorities, in case this could lead to reprisals" (Panel on the Independence of the Voluntary Sector 2012, 20). Private philanthropic patronage engenders similar debates, with many nonprofits accused of being beholden to their most generous donors or even purposely created to promote the views of their sponsors. Box 2.4 highlights criticism of the political role of government-funded nonprofits in the United Kingdom.

Unlike for-profit corporations, nonprofits must not distribute profits and cannot have individual shareholders who earn dividends from surpluses, but they can still generate considerable incomes, which individuals can access through salaries and other remuneration for services. They also may offer some form of cooperative, mutual association, or rotating credit "clubs," such as the *stokvel* in South Africa or the *susu* in West Africa and the Caribbean, which are largely informal syndicates that rotate a pool of funds among members. Professional and trade associations, such as an association of accountants or a business improvement district, which are constituted as nonprofits in most countries, may not in themselves distrib-

---

Box 2.4 Fake Charities and Sock Puppets

Nonprofits are subject to skepticism and backlash on a number of fronts. But perhaps the most virulent attacks come from those who object to their political role, particularly if the organization receives any funds from government. A UK website called Fake Charities defines its work in the following terms: "We define a Fake Charity as any organization registered as a UK charity that derives more than 10% of its income—and/or more than £1 million—from the government, *while also lobbying the government*. That lobbying can take the form of calling for new policies, changes to the law or increases in (their own) funding. Some of these organizations spend a large amount of their time lobbying the State to curtail our freedoms and not all charities are upfront about the amount of money they receive from the State. When an 'independent' charity takes a political stand or attempts to sway public opinion on matters of policy, we think you have a right to know whether they are being funded by the generosity of the public or by the largesse of the State. We think you have the right to know whether you're listening to a genuine grass-roots charity or are being fed PR from an 'astroturf' lobby group. This site exists to help you make up your own mind about who these campaigners are really working for." The Institute of Economic Affairs, a UK free-market think tank, maintains that state-funded nonprofits who lobby government create a "sock puppet" version of civil society, which creates the illusion of grassroots support causes but does not enjoy widespread support among the general public because they lobby for bigger government, higher taxes, greater regulation, and the creation of new agencies to oversee and enforce new laws.

Sources: See Fake Charities, http://www.devilskitchen.me.uk/2012/06/at-last -comprehensive-report-on-fake.html, emphasis in original; Institute of Economic Affairs, http://www.iea.org.uk/publications/research/sock-puppets-how-the-government -lobbies-itself-and-why.

---

ute surpluses, but they are created with the specific intent of improving the economic outcomes of their members.

The noncompulsory, or noncoercive, nature of nonprofits is distorted by different forms of membership organizations, including cooperatives, mutual associations, and business associations that limit benefits to members, as well as professional associations that control accreditation for those seeking to work in their fields. Similarly, many educational and social service nonprofits require affiliation or membership in order to gain full access to the benefits and services they provide, and in some countries people are compelled to belong to organizations by virtue of their religion, ethnicity, or residence.

Despite attempts to define nonprofits with normative and sacrosanct characteristics, they are not always altruistic or immune to exploitation. Neo-Nazi and terrorist groups may also be nonprofits, and any organization can fall prey to rent-seeking individuals or groups who choose to exploit them. The infamous "poverty lords" in poor neighborhoods live comfortably from the wealth they accrue through their control of funding for nonprofits in their neighborhoods. Although receiving relatively little attention in discussions on the sector, malfeasance by organizations, or by the "nonprofiteers" who use a variety of ruses to extract excessive benefits from even seemingly noble organizations, constitutes the "dark side" of nonprofits (D. H. Smith 2008).

Even the putative "helping the poor" mission of nonprofits is called into question when one analyzes the work of the range of organizations included in the nonprofit sector. In the United States, Pascuale Joassart-Marcelli (2012) noted that the majority of registered nonprofits are involved in the production of amenities that disproportionately benefit middle- and high-income communities, such as elite cultural and educational institutions. In many developing countries, the bias is often even more evident as the nonprofit legal form is used to establish separate and private provision of services for elite communities.

The Roles and Functions of Nonprofits

Nonprofits occupy an in-between space between governments and markets, beholden neither to the ballot box nor to the pursuit of profits. Ralph Kramer (1981) identified four key roles or functions: service provider, innovator, guardian of values, and advocate.

The service provider role of nonprofits is the one to which most attention is usually paid, both to understand why this sector has grown and to attempt to increase management effectiveness. The work of nonprofits is concentrated in those public goods and services that government and business are not willing or able to provide or that are too heterogeneous for government and business to adequately respond to. Nonprofit service provision generally focuses on quality-of-life issues—welfare, health, education, culture, environment, and leisure—whereas other areas have remained primarily the responsibility of the state—defense, public order, and foreign relations (although outsourcing is increasing even in these areas)—or have a stronger participation by the for-profit sector—infrastructure, energy, and communication. The proponents of service delivery through nonprofits claim that they have the capacity to be more sensitive to the needs of users and to respond in a more effective and innovative manner by providing the population a stake in the governance of public goods and services.

Nonprofits can serve as innovators to develop new projects and services as they are freed of the constraints imposed by voters or shareholders. If the raison d'être of nonprofits is the need to cover "excess demand" and "contract failure," then they must create innovative approaches to respond to the inadequacies of other sectors. Lester Salamon (1995) noted that often the nonprofit sector is the first to organize new collective goods, and governments assume responsibility for them later if they seek to extend them to a wider public, or the business sector commercializes them if marketable.

Through their social and civic action, nonprofits are seen as guardians of values, embodying within themselves, and fostering in others, the basic tenets of the democratic system, including altruism, social integration, self-help, cooperation, pluralism, and participation.

By participating in political and deliberative processes as experts, critics, watchdogs, and whistleblowers, nonprofits advocate on behalf of collective interests and help drive, or resist, social change. Nonprofits can be the essential organizing component of solidarity networks that seek to empower the population and facilitate political participation. Nonprofits help vector demands outside the usual channels, either as part of a continuing dialogue within a democratic system that complements election cycles or in dissent from authoritarian regimes.

These four functions are intertwined. In the course of service provision, nonprofits can innovate, foster democratic values, and implicate themselves in the political process. Although many nonprofits insist that they are "nonpolitical," in effect all take on some policy role, even if only by modeling desired changes. Conversely, they perpetuate the status quo of intervention strategies and funding distribution through traditional modes of service delivery (Minkoff 1994).

But the service, entrepreneurial, and innovative functions are undoubtedly less contentious than the expressive functions of advocacy, civic engagement, and cultural expression. Although many governments have historically preferred that nonprofits not meddle in service provision, the expressive, more political functions have drawn the most scrutiny and often mark the boundary between sanctioned and proscribed activities. Civic engagement and advocacy may be core to the work of nonprofits in the typologies above, but governments and political elites are often wary of such activities, and those that hold the purse strings, public and private, generally focus on the more immediate outcomes of services delivery. Public funding in many countries precludes any hint of political activity, and many private donors are reluctant to deal with the controversy and scrutiny that often result from efforts to influence political outcomes and public policy. The separation between service functions and expressive functions, whether such analysis is used to categorize specific activities or to distinguish between apolitical and political organizations, is a key fault line in discussions about the sector.

As noted previously, the virtuousness of the roles is also highly contested. Descriptions of the roles of nonprofits are tautological if they are a priori defined according to humanistic values and aims. A wider definition allows one to acknowledge that many nonprofits have little interest in promoting democratic or altruistic values. This refers not only to organizations such as neo-Nazi or exclusionary fundamentalist groups that are clearly antidemocratic but also to all nonprofits that seek to impose narrow interests over what may be considered a wider interest of the community. Moreover, nonprofits are often guilty of the same vices of which they often accuse governments and corporations, and the same market rivalry that exists between commercial firms is often mirrored in the competition between nonprofits that work in the same field (H.-R. Kim 2003). In some service areas, a small cartel of organizations monopolizes government grants and the channels of communication and consultation, and considerable effort is spent on preserving their dominant market share.

Moreover, although service delivery by nonprofits is often characterized as effective and responsive, little can be found in the research to demonstrate that they are more so than government or business entities (Anheier 2014). Many nonprofits provide second-rate delivery through underpaid and undertrained workers and volunteers. Other analysts question whether nonprofits, in fact, have innovative capacity. Kramer (1981) questioned whether innovation is a capacity inherent in nonprofits. He suggested that governmental organizations often seek to circumvent bureaucratic constraints by feeding ideas to nonprofits so that they will lobby for services that the officials want to see provided by their own administrations.

Another critique comes from the radical left, which sees nonprofits as part of the postindustrial adjustment to the crisis of capitalism and defines their primary role as entrenching the hegemony of dominant classes by providing a safe, less conflictive outlet for the "cheeky and restless" (Roelofs 1987, 2006). Rikki Abzug and Natalie Webb (1996) similarly ascribed to nonprofits a deliberate role in enabling capitalism, tracing a history in the United States of organizations specifically created to perpetuate the privilege of elites and to ameliorate the negative externalities of market economies in order to forestall the contagion of socialist ideologies from Europe. To Abzug and Webb, nonprofits historically served in the United States to mop up the mess of capitalism and to be the nursemaids of new for-profit endeavors, and they are playing a similar facilitating role in the implantation of global capitalism.

Coupled with the feminized imagery of nursemaids are the critiques that point to the gendered dimension of the nonprofit sector. It is a female-majority sector, particularly in social services, education, health, and arts. The caring mission is culturally defined as "women's work," and consequently work that can or should be done voluntarily or at low cost (Abzug and Webb 1996; Odendahl and O'Neill 1994). However, women do not necessarily lead the sector, which at executive levels mirrors many of the male-dominated hierarchies of public and for-profit organizations (Gibelman 2000; see also Box 3.9 on female employment in the nonprofit sector).

Such radical critiques are certainly not restricted to the United States, with commentators in other countries also asserting that the rise of the nonprofit sector diverts potential threats to the hegemony of current elites into "nonreformist reforms" that reinforce charity safety-net approaches and undermine attempts at structural reforms. In the developing world, critical analyses see nonprofits—usually defined in terms of bourgeoisie, elite nongovernmental organizations (NGOs)—as either, or both, ineffective or malevolent instruments of neocolonialism and neoliberalism (see the discussion on critiques of development in Chapter 7). Yet debates continue about whether even seemingly restricted spaces for mobilizations do in fact open up possibilities for actions that engender more profound structural changes in political systems (Bond 2008).

Classifying Nonprofits

Some researchers distinguish between member-serving nonprofits (e.g., self-help or mutual aid) from public-serving nonprofits (Anheier 2005, 2014), whereas others focus on the differences between service functions (direct provision of health, education, or welfare) and expressive functions (cultural expression, interest representation, or advocacy) (J. Douglas 1987; Salamon and Sokolowski 2010). Other classifications focus on whether nonprofits are primary service providers, secondary associations of providers, or tertiary associations of providers. Other classifications are based on whether the primary income of an organization is from philanthropy, from service contracts, or from entrepreneurial commercial activities (Hansmann 1980, 1987).

However, in order to encompass the whole range of possible organizations in the nonprofit sector, the tendency has been to create taxonomies based on organizations' subsectoral functions or focuses. The Johns Hopkins Comparative Nonprofit Sector Project (Salamon 1999; Salamon and Anheier 1997; United Nations 2003) built on existing national classification systems to create the International Classification of Nonprofit Organizations. This classification is the one currently used by the United Nations:

- Group 1: Culture and Recreation
- Group 2: Education and Research
- Group 3: Health
- Group 4: Social Services
- Group 5: Environment

• Group 6: Development and Housing
• Group 7: Law, Advocacy, and Politics
• Group 8: Philanthropic Intermediaries and Voluntarism Promotion
• Group 9: International Activities
• Group 10: Religion
• Group 11: Professional Associations and Unions
• Group 12: Not Elsewhere Classified

This classification is increasingly used as the international standard, although many countries continue to use their own earlier classifications enshrined in legislation or regulations, such as the US National Taxonomy of Exempt Entities (NTEE) and the Mexican classification of *donatarias autorizadas* (organizations authorized to receive tax-deductible donations). All such taxonomies present their own problems of application: some nonprofits do not easily fit the criteria for any one category, and others work in more than one sector. For example, Greenpeace, the international environmental advocacy organization, could be classified in either Group 5 or Group 7, or both, of the International Classification of Nonprofit Organizations, and if a union offers training programs, then it can be classified in both Group 2 and Group 11. Despite such disadvantages—and without entering into debates over the advantages of any one system over another—such classifications at least serve the function of offering a comprehensive overview of the array of organizations in the sector.

Notably, religious institutions, labor unions, and political parties are often excluded from discussions of the nonprofit sector (even though they are independent, voluntary, and nondistributory), particularly when they are engaged in their core activities of religious worship, representation of workers' rights, and the pursuit of political power. However, when they take on a wider range of activities, either through their existing structures or through affiliated organizations, they are then usually considered part of the nonprofit sector. The Salvation Army is a particularly intriguing example of a religious organization that is also one of the largest providers of social assistance around the world. Currently operating in 124 countries, the Salvation Army is one of the largest domestic social service organizations in many of them.

Similarly, the provision of education to workers and their communities crosses many organizational boundaries. Box 2.5 profiles the international federation that represents such organizations and demonstrates the complexities involved in classifying their structures and activities, both domestically and internationally.

Adding further complexities in classifying nonprofits are the various fault lines, real or perceived, that exist within the sector in any polity. The most common division is between larger professional, commercialized non-

---

Box 2.5 The International Federation of Workers' Education Associations

---

The International Federation of Workers' Education Associations (IFWEA) is the international organization responsible for the development of workers' education. Member organizations include national and international trade unions, independent workers' educational associations, NGOs, and foundations engaged in the provision of adult educational opportunities for workers and the communities in which they live throughout the world.

The IFWEA was established by the UK Workers' Educational Association in 1945, building on decades of bilateral contacts and a number of unsuccessful attempts in the 1920s to re-create an international federation that had succumbed to the rise of fascism in Europe. The goal of the new federation was to support the rebuilding of workers' education in postwar Europe. It later extended its reach, but membership continued to be constrained by the Cold War. Since the fall of the Soviet Union, it has expanded to all parts of the world and currently has more than 100 affiliates in some sixty-five countries. The part-time secretariat of the IFWEA was originally headquartered in London but was moved to Cape Town, South Africa, in 2007, where it is hosted by the Labour Research Service, a nonprofit organization affiliated with the South African labor unions.

Many IFWEA member organizations work under very difficult conditions, particularly where workers' rights are routinely violated or threatened. In these circumstances, IFWEA responds to requests for support from members facing repression or attack. Coordination of such solidarity makes up an important part of IFWEA's responsibilities. IFWEA, along with its partner organizations in the international trade union movement and labor-related development agencies, plays an important role in bringing together labor organizations in the global North and South, initiating development programs, and building new partnerships between trade unions and labor NGOs.

Source: See International Federation of Workers' Education Associations, http://www.ifwea.org/about-ifwea/ifwea-s-origins-history/.

---

profits and smaller community-based, primarily volunteer, organizations. In most jurisdictions, and in most subsectors, there is a small clutch of behemoth nonprofits that move the majority of funds in the sector, and a huge base of minnow organizations. In the United States for example, some 80 percent of registered nonprofits have an annual income of less than $100,000 to pay for at least one full-time employee, rented premises, and operational funds, which the vast majority of nonprofits fall below and operate only with part-time staff or volunteers. At the other end of the scale are the multibillion-dollar nonprofits, including the elite universities, large hospital conglomerates, and megacharities such as Goodwill Industries and the American Red Cross.

Whatever income threshold is used in any country to define a "live" operating organization (in many countries, an organization with a $100,000 annual income would be considered wealthy), the reality is that the large majority of registered organizations fall below it and operate only as a part-time, secondary activity of those involved. In every country, a small leading minority of organizations manages the vast majority of the economic activity of the sector, which often leads to concerns about nonprofit plutocracies or oligarchies that control fund-raising and sector-related policy development. These large organizations tend to dominate debates about the sector and are the ones that have the resources to actively and consistently participate in policy discussions. The demographic pyramid of the sector in any country is shaped more like an upturned thumbtack or pushpin, with a thin spike representing the small minority of large entities with considerable economic and social clout, balancing on a wide base of small organizations with legal identities but few, if any, full-time staff.

Outside this world of formal organizations is an even larger universe of informal associations and unincorporated organizations, as well as projects operating under the legal and fiscal sponsorship of other organizations, sometimes characterized as the grassroots front line of the sector. This informal sector includes groups as diverse as concerned neighbors who work together to improve local amenities, local sewing circles that serve primarily as a social outlet for members but also donate some of their outputs to local charities, and caste, clan, or kinship networks that create a mutual pool of funds to support entrepreneurial activities.

Estimates of the number of the unincorporated organizations are speculative at best. As noted earlier, the Australian Productivity Commission (2010) estimated that three times as many unincorporated organizations as incorporated ones exist in that country, but the commission conceded that little information is available on organizations that have chosen not to incorporate and that any estimates should be treated with caution. Even in the United States, where counts of registered organizations are fairly reliable, Michael O'Neill (2002) noted that when discussing informal organizations, "no one really knows how many [there are]." David Horton Smith (1997) argued that informal organizations are the "dark matter" that observers tend not to notice, even though in their aggregate they may have more economic and social impact than the formal sector. Considerable churning has taken place in the sector as new organizations are constantly being created and others disappear. The focus of policymaking and research tends to be on the larger organizations, but the smaller organizations that often fly under the radar and cling precariously to their continued existence may in fact be making contributions that are just as important to the collective goals of the sector, particularly in those countries where the sector is small, emerging, and somewhat under siege by a ruling elite wary of any independent organizing of its citizens.

Even though differences in size and political and economic clout are crucial, many other fault lines divide the sector. Differences are evident between the various industry subsectors, some of which may have little common ground between them (do local sports leagues have common interests with organizations promoting cultural identity?). But perhaps most important is the division between the "insiders" and "outsiders"—the organizations that enjoy the political and financial support of the decision-makers, the wealthy, and the influential, and those that do not (Grant 1995).

The Third Sector

The concept of a distinct third sector emerges from the analyses that separate government from nongovernment and for-profit from nonprofit. By convention, government is identified as the first sector, business as the second, and nonprofit as the third. The three sectors are also often characterized as "the Prince, the Merchant, and the Citizen" (Najam 1996).

Although the contemporary use of the term *third sector* can be traced back to the work of sociologists and organizational theorists in the 1960s and 1970s, particularly Amatai Etzioni (1967, 1973), its widespread recognition as a collective term for nonprofits is largely a result of its use in the US *Report of the Commission on Private Philanthropy and Public Needs* (see Filer Commission 1975). The third sector was defined by the commission by what it is not:

> It is not government—that is, its component organizations do not command the full power and authority of government, although some may exercise powerful influences over their members and some may even perform certain functions of government. . . . On the other hand, the [third sector] is not business. Its organizations do not exist to make profit and those that enjoy tax immunities are specifically prohibited from doing so, although near the boundaries of the sector many groups do serve primarily the economic interests of their members. (Filer Commission 1975, 31)

Beyond these three formal institutional sectors, some scholars identify a fourth sector, one that is made up of the more informal relationships within the family, among friends, and in a community (Offe 2000; Streek and Schmitter 1986; Van Til 2008), and debates occur over the order and hierarchy of the sectors. Wolfgang Streek and Philippe Schmitter (1986) suggested that community has always been one of the traditional three sectors and that "associations" are emerging as a new, fourth sector. The traditional three sectors can be associated with ideal models of society—the state with hierarchical control, the market with dispersed competition, and the community with spontaneous solidarity—and now a new model of organizational cooperation is being added through the emerging associations. Streek and Schmitter maintained that the history of democratic, industrialized societies consists of two main periods: the expansion of markets into preexisting communities in the nineteenth century and the expansion of the interventionist state into the market economy in the twentieth. In both of these periods, independent associations of all kinds were seen as impediments to the development of free markets and to the growth of the democratic state. This tendency to frame discussion of the nonprofit sector in terms of the actual or potential dysfunction of the others has continued to dominate debates.

The concept of a distinctive associative order that seeks to counterbalance other societal forces is not a product of contemporary social and political thought or practice. Early socialist theorists such as Claude Henri de Saint-Simon promoted the idea of "associationism" in the 1830s as an alternative to capitalism and antagonism, and Émile Durkheim spoke in the late 1800s of "organic solidarity" (primarily of occupational groups but also of other civil organizations) and its role in checking the excesses of both individual passions and oppressive bureaucracy. The notion of a third sector is based on a long tripartite theoretical tradition, but current discourse redefines the third sector in terms of nonprofit relations to the state and markets. The characteristic form of relations in the third sector is not the authority and hierarchy of governments and bureaucracies, nor is it driven by the market forces of the business sector, but instead it functions in a more horizontal manner and is primarily mission driven (Khagram, Riker, and Sikkink 2002).

A common visual representation of the sectors is a simple Venn diagram with three overlapping circles representing the institutional domains— government/state (first sector), markets (second sector), nonprofits (third sector)—and occasionally with a fourth circle to represent the family or community. Each sector has its prescribed roles and logics. The market creates economic wealth and provides private goods. Government provides and oversees public goods such as defense, basic infrastructure, and the rule of law and social services. Community and family provide identities, social networks, and support. Nonprofits have historically helped to fill in gaps left by the other sectors and to point out their failures. The evolution of modernity can be analyzed using the framework of the continuing search for a balance and compromises between the marketplace, the centralized state, associative action, and community realms as they vie for the blessing and loyalty of the population. A quick characterization of the global sectorial shifts notes that the nineteenth century was marked by the emergence and increasing dominance of private for-profit firms, the twentieth century by the rise of the state, and the beginning of the twenty-first century by the expansion of the nonprofit sector and socially responsible businesses.

That narrative of the rise of the third sector and its growing role in what might be considered to be government functions is both country and time bound, and it reflects pendulum swings in the relative size and salience of the government and philanthropy. In the 1970s in the United States, the Filer Commission (1975) noted "the growing role of government in what have been considered philanthropic activities" (16), and even in more state-centric Sweden, similar concerns arose that government was co-opting associations and taking over their functions (Boli 1992). In contrast, in developing countries, particularly ones with no fully functioning government, nonstate organizations, including informal local associations, international nonprofits, and even armed militias and criminal gangs, may provide the only semblance of formal social institutions.

Whether identified as a third or fourth sector, nonprofits occupy the definitional frontier between public institutions, the private marketplace, and family and community structures. Clear definitions are elusive and the various attempts to find neat fault lines between the sectors have only served to underline the demarcation challenges (see, for example, the section on social enterprise in Chapter 5).

Civil Society

Another term that needs early clarification is *civil society*, which will appear frequently throughout this book as the general equivalent of the nonprofit sector. The term dates back to ancient Greek and Roman philosophers, who considered a *koinonia politike* and *societas civilis* one in which good citizenship collectively shapes the nature of a society, referring to both the state and nonstate elements of a society (Götz 2010). In later eras, the focus of the discourse shifted to nonstate social structures, and debates have long taken place about the "civility" of nonstate social structures and the nature of the relationship between civil society (as associations, families, and individuals) and the state (Beng-Huat 2003; Muukkonen 2009; Van Til 2008). Through philosophical debates, ideological disputes, armed revolts, and nonviolent resistance, people have long sought to define the rights and obligations of citizens in societies in which power, whether nominally state or civil, was generally concentrated in the hands of small elite groups of enfranchised males (the monarchs, nobles, clergy, military, and wealthier landowners and merchants). The continuing struggles for freedom from the arbitrary oppression of rulers and for the freedom of association and assembly have been central to the establishment of an independent civil society.

Unlike the concept of the third sector, which focuses on organizational structures, civil society is primarily conceived as the "space" or "sphere" between the market, state, and family in which people organize, uncoerced, to pursue their interests (Edwards 2009; Van Til 2008; Walzer 1998). The parameters of this space are contested, with some commentators including for-profit corporations or familial networks in civil society, although most exclude both for-profit activities and family ties from their analyses. The goals are equally contested with some focusing on how the role of civil society is to build a "good" and democratic society, whereas others simply focus on the organized interests, whatever their ends (see the discussions in Cheema 2010; Colás 2002; Eberly 2008; Edwards 2009; Florini 2000; Fowler 2012; Kaldor 2000; Walker and Thompson 2008).

However, to organize, people need organizations. Most commentary about civil society as a conceptual realm is almost always immediately conflated with discussions of the role of civil society organizations. These are defined, similarly to nonprofits, as "private, voluntary associations, from neighborhood committees to interest groups and philanthropic enterprises" (Foley and Edwards 1996, 38). Analyses of civil society therefore generally focus on the role of its organizations in creating civic culture, promoting prodemocratic attitudes and citizen participation, and developing a pluralist base for political action and self-organization. Civil society, conceived either as a space or an array of organizations, is seen as both an impetus for democratic governance and a catalyst for change against a tyrannical government (Foley and Edwards 1996).

Two primary lines of reasoning can be found concerning the relationship between civil society and democratic political practice. The first considers that civil society organizations create social capital as schools for citizenship that teach democratic culture and foster trust and civil engagement (Putnam 1993). The second sees them as generating political capital by promoting pluralism. At the same time, proponents of both lines of reason acknowledge that civil society organizations can impede democratic consolidation when they are "narrow in scope, chauvinistic in content, stereotypical in form, and constructed around homogenizing impulses" (Farouk 2011, 93).

The political changes in the former Soviet Bloc countries of Eastern Europe in the late 1980s brought civil society into vogue as the descriptor for the burgeoning dissident movements and organizations that played a key role in the transitions to democracy. As a consequence, the term is now more often used in the context of emerging democracies and developing nations. But is a strong civil society an a priori condition of democracy or a

consequence of it? Michael Walzer (1992) postulated a "civil society paradox": a strong democratic civil society requires a strong democratic state.
The relationship between social and political capital can be causal, in both
directions, but it also can be substitutory (associative participation replaces
political participation) or even independent (one can be an active participant in associations that focus on one's own particular interests but disdain-
ful of those that seek to deliver wider public goods or of those that are traditional political institutions).

In *The Myth of Civil Society* (Encarnación 2003), Spain is characterized
as a country with a strong democracy but a weak civil society; in contrast,
Brazil is seen as having a weak democracy but a strong civil society (note that
although the book was written quite recently in the scheme of things, the situation in both countries has shifted significantly since then, with the strengthening of civil society in Spain and of democracy in Brazil). In *Exploring Civil
Society: Political and Cultural Contexts* (Glasius, Lewis, and Seckinelgin
2004), various authors posited that Western Europe and the United States are
rediscovering civil society; in Africa, civil society is the spearhead of neocolonialism; and in the Middle East, it represents hope for emancipation (the book
was written nearly a decade before the upheavals of 2011).

During the so-called Arab Spring of 2011, early commentators focused
on the role of civil society in building and maintaining the movements that
ousted one regime after another. But as this book is being published, the
evolution of the situation in many Arab countries clearly demonstrates that
the factionalism engendered by strong civil society organizations can be a
barrier to establishing pluralist democratic institutions. The Arab Spring
and the earlier color revolutions in former Soviet Union republics also
demonstrate how rapidly a country can switch from being characterized as
having a weak civil society, based on metrics that suggest low formal mem-
berships and frail organizations beholden to the state, to one characterized
as having a strong civil society of citizens willing to mobilize against corrupt or authoritarian regimes.

The emphasis of the civil society discourse on dissidence in transitional
countries provides the basis to query the generally positive, normative, and
heuristic analysis associated with its democratizing role. If civil society
actually exits, what would then be considered uncivil society (Bob 2011)?
(Note that morphology of the word *civil* is in itself useful here as one cannot as tidily posit an "un-nonprofit" or an "un-third" sector.) In authoritarian and transitional countries, external observers may laud the actions of
civil society organizations, but the domestic authorities are certainly more
wary and often regard them as destabilizing and even as enemies of the
state. Authoritarian regimes work actively to contain civil society actions
within narrow boundaries of approved, benign actions—often through a
discourse around the need for civic, not civil, organizations that collaborate

with the state to create an orderly society rather than engage in adversarial or competitive activities. As James Richter and Walter Hatch (2013) documented, Russia and China promote civil society to provide more efficient and effective delivery of public goods, as well as to help legitimize their regimes to their own citizens and to the international community. Both regimes manage the seeming contradiction between autocracy and civil society by promoting a network of GONGOs to create a regime-sponsored civil space, and they deploy an extensive repertoire of regulations, revenue controls, surveillance, and repression to ensure that more independent organizations to do not transgress acceptable boundaries.

Even in stable, prosperous democracies one can question whether the factional self-interest of some civil society organizations is creating uncivil, undemocratic dynamics. The prosperous and powerful have greater capacity to organize around their own interests, so the better-resourced factions can often appropriate civil society to push their agendas without the accountability associated with other democratic processes.

Whichever approach to civil society one is focusing on, the question of whether or not it can be equated with the nonprofit sector depends largely on the nature of the polity being examined. The concept of the nonprofit certainly does not capture the full essence of dissident movements such as Poland's Solidarność in the 1980s and is even less useful when discussing the armed militias of the Arab Spring. The use of the term *civil society* to describe dissidents and combatants evokes realms of action far beyond what most people think of when speaking of nonprofits. But once authoritarian regimes are overthrown, or they open spaces, however restricted, for the operation of independent organizations, the relationships between the terminologies become more complicated. Even before the Muammar Qaddafi regime was fully liquidated, the former opposition both established itself as the new legitimate government and spawned numerous new NGOs. Reports quickly emerged of the establishment of Libyan nonprofits in the liberated zones, and posttransition commentary often emphasized the key role played by these new local organizations and international nonprofits (see, for example, Applebaum 2012).

In countries where democracy is still nascent or continues to be uncertain, the term *civil society organization* is a useful operating concept that helps focus on dissidence from an authoritarian state. The term may continue to be used even when democracy is consolidated in order to underline the independence of the organizations, even as they start to take on more establishment roles in structured, government-sponsored service delivery and policy dialogues, rendering them more like the nonprofit sector in already-consolidated democracies.

The focus on dissidence and opposition to authoritarian regimes has imbued the term with a certain progressive aura. However, a conservative bent for civil society is reemerging, particularly in the English-speaking industrialized democracies. The Conservative Party–Liberal Democrat coalition that won government in 2010 in the United Kingdom argued through its Big Society rhetoric that social responsibilities that had been borne by the state should instead be in the hands of the citizenry and private sector. Prime Minister David Cameron specifically pointed to the need for civil society organizations to take more responsibility for the provision of public goods and services, with less government "involvement" (i.e., less government oversight and funding) and more volunteers and philanthropic support. Similar sentiments in favor of smaller government have been expressed in Australia by the conservative Liberal Party (although the Australian Liberals seem to deliberately avoid any reference to the UK Big Society debate). These conservative parties see personal initiative and market forces as the drivers of social action, an approach most often associated with neoliberal ideologies (see the discussion in Chapter 5 on neoliberalism and the Americanization of the nonprofit sector), and they specifically opt for the language of civil society to express this ideology. The coalition government in the United Kingdom changed the name of the Labour government cabinet-level Office of the Third Sector to the Office for Civil Society, and the Liberal Party in Australia has stated that it favors the term *civil society* to describe the sector because of the "broader role" that sector should be playing in providing public goods and services (Andrews 2012).

Nomenclature

As indicated in Chapter 1, the term *nonprofit* was chosen as the primary term to be used in this book because it is currently widely recognized as both a concept and descriptor in most countries, either in its English form or in its translation into other languages. All countries have some form of special incorporation or registration for organizations that can demonstrate that their activities generate a public benefit or common social good. These organizations can generate revenues but they cannot distribute any surpluses or profits, and instead of shareholders, they have some form of voluntary stewardship without pecuniary interests (unless members are also salaried employees). In exchange, these organizations usually receive fiscal advantages such as the exemption from certain taxes and fees and the conferring to donors the right to deduct some portion of the value of their contributions from the income they declare for taxation. Although the general concept of a nonprofit organization that delivers a public benefit is universal, the definition of the nondistribution restriction, the extent of tax exemptions, the tax deductibility of (or other incentives for) donations, and the ease of entry into the category differ considerably between countries (see the section in Chapter 3 on regulatory and institutional environments).

But *nonprofit* is a relative neologism, with the early research in English on the sector tending to favor the term *voluntary*, even in the United States (Robertson 1966; C. E. Smith and Freedman 1972; D. H. Smith 2012). Until the newer term came fully into vogue in the late 1970s, few people used the collective concept *nonprofit*—or the other terms analyzed below—but instead spoke of human services organizations, hospitals, or cultural organizations as separate entities, which had little in common (Frumkin 2005; Hall 1992). With the increase in the number and influence of these organizations, awareness that they constitute a sector of organizations with comparable goals and structures has increased. However, a unanimous nomenclature for this sector continues to elude professionals and researchers, and in its place continues to be a veritable potpourri of terms and definitions. The terms *third sector* and *civil society* have already been analyzed in this chapter, but numerous other terms are commonly used throughout the world, and their use varies considerably between countries. Moreover, a gap often can be found between the use of the lexicon by cognoscenti and by the general public. Few professionals in this field have not been confronted by someone who has scoffed, "I know some nonprofits that seem to make a lot of money," and had to patiently explain that the term refers not to the ability to generate surplus revenues but to the restrictions on their distribution.

In the following survey of the terms, I do not seek to define them but instead to lay out the parameters of their usage and indicate some of the debates around them. They convey overlapping concepts that can be differentiated according to the varying legal frameworks, degrees of separation from the state, participatory values, management styles, and the diverse political, economic, and social roles they imply. Some authors identify a hierarchy in which some of the terms are subsets of the broadest terms such as *third sector* (see, for example, Lewis 2007), whereas others refer to them as a roughly equivalent "family of concepts" (Muukkonen 2009). In common vernacular they are often used almost interchangeably, in effect creating a set of metonymies in which each single term is used as a substitute for the others. The choice of term depends as much on the custom of a country and the emphasis that one seeks to convey as on any purely academic or semantic definition. Each term has its own baggage and the nuances of meaning continue to be important for highlighting different approaches—as evidenced throughout this book—but considerable disorder can also be found in their definitions and use. Along with the previously cited terms *nonprofit, third sector*, and *civil society*, the terms most widely used to describe the sector are outlined below.

The term *charity* emphasizes the work with the poor and needy through the delivery of services and direct subsidies designed to lift people out of poverty or to relieve hardship. It is a traditional designation and often a key definition in legislation that regulates the sector (the English law known as the Statute of Charitable Uses of 1601 is widely acknowledged as a legal foundation for many of the "charity laws" around the world). As a descriptor for an organization or activity, the term is now considered somewhat dated and demeaning, as it is deemed to describe a more paternalistic form of assistance that has been superseded by more contemporary developmental and entrepreneurial approaches. However, it continues as a legal definition and is still common in public vernacular.

The terms *community* or *community-based* emphasize a link with citizens and the community service aspects. It is a common descriptor for the sector in the United Kingdom and Canada and is also widely used in Australia and New Zealand. In the United States, it is used primarily to designate smaller, more locally based organizations.

The term *nongovernmental organization* emphasizes the separation and independence from government. Its acronym, *NGO,* is perhaps the most widely used generic shorthand to describe nonprofits working in all fields, although in many countries a tendency can be found to equate NGO as an idea with international nonprofits, particularly humanitarian aid and advocacy organizations (see the discussion of international nomenclature in Chapter 6).

Social enterprise emphasizes the entrepreneurial and businesslike approach. A relatively new term, it has been adopted by the sector primarily since the late 1990s. Although some analysts define a social enterprise as a private commercial business with a social mission (and so outside the nonprofit sector), *social enterprise* is also increasingly used as a descriptor in the nonprofit sector to emphasize the new business-oriented managerial approach of many organizations (see the discussion on social enterprise in Chapter 5).

Voluntary emphasizes the noncompulsory, voluntary nature of participation in organizations and also reflects the extensive use of both volunteers and private, voluntary donations. It was previously in more common use in the United States and is still widely used as a descriptor for the sector in the United Kingdom and Canada. *Voluntary action* is a common descriptor of the dynamics of the sector.

Any attempt to fully describe the organizations and sector in any country needs to cover as many bases as possible. For example, the UK publication *Third Sector* describes itself as the "leading publication for everyone who needs to know what's going on in the voluntary and not-for-profit sector" and begins its daily online newsletter with the motto "the bulletin that delivers the top stories affecting charities, voluntary organizations and social enterprises" (*Third Sector* 2013).

The differences between the terms go beyond the purely semantic, and impassioned debates take place about which are the most effective for communicating a favorable image of the sector and its work. The chairman of the UK Royal National Institute of Blind People, Kevin Carey, recently declared that he would prefer that the organizations in the sector stop calling themselves charities and instead describe themselves as social enterprises, as the former now carries connotations of amateurism. He went on to say, "We are not taken seriously [as] we are called daft names like 'not-for-profits,' which tells you what we're not, 'third sector,' which relegates us below the other two, 'NGOs,' which says we're not government, and 'civil society,' whatever that means" (as cited in Ainsworth 2011, 1). Scott Hurrell, Chris Warhurst, and Dennis Nickson (2011) found that the label *voluntary* is a significant structural barrier to recruiting top professionals to the sector in Scotland as it "conjures up images of a volunteer army of Miss Marples wearing wooly cardigans and knitting tea cozies" (350).

In addition to these terms, many others are commonly associated with the sector. The terms *501(c)* and *501(c)(3)* are uniquely US terms that refer to the sections of the national Internal Revenue Code that regulate the taxation status of nonprofits. Nonprofits in the United States often identify themselves in writing and in spoken vernacular by their tax code status (e.g., "we are a 501(c)(3)"). Although only applicable to the United States, the predominance of US websites and literature means that these terms are also familiar to many outside the country. There are twenty-eight categories of 501(c) organizations, but 501(c)(3) is the largest subcategory, which confers tax deductibility for donations to charitable organizations and foundations. Two other large categories are 501(c)(4), civic leagues and social welfare organizations, and 501(c)(6), business associations and chambers of commerce (contributions to organizations in these categories are not tax deductible as charitable donations but may be deductible as business or professional expenses).

Association is the generic term for a group of individuals who voluntarily work together to accomplish a common purpose. However, it is now primarily used in the sector as the descriptor for member-based organizations that bring together professionals from a designated field or for umbrella organizations, such as industry associations, that represent other member organizations. At the same time, it is often used in English as a translation back from other languages, where it is used in civil law countries as the legal designation for nonprofits that have working capital only (i.e., no endowment; see the next paragraph on *foundation*) and a governance model based on the direct democracy of members.

In the United States and other common law countries, *foundation* describes an entity that falls into a legal category that refers primarily to grant-making organizations backed by an endowment. In civil law countries, the legal category generally refers only to the existence of the endowment and to governance through a board of directors, and foundations can equally be grant making or service providing. In some cases, nonprofits that are not technically foundations still have the term in their name for historical reasons or to convey prestige.

Nonstate, a generic descriptor for all organizations that are not directly controlled by a government, is seen as a neutral term that more easily incorporates trade unions, universities, professional associations, and even individuals that may not fall easily into definitions of the nonprofit sector. Some authors focus only on nonprofit, nonstate actors, whereas others also include for-profit corporations and their representatives.

Philanthropy, the generic term for the private giving of money, time, or other valuables for the purpose of producing a public good, is now mainly used to describe donations by prosperous individuals and foundations, although the adjective *philanthropic* is occasionally used to describe organizations and the sector.

Public benefit, the generic term for the provision of a social or public good, is now considered a somewhat archaic descriptor for individual organizations or the sector, but it often appears as a key operating concept in regulations conferring tax exemptions and incentives for donations. A number of countries have a formal "public benefit test" of the purposes and activities of organizations claiming nonprofit status.

Social is the generic term for human interaction, which as an adjective has taken on the connotation of "doing collective good." The terms *social organization* and *social sector* are used as descriptors, and the word also appears in key terms such as *social enterprise* and *social economy* (more on those terms below). In some European languages, a term equivalent to *social profit organization* is commonly used, and some advocate its adoption into English (see, for example, Gaudiani 2007).

Social economy is a general designation for economic activity with a collective or social purpose that falls between the private for-profit and public sectors, such as cooperatives and other mutual financial associations. It is a term primarily used in Continental Europe (i.e., in the French, German, and Spanish languages), but it is also often adopted back into English, both in the restricted sense of cooperatives but also often extended out to all economic activity that has a broader social purpose and so is often equated to the third sector.

Society is the generic term for a group of people with shared interests, customs, and norms. Apart from its use in the collective term *civil society*, it is also often used as a somewhat archaic name for an organization (e.g., the Cancer Society) or group of organizations (e.g., *historical societies*) and is often associated with more clandestine activities (e.g., *secret societies*).

Just as no consensus exists on the terms for individual nonprofits, there is also none on what to call coordinating bodies or industry associations that represent the interests of the sector. Researchers in different countries use labels such as *umbrella, second tier, peak, intermediary,* or *meta* to describe these organizations, and the names of the organizations use terms such as *association, council, federation, network,* and *partnership.*

One can also identify a grab bag of other related terms that, although not as widely used, still appear sporadically in the literature, including those used to describe organizations, such as *benevolent, grassroots, independent, informal, social benefit,* and *tax exempt,* as well as collective concepts such as *citizen sector, paragovernment, nonstatutory sector,* and *shadow sector.* Attempts are occasionally made to bring new language into the field. For example, Roger Lohmann (1992) argued that the term *commons,* a traditional designation for collective resources, should also be used as a descriptor for the sector because nonprofit organizations embody the basic characteristics of a commons, including free and uncoerced participation, a common purpose and shared resources, and a sense of fairness and mutuality among participants. David Horton Smith (2014) recently coined the terms *altruistics* and *voluntaristics* to refer to the academic disciplines that study all forms of action that involve altruism and voluntarism. When the sector is studied from the perspective of specific academic disciplines, other terms may be preferred, such as *social movement organization* in sociology and *interest group* in political science.

The differences in meaning of all these terms can be significant, but at the same time the terms are often more symbolic and cultural than substantive. Different countries, organizations, and disciplines simply have their own preferred jargon. A review of the names of institutions related to the sector in English-speaking countries demonstrates the complexities of nomenclature.

In the United States, the two largest national associations representing the sector are the National Council of Nonprofits and the Independent Sector. The academic association is the Association for Research on Nonprofit Organizations and Voluntary Action. The leading industry newspaper is the *Chronicle of Philanthropy*, a 2010 federal legislative proposal was the Nonprofit Sector and Community Solutions Act, and a 2009 report to the US Congress by the Congressional Research Service was titled *An Overview of the Nonprofit and Charitable Sector.*

In the United Kingdom, the national association is the National Council of Voluntary Organisations. In 2010 the newly elected coalition government created the Office for Civil Society to replace the previous Labour government's Office of the Third Sector, and the regulatory body is the Charity Commission.

Given the bilingual situation of Canada, the nomenclature of the sector is even more complicated. A 2001 national project was called the Voluntary Sector Initiative in anglophone Canada, and L'Initiative sur le Secteur Bénévole et Communautaire (the Voluntary and Community Sector Initiative) in francophone provinces. A major coordinating body is the Council for the Nonprofit Sector or Conseil pour le Secteur Communautaire (Council for the Community Sector). The Canada Revenue Agency registers qualifying organizations through its Charities Directorate and Direction des Organismes de Bienfaisance (Directorate of Charitable Organizations).

In India and Nepal, the terms *nonprofit* and *NGO* are used primarily to refer to international nonprofits or to service organizations run by local bourgeoisie elites, and in recent years they have acquired negative connotations of neocolonialism and exploitation. The term *rights-holders organization* is now commonly used by many local organizations to indicate that they are more representative of autochthonous voluntary action.

As discussions about the field have become more global, considerable cross-fertilization of terms has occurred. The term *third sector* is now not commonly used in the United States, even though it featured prominently in the seminal Filer Commission report, but it has become one of the most internationally accepted designations for the sector. For example, the International Society for Third Sector Research is the leading association for nonprofit academics from around the world, and the Spanish translation, *tercer sector,* is widely used in those countries where that language is spoken.

When working with languages other than English, one needs to understand the challenges of translations and the cultural nuances of the use of any term. The media in Poland commonly refer to nonprofits as *organizacje społeczne* (social organizations), but as it is the same term used by the former communist regime for mass movement organizations, it is now generally avoided by those working in the sector (who often use the English loanword *organizacje non-profit*). The Spanish *participación ciudadana* translates as "citizen participation," and whereas similar terms are used in English, in Spanish-speaking countries, it is a much more prominent concept in commentaries on the sector, as nonprofits now foster participation in policymaking and service delivery in realms from which citizens were previously excluded by authoritarian regimes.

Is There Even a Sector?

The fault lines and definitional problems outlined in the previous sections lead to a logical questioning of whether one can even legitimately claim that such a thing as an identifiable nonprofit sector exists. As Peter Hall

(1992) noted, what is now known as the nonprofit sector was "invented" as a single collective concept only starting in the 1960s. Even now, when the term is widely used, so many organizations resist categorization and so much interdependence and hybridization have taken place that any attempt to clearly delineate the sector is doomed to fail. At best, any definition of a sector described as a "loose and baggy monster" with fuzzy edges is subject to a multitude of caveats and clarifications (Corry 2010; Macmillan and Buckingham 2013). So is there a sector? Perhaps a pure epistemological answer must be that there is not: a sector should after all be defined by its boundaries, and the nonprofit sector, particularly when examined from an international and global perspective, has ambiguous and permeable margins that are almost impossible to discern.

At the same time, some commentators continue to argue that the collective significance of the elements that make nonprofits distinctive from other organizations does make a case for considering them a separate sector (Salamon 2010), even though certain outliers and hybrid organizations are bothersome exceptions, and affiliated organizations work in concert across the boundaries. Also, one must recognize that the existence of the sector is a fait accompli because when the word is used readers or listeners instinctively understand—or perhaps misunderstand—it, and the term conjures up a set of organizations. There is, borrowing Bertrand Russell's concept, "knowledge by acquaintance." Although this acquaintance may not coincide with others' conception of the sector, that factor does not necessarily take away from its heuristic value.

Most of this definitional angst emanates from within the nonprofit research discipline. As noted in Chapter 1, broader theoretical enquiry seems to have fewer qualms about identifying a distinct third sphere of social and economic activity. The boundaries, continuities, and conditionalities that separate or connect the sectors may be contested, but the social sciences comfortably posit the existence of the three distinct sectors.

The terms *nonprofit*, *third sector*, and *civil society*, whether referring to individual organizations or a collective sector, are currently in vogue, and a subset of organizations exists that almost all interlocutors would agree is part of that sector. As the US organization Board Source (2012) noted, "the idea of the nonprofits sector may be abstract, but the sector's role in our society is tangible and easily recognized" (11). That statement is applicable to almost every nation, and the existence of a sector is undoubtedly becoming more entrenched in the political, administrative, research, and popular discourses of a wide range of polities.

Readers of this book undoubtedly picked it up because they instinctively understood from the title what it was going to be about and made the choice to delve further into the topic. Perhaps we should be searching for more appropriate synoptic terms than *sector*—current proposals include *domain* (see Fowler 2012), *ecology* (see Read 2012), *ecosystem* (see Edwards 2011b), and *space* (see Kleiman 2011). But eschewing the familiar term and substituting it with any of the alternatives probably will not reduce the complexities or solve the definitional problem. Although clearly defining the sector may be impossible, a sector undoubtedly exists in the minds of readers, and exploring its boundaries is incumbent on them.

3

The Evolution of
the Nonprofit Sector

Despite a paucity of evidence about the outcomes of the work of nonprofits, contemporary societies have "voted with their feet" in favor of the perceived comparative advantage of the nonprofit sector. The substantial growth of the sector since the 1970s has been bolstered by the support of governments, for-profit businesses, and the general population, which all confer their trust in, and contribute resources to, nonprofits. The number of nonprofits has increased dramatically, and they have expanded their influence by developing both cooperative and competitive relationships with the government and for-profit sectors for policymaking and service delivery. The growth is also reflected in the expansion of the responsibilities and functions of individual nonprofits. The expanding role of the nonprofit that now manages Central Park in New York City is documented in Box 3.1.

Why the recent expansion of the nonprofit sector? The broadest context is the population ecology of the post–World War II period. The worldwide population has experienced exponential growth—from 2.5 billion in 1950 to 7 billion in 2013—and as a result, the number and complexity of all manner of organizations, whether government, for-profit, or nonprofit, have also boomed. The period from the 1960s to 1980s is widely cited as a time in which many processes and institutions, and indeed society itself, became increasingly codified and complex. The meme of the loss of simplicity and of innocence during those decades appears in a wide range of topics in industrialized countries: during this period, new legislation was introduced in areas as diverse as civil rights, consumer protection, and freedom of information; new business processes emerged, and having a master of business administration (MBA) became an entry-level qualification for many corporate jobs; formerly amateur sports became professionalized; and parents

---

**Box 3.1 A Nonprofit Organization
Takes Over the Management of Central Park**

Central Park in New York City is emblematic of how nonprofit organizations and private philanthropy have taken on the responsibility for what were previously considered to be government-funded and -managed services.

By the 1970s, the city-run Central Park had deteriorated significantly as funds were cut in successive financial crises. The wealthy citizens who lived near the park decided to take action, and the nonprofit Central Park Conservancy was founded in 1980 with the goal of restoring the park to its former splendor. The conservancy was successful in fund-raising and increasingly assumed management of specific restoration and recreational activities.

In 1998, the conservancy and the City of New York signed an agreement that transferred management of the park from the Department of Parks and Recreation to the conservancy, formalizing their then eighteen-year-old public-private partnership. The relationship was reaffirmed in 2006 when the agreement was renewed for an additional eight years. As the official manager of Central Park, the conservancy is responsible for the day-to-day maintenance and operation of the park. Presently, 80 percent of the park's maintenance operations staff is employed by the conservancy, which provides 85 percent of the $37.4 million annual budget through its fund-raising and investment revenue.

Central Park is bordered by Fifth Avenue and Central Park West, two of the most expensive residential streets in New York. The conservancy has been spectacularly successful in raising funds from its neighbors, including a $100 million donation in 2012 from a hedge fund manager. The success of this fund-raising by the conservancy has raised concerns about inequities between parks in different parts of the city. In the 2013 mayoral election, the candidates debated whether Central Park should transfer part of its donations to parks in poorer neighborhoods.

Source: See Central Park Conservancy, http://www.centralparknyc.org/about/.

---

started to accompany their children on their walks to school as "stranger danger" became a more widespread fear. With population growth and economic expansion, employment in all sectors has grown, but the nonprofit sector is growing faster than the other sectors (Salamon 2010; Salamon and Sokolowski 2010). Consequently, the key issues are not simply growth of the nonprofit sector but its relatively large growth and the rebalancing of responsibilities among the three sectors.

Although most of the analysis is focused on the balance between the government and nonprofit sectors and the outsourcing of formerly government functions, nonprofits are also making substantial inroads in areas formerly considered the exclusive domain of for-profit businesses. The business venturing and entrepreneurial activities of many nonprofits are creating a range of retail and service activities, which are competing directly with those of for-profit companies. Museum gift shops were until recently small, musty corners contributing little to institutional income; now they are glittering gift meccas that dominate the exit often along with smaller retail booths spread throughout the building. Some museums have even established autonomous stores in malls and other retail centers that directly compete with for-profit stores. In computing, the nonprofit Linux Foundation fosters the growth of free open-source software that competes with the commercial products of Microsoft and Apple, and a host of nonprofit actors have entered the media industry, blurring the line between journalism and activism. Depending on the tax treatment of such commercialized activities in the jurisdictions in which they operate, they may be offered directly by the nonprofit itself or through a for-profit subsidiary or affiliate.

Why does the state share its responsibilities with nonprofits if it has the legitimacy and authority of the political system? Why does the business sector support nonprofits with direct funding and other resources and appear to cede some potentially commercial markets to nonprofit providers? The literature on nonprofits identifies a wide range of drivers and dynamics that nurture the growth of the sector.

Economic Drivers

Economic theories that seek to explain the existence of nonprofits focus on the concepts of public versus private goods and the various "failures" that drive the demand for them (Salamon 1987; Steinberg 2006). Private goods can be bought and sold on the marketplace and are usually traded by for-profit companies; public goods are available to all because they are nonexcludable (i.e., they benefit all) and nonrivalrous (the use by one person does not directly create competition), so they are generally provided by the public sector. The public and private nature of goods may be determined by the economic marketplace, but they are also regulated by political and social considerations for the population as a whole or for specific subpopulations. Political bargaining and social expectations can deem that certain goods, such as education and health, should be more public than private, or that mostly private goods such as food and accommodation should be provided as public goods to eligible populations such as the poor, the elderly, or those who have served in the military. The major political ideologies have as their linchpins grand claims about whether societal outcomes should be provided through private or public means.

Nonprofits flourish when either, or both, "market failure" (for-profit firms have no interest in a good or few trust that it can be delivered with equity and accountability) and "government failure" (government cannot deliver a public good efficiently) have occurred. Burton Weisbrod (1977, 1988) argued that public goods provided by the state in exchange for citizens' taxes were generally targeted, for political and economic reasons, at the average citizen, which leaves a marketplace of excess demand for the production of public goods for those whose needs do not necessarily coincide with the average. This gap can be found both at the high end for those able to pay for such services in the marketplace (e.g., those who send their children to private schools) and at the low end for the marginalized, who must organize alternative provisions. Henry Hansmann (1980, 1987) focused on "contract failure," which posits that consumers prefer nonprofits because governments fail to provide services to all and for-profit businesses fail to offer assurances against exploitation. The preference for nonprofit service is driven by the trust that nonprofits will deliver responsive and nonexploitative services and will not abuse information asymmetries to further their own interests.

Nonprofits also face failure if they cannot deliver results. Lester Salamon (1987) noted that nonprofits are hampered by four potential failures: insufficiency (they cannot meet needs), particularism (their activities focus on a limited constituency), paternalism (they set the agenda with little end user input), and amateurism (they do not have the capacity to effectively manage programs). The shifting balances of the perceptions and realities of the failures of the three sectors drive the shifting relations between them.

Related to the failure theories are "choice" theories. "Rational choice," "public choice," and "social choice" are three variants of the theoretical frameworks that explore why individuals choose to engage in collective action and the subsequent consequences for social and political behavior. The widely acknowledged father of the choice discourse in relation to nonprofits is Mancur Olson, in particular through his book *The Logic of Collective Action* (1965). His thesis was that individuals will not cooperate to create public goods because a structural counterdynamic exists that makes such cooperation irrational. Since, by definition, any public good gained through collective action will be freely available to all, any one individual has no incentive to commit his or her personal resources to that action. Those who do not participate in the collective action can become "free riders" and enjoy the benefits, so the rational choice for individuals is to maximize their net benefits by withholding contributions or at least hedge their bets by minimizing them. According to this Olsonian rationality, if an organization relies solely on the value of public goods to induce member contributions, no collective action would take place.

But Olson recognized that coercion and incentives can drive collective action and that potential participants also respond to a number of seemingly extrarational incentives such as civic duty, morality, solidarity, and social status. Participation in collective action is not only a cost but also a benefit. The purely utility-maximizing, egocentric economic actor has not fared well in the real world. Despite the problem of free riders, collective action does indeed take place and is thriving (Rich 1988; Tarrow 1994), as nonprofits appear to have been remarkably adept at choice games.

Failure and choice equations tend to focus on demand conditions but do not necessarily explain the supply-side decisions to organize according to nonprofit principles where people have an option to choose between nonprofit and for-profit structures. What advantage could these organizations offer if they have a nondistribution constraint and so provide limited material returns to those delivering the good? Commentators note that ideological or religious missions are the ones that primarily encourage the creation of nonprofits, but nonprofits are further benefited by access to economic advantages—including reduced tax burden, the workforce contribution of volunteers, and access to government grants and private donations (Lyons 1993; Wolch 1990). Given the social mission of nonprofits, they provide possible solutions to free-rider problems and other possible negative externalities.

Equally important in supply-side dynamics is the economic growth of the second half of the twentieth century, which has created a favorable resource pool to drive nonprofit expansion. The post–World War II period has seen unprecedented accumulation of wealth in industrialized countries and a subsequent transfer of that wealth between generations. An increasing part of that wealth is being captured by nonprofits, not only through direct donations but also through the growth of a range of planned philanthropic giving vehicles, such as charitable bequests, donor-advised funds, and family foundations (Center on Wealth and Philanthropy 2010). The extent of wealth transfers to nonprofits is dependent on the enabling regulatory environment in any country, but increasingly such giving activity is being encouraged, and as a stronger middle class emerges in many developing nations, members of that class increasingly contribute to the nonprofit sector.

Social and Political Drivers

Sociologists and political scientists analyze the growth of the nonprofit sector in the context of changing political and social dynamics, including the civil rights and identity movements of the 1960s, the crisis of the welfare state, and the growth of the middle class. Akin to the more economics-based "failure" approaches discussed earlier, commentators identify a "democratic deficit" that can be characterized as an amalgam of deficits of ideology, integrity, representation, and, in the case of international nonprofits, sovereignty and reach (Clark 2008). The response to this deficit is couched both in pluralist values—organization is necessary in order to have one's voice heard—and in the call for organizational efficiency that has engendered the rise of new public management, governance, and third-party agency approaches to the provision of public goods and services that dictate that governments should steer, not row (Blair and Schroeder 1999; Denhardt and Denhardt 2003).

Analysts in the area of sociology theorize about the rise of new social movements in response to structural conflicts posed by late capitalist and postindustrial societies (Diani and Eyerman 1992). Three interrelated systemic dynamics have been identified: postindustrialism, a new class system, and a crisis in representation (M. Wallace and Jenkins 1995).

First, postindustrialism has left people with more freedom in terms of time and money. In industrialized countries, significant sectors of the population have had their material needs met and so now turn their attention to social issues. Similarly, postmaterial and culturalist interpretations see social movements in terms of lifestyle changes due to increasing wealth and leisure time offered by postindustrial society, combined with the breakdown of traditional social ties and the availability of new technologies.

Second, a new class system has emerged. Increased social activism has been engendered by new social and political cleavages resulting from the breakdown of class identification, particularly among professional classes and knowledge workers. New forms of organizations have emerged that do not represent traditional social divisions of class or religion.

Third, a crisis has taken place in representation. The vitality of new social movements is seen as a direct response to the dysfunctions of the traditional institutions of interest mediation and representation. Political parties and economic interest groups have failed to respond to popular demands and to feed those demands into the political system. These new social movements are vehicles for excluded people to gain access and influence within an established political system and to disrupt corporatist arrangements that seek to promote stability.

The literature on the new social movement paid relatively little attention to organizational forms, mostly speaking about movements in a general collective sense. At the same time, scholars began to recognize that social movements included a mixture of institutional and noninstitutional attributes that included formal organizations as well as looser forms of collective action and individual activists (Baggot 1995). Even when organizational forms were not specifically referenced, an implicit recognition of the need for organization in order to achieve the goals of the social movements could be identified. The most commonly used term for mobilizing structures was *social movement organizations*. These organizations are most closely analogous to nonprofits: they are nongovernmental by definition, and as they formalize their structures, they tend to adopt the legal frameworks used by nonprofits. As Sidney Tarrow (1994) noted, these organizations are "hosts of social movements that take advantage of opportunity structures provided in the modern State" (21). These organizations translate the public's changing values and issue interests into a potential force for change. They channel the energies of the movement, and they decide on the goals and strategies of the movement (Dalton and Keuchler 1990).

Political scientists generally concur in this analysis of the rise of more grassroots activism but couch the growth of the sector in industrialized democracies more in terms of the conflicts between factions of liberalism. Since the 1970s, welfare liberalism in the Western world has been losing ground to laissez-faire liberalism, a tendency accelerated by the collapse of the Soviet Union at the end of the 1980s. The resurgence of more market-oriented, neoliberal ideologies has resulted in the waning of the welfare state and the privatization of many of its functions.

Similar to sociology, mainstream political science literature tends to give scant attention to organizational forms. *Interest group* is the term most often used to suggest organizational structure, but unless the analysis focuses directly on the institutional dimensions of these groups, the legal structures, internal dynamics, and array of services provided by the organizations receive little mention. However, the literature on interest group organizations does note the exponential increase in their activity and projection in diverse countries since the 1970s—described, by the early 1990s, as an "explosion" (Dalton 1993; Knoke 1990; Richardson 1993). As the population of the West became more educated, articulate, and prosperous, and as knowledge and information become more widespread, new forms of political participation and oversight of the activities of government and the private sector emerged. People were disillusioned with traditional politics, and the new organizations provided a more rewarding style of political participation than membership of a political party. Single-issue organizations began to attract the young more readily than the grayer world of party politics and so could compete better than political parties or unions for the support and loyalty of the population in the marketplace of political activism (Minkoff 1994; Richardson 1993).

Scholars who focus on the organizational structures of the nonprofit sector tend to use a multidisciplinary approach, combining sociological perspectives on social movements and political science analyses of interest groups with organizational theories to explain the growth of the sector and to theorize about its outcomes. Key organizational theorists such as Peter

Drucker (1990, 1994) specifically link social dynamics and organizational forms by positing the rise of knowledge workers as key social actors and suggesting that nonprofits are the preferred organizational form for many of their interests.

The political science and sociology explanations for the rise of the non-profit sector provide a good illustration of the tendency to frame analyses of the dynamics in pluralist and progressive terms. Many analyses are normative, expressing both the desirability and inevitability of the growth of these organizations. However, little empirical evidence can be cited to corroborate that nonprofits deliver what they promise (Anheier 2014; Pestoff and Brandsen 2010). Nonprofits can be well financed, well managed, sensitive to the needs of the community, and more responsive to changing situations, but they can also be underfinanced, be forced to beg for funding in the cutthroat world of private donations, and provide deficient services due to untrained staff working with precarious labor contracts. Additionally, they are often not open to the same public scrutiny as public administrations, and their ability to promote pluralism may be questionable. As Paul DiMaggio and Helmut Anheier (1990) noted, "[nonprofits] are the protectors of pluralism and of privilege, instruments of democracy and of control, sources of innovation and of paralysis, partner and competitor of the State" (153). As an example, how nonprofit charity efforts served the German Nazi regime is illustrated in Box 3.2.

Resource Mobilization and New Technologies

John McCarthy and Mayer Zald (1977) attributed increases in activity of social movement organizations to increases in the effective use of resources. Their approach, known as resource mobilization theory, presumes that political dissatisfaction and a motivation for collective action are inherent in all societies, but the realization of collective interests is dependent on the capacity to obtain and effectively manage the resources necessary to sustain and expand organizations. As more resources are mobilized by both existing and emerging organizations, the sector grows, and the last decades of the twentieth century witnessed a growth in both potential resources for non-profits and in the capacity of organizations to secure and effectively use them. The imperative to mobilize resources, however, generates dependency on those that can confer them. A parallel resource dependency theory traces how the resultant principal-agent relations impose external controls on organizations (Pfeffer and Salancik 1978).

The contemporary version of resource mobilization theory focuses on the impact of new technologies on resource equations. Technology greatly reduces the transaction costs of creating and maintaining organizations and, as with all other areas of organizational and social life, greatly increases the

---

Box 3.2 Nazi Party Charity Campaigns

The Winterhilfswerk (winter aid work or winter relief) of the German Nazi Party was an annual fund-raising drive to finance charitable work. Using the slogan "none shall starve nor freeze," the Winterhilfswerk ran from 1933 to 1945 providing food, clothing, coal, and other items to less fortunate Germans during the winter months. The boys' youth association, the Hitlerjugend (Hitler Youth), and the girls' youth association, Bund Deutscher Mädel (German Girls' Association), were extremely active in collecting for the charity. The "Can Rattlers," as they became known, were relentless in ensuring that all good German citizens gave their share. Contributors were given reward collectibles including lapel pins, figurines, plaques, and booklets with Hitler's speeches. The high point of the drive was December 3, National Solidarity Day, when high-ranking party officials would take to the streets and ask for donations.

Neighbors and even family members were encouraged to report the names of those who had not contributed to their block leaders so that they could persuade them to do their duty. Recalcitrants often had their names published in local papers to remind them of their neglect.

Sources: See Mr. Boots Access Blog, http://wurmhoudt.blogspot.com.au/2013/07 /winterhilfswerk-winter-relief-for.html; Wikipedia, http://en.wikipedia.org/wiki/Winter hilfswerk.

---

productivity and reach of all activities and operations of nonprofits. With lowered barriers to entry, a single person with a website can in effect claim to be an organization. In the international arena, new communication technologies have eliminated many of the former barriers to cross-border operations and have fostered the growth of international organizations. The impact of new technologies on nonprofits cannot be overstated, but they are equally available to all three sectors. In some areas of civic action, advocacy, and fund-raising, new technologies may even present a threat to existing nonprofits by diminishing the need for their mediating role.

Certain subsectors of nonprofits are characterized as being behind the curve in their access and use of new technologies, constrained by their reliance on donated last-generation technologies. However, nonprofits such as Wikipedia (see Box 6.5) and Mozilla (see discussion of virtual volunteering, below) as well as nonprofit educational, arts, and health institutions are often in fact developing the new technologies and their applications. An extensive network of organizations and individuals also works to strengthen the capacity of nonprofits to use new technologies for administration, fund-raising, communication, and organizing. For-profit technology companies such as Google and Facebook offer apps and how-to guides for nonprofits;

nonprofit support organizations, such as TechSoup Global, which currently operates in forty-five countries, facilitate low-cost access to technology goods and services; and authors such as Heather Mansfield (2012) instruct the sector on how to use "social media for social good."

Government Sponsorship of Nonprofits

The growth of nonprofits since the 1970s has resulted as much from the evolving priorities policies of governments as from the organizational will of citizens. The role of the public sector is increasingly shifting from the production and management of goods and services to the facilitation and regulation of economic and social activities, and from centralized bureaucratic control to a more diluted authority based on interorganizational relationships. An earlier conception of nonprofits as an interference to the exercise of public power has given way to widespread support for their growth as an integral part of the governance approach to the provision of public goods and services through public-private partnerships. Governments, both conservative and progressive, foster nonprofits through public policies that devolve to them the delivery of service, as well as through the provision of infrastructure, technical assistance, training of personnel, and the enacting of favorable legal and taxation frameworks for their creation, finance, and protection. Above all, governments legitimate the activities of nonprofits through their integration into consultative mechanisms and service delivery strategies and so in effect consecrate them as gatekeepers between governments themselves and users.

Governments strengthen and expand nonprofit sectors by supporting the growth of existing organizations and fostering the creation of new ones to deliver initiatives that would have formerly been provided directly by government agencies. Government agencies are entering into prime contracts with large nonprofit organizations, which then subcontract to other nonprofits. The prime contractors, in effect, take on the contract management and oversight role of government. An increasing number of nonprofits are also being created specifically to directly support the provision of public goods and services still under government tutelage but facing cutbacks. New nonprofits, often designated as "friends-of" organizations, are being established to channel private donations to public services such as schools, parks, and cultural institutions. The relationship between government and nonprofits, therefore, can be described as a mixture of resource interdependency, principal-agent hierarchies, and mutual accountability (L. D. Brown and Jagadananda 2010; Saidel 1991). These relationships are increasingly couched in terms of collaboration (see the section on deliberate relations in Chapter 5), but the reality remains that in most areas of interaction, government in effect functions as a monopsony, the only "buyer" of what nonprofits "sell," with the resulting inequality of power between the purchaser and the provider.

Governments encourage and help build the nonprofit sector because they embrace the arguments in favor of the comparative advantage of nonprofits. Encouraging the use of extant nonprofits or fostering the creation of new ones allows governments to exploit the legitimacy that nonprofits enjoy and to make use of the administrative and economic efficiency they apparently represent. Such enabling also ensures a certain level of control over nonprofits and their activities by "defining-in" potentially provocative organizations so that they become part of the state-sponsored service delivery and consultative network (Abzug and Webb 1996; Gundelach and Torpe 1996; Roelofs 2003).

Government can be the catalyst that allows the sector to expand, but it can also be the impediment that restrains its activities. In the context of prosperous, democratic Australia, Clive Hamilton and Sarah Maddison (2007) used the metaphor of the long arms of government both embracing and constraining the sector. In other countries, the constraining can be outright repression. However, even in authoritarian and single-party societies, state-sponsored organizations can straddle the seemingly opposing worlds of top-down hierarchy and bottom-up local demands and produce surprisingly contradictory outcomes that can both reinforce centralized power hierarchies and provide spaces for contestation (Read 2012).

Governments promote nonprofits not only within their own borders but also as part of their external aid funding and international agendas, both directly through their own aid programs as well as through the program of intergovernmental and multilateral institutions. The democracy and governance programs of the US Agency for International Development (USAID) seek to develop a "politically active civil society" (see the discussion of the USAID CSO Sustainability Index in Chapter 4) and European Union programs for development of central and eastern Europe in the years after the collapse of the Soviet Bloc included substantial funds for the development of civil society organizations as a key element in the eventual integration of many of the countries into the union. The European Union continues an active program of capacity building for civil society around the world, including its direct funding of organizations such as the Civil Society Development Center in Turkey, a candidate for future integration into the union. Various intergovernmental initiatives, including the Open Government Partnership, seek to strengthen civil society and develop stronger dialogues between the sectors.

Nonprofits are also instruments of the cultural ambassadorship of many nations and of efforts to tap into the resources of the nations' diaspora. Ambassador organizations such as the French Alliance Française, German

Goethe Institute, Italian Dante Alighieri Society, and Spanish Instituto Cervantes are structured as government-sponsored nonprofits managing a global network of affiliated local organizations, usually established according to the nonprofit legislation and regulations of the jurisdictions in which they work. Official diaspora networks use a similar model. For example, Advance Australia, a US-based international nonprofit, was created under the auspices of the Australian government (see Box 3.3).

Box 3.3 Advance Australia

Advance Australia is a nonprofit organization headquartered in New York City with offices in Hong Kong, London, and San Francisco. Established in 2002, it forges connections between the 1 million Australians living abroad to promote opportunities for Australia and Australians around the globe and to foster the contribution of the Australia diaspora to economic and cultural life back home. The membership is over 20,000 in eighty countries. Advance Australia is supported by the Australian government through the Department of Foreign Affairs and Trade, Australian state governments, and global corporate partners and donors.

Source: See Advance Australia, http://advance.org/faqs/.

Business Sector Sponsorship of Nonprofits

The growth in the nonprofit sector has also been driven by increasing business sector interest in contributing to its activities. Boosters analyze this interest through the positive perspectives of altruism and the desire to give back to the communities that generate company profits (Kiran and Sharma 2011; Van Huijstee and Glasbergen 2010). Critical perspectives focus on the self-interest of tax minimization, the increased marketability of brands associated with philanthropic endeavors, and the role of nonprofits as fig leaves or smoke screens for mendacious activities (Neal 2008).

Large corporations and local small businesses have all contributed to nonprofits through monetary donations, in-kind contributions of products and services, pro bono expertise, employees' volunteering during company time, and the establishment of corporate foundations. When done formally, these contributions are presented as part of corporate social responsibility or corporate citizenship programs (which may also include other responsible business practices in areas such as environmental protection, labor relations, and corporate governance). Until the 1980s, corporate foundations were rare (Hall 1992), yet now most large corporations regard affiliated nonprofit foundations, which often carry the companies' names, as integral parts of their structure. The foundations manage corporate donations and in many instances implement their own programming. How a global news company has created a nonprofit foundation that projects its corporate image and values is illustrated in Box 3.4.

Another facet is cause marketing, often also referred to as cause-related marketing or marketized philanthropy, in which a private company promotes or supports the work of nonprofits through its marketing campaigns (Nickel and Eikenberry 2009). A recent series of advertisements by Levi's shows young people wearing the company's jeans as they "go forth and change the world" and provides information about how to donate directly to specific organizations (Levi's 2010). The Levi's campaign is the quintessential "doing well by doing good," which helps position a brand or product as one that cares about social outcomes. Usually such a campaign involves a company donating a certain percentage of its profit to a specific charity or cause or encouraging consumers to donate. An increasingly popular variation on this theme is the "buy one, give one" (also expressed as B1G1) transaction-based giving approach, in which the purchase of a product generates the donation of its equivalent to a charity. In a few instances, the product itself is the fund-raiser, such as Newman's Own, established by the actor Paul Newman, which donates all profits from the sale of the company's food products to charity.

Box 3.4 Thomson Reuters Foundation

Thomson Reuters Foundation is the charitable arm of the world's leading provider of news and information. According to its website, the foundation is "committed to empowering people in need around the world with trusted information and free legal assistance." A registered charity in the United States and the United Kingdom, the foundation seeks to leverage the skills, values, and expertise across Thomson Reuters to promote the rule of law, save lives in disasters, and improve standards of journalism. The website notes that "foundation initiatives stand for better governance, greater transparency, more effective humanitarian relief, and a robust global press. They are a call-to-action by our employees and partners. They are the embodiment of the Thomson Reuters Trust Principles of independence, integrity, and freedom from bias."

Source: See the Thomson Reuters Foundation, http://www.trust.org.

Also significant is the branding of celebrities such as sport stars and media personalities, who either act as spokespersons for nonprofits or, increasingly, create their own organizations and projects. Again, according to different perspectives, they have either a genuine commitment to using their fame to provide prominent support for charitable purposes or are cynically exploiting nonprofits to build their brands. In recent years, numerous charities run by "celanthropists" (a recently coined portmanteau of *celebrity* and *philanthropist*) such as the Haitian-born hip-hop artist Wyclef Jean and the pop artist Madonna have been embroiled in controversies over the work of nonprofits they have created in Haiti and Malawi, respectively.

Finally, the emergence of social enterprise discourse, which promotes the use of business models for creating social value (even though the resultant organizations most often use nonprofit institutional forms—see Chapter 5), strengthens the notion that business can and should be partnering with and promoting nonprofits. The rise of philanthrocapitalism, a form of social enterprise that involves "muscular philanthropy" by hands-on, wealthy donors (G. Jenkins 2011), has promoted business sector luminaries such as Richard Branson of Virgin and Mark Zuckerberg of Facebook as the new public faces of philanthropy.

A significant increase has taken place in such business sector activities (see, for example, the research on cause marketing cited in Nickel and Eikenberry 2009). Paul Newman sponsored the establishment in 1999 of the Committee Encouraging Corporate Philanthropy (CECP), which since 2005 has produced an annual report entitled *Giving in Numbers* (CECP 2014a), which focuses on US companies, and since 2013 an annual report entitled *Giving Around the Globe* (CECP 2014b), which looks at other regions. Both series document increases in corporate philanthropy and also highlight the differences between countries. Some countries, including Brazil, Indonesia, and China, mandate some form of corporate giving as a condition for certain licenses and permits; others, such as Russia, severely restrict corporate and individual tax deductions for philanthropy (see Box 3.12). A McKinsey global survey indicated that 76 percent of executives said corporate social responsibility efforts added to long-term shareholder value (McKinsey and Company 2009).

These activities are generally represented as a win-win situation. But for the nonprofit sector, potential hidden costs exist, including a shift in focus to more marketable causes and activities and a lowering of the "virtue threshold," whereby the public believes that by consuming they can meet social obligations (Buthe and Cheng 2014; Eikenberry 2009). Whatever the perspective taken on such business sector involvement in nonprofits, with little doubt, the cumulative impact in promoting the sector is considerable. The diverse impact of one corporation is illustrated in Box 3.5.

Box 3.5 Employee Volunteer Program Creates New Nonprofit

General Mills is one of the world's largest food companies, with brands
such as Cheerios, Häagen-Dazs, and Nature Valley. As part of its corporate social responsibility program, the company makes annual financial
contributions to philanthropic and charitable causes, totaling some $100
million worldwide in fiscal year 2010.

General Mills also encourages volunteering by its employees. One of
the volunteer projects created by a small group of the company's engineers and food scientists donated packaged food to schools in Malawi.
The program organizers decided they could reach more people if they
also offered their expertise to food producers in Africa and wanted to
extend their work through collaborations with other large food companies. Realizing that workers in competing companies would not want to
volunteer for a General Mills in-house project, they created an independent nonprofit, Partners in Food Solutions.

Partners in Food Solutions now attracts sponsorship and volunteers
from a wide range of food manufacturing and agribusinesses, as well as
from foundations and government aid agencies. It links the technical and
business expertise of employees at large multinational companies to
small- and medium-sized mills and food processors in the developing
world. The goal is to improve the ability of the local companies to produce high-quality, nutritious, and safe food at affordable prices and to
increase demand for the crops of smallholder farmers who supply them.

Sources: See Partners in Food Solutions, http://partnersinfoodsolutions.com/; General
Mills, http://www.generalmills.com/; Chronicle of Philanthropy, http://philanthropy.com
/article/General-Mills-s-In-House/128326/.

Nonprofit Sponsorship of Nonprofits

The nonprofit sector itself also drives its own growth. As individual nonprofits grow they often pursue expansion strategies through a network of
local and international branch offices, affiliates, and franchises (Oster
1996). Equally important, when the nonprofit sector gains a critical mass,
intermediary and representative organizations emerge that advocate on
behalf of the sector. Although much of the advocacy work of such organizations may involve the promotion of the policy interests of the publics
they represent, considerable effort is also focused on pursuing the organizational interests of the nonprofits themselves, which may not always coincide with interests of the constituents. This conflict of interests is particularly true for nonprofit industry associations that are specifically created to

promote the interests of member organizations. And in most jurisdictions, research institutes and other organizations promote philanthropy and proclaim the benefits of a strong nonprofit sector.

The expansion of government and business funding and of the economic and social spaces for nonprofit activity quickly become a priority agenda as does the reduction in compliance burdens on the governance of organizations and of their revenue flows. Box 3.6 describes some of the tensions that can arise when nonprofits advocate on behalf of their organizational interests, perhaps putting those interests ahead of a wider common good.

Box 3.6   Should the United States Reduce Tax Deductions for Charities?

In response to the fiscal crisis, the administration of Barack Obama proposed reducing the level of deductions for charitable donations that can be claimed by high-income earners. Nonprofit industry organizations lobbied hard to defeat any such attempt. Pablo Eisenberg (2011), a prominent commentator on nonprofit policy, disagreed with such actions. He wrote, "President Obama's repeated efforts to limit charity tax breaks for wealthy people have triggered fervent, if not frenetic, opposition by large nonprofits and their trade associations. The most recent flurry came after the president suggested limiting the value of all itemized deductions to pay for his jobs bill, an idea that appears to have died for now. But given the nature of the nation's money woes, odds are a similar measure will be proposed again soon."

Eisenberg continued by pointing out the flaws of the nonprofits' point of view. "Yet in their projection of a philanthropic Armageddon, these nonprofits seem to be ignoring several key considerations, including the inequity of the current tax system. They also fail to acknowledge the relatively minimal effect the change would have on charitable giving and the tiny portion of giving by large donors that goes to small, local organizations and charities that serve the needy."

Finally, he pointed out what he called the "hypocrisy of the nonprofit position." He said, "Instead of putting the national interest and common good first, those groups are pursuing their narrow self-interest. That the current tax code favors wealthy Americans is nowhere more pronounced than when it comes to itemized deductions, including those for charity. Wealthy Americans write off 35% of what they spend not just on charitable gifts but also on mortgage interest for their housing, medical expenses, and local taxes. Meanwhile, Americans in a lower tax bracket receive smaller write-offs, and those taxpayers who do not itemize receive no subsidies at all for their charity donations."

In the international arena, the expansion and strengthening of civil society organizations have been seen as key elements in supporting opposition to authoritarian regimes and in consolidating democratic transitions. Organizations such as the Soros Foundation have actively supported the growth of the nonprofit sector during regime change (see Box 3.7) and, along with others such as CIVICUS and the ICNL (see Chapter 4), continue to actively promote more favorable legal and political environments for nonprofits throughout the world.

Box 3.7 Soros Foundation

The Soros Foundation, founded by the financier George Soros, has been one of the most visible funders supporting the role of nonprofits during democratic transitions. Soros, a citizen of the United States born in Hungary, began his philanthropy in the late 1970s by providing scholarships for black students at the University of Cape Town and dissidents in Eastern Europe. In 1984, he established his first non-US-based foundation in Budapest, which distributed photocopiers to civil society organizations to break the Communist Party's control of information. The Soros Foundation also opened an office in China, but it was infiltrated by the authorities and closed down within a few years.

After the fall of the Berlin Wall, Soros Foundation offices were established throughout Eastern Europe and Central Asia to support efforts to promote democratic governance, human rights, and social reforms. The foundation also established the Central European University in Budapest as a center of teaching research and policy analysis in the region. In 1993, the Soros Foundation became the Open Society Institutes as part of a global expansion that is now a network of branches, offices, and semi-independent foundations in Africa, Asia, Latin America, and the Middle East. In 2010, the name of the organization was changed to the Open Society Foundations to better reflect its role as a funder for civil society groups around the world. The current budget is close to $1 billion.

Source: See the Soros Foundation, http://www.soros.org/about.

A New Nonprofit "Culture"?

A "culture" of a preference for nonprofits appears to be emerging. In many countries, nonprofits enjoy more trust, loyalty, and interest of citizens than other social actors and institutions, such as governments, unions, political parties, and commercial business. On a global level, the Edelman Trust Barometer (2012) indicated that since 2008 nonprofits have been the most trusted institutions globally, and that in sixteen of the twenty-five countries surveyed, they are more trusted than businesses (which are generally more trusted than the government). The nonprofit associational form is increasingly colonizing much of the political and social space formerly occupied by political parties and labor unions (see Box 5.2 for examples from the United States). Donations to nonprofits are rising, with many countries reporting a significant increase in tax-deductible giving (for data on Australia, see McGregor-Lowndes and Pelling 2013).

This new cachet is translated into a specific interest in working or volunteering in the nonprofit sector, which appears to be an increasing career and lifestyle choice in many countries. Even though volunteering rates around the world are relatively well documented (see Chapter 4), evidence of labor market manifestations of this cultural shift is more sporadic but increasingly persuasive. In the United States, a survey by the national daily newspaper *USA Today* and the Bipartisan Policy Center found twice as many people believe the best way to make positive changes in society is through volunteer organizations and charities, rather than through the government, and that younger people express a much stronger preference for working for nonprofits than for the government (Page 2013). There are numerous other reports that young people are expressing more interest in "purposeful work" in the nonprofit sector and in the social responsibility divisions of for-profit firms (see, for example, Korn 2011). As Peter Drucker (1994) noted, the third sector in the 1990s became an integral part of the emergence of a knowledge and service economy and was the sector of choice for those with a service mission seeking to meet the social challenges of modern life. *Crain's New York Business* ran a front-page story in 2010 about a new generation they dubbed "philanthroteens" and quoted the CEO of a New York–based nonprofit that facilitated youth social action, who noted that "the number of kids creating their own organizations and taking action for causes they care about is skyrocketing" (Kreinin Souccar 2011).

In many countries, volunteering and social service are increasingly being added to high school and college curricula (and at times even becoming a condition for graduation and college entrance), and high school graduates from developed countries are taking "gap years" before starting college, a sabbatical from formal education that often includes periods of volunteering, either domestically or internationally. Business schools report an increasing interest in social enterprise courses. The rise in social enterprise and its promise of both financial returns and the creation of social good are often presented as a solution to the problem of low pay in many nonprofit organizations, accompanied by the catchphrase "you can do good and do well."

Apparently increasing are "lifestyle" nonprofits, which are the personal project of individual entrepreneurs who in the past may have become participants in larger ventures but now find creating their own organizations viable. And a rise can also be witnessed in "encore careers" in which people who have been financially successful, or are simply dissatisfied with the direction their careers in other sectors have taken, switch to a nonprofit sector career they consider more attuned to their particular passions and their social values. The expansion of the nonprofit sector has created a larger labor market, which can provide potentially attractive options for career switchers and for surplus workers from downsized public and for-profit organizations. Many senior career switchers parlay their extensive contacts into successful careers in existing organizations or in their own start-ups. When former US secretary of state Hillary Clinton left that office, she stated in numerous interviews that her intention was to dedicate herself to philanthropy, advocacy, and the work of the Clinton Foundation. In Box 3.8, another example is provided of the increasingly common scenario of a former senior government official or business leader moving into an executive position in a nonprofit.

Pressure is increasing on the supply side for the creation and growth of the nonprofit sector, which may not necessarily coincide with demand. Phi-

---

**Box 3.8   A Former Government Minister
Becomes a Founder and CEO of a Nonprofit**

Former first deputy prime minister of Spain María Teresa Fernández de la Vega lost that job when the Socialist Party was voted out of office in 2010. Previously, she had a distinguished career as a lawyer, civil servant, and legislator, primarily focusing on justice issues.

In 2012, she reappeared in public life as the first president and CEO of the Fundación Mujeres por África (Women for Africa Foundation), a new international nonprofit based in Madrid, supported by some of Spain's largest companies and by political, sports, and artistic elites. The foundation continues the work Fernández de la Vega began as a government minister, when she organized a series of conferences on women in Africa that brought together government ministers from Europe and Africa, as well as prominent women from politics and business, to address issues of gender equality and empowerment.

Sources: See El País, http://sociedad.elpais.com/sociedad/2012/02/08/actualidad /1328711791_227111.html; Fundación Mujeres por África, http://mujeresporafrica.es /content/presidenta-biograf%C3%ADa.

lanthropy, volunteering, and support for nonprofits have evolved from being religious imperatives or political militancy and are now more akin to a cultural practice and perhaps even a fashion statement. Although some analysts celebrate the new level of interest in and support for the nonprofit sector, others lament the impact on the sector of the explosion in the number of organizations. They are often created more to respond to the career and lifestyle choices of the founders, a motivation that potentially fragments the sector, creates service redundancies and unnecessary competition for funding, and can complicate the development of coherent responses to social needs (Rosenman 2011). In certain fields such as health care and victims' services, memorial foundations and nonprofits are proliferating, created to honor a deceased loved one. These organizations compete for resources and policy attention with established organizations working in the same fields. When the loved one was a prominent celebrity, the new organization can often quickly crowd out existing organizations.

In the international arena, the explosion of nonprofits has led to an echoing of the same concerns about fragmentation and about the potential for fraud in the exploitation of the new interest in voluntary activities. The growth in popularity among young people for gap years of voluntary activities and in voluntourism for adults and early retirees (see Chapter 7) has apparently led unscrupulous operators in some developing countries to create reverse Potemkin village nonprofits (usually schools, orphanages, or employment programs) established primarily to provide tourists from the North with fleeting humanitarian experiences and to attract donations.

Volunteering

A defining feature of the sector is its voluntary soul, defined variously as one of three overlapping dimensions: the noncoercive, voluntary nature of participation in organizations; the stewardship of organizations by voluntary, independent boards; and the participation of volunteers in operations and service delivery.

The last dimension has experienced the most impact from the growth of interest in and support for the sector. Volunteering is defined in the broadest terms as the donation of time and effort to contribute to the common good, without expectation of material reward (UN Volunteers 2011), but these general principles are nuanced in each society by cultural and religious norms and by economic circumstances. The conceptual separation of the time spent on collective action from that spent on personal and professional endeavors, and the labeling of that collective action as volunteering, is very much an artifact of more industrialized, urbanized, and secular societies. Although attempts have been made to create international standards for research on volunteering (see Global Volunteer Measurement Project 2011; Salamon 2002b; and the discussion on measuring the nonprofit sector in Chapter 4), comparative research generally first notes the challenges of creating definitions robust enough to apply across cultures and economies.

In industrialized countries, volunteering is seen as a key policy instrument for building active citizenship and social capital as well as increasing service capacities. As the sector grows and garners increasing support from governments and business, and a philanthropic culture becomes a more central feature of many societies, nonprofits are seen as outlets for "giving back" but also for filling empty hours, finding friends, and building résumés (Einolf and Chambré 2011). Historically in Western industrialized democracies the mainstays of volunteering were the housewives in single-wage families, but economic and demographic shifts, including higher female participation in the active workforce, have meant that this demographic has become less predominant. Instead, the supply of volunteers in many countries now includes the following categories:

• Active elderly: People are living longer and staying active longer and use part of their retirement time to volunteer.
• Episodic volunteers: More people appear to be volunteering for one-off or short-term high-profile events, without developing a long-term commitment to an organization.
• Service learning: Schools and universities are increasingly introducing citizenship and volunteering components as part of the curriculum and as requirements for graduation.
• Internships: Many of those entering, or reentering, the workforce volunteer to gain experience and a foothold in the labor market. Many of these activities are structured as "internships" and may be in the nonprofit sector but also in commercial firms.
• Corporate volunteers: Corporations are providing opportunities for their employees to volunteer as part of corporate responsibility programs or as a staff development strategy to create a more positive corporate environment.
• Mutual obligation requirements: Welfare reform, alternative sentencing, and professional certification programs in many countries now require some form of community service or pro bono work (UN Volunteers 2011).

Volunteering is by definition uncoerced and nonobligatory, but service learning, internships, corporate volunteering, and mutual obligation requirements all have elements of the seemingly contrary notion of conditional or forced volunteering. As the demographics of the volunteer pool and the motivations for volunteering shift, the lines are increasingly blurred between altruistic and other forced or self-interested forms of volunteering. How is altruism reconciled with the multiple motivations or obligations that drive volunteering? How does one measure altruism when a government or a corporation encourages its citizens or employees to volunteer, and those who do not comply find themselves stigmatized; when considerable personal capital can be accumulated through volunteering (meeting friends, embellishing a résumé, or entering a select social circle); or when religious or social obligations require community service (D. H. Smith 1981)? Moreover, although one can find an assumption in public policy and practice that a social good is to be gained from the conditional obligations placed on students, welfare recipients, and those sentenced to community service, research suggests that institutional or forced volunteering does not encourage better citizenship but instead leads to negative and cynical views (Warburton and Smith 2003).

As the sector grows and takes on more responsibilities for the delivery of public services, volunteer work is becoming more professionalized and often requires volunteers to meet more stringent regulations. Nonprofits that provide services as diverse as home visits to the elderly, vacation visits for inner-city youth, phone-based crisis counseling, and literacy education are finding that providing such services with only volunteers is increasingly challenging. Funders require higher standards and qualified staff to meet contract targets, and regulatory authorities require documentation of the training and "good character" of volunteers. Many nonprofits that have in the past based their operations primarily on volunteers now face significant challenges in maintaining their former identity as they deal with the pressure to professionalize.

Technology has also enabled new forms of volunteering. Virtual volunteering allows volunteers to work remotely on the development of the digital assets of an organization (e.g., improve the website, create or maintain online materials, manage social media projects), to telecommute organizational tasks that can be done off-site (e.g., research and writing, outreach campaigns), or to provide formerly face-to-face services that can also be delivered online (e.g., mentoring and tutoring) (Cravens and Ellis 2000).

Open-source software projects, which involve the development of digital social goods primarily by volunteers, have resulted in the creation of thousands of software products. Two of the most widely known are the Linux operating system and the Firefox browser, both of which are coordinated through their respective foundations (whereas their products are commercialized through subsidiary corporations). The Mozilla Foundation, registered in the United States as a 501(c)(3) charity, declares in its manifesto that "the Internet is a global public resource that must remain open and accessible" (Mozilla Foundation 2013), and it retains 100 percent ownership of the subsidiary for-profit Mozilla Corporation. All profits from the Mozilla Corporation are invested back into Mozilla Foundation projects.

The Changing Nature of the Sector

As the sector has grown, it has gone through fundamental changes in many of the key paradigms that drive our understanding of its role and indeed of its essence. Two main themes can be found in these changes: the shifting relationships with government and the growth of "corporate" nonprofits that operate along business principles.

Evolving Relationships with Government

Since the beginning of the associational revolution, an evolution has taken place in the relationship between government and the nonprofit sector and consequently in the role of nonprofits in service delivery and policymaking. This evolution can be broken down into distinct eras. The dates given below are approximate (and overlapping) and represent developments primarily in Western industrialized democracies.

Conflict (1960–1985). The 1960s and 1970s saw the rise of new activist organizations, as formerly unstructured social movements gave rise to more formal social movement organizations, and existing nonprofits sought to become more involved in social action and policy deliberations. The initial response was that this emerging activism was superfluous to the democratic process and that the organizations were a disturbance to orderly policymaking. Nonprofits were not yet a significant part of service delivery infrastructure in most countries (except for a relatively small number of historical nonprofit educational, health, and cultural institutions). In the United States, the Great Society programs of the latter half of the 1960s began to provide new sources of funding for nonprofits.

Consultation (1970–1995). By the 1970s, the number of nonprofits and the level of their political activism had reached a critical mass and they could no longer be ignored. In response, a move was made to ameliorate the frictions created by the ever-increasing number of organizations through the establishment of formal processes of policy dialogues. Conflict started to give way to consultation, and new advisory and liaison committees were established as a way of formalizing the relationship between nonprofits and policymakers. Most of these consultation mechanisms continue to exist and they continue to be controversial, denounced by some as sham forums that in effect function more as marketing for determined policies. However, such consultation mechanisms continue to be a central feature of policymaking and service delivery.

Contracting (1980–2005). This era coincided with the rise of the new public management approach to the delivery of public goods and services. Conservatives attacked "big government" and pushed for privatization, and progressives attacked "universalist government" that could not effectively redistribute resources to those most in need or to the full diversity of modern societies and pushed for community organizations to have a greater role in service delivery. Government relationships with nonprofits began to be characterized by purchaser-provider paradigms. Funding initially flowed to a relatively small number of existing nonprofits through cost-recovery grants and subsidies, many of which were automatically renewed. But as the nonprofit sector grew and the focus of funding shifted from simply financing program outputs to requiring organizations to demonstrate significant outcomes, new funding models relied more on fixed-term and performance-based contracts or service agreements and on the creation of competitive quasi-markets.

The expansion of contracting saw the emergence of larger, more corporate nonprofits and shifted the focus of the sector from policy-related work to service delivery. Opposing views emerged of how expressive roles fared given the new emphasis on service delivery. Some argued that the closer relationships between the sectors would result in greater participation by nonprofits in policymaking. Others countered that because many nonprofits had come to rely on government contracts and on private philanthropy, they could no longer afford to bite the hand that feeds (see the section on advocacy in Chapter 7).

Corporatization and enterprise (1990–present). Professionalization of management and a greater focus on entrepreneurial approaches has increasingly become the markers of the sector. The new heroes of the sector are no longer the social activists and the grassroots community organizers of the first wave of sector growth, but new "CEO" leaders—most often with backgrounds in senior levels of government and the business sector—who can steward large complex organizations, as well as young entrepreneurs touting new approaches to resolving social challenges (see the section on social enterprise in Chapter 5). Although the primary focus is on service delivery, evolving communications technologies are also creating new discourses on expressive activities in which traditional nonprofits are bypassed as representative of constituencies. The policy relationships are between government and individual citizens directly, mediated not only by nonprofits but by social media and an emerging digital civil society (Bernholz, Cordelli, and Reich 2013a; Newsom and Dickey 2014).

As noted earlier, these eras represent the evolution of the nonprofit sector since the 1960s in Western industrial democracies. In other countries where more democratic structures have emerged only later, the evolution of the nonprofit sector has been quicker and more compressed, but the same elements of the eras and the same sequence are generally evident. And even though the four eras are represented here as different historical periods, the worldviews they embody also continue to coexist as the competing logics of the sector and the basis of ongoing debates about the roles and responsibilities of nonprofits.

Corporate Nonprofits

A defining feature of the growth and evolution of the sector has been the emergence of a small group of large, multidivisional nonprofits. Although relatively few in number, these large corporate nonprofits represent the overwhelming majority of the income of the sector, and they have an outsized profile and role. In the United States, less than 3 percent of the 1.5 million registered nonprofits have annual incomes of more than $5 million, yet that 3 percent represent some 90 percent of the income reported to the IRS (note that small nonprofits and religious institutions do not report income) (National Center for Charitable Statistics 2012). Throughout the 1970s and 1980s, as government and philanthropic funding became more readily available, many of the historic nonprofits and newer activist organizations grew and transformed themselves into large multiservice agencies.

Emblematic of this growth are the settlement houses and other similar institutions of late nineteenth-century social reform movements in industrialized democracies. For almost a century, they survived primarily on private philanthropy and contributions from religious institutions as solid, but relatively small, organizations. Their activities were often restricted to a single building, and new initiatives were generally spun off as separate autonomous entities. From the 1980s, large government contracts started to flow to them. They recruited executive officers with the capabilities to manage more complex structures and processes and employed their first dedicated development staff skilled in fund-raising from foundations and individuals. As a result, many became large multiservice and multisite agencies, managing numerous government contracts, cultivating a wider range of foundation and philanthropic donors, and developing fee-for-service programs. Organizations that had in the past worked with relatively simple structures and reduced staff relatively quickly became complex conglomerates.

The concept of managerialism was increasingly invoked in the nonprofit sector (as it was in the public sector) as a catchall phrase that sought to describe the application of management techniques and processes more often associated with the for-profit world. As a consequence, significant segments of the nonprofit sector have become more corporate than associative, more businesslike and more entrepreneurial, with managerial practices converging with those of private and public sectors (Anheier 2014; Bernholz, Cordelli, and Reich 2013b). Specific techniques for managing processes and for measuring and communicating outcomes abound, and business-speak, such as "return on investment" (often rebranded as "social return on investment") and "transformational leadership," is common currency. The sector is increasingly dominated by large professionalized organizations—a dynamic compounded by many funders, both government and private, who prefer to award contracts to larger, trusted organizations—and the organizations themselves are now led by a new technocratic elite.

The curricula vitae of contemporary nonprofit executives, particularly in larger organizations, demonstrate the shift. Whereas in the past the typical profile of a nonprofit leader would have been that of a community activist or social worker, it is now equally likely to be someone with experience at senior levels of business, law, politics, or the public sector. Many of the new leaders of the nonprofit sector are more adept at speaking the language of business and at tapping into philanthropy and power structures associated with financial centers. Patronage and power in the nonprofit sector appear to have shifted from a political to an economic focus, and a common aphorism in the social services subsector is that "the MBAs have pushed out the MSWs (master of social work)." These preferences may also explain why, despite the fact that women dominate employment in the lower ranks of the nonprofit sector, the higher ranks are still dominated by men (see Box 3.9).

Professionalization often involves changes in the "look and feel" of an organization, and growing organizations often experience a difficult balancing act when moving away from an existing "nonprofity" persona of a

---

Box 3.9 Female Employment in the Nonprofit Sector

Women make up the majority of the nonprofit workforce in most countries, but they are not the majority at either the executive or the board level. A 2011 report by the White House Project,[1] a US nonprofit that sought to advance women's leadership, found that although 73 percent of workers in the US nonprofit sector are women, only 45 percent of chief executives are women, and that number falls to 21 percent for nonprofits with annual incomes of $25 million or more. Furthermore, women chief executives have been losing ground relative to men in terms of salaries. Females earned only 66 percent of male salaries in 2011, compared with 71 percent in 2000. Finally, women account for 43 percent of the board seats among all nonprofits, but hold only 33 percent of the seats at nonprofits with annual incomes of $25 million or more.

Source: See YNPN Detroit (Young Nonprofit Professionals Network), http://ynpn detroit.wordpress.com/2011/01/23/women-leadership-and-the-nonprofit-sector/.
Note: 1. The White House Project ceased operations in early 2013 because of funding problems.

smaller, more casual, and collective entity based largely on volunteer input to an organization considered capable of effectively stewarding complex, high-budget projects. Like their counterparts in the for-profit world, nonprofit organizations are commonly driven by the impulse to grow and expand. However, the increasing professionalization of nonprofits in both service and expressive functions often leads to critiques from existing members and supporters that many organizations are moving too far from their voluntarist and activist roots. The rise of professionalized, meganonprofits is seen as bureaucratizing the sector and embedding nonprofits in government processes and thereby rendering them less able to respond to grassroots concerns and to win the support of volunteers. The New York Road Runners exemplifies these tensions (see Box 3.10).

Although such transformations are usually ascribed to service organizations, similar dynamics can be found in expressive organizations. William Maloney and Grant Jordan (1997) had already noted the rise of the "protest business" in the mid-1990s, which they claimed had transformed advocacy nonprofits into professional, bureaucratic, mainstream interest groups led by managers, staffed by professional analysts and advocates, and supported by sophisticated public relations and fund-raising departments. Transparency International, the anticorruption organization based in Berlin and established in 1993, now has an annual income of some $40 million for its secretariat, with additional income raised by the 100 national chapters throughout the world. The US environmental advocacy nonprofit Natural Resources Defense Council, started in 1970, now has an annual income of some $110 million and over 300 staff members in offices across the United States and in Beijing, China.

But has growth and professionalization led to an increase in the capacity of nonprofits to influence? According to the resource mobilization theory, the presence of professional staff is seen as a strong indicator of the capacity, or at least a potential, to influence, and the increasing participation of these organizations in policy debates appears to support that hypothesis. But growth and professionalization are also seen as distancing movements from their earlier base and possibly compromising them through a dependence on conditional donors, both public and private, who explicitly or implicitly set limits on their work. The protest business has long been derided by commentators who claim that it is "not grassroots but astroturf" and warn that such organizations generally survive at the expense of the movements that create them by compromising on the original objectives (Meyer and Imig 1993; M. Wallace and Jenkins 1995). Others, however, continue to maintain that even "checkbook organizations" contribute to pluralist democracy (Newton 1997), and certainly the ongoing concern about the influence of such advocacy organizations and of "big money" on policy outcomes is a constant theme of contemporary political discourse.

Box 3.10 The Growth of New York Road Runners

The New York Road Runners was founded in 1958 as a nonprofit running club with about forty members who, led by African American Olympian Ted Corbitt, opened their ranks to all: men and women, white and black, and fast and slow. Growth was gradual: the group only had about 250 members in 1970, the year that Road Runners staged the first New York City Marathon in Central Park. Road Runners continues to be the organizer of the marathon, as well as of dozens of other races and community fitness programs around New York, and contributes to running programs across the United States and abroad.

The current CEO is Mary Wittenberg, a former law firm partner who specialized in international trade deals for US banks. She joined Road Runners in 1998 as vice president and chief operating officer and in 2005 was named CEO. Under her leadership, the organization doubled its annual income to $60 million by 2012, and the field for the New York City Marathon has grown by nearly 30 percent, to 47,500 from 37,000, to become the largest in the world. Its youth programs have grown by more than ten times and now reach some 130,000 children in New York City and around the world. In 2012 the club gave more than $38,000 to a program for young runners in Angola.

Such growth has led to a collision of ideals. Some local runners say Wittenberg's expanding ambitions have eroded the ethos of Road Runners to serve amateur athletes in New York. The critics say that she has destroyed the intimacy of what started as a modest grassroots club for like-minded runners, and that the club has become "way too corporate," with board members chosen for their professional backgrounds rather than love of the sport. Rising entry fees have priced out lower-income runners and alienated some longtime Road Runners members.

Many of the disgruntled members have turned to new, smaller "boutique" running clubs, including those organized by commercial gymnasiums and other health and fitness industry businesses.

Sources: See *New York Times* (Online), http://www.nytimes.com/2012/10/14/sports/under-mary-wittenberg-the-new-york-city-marathon-is-thriving-so-whats-the-problem.html, and http://www.nytimes.com/2013/03/16/sports/new-york-road-runners-face-difficulty-months-after-marathon.html; New York Road Runners, http://www.nyrr.org/about-us/history.

National Differences in Nonprofit Sectors

In the commentaries on the role and rise of the nonprofit sector so far in this book, relatively few references have been made to different historical traditions or cultures. But the origin, function, and mode of operation of the nonprofit sector in each country reflect that country's unique circumstances (DiMaggio and Anheier 1990; E. James 1989; Kramer 1981; K. McCarthy, Hodgkinson, and Sumariwalla 1992; Pryor 2012; Salamon and Anheier 1997; Salamon and Sokolowski 2010; Skocpol 2011). The lawyers' association in one country may be a champion of human rights whereas in another it may only serve to protect the commercial interests of its members. In two countries with similar political regimes, one government may choose to encourage the formation of nonprofits whereas the other will move to restrict them.

The Determinants of Differences in Nonprofit Sectors

The nonprofit sector of every country is the result of its peculiar social, economic, and political history, which determines the legitimacy, structures, and functions of nonprofit organizations. Lester Salamon and Helmut Anheier (1992a, 1992b, 1998) spoke of "social origins" and "nonprofit regimes" whereas Helmut Anheier and Jeremy Kendall (2001) talked about "national scripts." Even though there is now a converging global discourse about the growth of the nonprofit sector and its increasing role in service delivery, policymaking, and economic life, fundamental historical differences between the sectors in different countries persist. Any contemporary growth is grafted onto the very different national rootstocks of the past evolution of the sector.

An oft-cited example is the contrast between the nonprofit sectors in the United States and France. The modern polities of both countries are largely the result of their eighteenth-century revolutions: Those fighting in the American Revolution (1775–1783) sought an end to the tyranny of the distant British Crown, and the resulting Constitution created a decentralized power structure that guaranteed freedom of speech and association and local independence. In contrast, those fighting in the French Revolution (1789–1799) sought to end the ancien régime of corrupt elites and local privileges, and the result was the centralization of power and the primacy of the collective interests of the state. The visiting Frenchman Alexis de Tocqueville in his two-part *Democracy in America*, published in the 1830s, famously praised the tendency to form associations and noted their key role in social and political life, and this tendency has continued to be the hallmark of US society, with its extensive nonprofit sector and strong philanthropic culture. In contrast, postrevolutionary France experienced no effective freedom of association, with systemic restrictions imposed by a centralized and interventionist state until a 1901 Law of Associations fully legalized the sector. But then in the twentieth century, the expanding French welfare state meant that provision of public goods and services remained primarily in the hands of the government and a restricted number of corporatist nonprofit organizations that had been absorbed into the welfare state apparatus (Archambault 2001; Ullman 1998). Even though France in the twentieth century has had an active social economy of collective and mutual organizations and since the 1980s has witnessed the establishment and consolidation of a new generation of more independent nonprofit organizations, the French nonprofit sector is comparatively smaller than the US sector and considerably more reliant for its funding on the continuing corporatist arrangements with government (Salamon and Sokolowski 2010). An intriguing coda to de Tocqueville's exaltation of the role of associations in the United States was that later, as a French legislator and government minister, he supported laws that restricted the freedom of association in order to ensure political stability.

Commentators note the higher rate of nonprofit development in Protestant and Anglo-Saxon common law societies as a result of a political, religious, and social culture that encourages self-organization (Anheier 1990). In Catholic, Continental European, and civil law countries, the tendency is to a greater obedience to the authority of the state and religious hierarchies. Consequently, the social contract for the service dimension of the welfare state (as opposed to the cash transfer dimension) in Catholic-Continental countries focuses on its funding and delivery by government institutions, whereas in Anglo-Saxon Protestant countries the voluntary sector has taken on a larger role. Other broad-brush portrayals of the differences between national sectors include the contrast between industrialized, democratic countries, where the growing numbers of nonprofits are seen as evidence of a hollowing out of government, and developing and authoritarian countries, where the growth is seen as a filling in of civil society.

Beyond these metanarratives, one can identify a more specific series of key path dependencies that determine the differences in social origins and national scripts for the nonprofit sector around the world. These include variations in the political and social environment, in economic conditions, and in the continuing institutional arrangements that regulate the sector.

Political and Social Context

Variations in dominant historical political discourses, and the shared symbolism and attitudes that derive from them, are the major root causes of differences between nonprofit sectors. Several political and social dynamics shape the size and role of nonprofits: the type of welfare regime the country has, the political-administrative traditions in service delivery, the strength of other social actors, demographics, and policy windows.

Welfare state regimes. Gøsta Esping-Andersen (1990) identified variations in the regimes of the welfare state in industrialized democracies based on their different patterns of working-class political formation, coalition building in the transition from a rural economy to middle-class society, and the institutionalization of class preferences and political behaviors. His analysis focused primarily on the social wage and labor market issues of the welfare state provisions that emerged after World War II, but subsequent authors have adopted his work to also trace how the different regimes confer political, economic, and social spaces to nonprofits (Salamon and Anheier 1998; M. Taylor 2010). Salamon and Anheier (1998) in their work on social origins identified four regime models based on two key dimensions: the extent of government social welfare spending and the scale of the nonprofit sector (see Table 3.1).

The varying roles of the government are also expressed in a number of related continuums that focus on its perceived strength (strong versus weak), size (big versus small), or openness to contestation (autocratic versus democratic). Strong, big, or authoritarian governments are generally inimical to the growth of nonprofit sectors, with the exception of a small group of designated regime-sponsored organizations. The resulting polities provide few opportunities for outside challengers to enter service delivery and policymaking spaces (Dalton 1993; Thomas 1993).

Under the strongest and most authoritarian regimes, rights of association are limited, and any nonprofits that waver from the strict parameters imposed by the regime will find themselves hounded and their workers threatened. Various versions of the large/strong/authoritarian government discourse focus on clientelism, the capacity of government to control the

Table 3.1 Welfare Regimes and Nonprofit Roles

	Small Nonprofit Sector	Large Nonprofit Sector
Low government welfare spending	Statist: Government provides only limited social welfare programs and also controls and constrains development of the nonprofit sector (e.g., Japan)	Liberal: Government provision of social welfare programs is resisted, and services are left in the hands of markets and the nonprofit sector (e.g., the United States)
High government welfare spending	Social democratic: Extensive welfare service is provided by the government; nonprofits focus on recreation, hobby, and volunteer-based advocacy (e.g., Sweden)	Corporatist: Government-funded welfare services are provided through corporatist arrangements (stable partnerships) with large faith-, union-, and employer-based nonprofits (e.g., Germany)

Source: Anheier 2014.

nonprofit sector and to corral it into prescribed social and political spaces. At the same time, some analysts note that nonprofit activity is not necessarily correlated with weak or strong government as with the civil society paradox quoted earlier. Strong government and strong nonprofits may be equally mutually supportive whereas weak government may also be accompanied by a weak nonprofit sector (Wilson 1990).

Kevin Brown and Susan Kenny (2000) provided an updated perspective on welfare regimes in postmodern societies and on the expanding role of the private sector in providing public goods and in supporting the nonprofit sector. Their rubric was based on concepts of citizenship across two dimensions: passive versus active and consumer (market) versus collective. They identified six regimes, each with different roles for nonprofits (see Table 3.2).

These frameworks illustrate how expectations of the roles of nonprofits under different regimes may serve to legitimize, or delegitimize, their participation in service delivery and policymaking. However, nonprofits are by definition independent, and many do not necessarily abide by the functions nominally ascribed to them by dominant ideologies or by the evolving social, economic, or cultural context in which they operate. Increasingly,

Table 3.2 Postmodern Welfare Regimes and Nonprofit Roles

	Passive Citizenship	Active Citizenship
Consumer citizenship	McWelfare: Corporations become surrogate state providers. Nonprofits align themselves with corporations or are created by them.	Welfare.com: Nonprofits aligned with corporations, but new niche markets allow more choice for consumers with a high level of connectivity.
Consumer/ communitarian citizenship	Contractual welfare: The nonprofit sector is likely to expand, with bifurcation between state contractors and others.	Market-bounded associationalism: Nonprofits are strong, in an environment with a high level of social capital and civil society, but experience stronger market influences.
Communitarian citizenship	Social democratic welfare: Nonprofits remain largely concentrated on nonwelfare concerns, with the state being more dominant.	State-bounded associationalism: Nonprofits are strong, in an environment with a high level of social capital and civil society, but are nested within more state-determined frameworks.

Source: Adapted from Brown and Kenny 2000.

nonprofits in traditionally state-centric industrialized countries such as France and Spain are playing a greater role in service delivery and policy-making, and a broad range of nonprofit actors are emerging to challenge the hegemony of the large corporatist providers in countries such as Germany. Some authors postulate the existence of ideological cycles that move society between competing views of collective responsibility and individualism (Dalton 1993), asserting that endogenous mechanisms push citizens back and forth between a preference for more private, individual choices and more collective choices. Each alternative brings about its own cycle of disappointment and backlash.

Political-administrative traditions in service delivery. In addition to macro-welfare-regime debates, a range of mesolevel political and administrative arrangements may favor plurality in the delivery of key services. Schools, universities, hospitals, aged-care facilities, emergency services, or museums can be government run, for profit, or nonprofit for historical reasons that are not always in accord with broader political debates. Throughout Africa, many of the legal and institutional structures of the former colonial powers have survived independence, and contemporary nonprofit sectors build on traditions inherited from former European settler communities (Shivji 2007).

Strength of other social actors. One of the core discourses regarding the rise of nonprofits has been that they are filling a void left by the waning of other, more traditional social actors—religious institutions, labor unions, political parties, and other historical collective and mutual structures. Nonprofits are potentially offering a new, more responsive outlet for the political, economic, and social interests of the population. The residual strength of the traditional actors and their relationships to the state are key factors in determining the size and shape of the nonprofit sector, both in terms of competing with nonprofits for the loyalties of the population and in creating their own new affiliates using the organization forms and legal structures of the nonprofit sector.

Religious institutions, most notably Catholic and Islamic in those countries where they are majority religions, have traditionally occupied much of the social and political space that nonprofits are moving into. Equally important, they have historically been the major recipients of the donations of their adherents, often through religious compulsions such as tithing in Christianity, *maaser* in Judaism, *zakat* in Islam, and *dasvand* in Sikhism. In most industrialized countries, attendance in and contributions to traditional religious institutions have been dwindling considerably (some increase in attendance has occurred at newer charismatic religions, but this increase has not generally had any great impact on overall attendance figures). In countries where faith-based institutions continue to be strong, those institutions often restrict the growth of the secular nonprofit sector.

Similarly, unions and political parties either maintain the loyalty of the population or concede space to the nonprofit sector. But as noted earlier, religious institutions, unions, and political parties have also played a role in the development of the nonprofit sector as they have increasingly recognized that future ties with their constituencies would be well served by collaborating with the emerging sector and by creating affiliated organizations. The new nonprofits may maintain close ties with traditional social actors, and, in a trend that is not unusual, those affiliations are often part of the public identity of nonprofit organizations. European political parties generally continue to dominate interest articulation, so close connections are often formed between parties and nonprofits through vertical integration dynamics. These connections can limit the ability of nonprofits to operate independently on key issues and often lead to a loss of funding when regimes change.

Demographics. Various sociodemographic realities can shape the parameters of the nonprofit sector. A wide range of such factors includes the following:

• Population size: In countries with smaller populations, particularly in those with only a tiny educated elite, personal relations and patronage may inhibit the establishment of an independent nonprofit sector.

• Religious and ethnic diversity: In more diverse communities, nonprofits may be organized around ethnic or religious fault lines. Some may work to bridge divides; however, others may, intentionally or unintentionally, entrench the separation and tension between groups. Ethnic and religious homogeneity has long been cited as one of the reasons why the citizens of social democratic countries are prepared to support higher taxes and government intervention (as the benefits go to people who are "like us").

• Age pyramid: Older populations, particularly those who are active after retirement, can support the nonprofit sector with monetary contributions and volunteering.

• Female workforce participation: Females are traditionally the majority of volunteers and the majority of employees in service industries. Female participation in the workforce can increase both the demand for services, which nonprofits can provide, such as child care, and the supply of workers interested in nonprofit careers.

• Downsizing of public and private organizations: Retrenchments can create a pool of unemployed highly skilled workers who may seek future employment in the nonprofit sector. They may either start new organizations, and so lead to the increase in the number of organizations, or join existing organizations and expand the skills capital of the sector.

• Rural-urban divide: Rural nonprofits face considerably more funding and operational challenges than their urban counterparts, due to higher incidences of poverty that are generally evident in rural areas and the complex logistics of serving a more dispersed population.

Policy windows. The concept of specific historic opportunities—"windows" that open or close—for political and administrative change is well established in political science (Kingdon 1995). The same concept is also applicable to the development of the nonprofit sector. The narratives of the expansion of the nonprofit sector in many countries focus on a few key events that have given impetus to its growth. Major historical moments such as the restoration of democratic institutions evidently create new opportunities, but other events such as natural disasters can also provide an opening for nonprofits to demonstrate their worth to the wider society. How the April 2011 earthquake and tsunami in Japan has given impetus to its nonprofit sector is illustrated in Box 3.11.

Economic Context

The size and nature of the nonprofit sector in any country is closely tied to that country's economic conditions, with industrialized countries on average having nonprofit sectors proportionally more than three times larger than developing countries (Pryor 2012; Salamon and Sokolowski 2010). Advanced industrial democracies are characterized by an increase in middle- and upper-class urban dwellers and a breakdown in traditional class consciousness, and two of the outcomes of such changes in social relationships are an increase in postindustrial, postmaterial concerns and an increase in support for and participation in nonprofits (M. Wallace and Jenkins 1995). New social and political concerns are reinforced by the availability of more discretionary time for participation in nonprofits, as well as more public and private funds for underwriting nonprofit activities (Richardson 1993; Thomas 1993; M. Wallace and Jenkins 1995).

The inverse is true in lower-income, developing countries: public funds are scarce, private donations are limited, and few opportunities exist for nonprofits to generate meaningful local revenues through fees for services or business venturing (with the exception of nonprofit organizations created by local elites to provide education, health, or recreational services to their own communities). Whereas in industrialized countries nonprofits receive most of their funds from domestic sources, in developing countries the majority of funds are received from external sources including official development aid, international philanthropy, and contributions from the local affiliates of multinational corporations.

Box 3.11 Changes in the Nonprofit Sector in Japan

Japan lacks a tradition of private philanthropy, and support for the needy is often expected to come from the family. There are a range of public interest corporations and associations operating under the close control of the government, but officials have tended to regard independent nonprofits as meddlesome amateurs.

For most of Japan's history, qualifying for favorable tax treatment, which was almost guaranteed for charities in the West, was nearly impossible. Of the some 45,000 registered, specified nonprofit corporations in 2010, only some 230 had an approved tax status that allowed for tax deductibility of donations. The process to qualify was so cumbersome and opaque that few nonprofits did. Hundreds of pages of documents had to be filed every few years. Organizations had to get the approval of a ministry related to their area of activity, giving bureaucrats a virtual power of veto over their operations. And nonprofits had to spend 70 percent of their donations over five years, meaning they could not build up large endowments.

Now, many of these impediments have disappeared. Legislation more favorable to nonprofits, which had languished with little parliamentary support for years, was given a boost by appreciation of the efforts of nonprofits to assist in the response to the March 2011 earthquake and tsunami. A law that passed on June 2011 significantly eases the process of getting favorable status. Certification is done by municipal authorities rather than the national tax agency, which tends to see every nonprofit as a net loss to the national coffers. An excessive "public support test" that hampered eligibility has been scrapped. Contributions are almost 50 percent tax deductible, compared with less than 10 percent prior to the law.

Nonprofit lobby groups called it a dramatic change and estimated that as many as 70 percent of existing nonprofits in 2011 would eventually achieve the new tax status. However, by 2014 there were still only 670 specified nonprofit corporations with approved status for tax-deductible donations.

Sources: See *The Economist,* http://www.economist.com/node/18929259; Japan Association of Charitable Organizations, http://www.kohokyo.or.jp/english/Source /databook2014.pdf.

The economic strength of a country and the sources of funding for its nonprofit sector are often expressed as the difference between aid-donor and aid-receiving countries. Of the nearly 200 sovereign states and territories recognized by the United Nations, some 152 are aid receiving (Organisation for Economic Co-operation and Development [OECD] 2011), although some of those with stronger economies, such as Brazil, Russia, India, China, and

South Africa (BRICS), as well as Mexico, Indonesia, South Korea, and Turkey (MISTs), are now both recipients and donors. South Korea is the only country that has since the 1980s moved definitively from being a recipient country to a donor country, although the global financial crises may see countries such as Greece, Ireland, and Iceland slip out of the ranks of purely donors. In those countries that are on the cusp of donor status, a widening debate is occurring about whether they should still be receiving aid.

The relationship between economic development and the size of the nonprofit sector is not necessarily linear. Economic development will not engender a larger nonprofit sector if it does not also generate macroeconomic stability and a philanthropic culture among the more prosperous. Nuno Themudo (2013) applied the Kuznets curve theory of development inequality to the nonprofit sector to demonstrate why developing countries may first experience a waning of their nonprofit sector. The economic systems of many countries favor the accumulation of wealth and permit the largely unfettered transfer of wealth between generations. If the political system and culture are primarily exploitative and extractive, relatively little government or donor support will be found for nonprofits. However, when the culture is more distributive and philanthropic, wealth accumulation can facilitate the growth of the sector. The United States is probably the most emblematic example of the latter in that the accumulation of wealth is deeply embedded in the economic system, but so is a philanthropic culture. The United States has a low tax regime, but broad cross sections of the population have also internalized the obligation to donate, whether they are the robber barons of the late nineteenth and early twentieth century who established the large foundations that continue to be influential 100 years later, the contemporary technology and finance billionaires such as Bill Gates or Warren Buffett who have signed a Giving Pledge (see Box 6.15) to dedicate the majority of their wealth to philanthropy, the more humble parishioners who support their church, or those of all incomes who regularly give to a range of nonprofit organizations.

Regulatory and Institutional Environments

The architecture of public authority and the regulatory institutions, rules, and processes within each polity are the current "peace treaties" of past battles (Richardson 1993). They also become in effect institutional policy actors in their own right, generating enduring bureaucratic logics and path dependency that determine the growth or constraint of the sector.

The legal and administrative regimes in each country determine key elements of the national nonprofit sector. Legal systems based on common law, civil law (e.g., Napoleonic code), or religious law (e.g., sharia) differ in how they structure nonprofit organizations and regulate their relationships with the state and other social actors. This situation reflects the traditional interplay between legal, political, and religious structures—as noted earlier, numerous studies have demonstrated that Protestant, Anglo-Saxon, common law societies tend to have more extensive nonprofit sectors than Catholic, civil law countries or those significantly influenced by religious law (Anheier 1990).

The distribution of powers among branches of government, the distribution of responsibilities among executive agencies, and the centralization-decentralization of administrative structures determine the possibility of regional or industry variations. Various researchers have identified the key elements of legislative and regulatory frameworks that potentially foster or hinder the supply and demand factors that can determine the parameters of the nonprofit sector in any country (Bloodgood, Tremblay-Boire, and Prakash 2014; ICNL 2013; Salamon and Toepler 1997). Freedom of association and assembly is the sine qua non of a strong, independent nonprofit sector. But it is also dependent on the ease and flexibility of incorporation and registration, the regulations covering the operations of the organizations and the fiscal regimes they operate in, and the right (or power) of the government to intervene in, or to terminate, an organization, particularly if that organization engages in political contestation.

The financial health of the sector depends on the tax and fiscal benefits for nonprofits, including the incentives provided for domestic individual and corporate philanthropy, control over foreign donations, provisions for earned income, and the enabling mechanisms for public-private partnerships, including the transparency of the processes of government grant making, contracting, and accountability for such funds.

The regulatory incentives for private philanthropy are among the most visible markers of institutional support for the nonprofit sector. The number of organizations eligible to receive tax-deductible donations, the possibilities available to individuals and corporations for making donations and their tax deductibility, and control over foreign donations vary considerably between countries (Bloodgood, Tremblay-Boire, and Prakash 2014; ICNL 2013; Moore and Rutzen 2011; Salamon and Toepler 1997). Some examples of the variations are outlined below.

Some 1 million organizations in the United States are in the 501(c)(3) category of the tax code, which confers deductibility for charitable donations, whereas in Japan, until recently, only some 230 specified nonprofit organizations had an equivalent status (as indicated in Box 3.11, this category was expanded after the 2011 tsunami), and in the Philippines only 300 organizations have attainted such a status. In the United States, eligibility is determined directly by the government agency the Internal Revenue Service (IRS); in the Philippines it is determined by an independent commission formed from existing nonprofits.

How and how much taxpayers can give varies from country to country. The taxation systems of some countries (e.g., Spain and Hungary) incorporate a charity designation scheme, whereby taxpayers can choose to designate some portion of their tax liability to charitable purposes. These funds—usually around 1 percent of the liability—are either pooled and then assigned to nonprofits through a competitive scheme, or taxpayers can directly designate specific nonprofits as recipients. Australian taxpayers can claim deductions for charitable donations up to the equivalent of 100 percent of their incomes; on the other hand, deductions are capped at 7 percent of individual income in Mexico.

International nonprofits that have affiliates in different countries find that their statuses may vary, even between countries with seemingly similar systems. Greenpeace New Zealand lost its charity status (and so could not receive tax-deductible donations), even though many Greenpeace affiliates around the world continue to be registered for tax-deductible donations (although in almost all countries they must work around regulatory restrictions on political activities by nonprofits with tax-deductible status).

In 2012, the United Kingdom introduced a new provision in the tax code to reduce the rate of inheritance tax from 40 percent to 36 percent for anyone who leaves at least 10 percent of their estate to charity. The United Kingdom also has a Gift Aid system, which allows nonprofits to supplement donations by claiming a refund from the tax office for part of the tax the donor would have paid on the income they chose to donate.

Although many countries now provide relatively generous tax incentives for private and corporate contributions to nonprofits, some continue to keep a tight leash. Box 3.12 documents the tight restrictions on philanthropy in Russia.

Other Social-Cultural Norms

Each country has its particular moral ecology that has a potential impact on the nonprofit sector. This ecology consists of an ill-defined set of cultural values and behaviors, including trust in institutions and in other people, tolerance for corruption, willingness to donate to nonprofit organizations, or disposition to volunteering. These behaviors are reflections of the political and economic realities outlined above but also become operating factors in themselves.

When confronted with a beggar, what will people with the means to help do and why? One option is to give alms because they trust that beggars will be best able to alleviate their plight through such direct contributions, or conversely they mistrust panhandlers, assuming they will use the money for drugs or alcohol and instead resolve to donate to a nonprofit (or support government policies to alleviate poverty). Mexicans tend to give alms directly to the poor and distrust institutions (Layton 2009); conversely, in the United States, people tend to distrust beggars but may give generously to charities (and governments and nonprofits regularly run public cam-

---

Box 3.12 Tax-Deductible Donations in Russia

In Russia, private entities cannot claim a tax deduction or credit at the federal level for contributions made to nonprofits. Individuals may deduct from taxable income any monetary donations to scientific, cultural, health care, educational, sports-related, and social security organizations up to 25 percent of their total income. However, with the exception of sports organizations, the recipient organization must be state subsidized or state owned for the donation to qualify as deductible. Thus, donations to fully independent nonprofit schools, museums, or health care providers do not qualify for a tax deduction. Deductible donations can only be made directly to the beneficiary organization, so donations to umbrella organizations or other intermediaries that redistribute the funds to other nonprofits (such as a "community chest") are not tax deductible. Deductions for individuals can be claimed only for monetary donations; in-kind donations are not eligible for deductions.

Source: See Council on Foundations, http://www.usig.org/countryinfo/russia.asp #deductiblity.

---

paigns to discourage panhandling). The need to engender a "culture of philanthropy" is a common theme in debates on how best to strengthen nonprofit sectors.

Equally important are societal attitudes toward paying taxes. Should there be a high rate of taxation on individual and corporate incomes, which then should be used to pay for public services and subsidize nonprofits, or should taxes be low, leaving to individual citizens and corporations the choice over how to distribute their income surpluses? Various research projects, most notably the European Values Study (2011) and the World Values Survey (2011), were conducted to capture the differences in such values based on extensive national-level survey data. Using such data, cultural groupings have been constructed similar to those used later in this book to classify nonprofit sectors in different countries.

Cultural Frames

The sum total of the above dialectics, undercurrents, and accommodations allows for the creation of a variant of the social origins analysis and identification of a number of distinct cultural frames that describe the nonprofit sector in different countries. Past taxonomies of the differences between national nonprofit sectors have focused on welfare state dynamics in industrialized democracies, on the distinction between developing and industrialized countries, and on regional cultural and political groupings (Anheier 2005; Boli 1992; Bullain and Toftisova 2005; K. McCarthy, Hodgkinson, and Sumariwalla 1992; Salamon et al. 1999; Salamon and Sokolowski 2010; M. Taylor et al. 2009). These factors remain crucial to understanding the national differences as they have engendered a habitus of structures and actions (Ebrahim 2005; M. Taylor et al. 2009). However, nonprofit sectors are expanding under almost all political regimes, and in a globalized world, with its heightened information flows and convergences in policy and practices, such taxonomies need to be updated. In Chapter 4 the comparative research on national nonprofit sectors and the cultural frames are examined in greater depth. But even within each cultural frame, seemingly similar countries continue to have their quirks (see Box 3.13).

Box 3.13 Quirks of the Sectors in English-Speaking Countries

The nonprofit sector in any particular country has a number of significant features or dynamics that distinguish it from other countries with a similar cultural frame. Examples of distinctive quirks in English-speaking countries include the following from the United Kingdom, Australia, and Canada.

In the United Kingdom, *commissioning,* a term that is generally not used in other English-speaking countries, is currently the favored descriptor for government outsourcing and contracting of services to nonprofits. The term is used to acknowledge the idea that collaboration between government and nonprofits does not involve just the transfer of funds but also of powers and responsibilities.

In Australia, nonprofit military veterans organizations and sports clubs have licenses to offer gaming and slot machines. As a result, many Returned and Services League clubs and football clubs are large, casino-like entertainment complexes with high incomes. In their public relations they focus on their role as "community clubs" that use their incomes to provide social and recreational services to the disadvantaged in their localities and to support local nonprofits. Critics claim they designate only a miniscule part of their profits to charitable activities.

In Canada, the bilingual, bicultural situation means that two nonprofit traditions coexist: the anglophone "voluntary sector" and the francophone *secteur bénévole et communautaire* (voluntary and community sector). Like their counterparts in France, nonprofit organizations in francophone provinces function under civil law and have a strong tradition of focusing on collective social action.

4

Comparing National Nonprofit Sectors

There are three kinds of lies: lies, damn lies, and statistics.
—*Aphorism attributed variously to Mark Twain, Benjamin Disraeli, and Leonard Henry Courtney*

Although the benefits of studying nonprofit sectors around the world are evident, one should also be aware of the difficulties of international comparisons. Rod Hague and Martin Harrop (2010) identified the four main difficulties: definitions, data, expert fallibility, and limitations of the method itself.

First, as has been discussed in earlier chapters, definitions and structures of organizations continue to vary considerably from country to country. The differing forms of incorporation and their implications for tax exemptions and incentives for donations have a significant impact on attempts to document and analyze the sector. In some countries, a larger informal sector may result from bureaucratic barriers to incorporation or because of government restraints on nonprofit activities. In some countries, organizations that would operate as nonprofits elsewhere choose to register as business entities.

Second, obtaining accurate data from many countries is extremely difficult. The methods of collecting data may be partial and inaccurate; resources may not exist to make even that data available to researchers; or the country may not have a tradition of transparency. In Spain, for example, the tax returns of foundations have the same legal status as those of corporations and private individuals and so are covered by privacy provisions. Their annual reports are filed with one of over fifty separate national and local administrative registries, which are public but difficult to access (Rey and Alvarez 2011).

Third, the people who compile statistics and who write case studies and commentaries about the nonprofit sector in other countries are limited in certain ways in their skills and understanding of what they are researching. Their capabilities in interpreting differences in data and definitions and in understanding the different cultural and social contexts of their work will have a direct impact on their capacity to analyze the work of nonprofits. Do the researchers speak the language of the country they are studying and have they spent sufficient time there to truly understand the context?

Fourth and finally, in any research, choices are made about how to apply the method. If one is comparing nonprofits in different countries, on what data is the method based? Put simply, too many variables influence the makeup of the nonprofit sector and too few countries are available from which to gather reliable information. How the comparative method is applied, and which countries are used for the comparisons, will significantly influence the results.

Research on nonprofits around the world offers multiple examples of the challenges of documenting and comparing sectors between countries and of interpreting long cultural histories of associative life through the lens of contemporary conceptual frameworks. Civil society and social capital were identified in Chapter 2 as key concepts, but attempts to apply them in different cultural contexts are often problematic. For example, the Chinese word *guanxi* and Melanesian word *wantok* both describe traditional relationship networks that help individuals and groups articulate their interests and are often likened to the Western concept of social capital. But they are also seen as corrupting influences that potentially generate cronyism and nepotism. As an example, the challenges of applying nonprofit sector concepts to traditional collective structures in Japan are illustrated in Box 4.1.

Historical Comparisons

The focus of this chapter is on comparing contemporary national nonprofit sectors, but social origins and path dependency approaches to the study of nonprofits are based on understanding how the history of each polity has conditioned current dynamics. In industrialized countries, guilds and fraternal societies that once dominated the associative sector have become a shadow of their former selves, mutual financial institutions such as local savings and loans societies have amalgamated and demutualized, and trade unions, mainstream religions, and political parties have all seen membership and attendance plummet. In developing countries, traditional associative structures based on ethnicities, religions, kinship, localities, or trades are being swept away as "modernization," "development," and "globalization" (all highly contested concepts) take hold. Political transitions transform former clandestine opposition networks into new legal organizations or simply foster new spaces of independent, nonstate action.

Box 4.1 Should *Jichikai* Be Considered Nonprofits?

Japan is often characterized as having a comparatively small nonprofit sector (see Table 3.1 and Box 3.11), a ranking based on the relatively low number of organizations incorporated under a 1998 law on nonprofit organizations and on the small number of these organizations eligible for tax-deductible donations.

However, Japan has a long history of local communal life with neighbors taking an active part in the maintenance and beautification of public spaces and ensuring the well-being of others in the community. The formal structures of this neighborhood life are associations known as *jichikai* (also rendered in English as *chihi-kei* and usually translated as "neighborhood or community associations"), which are present in almost every locality. Neighbors pay dues and the association provides sanitation, security, recreation, and social services, as well as institutional links to local government. Participation is voluntary, but members of the community face strong cultural pressure to belong and nonparticipation would leave one branded as an outsider, particularly in rural areas and older urban neighborhoods.

During World War II, the *jichikai* were used for home front mobilization and after the war were initially disbanded by the occupying forces as antidemocratic remnants of the old regime. But they were soon reestablished and are now considered to be a key element of Japanese social cohesion (Applbaum 1996). Nonetheless, they are often overlooked in research on nonprofits in Japan, with many observers regarding the *jichikai* more as part of the government apparatus. They are generally regarded as conceptually separate from modern independent nonprofits in Japan, even though analogous organizations with the same goals and activities would be considered the core of the community-based nonprofit sector in many other countries.

In addition, a number of other public corporations in Japan have traditionally carried out activities often associated with the nonprofit sector, including public benefit corporations (*koeki hojin*), school corporations (*gakko hojin*), social welfare corporations (*shakai fukushi hojin*), readjustment relief corporations (*kosei hogo hojin*), and religious corporations (*shukyo hojin*). Some 230,000 of these organizations are in operation, but because they are generally well established and under strong government control, they are also often excluded from discussion of the nonprofit sector in Japan.

Source: See Nonprofit Japan, "Overview of Nonprofit Sector in Japan," http://nonprofit japan.home.igc.org.

In the cultural frames outlined below, historical change is a constant theme in the analysis of the forces that have created the contemporary sectors. National narratives from around the world describe "new" or "modern" sectors that reflect the changes documented in earlier chapters. Although collective voluntary action has a long history within each national context, the contemporary nonprofit sector is clearly distinct from earlier structures that were rooted in faith-based organizations, political parties, labor movements, or other traditional bonds. The new sector is more secularized, universalist, professionalized, commercialized, results oriented, and globalized than earlier iterations. In the narratives of the contemporary dynamics of a wide range of countries, the nonprofit sector is cited as larger, more influential, and more integrated into national policymaking and service delivery than at any time in recent history (see, for example, Government of Liberia 2008). The histories of many individual organizations also reflect such evolutions, as can be seen in Box 4.2, which documents the growth of an iconic Argentinean organization.

Box 4.2 Madres de Plaza de Mayo

Madres de Plaza de Mayo (Mothers of May Square) began in 1977 as a small group of mothers who protested outside the Argentinean president's office seeking information about their children who had been detained and "disappeared" by the military as part of its "Dirty War" against opponents of the regime. The fourteen founders had met in the corridors of police stations and army barracks as they fought to locate their missing sons and daughters.

Their weekly protests were held in the square outside the presidential office, which has been a focal point of political life in Argentina since the May 1810 revolution for independence from Spain. The mothers walked continually around the center of the square, as they were prohibited from congregating, and they wore white scarves embroidered with the names of their children because they were not allowed to carry placards. Their protests were met with fierce repression, and numerous mothers and their supporters were arrested and ended up among the disappeared. Years later, the remains of three of the original group were located and exhumed (one was reburied in the square). The surviving members persisted in their protests, and the organization grew and garnered international support and celebrity while continuing to demand answers from the military government about the fate of their children. With the return to civilian government in 1983, Madres continued to press the government to investigate the crimes of the Dirty War.

continues

Box 4.2 continued

In 1986, Madres split into two factions. The Madres de Plaza de Mayo–Línea Fundadora (Mothers of May Square–Founding Line) continued to focus on recovering remains and bringing perpetrators to justice. The Asociación Madres de Plaza de Mayo (Association of the Mothers of May Square), headed by Hebe de Bonafini, the president of Madres since 1979, sought to continue the work of their children. It began to be more active in a range of progressive political causes and in service provision, establishing a newspaper, a radio station, and a university. Hebe de Bonafini and the association faction developed close ties to the administration of the center-left president Néstor Kirchner, elected in 2003, and to his wife and successor Cristina Fernández de Kirchner. In 2008, it established a federally funded housing program, Sueños Compartidos, to build thousands of new housing units and other facilities for the poor throughout the country.

The Asociación Madres de Plaza de Mayo has evolved from a small group of dissident mothers under attack by an authoritarian regime to a multimillion-dollar advocacy and service conglomerate of affiliated organizations and projects working in partnership with an elected democratic government. However, its rapid growth in recent years appears to have overwhelmed the administrative capacities of its principals. In 2011, widespread fraud was uncovered in the Sueños Compartidos program and the contract was rescinded, and in 2014 the university was taken over by the government after accumulating a large deficit.

Source: See Asociación Madres de Plaza de Mayo, http://www.madres.org/; DeMars 2005.

Comparative Research Projects

Statistics on the nonprofit sector are constantly improving. Researchers and international organizations are addressing the methodological challenges, and considerable work has been done to standardize definitions and data collection methodologies internationally. Five key research projects have made a significant contribution to the understanding of the nonprofit sector worldwide. However, each one covers only a limited number of countries, so all have significant gaps. Furthermore, no single study covers China, India, and the United States, the three most populous countries. Collectively, the studies cover only 124 of the some 200 recognized states and territories in the world (although they do cover the great majority of the world population, and for some missing countries such as Haiti, extensive documentation can be found elsewhere). Figure 4.1 indicates the countries covered by each of the research projects, which are detailed below.

Figure 4.1   Countries and Territories Included in the Research Projects

Johns Hopkins University Comparative Nonprofit Sector Project

http://ccss.jhu.edu/research-projects/comparative-nonprofit-sector-project/; various publications are available for each country, with dates starting in 1996

45 countries: Argentina, Australia, Austria, Belgium, Brazil, Canada, Chile, Colombia, Czech Republic, Denmark, Egypt, Finland, France, Germany, Ghana, Hungary, India, Ireland, Israel, Italy, Japan, Kenya, Lebanon, Mexico, Morocco, Netherlands, New Zealand, Norway, Pakistan, Peru, Philippines, Poland, Portugal, Romania, Slovakia, South Africa, South Korea, Spain, Sweden, Switzerland, Tanzania, Thailand, Uganda, United Kingdom, United States

National Satellite Accounts (Johns Hopkins University/United Nations/National Statistics Agencies)

http://ccss.jhu.edu/research-projects/un-nonprofit-handbook/un-handbook-publications/; draft reports are available on the Internet from other countries, see Government of India 2009

16 countries: Australia, Belgium, Brazil, Canada, Czech Republic, France, Israel, Japan, Kyrgyzstan, Mexico, New Zealand, Norway, Philippines, Portugal, Thailand, United States

CIVICUS Civil Society Index

http://www.civicus.org/csi/index.php

71 countries and territories: Albania, Argentina, Armenia, Azerbaijan, Belarus, Bolivia, Bulgaria, Canada, Chile, China, Croatia, Cyprus (South), Czech Republic, Ecuador, Egypt, Estonia, Fiji, Georgia, Germany, Ghana, Greece, Guatemala, Guinea, Honduras, Hong Kong, India (state of Orissa only), Indonesia, Italy, Jamaica, Japan, Jordan, Kazakhstan, Kosovo, Lebanon, Liberia, Macedonia, Mexico, Mongolia, Montenegro, Morocco, Mozambique, Nepal, Netherlands, New Zealand, Nicaragua, Nigeria, Northern Ireland, Pakistan, Philippines, Poland, Romania, Russia, Rwanda, Scotland, Senegal, Serbia, Sierra Leone, Slovenia, South Africa, South Korea, Taiwan, Tanzania, Togo, Turkey, Uganda, Ukraine, Uruguay, Vietnam, Venezuela, Wales, Zambia

continues

Johns Hopkins University Comparative Nonprofit Sector Project

The Johns Hopkins University Comparative Nonprofit Sector Project, which began in 1990, was the first systematic international effort to analyze the size, scope, structure, financing, and roles of the nonprofit sector around the world. The project sought to increase practical and theoretical knowledge about the nonprofit sectors and to help provide a basis for informed public policy and private philanthropy. The objective of the project was to understand the factors that encouraged or hindered the growth of the sector in each country and to evaluate the impact of its contributions. Almost every contemporary study and profile of the nonprofit sector makes some reference to this seminal work.

Figure 4.1 continued

USAID CSO Sustainability Index

Central and Eastern Europe and Eurasia

http://www.usaid.gov/europe-eurasia-civil-society/cso-sustainability-2012

29 countries: Albania, Armenia, Azerbaijan, Belarus, Bosnia and Herzegovina, Bulgaria, Croatia, Czech Republic, Estonia, Georgia, Hungary, Kazakhstan, Kosovo, Kyrgyzstan, Latvia, Lithuania, Macedonia, Moldova, Montenegro, Poland, Romania, Russia, Serbia, Slovakia, Slovenia, Tajikistan, Turkmenistan, Ukraine, Uzbekistan

Sub-Saharan Africa

http://www.usaid.gov/africa-civil-society

25 countries: Angola, Botswana, Burundi, Democratic Republic of Congo, Ethiopia, Gabon, Gambia, Ghana, Guinea, Kenya, Liberia, Malawi, Mali, Mozambique, Nigeria, Rwanda, Senegal, Sierra Leone, South Africa, South Sudan, Sudan, Tanzania, Uganda, Zambia, Zimbabwe

International Center for Not-for-Profit Law (ICNL)

http://www.icnl.org/research/monitor/index.html; list only includes NGO Law Monitor country reports, but reports on regional intergovernmental entities are also published by ICNL, and various documents from other countries can be accessed through the site

41 countries: Afghanistan, Algeria, Azerbaijan, Bangladesh, Belarus, Cambodia, China, Colombia, Ecuador, Egypt, El Salavador, Ethiopia, Honduras, Indonesia, Iraq, Jordan, Kenya, Lebanon, Malaysia, Mexico, Morocco, Nepal, Nicaragua, Nigeria, Pakistan, Palestine, Panama, Peru, Russia, Rwanda, Saudi Arabia, Sierra Leone, South Africa, Tajikistan, Turkey, Turkmenistan, Uganda, Uzbekistan, Venezuela, Yemen, Zimbabwe

---

The project has both documented the growth of nonprofit sectors around the world and fostered it. A goal of the project had always been to improve awareness and build local capacity (Salamon and Sokolowski 2010). One of the founding principal researchers of the study is credited with coining the phrase "global associational revolution" (Salamon 1994), and the globe-trotting activities of Lester Salamon and other early project researchers such as Helmut Anheier, along with their extensive network of local associates, have generated considerable academic research and public policy interest in the sector. Disciples have set up research and advocacy organizations in a number of countries as platforms for policy discussions and for the drafting of legislation favorable to the sector.

The first phases of the project established the structural-functional definition quoted in Chapter 2, which has become the world standard, and collected available data on the sector in forty-five countries (see the list in Figure 4.1). The field research was done primarily in the period from 1995 to

1998, and the results were published in various working papers and books, including *Global Civil Society: An Overview* (Salamon, Sokolowski, and List 2003). Given the differences in definitions and legal structures of organizations and the dearth of reliable statistics, the project used mixed methodology to document the scope of the sector in the countries researched. It combined official economic and population statistics with a variety of estimating techniques, as well as data assembled by umbrella groups and some limited original survey work. Newer project publications can be found, including a 2010 third edition of *Global Civil Society: Dimensions of the Nonprofit Sector* (Salamon and Sokolowski 2010), but they are based primarily on forward projections from the initial data. The project has provided the fundamental framework for continuing research comparing nonprofit sectors, and it continues to be the most widely disseminated and quoted comparative work.

The various project publications contain numerous tables and graphs, which compare countries on key metrics. Figure 4.2 shows two extracts from the 2003 publication that illustrate the mix of service and expressive functions and the mix of revenues from earned income, government subsidies, and philanthropy.

These and other key indicators were used in the 2003 publication to define patterns or clusters divided into two main groupings: (1) developed and (2) developing and transitional countries. The developed countries were broken down according to their welfare state regimes into the subclusters: Anglo-Saxon, Nordic welfare, European welfare partnerships, and Asian industrialized. The developing and transitional countries were broken down by regions into the subclusters of Latin America, Africa, and Central and Eastern Europe.

In the 2010 edition of *Civil Society*, updated definitions of the patterns were based on the combination of five factors: the size of the nonprofit workforce, the share of the nonprofit workforce that is made up of volunteers, the level of government support, the level of philanthropic support, and the share of organizations that focus more on expressive functions than service functions. The five patterns were identified as liberal, welfare partnership, social democratic, statist, and traditional (Salamon and Sokolowski 2010).

National Satellite Accounts

Despite the significant contribution of the Johns Hopkins project in creating comparative frameworks, significant gaps in knowledge about the nonprofit sector continue to exist. As Salamon (2010), the principal researcher, noted:

> The nonprofit or civil society sector remains the invisible subcontinent on the social landscape of most countries, poorly understood by policymakers and the public at large, often encumbered by legal limitations, and inadequately utilized as a mechanism for addressing public problems. One reason for this is the lack of basic information on its scope, structure, financing, and contribution in most parts of the world. (167)

Figure 4.2 Selected Results of the Comparative Nonprofit Sector Project

A. Service and Expressive Functions

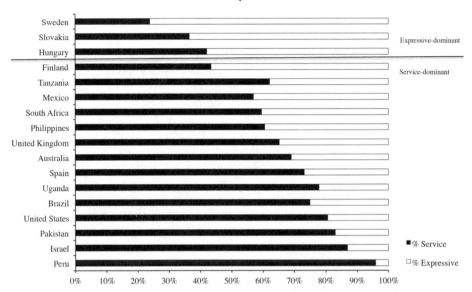

B. Sources of Income

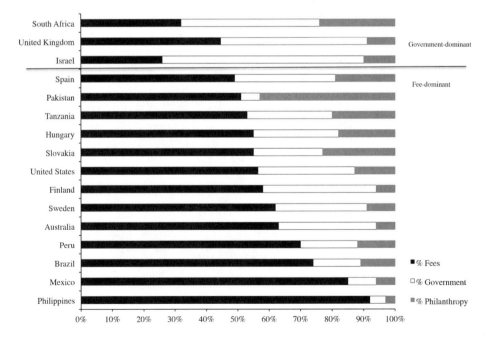

Source: Salamon, Sokolowski, and List 2003.

In order to try to create a more accurately comparative database, Salamon and his collaborators have shifted their efforts in recent years to institutionalizing the measurement of the nonprofit sector by working with the UN Statistics Division and with the statistics agencies of individual countries to create international standards for calculating the contribution of nonprofits to national economies. The focus has been on creating nonprofit satellite accounts as part of the UN System of National Accounts, the official international system of collecting and reporting economic statistics, which has until now consigned nonprofits to "statistical oblivion" (Salamon 2002b). The collaboration between the Johns Hopkins project and the UN Statistics Division has resulted in the publication of the *Handbook on Nonprofit Institutions in the System of National Accounts* (United Nations 2003) and subsequent efforts to implement satellite accounts at national levels around the world. By 2011, sixteen countries had produced satellite accounts, and thirty more had made formal commitments to implement them in the near future (see the list of countries in Table 4.1). A parallel collaboration with the International Labour Organization produced the *Manual on the Measurement of Volunteer Work* for gathering data on the contribution of formal and informal volunteering to the economy of a country (Global Volunteer Measurement Project 2011).

The first sixteen countries to complete satellite accounts show the following results for the contribution of nonprofit institutions to gross domestic product (GDP), including the contributions of volunteers (see Table 4.1).

Table 4.1 Contribution of Nonprofit Institutions to GDP

Country	Nonprofit Contribution to GDP (percentage)	Research Year
Canada	8.1	2008
Israel	7.1	2007
Mozambique	6.7	2003
United States	6.6	2009
Belgium	5.8	2008
New Zealand	5.3	2004
Japan	5.2	2004
Australia	4.9	2007
France	4.7	2002
Norway	4.6	2009
Brazil	3.4	2002
Kyrgyzstan	2.3	2008
Mexico	2.2	2008
Portugal	2.0	2006
Czech Republic	1.6	2009
Thailand	0.8	2008

Source: Salamon 2010.

Among the initial findings from the first countries with nonprofit satellite accounts was the following:

• The nonprofit sector is a considerable economic force, accounting on average for 5 percent of the GDP. It is on a par with or exceeds the GDP contribution of other major industries, such as utilities (gas, water, and electricity—averaging 2.3 percent of GDP), construction (5.1 percent of GDP), and financial intermediation (banks, insurance companies, and financial services firms—5.6 percent of GDP).

• About a quarter of the value added by nonprofits comes from the work of volunteers, underscoring again the crucial importance of capturing volunteer work in economic statistics.

• Nonprofits are a highly dynamic and fast-growing element of the economy. In the countries in which historical data are available, the nonprofit sector's contribution to GDP has been growing at an average rate that is twice the growth rate of GDP over recent years (8.1 percent per year vs. 4.1 percent).

CIVICUS Civil Society Index

CIVICUS World Alliance for Citizen Participation works to strengthen citizen action and civil society throughout the world, especially in areas where participatory democracy and freedom of association are threatened. The first meeting was held in Barcelona in 1993, and the secretariat was initially established in Washington, DC, but moved to Johannesburg, South Africa, in 2002. One of the signature projects of CIVICUS is the Civil Society Index (CSI), an assessment tool that measures the strength of civil society in different countries. The two phases of CSI, 2003–2006 and 2008–2010, covered a total of seventy-one countries (see the list of countries in Figure 4.1). It focused on four dimensions: the structure of civil society, the external environment in which civil society exists and functions, the values practiced and promoted in the civil society arena, and the impact of activities pursued by civil society actors. These four dimensions are measured using a core set of seventy-four universal quantitative and qualitative indicators, and country teams are encouraged to adapt and add their own indicators to ensure contextual validity. Each dimension is assigned a score of 1 to 3, and the results for a country are represented graphically as a "civil society diamond." Figure 4.3 shows the diamond for Sierra Leone.

The diamonds are accompanied by narrative reports. In Box 4.3, the report for Sierra Leone is summarized.

CIVICUS continues to explore methodologies for measuring and comparing civil society in countries around the world. In 2012 CVICUS released its first annual global *State of Civil Society*, which combined a review of the trends having an impact on national civil societies around the world with the

Figure 4.3 Civil Society Diamond for Sierra Leone

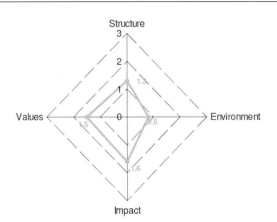

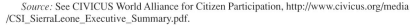

Source: See CIVICUS World Alliance for Citizen Participation, http://www.civicus.org/media /CSI_SierraLeone_Executive_Summary.pdf.

national profiles that resulted from the second phase of its survey (CIVICUS 2012). The 2013 *State of Civil Society* examined the enabling environments for civil society and focused on emblematic case studies from around the world (CIVICUS 2013a). In 2013, CIVICUS launched a new Enabling Environment Index (CIVICUS 2013b), which documents the socioeconomic, sociocultural, and governance environments at national levels that enable or hinder the development and operations of civil society. The new index was created to complement the existing CSI due to the need to cover the broader definition of civil society as a space or sphere and not just as organizations. The Enabling Environment Index is calculated using seventy-one indicators gleaned from available sources such as the UN Human Development Index, the World Values Survey, and the World Bank World Development Indicators. The first edition covers 109 countries, selected on the basis of data availability. According to CIVICUS the new index demonstrates the strong correlation between socioeconomic development and the enabling environment for civil society. The top ranked countries were New Zealand, Canada, Australia, Denmark, and Norway, whereas the worst ranked were Gambia, Burundi, Iran, Uzbekistan, and the Democratic Republic of Congo (CIVICUS 2013b).

USAID CSO Sustainability Index

USAID, the development agency of the US government, as part of its democracy and governance program, has been publishing annual reports since 1997 on the state of the nonprofit sector in twenty-nine countries in Central and Eastern Europe and Eurasia and in 2010 began publishing reports on twenty-

Box 4.3 A Critical Time for Civil Society in Sierra Leone

The CSI report indicates that civil society organizations played a strong and influential role in bringing democratic change to the country and that they continue to play an important role in rebuilding after years of civil war.

The report focuses on the strengths, weaknesses, and opportunities of and threats to civil society in Sierra Leone against the backdrop of a relatively democratic state. The civil society diamond that emerged documents a civil society facing challenges characterized by weak organization and poor resources. The lack of sustainability of financial resources has been identified as a potential threat to the work of civil society organizations, especially since most of their funds come from foreign donors. Civil society in Sierra Leone also faces structural problems centered on the fragmentation caused by the differences between urban-based professional and community-based forms of organizations.

The environment for civil society in Sierra Leone constitutes the weakest dimension, characterized by low social trust, with two-thirds of the respondents to a survey not trusting fellow citizens. The levels of social tolerance remain low, particularly toward people living with the human immunodeficiency virus (HIV) and the resultant acquired immune deficiency syndrome (AIDS), homosexuals, and people of a different race. The environment is further hampered by rampant poverty. The government has made modest gains in the area of human rights through the creation of structures and institutions to ensure the protection of human rights, and the rural population has been empowered to participate in local governance issues in their respective local councils.

The report also reveals that civil society organizations do not practice good governance and gender equity and are often characterized by a culture of secrecy and corruption. Most organizations lack internal democracy, accountability, and transparency, and their leadership is mostly concentrated in the hands of the respective founders.

Sources: See CIVICUS World Alliance for Citizen Participation, http://civicus.org /index.php/en/media-centre-129/reports-and-publications/csi-reports/africa-country -reports/325-sierra-leone, and http://www.civicus.org/media/CSI_SierraLeone_Executive _Summary.pdf.

five countries in sub-Saharan Africa (see the list of countries in Figure 4.1). The reports, initially titled *NGO Sustainability Index,* but later changed to *CSO Sustainability Index* (USAID 2011a, 2011b), analyze and assign scores to seven interrelated dimensions: legal environment, organizational capacity, financial viability, advocacy, service provision, infrastructure, and public image. These are then averaged to produce an overall sustainability score. Scores are in the range of 1 to 7, with a lower score signifying greater sustainability. A panel of civil society practitioners and experts in each country assesses the sector's performance and a Washington, DC–based editorial committee of technical and regional experts reviews the local panels' findings. Based on their scores, countries are classified as either sustainability enhanced, sustainability evolving, or sustainability impeded. Figure 4.4 shows the scores for the Central and Eastern European and Eurasian countries.

The scores are accompanied by narrative reports that outline the recent developments having an impact on the nonprofit sectors in the different countries. In Box 4.4, the 2013 regional report for sub-Saharan Africa is summarized.

Figure 4.4 Sustainability Index Scores

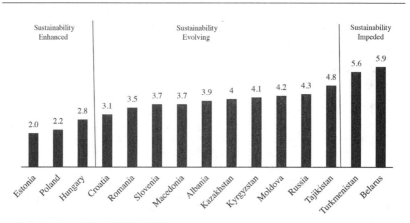

Source: Adapted from USAID 2011a.

Box 4.4 CSO Sustainability in Sub-Saharan Africa

According to the *2013 CSO Sustainability Index,* "CSOs in sub-Saharan Africa are growing in their role as critical responders to emerging national issues and needs, through advocacy initiatives and provision of needed services." The report highlights continued areas of weakness that impede sustainability in the region: "Notably, in many countries in the region, CSOs—particularly those focused on advocacy and human rights—are facing increasing restrictions or threats of restrictions on their work. In addition, even the most sustainable CSO sectors continue to lack access to critical technical and financial resources, thereby undermining growth in most other dimensions of sustainability."

Source: 2013 CSO Sustainability Index for Sub-Saharan Africa, http://www.usaid
.gov/africa-civil-society.

International Center for Not-for-Profit Law

The ICNL promotes an enabling legal environment for freedom of association and public participation around the world by brokering the flow of knowledge about legislation and regulations and by providing technical assistance to governments and nonprofit organizations. ICNL has offices in Washington, DC; Budapest, Hungary; Almaty, Kazakhstan; and Kiev, Ukraine, and representatives in Asia, the Pacific, and the Middle East, as well as a substantial online presence. The ICNL online library contains more than 2,900 resources from 165 countries and territories in forty-two different languages, and ICNL publishes the *NGO Law Monitor*, the *International Journal for Not-for-Profit Law*, and numerous thematic reports and analytical articles. The resources are somewhat patchy: the online library holdings for any particular country may be as sparse as one single form, and the *NGO Law Monitor* covers only forty-one countries, but the profiles in the *Monitor* are continually updated, so ICNL is a useful resource for current information about those countries. In Box 4.5 are given various snapshots from the information on Venezuela, Rwanda, and Saudi Arabia.

ICNL also collaborates with other organizations to develop and evaluate tools for assessing the enabling environments for civil society. A recent issue of its journal compared eight assessment tools, and ICNL and CIVICUS have jointly developed a guide for researchers and advocates (ICNL 2014).

Comparing the Studies

The five research projects detailed in Figure 4.1 and the preceding sections are an invaluable resource for understanding the domestic nonprofit sectors of different countries. However, they also highlight the reality that no single authoritative source provides comprehensive current data on the nonprofit sector in all countries. The research projects generally rely on local partners, and although each project has a standard common methodology, these partners put their own spin on the research. This flexibility in approach allows projects to adjust for cultural differences but also exposes the results to possible bias errors. How the same indicator, charitable giving, is evaluated and ranked in the CIVICUS CSI reports from Germany and Guinea is demonstrated in Box 4.6.

No countries are the subject of all five research projects, and only four countries (Czech Republic, Mexico, South Africa, and Uganda) are included in at least four projects. For countries included in two or more research projects, apparent inconsistencies and contradictions can be found in the data and narratives in the different reports. In Table 4.1, Mozambique, a country that is generally characterized as a typical developing country with a weak nonprofit sector, appears near the top of the list in terms of the nonprofit sector contribution to GDP, whereas Norway, which is usually characterized as having a robust nonprofit sector, is toward the bottom. Such discrepancies underline the need to understand the local context of each country. The large contribution of the nonprofit sector in Mozambique may be due to the outsized influence of large foreign donors and international organizations in a developing country, as well as by the tendency of elites in developing countries to support the private provision

---

Box 4.5   ICNL Snapshots of Civil Society:
Venezuela, Rwanda, and Saudi Arabia

In Venezuela, the National Assembly on December 21, 2010, passed the Law for Protection of Political Liberty and National Self-Determination, which targets NGOs dedicated to the "defense of political rights" or other "political objectives." Specifically, it precludes these organizations from possessing assets or receiving any income from foreign sources. Noncompliance could lead to a fine of double the amount received from the foreign source. In addition, these organizations reportedly will be prohibited from hosting a foreign citizen who speaks out in a manner that might offend state institutions or senior officials, or that might go against the exercise of state sovereignty. Noncompliance with this provision could subject representatives of the Venezuelan organization to monetary fines and a loss of "political rights" for five to eight years.

Civil society in Rwanda remains in an embryonic state due to a variety of practical constraints. The overwhelming majority of Rwandans suffer from extreme poverty; about two-thirds of the entire population lives on less than $1 per day. Such poverty deters engagement in any activity that is not directly productive. The lack of education limits the ability of people to access various sources of information and limits the capacity to interact with formal institutions of the state. Grassroots associations are focused on issues of livelihood, with little capacity to engage on public policy issues in a more strategic way. This situation in turn has made it difficult for urban-based advocacy organizations to make connections to the grassroots.

In Saudi Arabia, although hundreds of organizations work in various fields, civil society remains underdeveloped due to a weak legal framework, lack of transparency, and a lack of experience in establishing effective and sustainable institutions. This environment exists despite Saudi society's cultural and social heritage and religious laws that call for civic work in various spheres. Modern state institutions have adopted a central administrative approach. As a result, civil society organizations are restrained by a legal framework that limits their effectiveness and diversity.

Source: See ICNL, Country Profiles, http://www.icnl.org.

of key services such as health and education through nonprofit organizations separate from inadequate government systems. The small relative size of the nonprofit contribution in Norway may be due to the outsized revenue that the country derives from North Sea oil and gas.

Box 4.6 CIVICUS CSI Results for Charitable Giving: Germany and Guinea

---

In Germany, the report by the Maecenata Institute of Philanthropy and Civil Society at the Humboldt University in Berlin gives Germany a midlevel grade (2 out of a possible 3) on charitable giving based on the following justification: Charitable giving includes regular donations, defined as money given at least once a year to a nonprofit. According to a prominent national donation monitor, 41 percent of the total population aged fourteen and above made donations in 1999. This percentage accounted for 37 percent (2000), 40 percent (2001), and 47 percent (2002) in subsequent years. For 2003, 45 percent was indicated. Another national statistics monitor had similar figures in 1996, with 41 percent of the population in West Germany and 32 percent in East Germany having made donations. Moreover, reference is made to the scope of donations in kind, with 41 percent of East Germans and 35 percent of West Germans making such donations in 1996, which corresponds to an average monetary value of about 107 euros and 148 euros, respectively. In Germany, a total of 3.87 billion euros was donated, with private donations accounting for 60 percent, inheritances for 20 percent, and corporate donations for 20 percent. Older people are more likely to donate than younger people, individuals in permanent employment are more likely to make donations than the unemployed, and individuals with higher incomes are likewise more likely to make donations than those with lower incomes. However, donations are not solely influenced by economic situations. For example, idealistic values also play a significant role, and membership of a particular religion exerts influence on the likelihood of donations.

In Guinea, the report by the National Council for Guinean Civil Society Organizations gives Guinea the highest grade (3 out of a possible 3) for charitable giving based on the following justification: In Guinea, gathering statistics on charitable donations is difficult, as no database contains information on such donations. Guinean people tend to give in mosques or churches or give money to people anonymously. But charity seems to be a habit of the population. A community survey reported that a high level of citizens (87.8 percent) donate to charity on a regular basis, generating an indicator score of 3. It would, however, be necessary to do a more extensive survey on this issue in order to obtain more reliable data.

Source: See CIVICUS, Civil Society Index, http://www.civicus.org/csi/index.php.

The differences between results in research reports are largely due to differences in methodologies and access to information but also to the different orientations and agendas of the participants. The national satellite accounts that are part of the UN System of National Accounts and the ICNL may be the most impartial, but they also focus only on the economic and legal dimensions of the sectors, respectively, and so may not capture many of the wider social and political implications. The other projects have more specific normative agendas: the Johns Hopkins project clearly stated from the outset that a goal was to improve awareness, CIVICUS is a nonprofit created specifically to strengthen citizen action and civil society, and USAID is a US government agency that through its democracy and governance program seeks to promote sustainable democracy through diplomatic efforts and the support of government institutions and civil society. One should expect that local partners would have different dialogues with a university research center, a nonprofit advocacy organization, and an agency of the US government.

While the coverage of the sector around the world is substantial, the most significant gap in the research is the small representation of Arab countries. Prior to the current political upheavals in the region, the preponderance of authoritarian and single-party regimes in the second half of the twentieth century kept their formerly more independent civil societies on a tight leash (R. A. Brown and Pierce 2013), restricting the work of internal and external researchers. Another factor has been the historic institutionalization of charity and social services through Islamic organizations, based on the religious precepts of *zakat*, *sadaqah*, and *waqf* (see Box 4.7). Research on the operations and finances of faith-based institutions from all religions has been particularly challenging. In a few countries, the social service dimensions of their work are delivered through separately incorporated nonprofit organizations and so are subject to the same oversight and transparency requirements as other nonprofits. In most countries, however, social services are generally provided directly by the religious institutions themselves and so continue to be outside the full accounting of the taxation system or other regulatory oversight. This latter situation is the reality in most Arab countries. In 2011, Forbes Middle East published its first list of the most transparent charities in the Arab world (*Al Bawaba* 2011; Forbes Middle East 2013). In a region of some 370 million people, *Forbes* could rank only 54 of the 337 charities surveyed, as the remainder could not supply sufficiently independently audited financial statements. Of the twenty-two Arab countries, five were absent from the list because their ministries refused to provide lists of charities, and four countries were excluded due to political turmoil. In the second list covering 2012, only 61 charities from 2,050 surveyed were deemed sufficiently transparent to be included (Forbes Middle East 2013).

Box 4.7 Islamic Concepts of Philanthropy

Zakat, or charity, is one of the five pillars of Islam. All Muslims are expected to pay *zakat fitrah,* a donation at the end of Ramadan, generally equivalent to the price of one meal. Those whose means place them above *nisab,* a poverty threshold, must also pay *zakat al-mal,* generally interpreted as 2.5 percent of net income and savings. These two types of charity are obligatory. Anything that exceeds this basic obligation is called *sadaqah* and is considered to be voluntary charity. In addition to *zakat* and *sadaqah,* Islam encourages other charitable traditions. *Waqf* refers to an endowment for charitable purposes that is to be held by a trust in perpetuity. It is generally translated into English as "foundation."

The application of this concept to the work of nonprofits varies greatly between countries with Islamic populations. In general, *zakat* and *sadaqah* go to religious institutions that may use the money for charitable purposes. As with all religions, the expenditure of such funds is generally not open to public scrutiny.

In national taxation regimes, *zakat* is generally treated as a charitable donation, and corresponding income deductions are allowed. A few governments do not allow deductions but pass on the taxes collected on *zakat* to Islamic organizations. In countries with more established independent nonprofits, Islamic service organizations may directly seek *zakat* donations, and some even incorporate the concept into their names, including the Zakat Foundation of America, the Zakat Foundation of India, and the Malaysian nonprofit Rumah Zakat. The Islamic Development Bank (2005) encourages the use of *zakat* and *waqf* as key elements of poverty reduction strategies.

Other Possible Indicators of Nonprofit Activities

In addition to the research projects outlined above, a number of other international comparative indexes are relevant to the nonprofits, either because they focus on issues that have a direct impact on the sector or because they document key determinants of the enabling environment.

The most directly significant of these indexes are those related to philanthropy and volunteering (i.e., the giving of money and time to nonprofits). In 2010 the UK Charities Aid Foundation began publishing the World Giving Index based on data from the Civic Engagement Index of Gallup WorldView poll, an ongoing survey project carried out in 153 countries covering 95 percent of the adult population of the world (Charities Aid Foundation 2010, 2011, 2012). Included in the Gallup survey are questions about whether respondents have in the previous month donated money or volunteered time to an organization or helped a stranger. The Charities Aid Foundation uses this data to generate the World Giving Index. As with the research projects cited above, the index has significant measurement challenges, including how to weigh the impact of formal organizations against informal solidarity networks. Many countries that in other research reports are characterized as having small and weak nonprofit sectors appear near the top of the index table. For example, Sierra Leone and Guinea are both ranked in the top twenty of giving countries because large numbers of respondents indicate that they help strangers. The index highlights significant differences in patterns of giving, with people in poorer countries primarily tending to help strangers, whereas those in richer countries also give money. Figure 4.5 compares regions on the three indicators used.

The Charities Aid Foundation has also produced other comparative reports, most notably the earlier *International Comparisons of Charitable Giving* (Charities Aid Foundation 2006), which compares charitable giving as a proportion of the GDP in twelve countries. Of the twelve countries, the United States had the highest rate of giving, with charitable contributions accounting for 1.67 percent of GDP, whereas they made up only 0.17 percent in France.

Figure 4.5 Giving by Regions

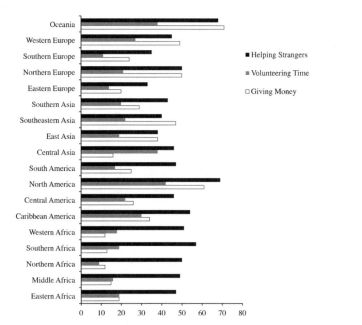

Source: Charities Aid Foundation 2012.

The Center for Global Prosperity of the Hudson Institute in the United States has also begun a series of reports on giving around the world. The *Index of Global Philanthropy and Remittances 2013* (Hudson Institute 2013a) is focused on financial transfers from developed to developing countries, comparing philanthropy and migrant remittances to official development aid and private capital transfers. Philanthropic transfers represent 0.25 percent of US GDP but only 0.085 percent of Norway's; in contrast, Norway dedicates more than 1 percent of its GDP to official aid, whereas the United States dedicates only 0.2 percent (see further discussion on financial transfers in Chapter 7 and Table 7.1). The Center for Global Prosperity has also published *Philanthropic Freedom: A Pilot Study* (Hudson Institute 2013b), in which the authors analyze the ease of creating nonprofit organizations and the institutional incentives for philanthropy in thirteen countries. Countries such as Holland and the United States had few barriers to the creation of nonprofits and significant incentives for giving; on the other hand, China and Russia have high barriers and few incentives.

In 2013, a UK consultancy launched the Big Mac Philanthropy Index, which measures relative generosity of charitable donations in thirty-eight countries using the Big Mac Index developed by *The Economist* magazine as the unit of comparison (Management Centre 2013). The Big Mac Philanthropy Index corrects for differences in national costs of living by pegging the value of donations to the local cost of a Big Mac hamburger, but it is still subject to error as it is based on the donations to only a small group of large international charities that operate in all the countries, even though they may be structurally and culturally very different in each. However, it does provide some "food for thought" (pun intended) as it seemingly contradicts many of the findings of other research. The index ranks the citizens of Singapore and Malaysia as among the most generous, even though those two countries are generally considered to have small nonprofit sectors, whereas countries such as Sweden and the Netherlands, two countries with large nonprofit sectors, are among the least generous.

From its very beginnings, the Johns Hopkins University Comparative Nonprofit Sector project, outlined earlier, sought to document the contribution of volunteers to the nonprofit sector and the economy. The successor entity to the original project, the Johns Hopkins Center for Civil Society Studies, continues to work with the United Nations and the International Labour Organization to improve data gathering on the contribution of volunteering to the economy through the *Manual on the Measurement of Volunteer Work* and the Global Volunteer Measurement Project (Global Volunteer Measurement Project 2011). In a related project, in 2011 the UN Volunteers office launched the *State of the World's Volunteerism Report* (UN Volunteers 2011), in which the organization sought to document the diverse forms of domestic and international volunteering. Authors of the report acknowledged the diverse form of indigenous collective action and noted that uncompensated activities to assist other individuals and strengthen communities are evident in all societies, even though the term *volunteering* is not necessarily used to describe them.

Numerous other research studies and surveys document political and social support for freedom of association, the strength of social capital, trust in institutions, resource availability, and other markers of a favorable environment for independent collective action and the development of the nonprofit sector. The World Values Survey, currently carried out in eighty-seven countries by the World Values Survey Association (a nonprofit association headquartered in Stockholm), documents a wide range of individuals' attitudes and actions, including membership in voluntary organizations, trust in other individuals and key social institutions, and the importance (or not) of their living in a democratic society (World Values Survey 2013). One of the products of the World Values Survey is a cultural map on which countries are clustered according to the correlation of two key social dimensions: whether their societies adhere more to religious-traditional values or to secular-rational values, and whether the population focuses more on survival or self-expression (a substitute for level of economic development) (World Values Survey 2011). In addition to the World Values Survey, regional studies such as the European Values Study (European Values Study 2011) and the European Social Survey (European Social Survey 2013) document similar sets of social and cultural determinants.

The Edelman Trust Barometer measures the public's trust in business, government, NGOs, and the media (these are the terms used by the Edelman researchers) in twenty-five countries. Globally, NGOs are the most trusted institutions, with 58 percent of the "informed public" in 2012 indicating that they trust that NGOs "do what is right" (compared to 53 percent who say the same about business, 52 percent about media, and 43 percent about government) (Edelman Trust Barometer 2012). Trust in all institutions varies considerably between the countries surveyed, but most significantly, trust in NGOs has increased dramatically in emerging countries such as China and India.

Numerous indicators and indexes focus on key concepts such as development, freedom, peace, prosperity, and stability, which are predictors of the enabling conditions for nonprofits. These include the Fragile State Index, Freedom House's Freedom in the World Index, the Global Peace Index, the Human Development Index from the UN Development Programme, the Legatum Prosperity Index, the Transparency International Corruption Perceptions Index, the World Bank World Development Report, the World Bank Indicators Database, the World Bank Worldwide Governance Indicators, and the Cingranelli-Richards (CIRI) Human Rights Dataset.

Given the key role of the faith-based organizations in the nonprofit sector, studies on religious freedom and related activities are another useful source for data. The Association of Religion Data Archives has regional and national data on faith-related activities. The data is aggregated from a number of sources, including the Center for Religious Freedom at the Hudson Institute.

The question of the role of faith-based organizations and their impact in understanding the differences in the size and scope of nonprofit sectors around the world is yet to be fully explored at an international comparative level. That much of the work associated with the nonprofit sector is carried out by faith-based organizations, either directly or in the guise of faith-related nonprofits, is easily discernible. In countries where a certain religion is state sponsored, the organizations associated with that faith will occupy much of the social and economic spaces that are occupied by more independent, secular nonprofits in other countries, but no studies appear to have been done that quantify the extent of the crowding out or competition between faith-based and secular organizations. That a large portion of all philanthropy goes to faith-based organizations has been documented (in the United States and Australia, where statistics on giving are divided by sector, approximately one-third of all private donations go to religious organizations), but no reliable statistics appear to have been gathered on what goes to purely faith-related purposes as opposed to more secular social service.

The Cultural Frames Revisited

In the following sections, distinct cultural frames are presented as the archetypes of the current dynamics of national nonprofit sectors operating under different economic, political, and social regimes. They are similar to those based on welfare regimes (Anheier 2014; K. M. Brown and Kenny 2000; Esping-Andersen 1990) and the patterns and clusters that emerged from the Johns Hopkins project (Salamon 2010; Salamon and Sokolowski 2010), but the frames presented below also incorporate contemporary political and social dynamics that are reshaping and transcending those earlier categories.

The frames are not strict templates but instead represent patterns of development of the nonprofit sectors and their relationships with their respective governments and business sectors. Nor are the frames clearly separate: there are overlaps and certain convergence (see the discussion on the convergence to an "American model" in Chapter 5), and some of the purported differences, which are often based on prevailing historical and cultural narratives, may not necessarily be supported by other research data. Peter Baldwin (2009) in *The Narcissism of Minor Differences: How America and Europe Are Alike* drew on available statistical and survey data to argue that, despite popular narratives of the cultural and social gulf between

Europe and the United States, they are very much alike on a wide array of metrics, including key civil society markers such as trust in government and volunteering.

The frames described below can be represented graphically by focusing on two key interrelated continuums: (1) the relative dominance of the state or civil society (given the arguments outlined in Chapter 2 about the definition of civil society, it is a better descriptor for the purposes of comparison than the term *nonprofit*); and (2) the level of economic development of the country. The continuum of dominance between state and civil society reflects the political and social environmental issues outlined in earlier chapters, as well as the quantitative and qualitative research projects outlined in this chapter. Economic development can also be plotted along a continuum by measuring gross national income per capita (the standard used by the World Bank to classify countries as high-, middle-, or low-income). Using these two continuums, one can map the general contours of the frames and the relationship between them (see Figure 4.6).

Figure 4.6 includes a frame, FRACAS (fragile and conflict-affected states), which describes a small group of the least developed countries, in which government institutions function only marginally and cannot control

Figure 4.6 The Nonprofit Sector Cultural Frames

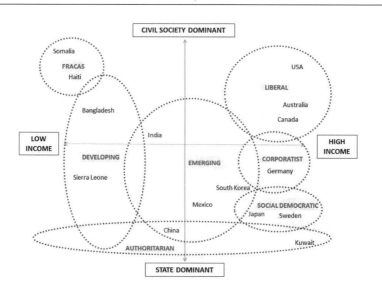

or provide services to their entire territory. The country may be divided between warring factions, and the few formal service delivery structures are often controlled by militia groups. Depending on the security situation, peacekeeping operations and disaster relief and humanitarian aid organizations (including UN and regional multilateral entities such as the African Union and international nonprofit emergency aid organizations) may have a significant presence, operating mostly independently from the government. These FRACAS countries provide "outlier" examples of a distorted form of civil society. Although the existence of the FRACAS frame is important to acknowledge, it is not directly discussed below, as it involves processes of state construction and international statecraft generally outside the scope of discussions of a nonprofit sector. At the same time, many of the challenges of operating under such conditions will be addressed in later chapters of this book.

Applying the terms *nonprofit sector*, *civil society*, or *third sector* to the configurations of social and political structures in failed states and in authoritarian and emerging countries again highlights the definitional challenges and the use of exogenous frameworks of the global North. However, a clear tendency can be found to describe the diversity of dynamics in different countries using the same evolving globalized nomenclature. For example, among the sources documenting the sector in Malaysia, a 1973 monograph titled *Blood, Believer and Brother: The Development of Voluntary Associations in Malaysia* is focused on kinship networks, trade associations, and guilds (S. A. Douglas and Pedersen 1973). A 2003 book focused on essentially the same set of organizations is titled *Social Movements in Malaysia: From Moral Communities to NGOs*, in which the authors noted that "while the specific shape of many contemporary NGOs may be new, they often build on a long history of social networks and associations" (M. Weiss and Hassan 2003, 1). In a 2011 article titled "The Limits of Civil Society in Democratising the State: The Malaysian Case," in the *Kaijian Malaysia: Journal of Malaysian Studies*, the author noted that Malaysian civil society organizations "come in a confusing array of manifestations, from academic and professional groups to grassroots groups, business-oriented groups, charity organizations, and, most of all, ethnic and religious groups" (Farouk 2011, 105). The same semantic shifts can be found in the documentation of any of the countries described in the frames below.

The descriptions of the frames minimize reference to race, religion, and region, even though previous analyses of nonprofit sectors around the world have generally included categories based directly on such factors. David Schak and Wayne Hudson (2003) posited the existence of an Asian model based on the Confucian concepts of morally binding loyalty, piety, and etiquette, which have been translated into social contracts that lead to greater subservience to the authority of the state. Some typologies often included a separate category for Islamic countries based on the charity pillars that are fundamental to the practice of Islam (see Box 4.7). The broad category of developing countries is often broken down into regions such as Latin America, where the Catholic Church has played such a dominant role, and Africa, where the legacy of colonialism and exploitation have entrenched underdevelopment and where nearly all of the FRACAS countries are clustered. The work of nonprofit researchers who use such cultural-religious categories is buttressed by broader social research such as the World Values Survey (2011), quoted earlier.

However, although documenting and analyzing regional, religious, and cultural influences are essential, and although many of these influences are discussed in this book, they are increasingly less relevant as the defining feature of typologies. The groundbreaking comparative work of researchers such as Kathleen McCarthy, Virginia Hodgkinson, and Russy Sumariwalla (1992) is "only" a little over twenty years old, yet to read about categories based on the formerly communist Eastern Europe, on Islam, and on regional groups is somewhat jarring in a swiftly changing world. Much of Eastern Europe is now part of the European Union; South Korea has firmly taken its place among high-income aid-donor nations; African countries such as Botswana, Ghana, and South Africa appear to have consolidated their democratic institutions and are rapidly developing; other African nations have more in common with the situation in some areas of the Pacific Island region; and Cuba, increasingly along with Venezuela and Nicaragua, shares the state-centric tics of East Asian and African regimes. This book was written while the Arab Spring was unfolding, and the outcomes of those events will take years to evaluate, but given the differences that have already emerged between the countries caught up in the upheavals, any doubts about whether to include a single Arab category were definitively put to rest. Any categorizations of the nonprofit sector and the activities of its organizations are increasingly cross-cultural and cross-regional.

Liberal

Although the label *liberal* is often used, particularly in the United States, as a synonym of *progressive*, the term is used here as a descriptor for the nonprofit sector in the traditional sense of classic pluralist liberalism, which espouses freedom of speech and association and limited government (the latter generally regarded as a more conservative agenda). In contemporary discourse, particularly by European commentators, classic liberalism is also often referred to as neoliberalism to signify the late twentieth-century resurgence of ideologies that seek a reduction in the size and scope of government, focusing particularly on competitive market principles and outsourcing.

Countries in the liberal frame have a long tradition of individual free-doms, independent associational life, and less centralized government. In the current context, they are now also characterized by strong nonprofit sectors that represent a significant proportion of national economic activity. The frame is generally correlated with industrialized English-speaking countries, which have in common pluralist historical-political arrangements that encourage independent associational life and self-organizing, cultural norms that promote philanthropy and voluntary action, and a range of more recent institutional arrangements that seek to consolidate and expand the nonprofit sector. The United States is the emblematic liberal country with a long history of smaller government and strong nonprofits, whereas others such as Australia, Canada, and the United Kingdom have combined liberal-ism with the development of stronger welfare state provisions introduced in the early to mid-twentieth century.

Since the 1970s, the nonprofit sectors in all these countries have grown considerably for all the combined "conservative" and "progressive" reasons identified in previous chapters. The widespread impact of new public man-agement and public sector reforms by the various governments since the 1980s has made contracting out, consultation, and coproduction central organizing principles in liberal countries. In these countries, considerable government funding of nonprofit organizations but also relatively high lev-els of private philanthropy and volunteering, as well as extensive entrepre-neurial activities, have resulted in significant income for some organiza-tions. The management of larger nonprofits is increasingly professionalized and entrepreneurial, and significant emphasis has been placed on service delivery over expressive functions, with the latter increasingly corralled into the work of a small group of nonprofits that openly identify as advo-cacy organizations. Advocacy relationships with government are based on the perceived strength of the nonprofit sector and its capacity to mobilize the will of the wider population, but they are also mediated by the density of the new institutional relationships between governments and nonprofits created by extensive consultative and contracting processes.

In Chapter 5, I will take a more detailed look at the US version of the neoliberal frame and explore how it is being emulated in other countries.

Social Democratic

In the social democratic frame, the state takes the primary responsibility to both finance and deliver social, educational, and health services through high levels of taxation and public spending. This model, for much of the twentieth century, has characterized the Scandinavian countries, most emblematically Sweden, which has a level of public spending that repre-sents some 52.5 percent of GDP (as compared to 38.9 percent in the United

States), supported by a higher taxation burden (47.9 percent, versus 26.9 percent in the United States).

The outcomes expected from a larger government sector are also reflected in the expectations of other economic sectors including commercial enterprises. The social economy of cooperatives and mutual organizations has played a larger role than in liberal countries, labor unions have maintained high membership relative to other industrialized democracies, and corporate social responsibility has been more ingrained as standard business practice. Social outcomes such as universal health care, accessible public education, and the greater equality of women—typical policy and programmatic goals of nonprofits in other countries—are achieved through a range of government-led policies and programs and labor market mechanisms. Instead of the more market-based economy of liberal countries, the reference here is to a social market economy that seeks to limit inequalities and deliver the possibility for more universally equal welfare.

Because the state is more dominant, relatively few service delivery nonprofit organizations can be found, and only a restricted number of volunteers engaged in service delivery. However, the nonprofit sectors in social democratic countries are still large numerically and play a significant role in social, political, and economic life. The nonprofit sector in Scandinavia has a long tradition in both religious charity and progressive social movements, which led to the emergence of the welfare state from the 1930s and the assumption by the state of core service provision. These societies are affluent, and the population has significant surplus income and time. An expansive network has developed of small volunteer-based, member-serving organizations that have self-organizing and expressive functions as their central principles. Social democratic countries still see a high level of volunteering, but it is focused on advocacy, professional associations, and sports and recreation organizations, and a significant portion of the income of these organizations is fee for services. A strong international aid subsector has also developed as private donations to charitable activities generally have had an external focus.

Since the 1980s, however, the role of the state has been significantly rolled back in social democratic countries. What for most of the twentieth century had been conceptualized as an advocacy and member-oriented "popular movement sphere" is being reconceptualized as a sector that also collaborates with the state in service delivery (Reuter, Wijkström, and von Essen 2012). Privatization of government services in areas such as health, education, and welfare is still relatively modest compared with other industrialized countries, and new contracting processes include the commercial sector as much as the nonprofit sector. A certain assumption appears to have been made that the traditional nonprofit sector does not have a particular interest in assuming a service role and that nonprofits generally do not have the capacity or skill base needed for the management of larger-scale service delivery (Pestoff 2009).

Corporatist

In the most general sense, the term *corporatist* describes a society in which the state, as the central actor in a strict hierarchy of power relations, apportions certain roles to other major actors. Strictly speaking, therefore, the social democratic countries identified in the previous frame are also corporatist (as are the authoritarian countries described below). However, for the purposes of this taxonomy, *corporatist* refers to those democratic countries in which historical partnerships involve the devolution and delegation of legal and administrative responsibility for social service delivery to a set of intermediary nonprofit conglomerates, primarily faith-based organizations and labor unions. Although these nonprofit organizations are separate from their respective governments, the long-standing institutional arrangements blur the distinctions, and their work is embedded into the dynamics of the social market economy and the welfare state. Government raises the revenue or creates processes that institutionalize revenue generation (e.g., compulsory salary deductions to pay for health and pension benefits), but only a small number of key nonprofits, entrenched in the welfare state apparatus, manage and deliver the services.

This frame refers primarily to Continental European countries such as Germany and Belgium. These countries have nongovernment sectors based on ideological-religious divisions and have developed stable collaborative links between government and a few selected NGOs. Their nonprofit sectors are large in terms of economic activity and employment but are relatively small in number with a few dominant service providers supported by tax revenues that flow through the historical corporatist arrangements. The vertical integration dynamics, often referred to as "pillarization," are also reflected in decisionmaking and social action structures that link political parties with mass organizations such as unions and associations.

Some authors have suggested that a convergence can be identified between US and European interest mediation, and already in the early 1990s, some declared that "corporatism is dead" (Richardson 1993). Wolfgang Streek and Philippe Schmitter (1986) and Clive Thomas (1993) suggested that Europe was witnessing changes in social structures and political systems that undermined corporatism and that processes of intermediation were moving toward a US-like pattern of disjointed pluralism because of increased differentiation of social structures and collective interests, as well as market instability and technological shifts. But despite such shifts, the traditional corporatist structures have persisted and continue to play a central role in policymaking and service delivery, even though the early decades of the twenty-first century have seen an increasing use of competitive bidding for services and the diversification of the nonprofit sector.

Emerging

This frame brings together those countries that have, since the late 1980s, experienced a relatively peaceful transition to democracy and have established relatively stable and solid economies. The word *relatively* is key here, as some "emerging" countries have seen considerable civil unrest and violence, and so democratic institutions and rule of law have not fully consolidated, and their economies are not yet on solid footings. In this frame can be included the postsocialist countries of Central and Eastern Europe and Eurasia, the former military dictatorships of Central and South America, and the former authoritarian regimes in Africa and Asia. The Arab Spring was seen as potentially propelling a number of Middle East countries into this category, but that is still a work in progress.

The civil society discourse outlined in Chapter 2 has been a central analytical concept in commentary on the transitions of the above governments to democracy, with civil society organizations, in their broadest definition, which may include clandestine labor unions and dissident citizens' organizations, identified as key actors in forcing political change. Once a transition takes place, the country often experiences a sudden influx of Western nonprofits (some of which may have already been supporting dissidents under the previous regime), working alone or with local partners, and a sweeping restructuring of autochthonous organizations. The government-sponsored mass movement social and professional organizations that existed under the old regime convert to more democratic operations or disappear, former dissident and clandestine organizations become legal, and new organizations quickly appear (perhaps including the revival of historic organizations suppressed by the authoritarian regime). Some of these organizations eventually transform into full-fledged political parties and focus their energies on electoral politics, but others become independent nonprofits as the relevant enabling legislation is enacted under the new democratic government. The emerging civil society organizations are generally seen as preventative measures against the return of past tyrannies.

Once those organizations interested in electoral politics have reestablished themselves as political parties, the remaining nonprofit sector is often dominated by culture, recreation, and professional associations, the realm of organizations typically encouraged under authoritarian regimes. The conversion of organizations that existed under the old regime presents a considerable challenge: for example, a lawyers' association, which was previously dominated by loyal regime cadres whose role was to ensure that the legal profession remained subservient to authorities, must now become an independent organization defending the rights of members and acting as a watchdog for the rule of law.

Often a significant initial surge of new organizations is created in the new climate of entrepreneurial fervor. However, many prove to be unsustainable, as the development of independent nongovernmental action is fragile and often tainted both by the legacy of mass movement associations under the previous authoritarian regime and by corruption in the new organizations (M. Taylor et al. 2009). Nonprofits in transitional countries generally play a crucial role in advancing democracy and providing essential services, but the "dark side" of the sector also emerges, and often considerable concern arises about corruption and rent seeking. In one Eastern European country, many nonprofits appeared in the 1990s whose only apparent assets were foreign luxury automobiles, because a tax loophole allowed nonprofits to import them without the steep duties experienced by individuals or for-profit firms. The initial posttransition surge in nonprofit numbers quickly reaches a peak and is often followed by a steep drop as unsustainable organizations fold and questionable ones are closed by the authorities.

The emerging nonprofit sector often survives precariously on the margins caught in a complicated dance of relationships with the government authorities. The first new organizations are often under the auspices of political parties, unions, and religious organizations and must sustain themselves in a social context that has low levels of giving and volunteering. The service functions of the nonprofit sector expand as funding becomes available either through foreign donors, or from the new government, which may increasingly encourage their activities and begin to contract with the sector, but expressive functions are more contested. As transitions consolidate, many organizations face funding shortages if foreign donors withdraw and shift their focus to the latest zones of instability and conflict.

With regime change, former opposition activists generally move into the corridors of power. Once they are part of the new government institutions they often regard independent organizations with considerable suspicion as the refuges of disloyal former comrades or of disgruntled members of the past regime (and this description may sometimes be apt, especially of the new organizations that emerge). New nonprofits may be accused of acting as an illegal opposition or of corrupt behavior, and yesterday's activist heroes working in these organizations are recast as today's villains. The distinction between nongovernment and antigovernment may become blurred, particularly when political tensions rise. The participation of civil society organizations in regime changes around the world has fueled the distrust of many governments, particularly those sliding back toward authoritarian tendencies, and a significant amount of wariness can be found around what is commonly characterized as "foreign influence" on internal issues (Rutzen 2015). Nonprofit organizations focusing on advocacy and watchdog activities often work at considerable personal peril to those involved—the all too frequent harassment and even murder of human rights activists and nonprofit social service workers around the world are sad testament to the dangers such workers face.

Tensions can arise between a top-down externally fostered sector and a bottom-up indigenous recovery of historic organizations and development of new local organizations. As transitions consolidate, foreign governments, aid organizations, and individual nonprofits take an active role in developing civil society organizations. Government-sponsored aid such as the European Union's programs for funding civil society in Central and Eastern Europe in the post-1989 transitions and nonprofit democracy projects such as the Open Society Foundations (see Box 3.7) and CIVICUS (see Box 7.1) are joined by individual nonprofit organizations from other countries that seek to reproduce their work in this new fertile ground. The more benevolent view is that this intervention seeks to aid local citizens to build capacity for collective action and stabilize democratic institutions, but critics see more nefarious agendas to implant capitalism or to serve the other interests of external funders (Abzug and Webb 1996; T. Wallace 2003).

The outcomes of transitions have been mixed (for reasons rarely determined by the nonprofit sector). Central and Eastern European countries have joined the European Union, and Brazil has moved from the twenty-year military dictatorship of the 1960s to the 1980s to its current status as a stable democracy with one of the fastest growing economies. However, other countries, such as some of the Eurasian former Soviet republics, have faced greater challenges and have slipped back into authoritarian habits and economic instability (see Box 4.8 for the example of Kazakhstan).

Developing

The preceding frames have focused on industrialized countries and those on the threshold. At the lower end of the economic scale are the low- and lower-middle-income developing nations. The world's poorest countries are defined officially as having a low GDP per capita (in 2012 it was less than $1,005 per capita in low-income countries and $1,006–$3,975 in lower-middle-income countries), as well as weak human assets (poor health, low level of education, etc.) and a high degree of economic vulnerability. The poorest countries are often subject to widespread internal conflicts, suffer from extensive corruption, and lack political and social stability. Governments are often autocratic and split into opposing factions, with guerrillas or warlords controlling parts of the country. They are also often kleptocracies, in which oligarchs pillage the wealth of the country to fuel luxury lifestyles while the vast majority of the population lives in poverty. The state does not provide reliable public services or protect citizens, and any

---

Box 4.8 Nonprofits in Kazakhstan

Kazakhstan is a republic in Central Asia that gained independence with the breakup of the Soviet Union. The population is 17 million; 70 percent are Muslims and 24 percent Christian, primarily Russian Orthodox. It is a democratic republic but has had only one president since independence, Nursultan Nazarbayev, who in the last election won over 90 percent of the vote.

Recent studies find that Western-style professional nonprofits in Kazakhstan are weak and unsustainable. Most of these nonprofits have developed strong dependency on foreign donors for funds and do not yet have a strong local support network. The explanations for this institutional ineffectiveness include a disconnect from local traditions, the low visibility of nonprofits, and an unsupportive government. A survey of the general population suggests that people in Kazakhstan know very little about nonprofits and do not appreciate their utility. The inability of civil society organizations to reach out to local people may largely be a result of a fundamental cultural mismatch, as the local culture is in striking dissonance with the cultures of the donor countries that have created the nonprofit agenda in Kazakhstan.

Source: See Borzaga and Fazzi 2010.

---

independent organizations that might threaten the hegemony of the elites are often violently repressed. Even in those poor countries that operate with a more open, democratic regime, bourgeoisie elites dominate economic and political life (with a handful of prominent families controlling wealth and political patronage).

Many important grassroots efforts are being made to achieve change, but they are often overwhelmed by wider economic forces and direct repression by the despots in power. These countries usually have a long history of traditional collective structures and associational life, as well as of colonial missionary and charity work, and since the 1990s they have witnessed the emergence of a professional nonprofit sector. The new nonprofits include both foreign international nonprofits and autochthonous nonprofits that have successfully tapped into international funding streams or created alliances with international partners.

A significant facet of the sector in these countries is the substantial presence of foreign nonprofits and the dominant role of foreign funding to local organizations (Shivji 2007). Workers in nonprofits funded from external sources are among the higher paid workers in the local labor markets. Foreign expatriates, whose salaries are generally benchmarked to their home country, enjoy a lifestyle on par with local elites, and locals with jobs in organizations funded from external sources are often among the fortunate minority that has a stable living-wage income from guaranteed sources. Unlike nonprofit employees in industrialized countries, who are usually at the lower end of the pay scale, those who work in nonprofit organizations in low-income countries are generally a privileged class. Furthermore, local nonprofit employees are often highly qualified professionals (engineers, lawyers, and academics) who take secondary employment in nonprofits, often significantly below their skill set, because they find that they earn more working as drivers, interpreters, or midlevel administrators on an internationally funded project than they would in their own professions. Many of the usual organizational hierarchies are also significantly different from those in industrialized countries, with the executive staff in international nonprofits being relatively young expatriates, often females, who may not speak the local language but rely on bilingual local staff as interlocutors. In order to develop a cadre of qualified professionals, a boom has taken place in nonprofit studies at universities in developing countries that combine both managerial and development issues (Mirabella et al. 2007).

The political and social consequences of external funding and external pressure are often a source of some friction. As international nonprofits have assured sources of their own income and are beholden more to their own members and contributors than to local authorities, questions of accountability and ownership of policies arise. Haiti is often presented as the prototypical case of a country in which NGOs have become more powerful than the government through the donations they bring to the country and their subsequent capacity and power to influence policy and program agendas (see Box 8.6).

Given the weakness of governments in many developing countries and their lack of capacity to regulate nonprofits, other processes have been developed to oversee the involvement of international nonprofits. The United Nations has encouraged the development of "policy documents," which provide guidelines for the operations of nonprofits in different countries (see, for example, Government of Liberia 2008). These policies in effect constitute the legal framework for regulating the activities of NGOs in the absence of local legislation.

International nonprofits seek to play a significant part in the economic development and democratization of a number of countries, but they face the reality that both governments and opposition may be reticent about their activities (Roelofs 2006). Suspicious and fearful governments are putting limits on nonprofit activities, and where unrest and insurgency are present, armed oppositions often target nonprofit aid workers, as they see them as representing foreign interests by propping up the extant corrupt regime and imposing external values, habits, and systems that are at odds with local customs. Externally funded nonprofits are often seen as inhibiting the development of indigenous civil society and distracting from the development of more political organizations that could push for structural changes (Banks and Hulme 2012; M. Taylor et al. 2009).

An extensive informal grassroots associational sector based on traditional family, clan, language group, caste, tribe, or village is still usually in existence. As the new professional sector takes root, it often butts up against these extant social structures. In all countries, a tension can be found between large corporate nonprofits and small grassroots organizations, but in developing countries a particularly sharp divide often develops between traditional collective structures and a newer generation of professionalized nonprofits funded by external donors and favored by local elites. The newer sector is generally in the hands of expatriates who have settled in the country or local elites who can more effectively operate in international environments (a situation that is particularly evident where only a small educated minority speak English or French, the most common languages in international organizations). They are commonly accused of claiming to represent the interests of poor and rural communities without really understanding their true needs and of treating them more as "stakeholder" recipients of largesse than "rights-holders" who should determine program policies and strategies (Suleiman 2013; Tanaka 2010).

The divide between the grassroots and the elites is also evident in the existence of a small sector of cultural, educational, and health nonprofits created to meet the needs of the prosperous in the absence of government services. The best schools, hospitals, and cultural institutions in many developing countries are often constituted as nonprofits, but generally provide few services to the poor and disenfranchised.

Organizations in developing countries are also often based on the leadership and patronage of a powerful "big man" or other charismatic entrepreneurs who become the patriarchs (occasionally, the matriarchs) of dynastic structures that dominate many nonprofit organizations. They may have achieved their status through traditional ruling lineages or through guile and violence, but participation in organizations with ties to these individuals can be key to survival or sustenance in societies bedeviled by corruption and violence (Hyden 2010).

The relationship between organized crime and nonprofits again becomes an issue, as some criminal gangs operate services akin to nonprofits in the areas they control, and they may also use nonprofit organizations as fronts for their activities in an environment in which the state cannot provide oversight or is riddled with corruption. Transparency can also be problematic. Few institutional structures may be available to promote or oversee the transparency of organizations, whether public, private, or nonprofit, and little infrastructure may be in place for gathering and disseminating material about the operations and finances of nonprofits. Transparency may even be seen to endanger workers, and in some countries nonprofits deliberately do not publicly declare their income, as doing so may make them more visible targets for extortion and theft.

Authoritarian

A final group, which straddles the economic divide, is that of illiberal single-party and authoritarian regimes in which any political or social organizations not associated with the dominant regime (or dominant religion in the case of theocracies) are banned or allowed only limited participation. Although a clustering of such regimes can be found at the bottom end of the economic scale, a few higher-income countries have authoritarian governments or are dominated by a single leader or party that curbs political freedoms. In the 2011 Freedom in the World report, 60 of the 194 countries studied were designated "partly free" (31 percent of the countries, or 22 percent of the global population), and 47 were "not free" (24 percent of the countries, or 35 percent of the global population—of which more than half live in China). In these countries, considerable institutional and informal barriers can be found to the operations of independent nonprofits, both domestic and international, although international nonprofits may be given marginally more leeway within the strict constraints of the activities deemed acceptable to the regime (Freedom House 2011).

The most autocratic, predatory, and extractive regimes use "hard power" repression, including the detention, torture, and murder of those considered a threat. The focus of repression is most directly on rivals, but those who suffer persecution also usually include any watchdog organizations seeking to expose human rights violations or corruption, and even social service, community development, or educational organizations that are working outside the narrow parameters allowed by the regime. Criminal gangs and militias working for oligarchs may also be operating with relative impunity to target nonprofits seen as jeopardizing their interests. When armed conflict is present, militias may target service and aid nonprofits whose activities they regard as legitimating or propping up their opponents.

More developmental and distributary single-party regimes use "soft power" controls—barriers to registration, regulations on permitted activities, and constraints on funding and income generation, as well as monitoring provisions that make the continued existence of the organization subject to the veto of the authorities (ICNL 2013; J. Richter and Hatch 2013). These go hand in hand with general laws that restrict the right of association and protest, control the press, and hinder transparency (see examples from sub-Saharan Africa in ICNL 2014). The government has the right, or simply the power, to shut down any organizations whose activities are no longer sanctioned and to detain recalcitrant holdouts. Attempts to maintain independent organizations are quickly met with pressures toward clientelism and co-optation, and those that do not conform are forced to act at the margins under constant vigilance and harassment. Service-focused nonprofits may be tolerated, or even encouraged, if they are seen as complementing government service provision on approved issues, although advocacy and cultural organizations may also be permitted if they are seen as buoying the legitimacy of the regime and aiding in providing a voice in international forums.

The reluctance to open spaces for the work of nonprofits may also be based as much on models of economic growth as on political restrictions. A number of East Asian countries based their economic growth of the 1980s and 1990s on state-centric "paternalist" models that celebrated thrift, hard work, and duty to family and society and eschewed the creation of Western-style welfare states as superfluous to societies in which employers and family provided the safety net. Policy development was state controlled, and attempts to provide services received little encouragement, resulting in a restricted political or operational space for a nonprofit sector.

In many authoritarian and single-party regimes government-sponsored organizations take on the form and use the language of nonprofits. These are most often mass movement, party-based organizations tightly controlled by the ruling regime, which usually focus on cultural and recreational activities but also on charitable work. Typically, the wife of the president-dictator is the head of the national women's mass movement organization and a charity figurehead. Given the pervasive intrusion of authoritarian governments in their citizens' lives, much less distinction can be made between the public and private, and many social and economic privileges are typically dependent on membership in such organizations, although they are formally voluntary. The politics of language play an important role, with authoritarian-minded regimes adopting variants of democratic terminology, such as *realistic democracy* and *state democracy,* to describe their rule and to legitimize the organizations it engenders.

Many authoritarian countries also have "nonprofit sectors in exile." Those who fled the regime and have found refuge in democratic countries form "solidarity committees," often in conjunction with local activists. Although these committees usually have the overtly political goal of regime change in their country of origin, they often also maintain some type of aid and cultural exchange activities that link the country of exile with their homeland. The refugees in exile are schooled in the nonprofit sector and regulatory regime of the host country and often take that orientation back with them when a transition establishes a more pluralistic system that permits return.

Moving Between Frames

The quantitative comparative research projects and the qualitative narratives of the cultural frames are essential tools for understanding the nonprofit sector in any country. At the same time, all nonprofit sectors are in constant evolution, both in their metrics and in how they are perceived by researchers and the public. This evolution may be the result of incremental changes in the factors that determine the national scripts or may be marked by sudden shifts. Inchoon Kim and Changsoon Hwang (2002) described three "stages" of evolution of the nonprofit sector in South Korea since the end of the Korean War. These stages may be unique to South Korea but nevertheless reflect the shifts in many other countries that have experienced regime change and economic growth.

In the first stage, until the early 1960s, the primary goal of the state was to maintain national security. Nonprofit organizations were service oriented, providing welfare services or implementing development projects for the poor, and were mostly established and supported by foreign aid. Korean society was still agrarian, and community, religious, and ancestral associations were popular.

The second stage began with the 1961 military coup and was characterized by an authoritarian developmental state. Independent civil activity was permitted only within a limited political space, but the country also experienced rapid economic growth. Three distinct subsectors of organizations emerged: (1) government-sponsored social organizations mobilized the population for national development and to publicize government policies; (2) nonpolitical education and service-oriented organizations began to play a significant role in providing public goods and social services; and (3) underground student activities and political opposition groups agitated against the regime but were severely oppressed.

The third stage began with the end of the authoritarian regime in June 1987. The dramatic rise of citizens' and labor movements and other nonprofits during the immediate postdemocratization period added important new players. The earlier leader groups, such as student organizations and underground groups, were gradually replaced by new organizations. The decade of the 1990s is considered by many as "the age of civil society." The nonprofit sector has now grown into a highly visible and independent element in Korean society, with a wide range of both service and expressive organizations.

The growing wealth of the population and diaspora philanthropy (see Chapter 7) have contributed to the establishment of a considerable donor base that supports domestic and international activities. New Korean international nonprofits are beginning to make their mark around the world (see Box 4.9).

Box 4.9 Global Civic Sharing

Global Civic Sharing (GCS) is an international nonprofit providing development aid to needy communities in Asia and Africa. Established in 1998 and based in Seoul, it currently works in Vietnam, Mongolia, East Timor, Myanmar, Rwanda, and Kenya. Its objectives are to carry out development assistance projects, support civil society empowerment, provide emergency relief assistance to victims of natural disasters and conflicts, promote the participation of young Koreans in voluntary activities and global exchange programs, and implement research and campaigns for policymaking. GCS has an annual budget of $2.4 million and manages the following programs:

• Vocational training: Empowers local people by providing them with training opportunities to develop Korean-language and computer skills. The programs target the socially marginalized who have limited educational and employment opportunities.
• Education: Focuses on youth and university students, equipping them with the experience and training needed to develop better leadership and accountability in global issues.
• Advocacy: Promotes research on foreign aid policies and strategies, participates in national and international seminars, and organizes various antipoverty campaigns.
• Fellowship: Sends volunteers to developing countries to gain experience working in the field of international development cooperation. Since November 2004, approximately fifty South Korean volunteers have been sent to seven different countries for a span of one to two years, conducting various income-generation, community-education, and civil-society exchange projects.

Source: See Global Civic Sharing, http://www.gcs.or.kr/eng/.

5

The Globalization of Ideas

The previous chapter was focused on the differences between national nonprofit sectors. But increasingly similarities can also be found. As ideas move between countries more easily through information technologies, and individuals circulate more freely for education and employment, a convergence is taking place in the key elements of the nonprofit sectors around the world. In this chapter, I examine whether an American model is becoming the dominant operating framework around the world and look at converging discourses about government-nonprofit relations and social enterprise.

The Triumph of the "American" Model?

> The American social revolution that Alexis de Tocqueville observed in the early nineteenth century, of citizens joining groups of every conceivable kind, is about to go global, forever changing the relationship between citizens and their governments, and governments with each other. The Arab revolutions are but the first taste of this larger change.
>
> —Ann-Marie Slaughter,
> "Problems Will Be Global—And Solutions Will Be, Too"

As was emphasized in the first chapters, a worldwide expansion of the nonprofit sector has taken place: in countries with a longer tradition of an active nonprofit sector, a significant growth spurt has taken place, and in countries where independent nonprofits have in the past been largely absent, clear evidence can be found of the emergence of a growing and newly confident sector seeking wider legitimacy.

131

Each country is unique, subject to the path dependency generated by its national historical baggage, by contemporary institutional transformations, and by the personal dynamics of key policy entrepreneurs or champions. But decontextualized, the rhetorics and processes of change in countries around the world seem remarkably similar, with a marked convergence in discourses and models. A common international trend is seen in the increased capacity of the population for independent organizing and action, a change in public expectations of the role of nonprofits, a shift to governance and partnership approaches that involve third-party arrangements and the privatization of the public sector, an increase in commercialization and marketization of the work of nonprofits, and the corporatization of an elite segment of the nonprofit sector.

The quote from Slaughter above suggests that this convergence is to a US-style combination of neo-Tocquevillian civic participation and neoliberal outsourcing in search of efficient and effective service delivery. Similarly, Don Eberly (2008) saw compassion, in the form of a bottom-up organized civil society, as "America's most consequential export."

Are these claims mere chauvinism, or do they truly reflect a global Americanization of nonprofit sectors and of the broader economic and social systems and cultures? The US nonprofit sector is not the largest in numbers—that distinction goes to India—but in terms of its economic strength and influence within its own domestic polity and international discourses, it is arguably the world's most powerful. The international flow of ideas about the nonprofit sector is largely driven by the economic muscle of US foundations, government aid programs, and the sheer volume of US academic and professional publications that directly spread the nonprofit gospel, as well as by a range of institutional counterparts that promote wider concepts such as democracy, transparency, and civil and human rights, which are correlated with a stronger nonprofit sector (DeMars 2005; Hammack and Heydemann 2009). The US nonprofit model is one more of the economic and cultural artifacts the United States exports, along with Coca-Cola and Hollywood movies (Hunter and Yates 2002).

The US nonprofit model is also driven at more microlevels by human mobility. A growing global cadre of nonprofit professionals has worked or studied in the United States, absorbed its worldview, and then returned home or moved on to other countries. Furthermore, strong diaspora philanthropy links have been created between immigrant communities in the United States and their home countries. The sum of these dynamics is resulting in a "mimetic and normative isomorphism" (Abzug and Webb 1996; Anheier 2005; DiMaggio and Powell 1983), as the globe-trotting cadre grows and US nonprofit workers and consultants are called on to share their wisdom with colleagues in emerging democracies. In Box 5.1 is illustrated how an Africa-focused nonprofit was established in Hungary by a diaspora entrepreneur influenced by a US organization.

Box 5.1   Afrikáért Alapítvány

Afrikáért Alapítvány (Foundation for Africa) is a small Hungarian non-profit aid organization that "facilitates development, aid and the forming of civil society through providing help in the fields of education, society and health care in Africa and organizing cultural programs and lectures to introduce the continent to Hungary." Afrikáért Alapítvány focuses on education, social issues, and health care in the Democratic Republic of Congo. It helps maintain a school and orphanage in the capital, Kinshasa, and provides medicine and surgical instruments for several health care centers in the capital and rural areas. In 2007, Afrikáért Alapítvány began a program of humanitarian tourism, in cooperation with a US partner organization.

Afrikáért Alapítvány was registered in Hungary in 2002 and in the Democratic Republic of Congo in 2004. The founder and executive director, France Mutombo Tshimuanga, is a citizen of the Democratic Republic of Congo who studied theology in Hungary and later married and settled there. In 1999, he participated in a humanitarian mission organized by the US evangelical organization Steps to Life, and his experiences from that trip prompted him to found an organization in his country of residence to provide aid to his homeland.

Source: See Afrikáért Alapítvány, http://afrikaert.hu/en/.

What Is the US Model?

The United States is the quintessential liberal country with an extensive and powerful nonprofit sector. Some commentators compare its influence—with only the merest hint of hyperbole or jest—to that of the military, defense, and security industries by speaking of a "nonprofit industrial complex" (Buffett 2013; Incite 2007).

The path dependency of the US national script is well documented: the cultural, political, and institutional roots of the contemporary sector can be traced back to the collective ethos of the colonial settler communities and to the protection of individual liberties and voluntary association embodied in the founding charters of the new nation (Hall 1992, 2010). The US nonprofit sector has grown dramatically in the past decades, but the conditions for its growth continue to be attributed to a historical predisposition. However, if one releases the narrative from its historical moorings and takes a snapshot of the current US nonprofit sector, one can distill the following defining elements of the political, economic, and social climate and of the most salient characteristics of the sector.

Political, economic, and social climate. A social-cultural preference for "smaller government" and a profound distrust of political institutions and centralized authority are expressed. The most visible manifestations of these attitudes are a resistance to higher taxation and the widespread disparagement of the quality and effectiveness of government service delivery.

Paired to the preference for small government is the exaltation of market forces and of private solutions to social challenges. The US economic system facilitates the accumulation of individual wealth and accepts considerable wealth disparities, but considerable institutional and social incentives can also be identified for nonprofit charitable activity, which has engendered a culture of philanthropy and a high level of trust in nonprofits.

Relatively few administrative barriers exist to inhibit the creation and registration of nonprofit organizations and to qualify donations for tax deductibility. The administrative process is relatively simple, quick, and cheap, with low rejection rates, as regulating bodies seek to be inclusive rather than exclusive. Nonprofit status confers substantial tax-exempt and tax-deductible benefits, and generous tax incentives are offered for private and corporate donations.

Federal, state, and local governments have diminishing capacities to operate unilaterally, so private-public partnerships and outsourcing of public goods and services to private organizations, both for-profit and nonprofit, are strongly relied upon in a series of "third-party government" or "indirect government" arrangements. In social policy areas, a general institutional preference can be identified for contracting with nonprofit organizations. With the growing role of the nonprofit sector, a conceptual and operational redefinition of the "public sector" has come to include nonprofits.

For-profit corporations play a significant role in funding, promoting, and partnering with nonprofits. Donations, sponsorships, and other corporate contributions to the nonprofit sector are high, and senior corporate employees who distribute these resources, such as the "vice president for corporate responsibility," play key roles in determining nonprofit sector strategies and outcomes.

Market and businesslike solutions to social concerns and increasing hybridizations of organizational structures and activities are ever more emphasized. Social enterprise initiatives based on individual entrepreneurs play an increasingly central role in the ideation of the nonprofit sector. New forms of incorporation and new financial instruments are being developed to combine business principles with social missions.

Third-party and contracting arrangements are regulated through performance-based competitive tendering processes that require increasingly complex processes of accountability and transparency. The tax returns of nonprofits are public documents, and numerous organizations provide access to those documents to facilitate oversight and analysis.

The decreasing participation in and support for traditional social actors—religions, unions, political parties, and mutual societies—have opened up social and political space for independent nonprofits with looser partisan affiliations (see Box 5.2).

Box 5.2 Nonprofits as Political Parties and Labor Unions

Political parties have long used a range of nonprofit legal structures for their organizations, but a new generation of political groups present themselves not as parties but as movements or organizations that identify as nonprofits.

The Tea Party describes itself as "a national grassroots organization." Tea Party Patriots, Inc., operates as a social welfare organization organized under section 501(c)(4) of the Internal Revenue Code.

MoveOn.org describes itself as a "community of more than 8 million from all walks of life who use innovative technology to lead, participate in, and win campaigns for progressive change." The MoveOn family of organizations includes MoveOn.org Civic Action, a 501(c)(4) nonprofit organization that focuses on education and advocacy, providing civic engagement tools to the public and building the progressive movement, and MoveOn.org Political Action, a federal political action committee (PAC), that focuses on demonstrating MoveOn members' power at the ballot box.

A similar dynamic is evident in labor organizations. Although labor unions make up one of the 501c categories—501(c)(5)—and the union movement has long been the breeding ground for many spin-off nonprofits, the United States has witnessed the emergence of new nonprofits with no formal institutional ties to traditional unions but still focused on promoting workers' rights in the United States and around the world. These organizations, identified as "alt-labor" by those seeking to emphasize commonalities with the union movement or as part of the new mutualism by those who seek to minimize them, include the Freelancers Union for independent workers; the Organization United for Respect, also known as OUR Walmart, a Walmart employees group; and the Fair Labor Association, which focuses on labor rights around the world.

Sector characteristics. Much of the focus and energy of nonprofits is spent on cultivating relationships with corporations, foundations, and individual donors. This effort is driven by a strong and aggressive fund-raising industry that captures increasing amounts of private donations from individuals and corporations. Emphasis on earned income activities is increasing, with the introduction of new or increased fees for services and monetization of formerly free services.

Although nonprofits are generally seen as independent with few formal partisan affiliations, extensive connections can be found with individual members of the political and economic elites. Nonprofits can provide a key political base and have become centers of patronage: many elected officials, particularly at more local levels, have worked in nonprofits previous to holding office, and most elected officials, along with most business executives, serve on boards or are active members and supporters of numerous nonprofits.

The "high end" of the sector is increasingly professionalized and corporatized, and a large labor market exists for nonprofit employees. Although frontline wages and benefits in the sector are generally lower than many equivalent public and private sector positions, well-remunerated positions are increasing at the executive level in the larger professionalized organizations, often exceeding the salaries of equivalent positions in the public sector. Senior staff moves through a "revolving door" between the public, for-profit, and nonprofit sectors, and previous government or business experience is increasingly required for executive positions in larger nonprofits.

Strong industry associations at sector and subsector levels lobby in the interests of their member organizations, and an extensive support network of nonprofit and for-profit capacity-building entities, think tanks, and organizational consultants has formed.

Teaching and research in nonprofit issues have become a substantial discipline in universities and other higher education institutions, which provide an increasing array of undergraduate and graduate degrees and continuing education programs in nonprofit policy and management.

Given this political, economic, and social climate and these sector characteristics, the equilibrium in the social contract between the state and its citizens has moved away from the funding of many public goods and services through tax revenues and their provision by government employees. Historically in the United States, nonprofit organizations have had a significant presence in higher education, health, and culture, but the mid-twentieth century saw the growth of a social and political consensus also grew that tax revenues should pay for, and government agencies should deliver, services in key areas such as primary and secondary education, child protection, arts and culture, and parks and recreation.

This consensus has largely disappeared over the past thirty years, and many public goods and services that in other countries are directly publicly funded and government operated, or closely associated with government, are provided by nonprofits in the United States and increasingly supported by private funding. These goods and services include national public radio and television networks, broad swathes of health and social service provision, and public amenities such as parks. An increasing amount of public infrastructure (buildings, parks, monuments, etc.) is sponsored by, and often named after, major donors, and increasingly the default option for funding new social initiatives is to seek private funding.

Nonprofit activity has long been touted as an integral element of the economic and social development of the United States (Drucker 1990, 1994; Filer Commission 1975), and it continues to be a key marker of contemporary public affairs. As Gaudiani (2007) noted, "the U.S. government recognized, perhaps earlier than any other democratic country, that [the nonprofit sector] was essential to economic and political growth . . . [and that nonprofits] supported the entrepreneurialism, comity, stability, and innovation that America has used to prosper over time" (1).

The sector is generally considered to be a driver of progressive reforms, notwithstanding the substantial presence of deeply conservative nonprofits such as the National Rifle Association and the Christian Coalition of America. However, the boundaries of reform continue to be highly contested. As noted in Chapter 2, a broad spectrum of progressive liberals, neopluralists, and neomarxists (often buttressed by conservative critics) combine ideological, structural, and operational analyses to argue that the operations of nonprofits help legitimize economic structures that have fostered the accumulation of private wealth and so mask exploitation and perpetuate societal hierarchies (Abzug and Webb 1996; Brecher and Wise 2008; Fisher 1998; Incite 2007; Joassart-Marcelli 2012; Roelofs 2003, 2006; T. Wallace 2003).

Is There Convergence to the US Model?

US nonprofits are supported by a strong philanthropic culture that contributes a significantly larger share of GDP than other countries to both domestic issues and international aid (Charities Aid Foundation 2006, 2011; Hudson Institute 2012). The large, powerful nonprofit sector enjoys a high level of public trust and demonstrates a strong entrepreneurial spirit, combined with highly developed governance processes and strong transparency mechanisms. The nonprofit sector increasingly operates within a performance framework that is seeking to document and disseminate its achievements. A strong skill base underlies the sector, and a substantial labor market can compete with other sectors for the best and brightest professional talent. Powerful industry associations lobby on behalf of the sector, and knowledge generation is supported by an extensive network of education and research through universities, think tanks, and consulting companies. The tax returns of some 1.6 million registered nonprofit organizations are freely available in the public domain through organizations such as GuideStar, Charity Navigator, Pro-

Publica, and the Urban Institute's National Center for Charitable Statistics, which all provide open-source data tools that allow interested observers to dissect the sector from multiple perspectives.

The US nonprofit sector has long been admired by foreign commentators (Skocpol 2011), and the expansion of national nonprofit sectors around the world appears to reflect an increasingly shared discourse ostensibly based on these US templates. Practical examples abound in both the developed and developing world:

• In Newcastle, Australia, local government subcommittees charged with reviving neglected commercial areas of the city have been converted to independent nonprofit business improvement associations.

• A German foundation sponsors an annual study tour to the United States, which focuses on teaching fund-raising to executives of nonprofits so that they can attract donations to organizations that have previously been fully supported by tax revenues.

• In India, new private foundations are being created to restore historical monuments that have fallen into disrepair under government tutelage.

• In Latvia, public universities are for the first time creating foundations to attract alumni donations.

• The Mexican government is working closely with local and foreign foundations to develop strategies for expanding and strengthening the nonprofit sector, which has traditionally been one of the smallest in Latin America.

The US philanthropic culture and environment are used as a benchmark to which other countries aspire (Charities Aid Foundation 2014), and US entities are frequently called on to teach about fund-raising and resource development. The educational outreach of the Kennedy Center, the Washington, DC, performing arts center, is profiled in Box 5.3.

On a more conceptual level, policy shifts and official discourses also indicate convergence, with an increasingly worldwide accord in favor of expanding the nonprofit sector and encouraging it to deliver a greater share of public goods and services. In 1999, the Labor Party prime minister of the United Kingdom, Tony Blair, and the Social Democrat chancellor of Germany, Gerhard Schroeder, jointly issued their Third Way/Die Neue Mitte (New Middle) manifesto culminating more than a decade of social democrat governments around the world embracing new public management approaches. The Third Way ideology sought to combine neoliberalism with a communitarian agenda. Although the manifesto itself did not directly address the role of nonprofits—indeed it makes no explicit mention of them—it contained language such as "the State should not row, but steer," and "the public sector bureaucracy at all levels must be reduced," which pro-

Box 5.3 Kennedy Center Teaches Fund-Raising to the World

Cultural diplomacy usually comes in the form of a traveling art exhibit or a celebrity visit to a war-torn country. But a new kind of diplomacy is taking place at the Kennedy Center. Since 2006, arts managers from around the world have been coming to Washington, DC, for training on how to improve their organizations back home. Each year's cohort of fellows comes from every corner of the globe: Pakistan, Russia, Ecuador, Zanzibar, Cambodia, and China, to name a few.

In most of these countries, nonprofit staples such as capital campaigns and membership drives are unheard of. "The funding system in the US is different than most of the world," said Kennedy Center president Michael Kaiser. "We developed this private philanthropy model because of a separation of art and state that really emerged from the Puritans who thought that music and dance were evil. Today, an entire American industry, known as fund-raising for nonprofits, has evolved from that evil."

But the question remains: How applicable are these US tools in, say, Nigeria? According to Michael Kaiser, "we're not saying our culture is important; we're saying your culture is important, and we want to make your organizations more robust." The program teaches the participants to apply fund-raising tools in the context of their cultures.

Source: See E. Blair 2011.

moted the opening of government services to contestation and decentralization and so elevated nonprofits to a more central role in service delivery and policymaking (Blair and Schroeder 1999). While the labels *Third Way* and *Neue Mitte* quickly fell out of favor, as they were too closely identified with the personal political projects of the respective British and German leaders, Blair and Schroeder's attempt to create a middle path between statism and neoliberalism helped reframe discourses on the role of nonstate actors.

Even though commentators note the continuing differences between neoliberals, who seek change through marketization, and social democrats, who stress active citizenship, at an operational level the impact of each of these contrasting ideologies is comparable: government retrenchment and an expanded nonprofit sector. The expansion of outsourcing is generally cited as a conservative, neoliberal agenda, but progressive agendas use the language of citizen participation, coproduction, and entrepreneurship to also seek a devolution of the delivery of public goods (Anheier 2005; Pestoff and Brandsen 2010).

Since the Blair-Schroeder era, the shift to the nonprofit sector has become even more evident in the English-speaking industrialized world, particularly where conservative governments have gained office. The Big Society rhetoric of the UK Conservative Party–Liberal Democrat coalition that won government in 2010 highlighted the importance of volunteering and local decisionmaking in responding to community needs through the provision of services previously delivered by the state, and the government has continued to open more public services to be run by the private and voluntary sector. In 2011, the ongoing reforms of the government of Conservative Stephen Harper in Canada were dubbed as being "inspired by British Prime Minister David Cameron's Big Society experiment, in which social responsibilities that traditionally fell to the State are put in the hands of the citizenry and private sector" (Curry 2011).

In Sweden, the quintessential social democratic country, a parliamentary panel known as the Ansvarsutredning (Responsibility Investigation) focused on the need for citizens to take greater responsibility for their own welfare by becoming coproducers of the services they use (Pestoff 2009). Even state-centric Asian regimes are increasing opening spaces for civil society to participate in service delivery. Although Asian welfare provisions are still lean by Western standards, that region is experiencing a rising prosperity and a growing middle class that has less faith in the state-centered outcomes offered under current regimes. As many developing nations around the world surpass the level of wealth that in the early twentieth century helped drive the creation of the welfare state in industrialized democracies, the search is increasing for institutional structures that can help redress inequalities.

The nonprofit sector is even injecting itself into the different national narratives that describe revolving door sinecures for former legislators and senior civil servants. The nonprofit sector has long offered such opportunities in the United States, but more recently the French term *pantouflage* and the Japanese *amakduri,* which previously focused only on the flow between government and government-run corporations or private sector jobs, have in the popular vernacular now also been extended to include nonprofits.

The narratives and statistics from around the world indicate an inexorable drift toward the upper top right of Figure 4.6, and certainly most countries are becoming a little more "American." But does the convergence have limits? Will the sum of incremental changes eventually institute the US system everywhere? Will an inevitable "death spiral" occur in which atrophied government services reach out to private initiative to top-up funding, only to find that when they are successful, legislators use that as an excuse to further reduce tax revenue funding and for citizens to pay fewer taxes? Will increasingly effective fund-raisers in more countries convince the public that nonprofits are better than government at providing certain services, and so they should give directly to nonprofits instead of paying taxes? Competing ideologies may still coexist, but is the "American way" winning most of the battles and eventually the war, if for no other reason than the dynamics of unintended consequences?

In recent years, controversies have occurred over philanthropy and foundation activities in countries around the world that seem positively quaint when seen from a US perspective. In China and Australia, protests have erupted when universities have named buildings after prominent donors (universities in those two countries are mostly public sector institutions and until recently their buildings were generally only named to honor distinguished scholars and public figures). In Barcelona, Spain, when the city council allowed the Fundació Barcelona Comerç, the coordinating body for the business improvement associations in the city, to install a seasonal fee-based ice-skating rink in the main square, protesters railed against the privatization of a public space. Perhaps the most important feature of all these cases is not that protests were made against commercialization, but that they essentially fell on deaf ears, and such philanthropic activities are now becoming the new norm in those countries.

Now, since the global financial crisis of 2008, considerable cutbacks have been made in government funding for social services, education, culture, and international aid, and organizations providing these services are increasingly looking toward philanthropy for support. As industrialized democracies become less able and willing to continue to function as twentieth-century welfare states, their citizens look elsewhere for what they had expected the state to provide.

What label should be put on such dynamics of potential homogenization with a political and cultural norm? Is this process one of "Americanization," "Westernization," "modernization," "neoliberalization," or even the much-debated "end of history" triumph of liberal democracy? Is this part of the global imposition of the US model? Is it an inexorable consequence of a more democratic and prosperous world that is fostering universal desires for self-organization? Or is it simply organizational isomorphism driven by the easy instant availability of information about good practice? With the influx of foreign advisers into transitional countries, will traditional grassroots collective structure and formerly clandestine political oppositions (historically described with terms such as *community, social capital, civil society, social movements,* or *political activism*) inevitably be transformed into a contemporary nonprofit sector? Which model does the emerging sector reflect?

Perhaps a cultural-generational dynamic is being fostered by the emergence of a globally connected "NGO generation" that has fully assumed postindustrial cosmopolitan values and places an increasing trust in independent collective action and nongovernmental organizing. A "Bono–Angelina Jolie effect" may even be taking place as youth around the world seek to mimic the charitable work of celebrities. In recent years, many countries have adopted the US custom of Halloween and trick-or-treat, so why shouldn't they adopt its nonprofit culture?

Instead of a convergence to a US-inspired neoliberal model, an evolution may be trending toward the newer, emerging postneoliberal frameworks such as neocorporatism (Reuter, Wijkström, and von Essen 2012), a resurrection of the mutualist and cooperative ideals of the sector through new mutualism (Birchall 2001), or the renewal of social economies through the blurring of the sectors and social enterprise. The global reach of US political and cultural influences may be combining in different countries with existing models to create new dynamics that have yet to be labeled. Does the terminology exist to describe the different national variants of the emerging postindustrial, postpartisan political cultures that promote values such as self-administration, voluntary community service, and citizenship, all of which embody some version of shifting the power from political elites and bureaucracies and dispersing it to a broader range of collective actors?

Convergence to a US model is contingent on the continued hegemony of US power and of the Western democratic model, yet a steady stream of authors portend their decline (Kupchan 2012; Zakaria 2009). The Japanese decade-long stagnation and the recent global financial crisis have engendered reticence toward market-based, small-government ideologies. Meanwhile the rise of China and its increasing economic and political influence mean a more state-centric model is regarded more favorably by governments and the public, particularly in those developing nations and in nations where the regime has already had an authoritarian bent.

The Washington Consensus of the post–World War II period may have entrenched neoliberalism in many parts of the world, but according to Stefan Halper (2012), a "Beijing Consensus" is now also emerging, based on neoauthoritarian state capitalism in which nonstate actors (for-profit or nonprofit) are allowed to operate, but only within the narrow parameters permitted by the ruling regime. In 2013, an internal document of the Communist Party of China, known as Document 9, warned against subversive Western tendencies, including "constitutional democracy," "universal values of human rights," "civic participation," and "pro-market neoliberalism" (Buckley 2013). In 2014, the prime minister of Hungary, Viktor Orbán, declared that his country would follow "illiberal nationalism" and that "nations whose systems are capable of making us competitive in the global economy are not Western, not liberal, not liberal democracies, maybe not even democracies" (*Washington Post* 2014).

Many authoritarian and illiberal regimes around the world share such sentiments, although they may have allowed a nascent nonprofit sector to gain a foothold. Even when the growth of the nonprofit sector is not necessarily seen as such a direct threat, the primary alternatives to neoliberalism currently being touted usually signify greater state control of nonprofits. As South-South dialogues between developing countries increasingly compete with the earlier North-South development logics, new paradigms for the nonprofit sector may emerge.

Key structural constraints continue to hold back convergence to a US model. The size of the US economy and its institutional and social incentives that favor giving generate a large philanthropic funding pool that is unlikely to be replicated in other countries. Moreover, in the United States, the large historic nonprofit institutions—universities, hospitals, and cultural institutions—power the philanthropic culture and help assure continued public and regulatory support for the sector, but their equivalents in other countries are likely to remain primarily in government hands.

The nonprofit sectors in almost all countries will continue to expand, so in some ways they are all becoming more like those in the United States and other liberal industrialized democracies. But cultural, ideological, and structural "glass ceilings" also make the full adoption of the US model unlikely (Charities Aid Foundation 2014). The cultural frames outlined in Chapter 4 remain as important moorings that cannot be easily cast off. Although both mistrust in the ability of current governments around the world to deliver services and the clamor for expanded spaces of nonstate actions are increasing, nonprofits in other countries are unlikely to be handed the reins of such a broad swath of services as in the United States or to be allowed to so openly engage in contestation.

Compacts and Deliberate Relations

Governments and nonprofits are inextricably linked in a complex series of interactions that configure their joint and separate interests. Nonprofits are independent organizations, but they almost invariably seek some "good" for their members, constituencies, or clients that involves extensive dealings with governments. Likewise, governments are increasingly dependent on nonprofits for service delivery, policy input, and the promotion of civic action. Governments, through the control of institutional legitimacy and capacity to confer fiscal advantages or financial support, are the crucial enablers of nonprofit endeavors.

The most commonly referenced typologies that seek to describe and analyze these interdependent relationships focus on their modes or attributes. Adil Najam (2000) described four categories of relationships based on the ends and means of governments and the corresponding nonprofits: cooperation, when both have similar ends and similar means; confrontation, in the case of dissimilar ends and dissimilar means; complementarity, in the case of similar ends but dissimilar means; and co-optation, in the case of dissimilar ends but similar means. In a comparable vein, Dennis Young (2006) identified supplementary, complementary, and adversarial as the three dominant modes of relationships between the sectors. The modes are not mutually exclusive, and the political economy of the operational environment determines whether the continuing dynamics between the sectors are primarily either vertical and hierarchical or horizontal and collaborative. Janet Saidel (2011) mapped intersectoral dynamics along a continuum, from governance by proxy, in which a transactional, principal-agent dynamic dominates, to relational governance, in which partnerships are the mode of interaction.

The policy agendas that have shaped the increasing salience of nonprofits are shifting and often contradictory—collaborative symbiosis coexists with head-butting antagonism within the panoply of government-nonprofit relations—but in recent years dominant themes seem to be emerging. Advocates for the nonprofit sector are generally seeking explicit recognition of the key role it increasingly plays in delivering services and promoting civil action. They seek greater stability and coherence in the currently uncoordinated and inefficient flows of funding from governments, and they seek some delineation of the independence of the sector and protection for the right to advocate on behalf of constituencies. Legislators and bureaucrats are generally seeking to strengthen the nonprofit sector but are also seeking to foster more "discipline" in terms of performance and transparency in the services delivered by nonprofits and in the input they provide to the policy process. Multiple uncertainties can be found in the relationships between the sectors (Saidel 2011), and all parties have an interest in promoting processes that might reduce them.

The growth of the nonprofit sector in the past decades and its greater salience in the delivery of public goods and services in countries around the world have led to the development of new processes and institutions for managing the relations between nonprofits and governments. As transactions between the sectors have increased, a trend has developed toward more collaborative forms of relations and an institutionalization of the conduits of interactions (Salamon 2006). These new "deliberate relations," as Susan Carter and Paula Speevak Sladowski (2008) called them, go beyond specific contract or advisory relations that focus on a single agency, program, or project. Instead, they are developed to foster stronger government-nonprofit relations across a range of service delivery and policymaking functions and to bring some order to the somewhat chaotic nature of the former haphazard growth. They include the establishment of new government lead agencies or executive appointments that focus on nonprofit relations (e.g., office for the third sector, commissioner for volunteering), as well as new nonprofit coordinating bodies and trade associations that seek to mediate relations with governments and push for more favorable treatment for nonprofits. Even where new formal instrumentalities are not being created, the two sectors may use existing structures to create new processes that foster broader and deeper deliberate relations.

A recent Canadian document illustrates the extent of these deliberate relations:

> Interest in strengthening relationships between governments and the non-profit voluntary sector has resurfaced in several Canadian provinces and territories over the past few years. Leadership organizations, chambers, networks, and councils, in the non-profit/voluntary sector, have been gaining momentum as they build connections, cohesion, and capacity within the sector. Government departments, units, and branches have broadened their scope from volunteer recognition to recognizing the contributions that voluntary organizations make to society. With each sector coming to the table possessing renewed energy and a clearer focus, there is even greater will to work collaboratively and to leverage their collective capacity to build resilient communities. (Centre for Voluntary Sector Research and Development 2009, 1)

Compacts

Since the mid-1990s, the efforts to strengthen deliberate relations have resulted, in many countries, in the creation of formal sector-level framework agreements that commit the parties to joint operating principles and specific actions to increase collaborations. The first such agreement, the Compact on Relations Between Government and the Voluntary and Community Sector in England, was signed in 1998. The term *compact* has since become the most commonly used descriptor for such agreements, but other terms such as *accord, charter, concordat, cooperation program, protocol, partnership*, and *strategy* are also used to describe analogous agreements in different countries (Casey et al. 2010). In their review of such agreements in Europe, Nilda Bullain and Radost Toftisova (2005) used the generic term *policy documents for cooperation.*

Despite very different histories of nonprofit development and current operating models, countries as diverse as Australia, Canada, Estonia, France, Spain, and Sweden have all developed some form of compact. Many others, although not signing formal compacts, have strengthened deliberate relations through the establishment of new government and nonprofit coordinating structures (Bullain and Toftisova 2005; Casey et al. 2010; Kendall 2003; Osborne and McLaughlin 2002; Reuter, Wijkström, and von Essen 2012). Intergovernmental organizations have also sought to better incorporate nonprofits into their deliberations and service delivery (see Chapter 8).

Compacts signed with democratic governments and intergovernmental institutions are generally written to strengthen nonprofits and guarantee their independence, but authoritarian and transitional governments are often seeking to control a nascent sector that is regarded with suspicion by ruling elites. A number of countries have in recent years imposed top-down "agreements" or adopted laws that constrain the formation and operation of nonprofits and give significant oversight discretion to government (ICNL 2013). Although the purpose is control, these laws paradoxically still serve as an acknowledgment of the growing role of nonprofits.

Considerable variations can be found between countries and institutions in the characteristics and outcomes of these initiatives, but they mostly appear to have helped nonprofits to gain a stronger footing and develop more horizontal relations with governments and international intergovernmental instrumentalities and have allowed these to require more accountable service delivery and policy inputs from nonprofits. The first paragraphs from the foreword of the original English compact described above illustrate the principles and objectives embodied in these agreements:

> The voluntary and community sector has a vital role in society as the nation's "third sector," working alongside the State and the market. Through its engagement of volunteers, the services it provides and the support it gives to individuals and groups, its contribution to community and civil life is immense, invaluable and irreplaceable.
>
> This Compact is aimed at creating a new approach to partnership between Government and the voluntary and community sector. It provides a framework to enable relations to be carried out differently and better than before. (Home Office 1998)

Compacts are high-level, formal enabling instruments that define the institutional relationship between government and nonprofits, but they are only the tip of the iceberg of the much wider base of multiple formal and informal processes that have emerged in the context of the tendency to strengthen deliberate relations.

As Jeremy Kendall (2003) and Nicholas Fyfe (2005) noted, the creation of compacts in England and other jurisdictions in the United Kingdom was integral to the Third Way political philosophy of Tony Blair's Labour government. However, as noted throughout this book, such rapprochement between nonprofits and governments and the mainstreaming of nonprofits as service providers and participants in policy negotiations have not been unique to the United Kingdom nor restricted to fellow travelers of Third Way philosophies. New collaborative public-private partnerships between governments and nonprofits are embedded in the various national variants of new public management and governance approaches to the management of public goods and services (Casey and Dalton 2006; Kendall 2003; Osborne and McLaughlin 2002). Despite the significantly different social origins of government-nonprofit relations in different countries, a global trend can be identified in new paradigms of collaboration and institutionalization (Carter and Speevak Sladowski 2008; S. R. Smith 2012). Compacts and other processes of deliberate relations are an attempt to go beyond previous purchaser-provider relationships between governments and nonprofits and move to a more mutual obligation approach that replaces a "contract culture" with a "partnership culture" (Kendall 2003). The rhetoric of these dynamics alludes to the aspiration for collaborative coproduction and relational governance that marks much of contemporary government-nonprofit relations.

Impact of Deliberate Relations

The efforts to establish more deliberate relations are credited by some with the potential to transform the relationship between governments and nonprofits, but others caution against underestimating the challenges of redressing the inherent imbalances in the existing purchaser-provider relations. In particular, some compacts appear to have helped structure more horizontal relations, whereas others fail to live up to initial expectations and may even entrench skepticism among the nonprofit partners (Casey et al. 2010; Elson 2006; Kendall 2009; Lyons and Dalton 2011).

Moreover, in almost every country, an "aspiration gap" appears to be present. In other words, those who structure the deliberate relations and compacts aspire to embrace the widest possible definition of the nonprofit sector, but the nonprofits that are active and the participants who engage in the compact processes tend to be more restricted in scope. Generally, the nonprofits providing social and human services are the ones most engaged in the compact processes, as the focus tends to be on improving procurement procedures and service outcomes in these areas. Nonprofits outside this ambit tend to have less interest in compacts, except when they involve possible changes to regulatory frameworks or tax structures.

Even within the social and human services, some organizations are more engaged than others. One of the consequences, intended or unintended, of the development and implementation of compacts appears to be a certain bifurcation of the nonprofit sector into a compact subsector, which works in close relationship with the government, and a noncompact subsector, which remains more remote (Fyfe 2005). Although this split may be currently defined by the interest and capacity of nonprofits to engage in contemporary compact processes, a similar dynamic that divides the insiders (who benefit from their close relationships with legislators and bureaucrats) from the outsiders (who work on the margins) has long been identified as a feature of government-nonprofits relations (Grant 1995).

In the United States, there is currently no broad, sector-to-sector agreement that would be the direct equivalent of the compacts that have emerged in numerous other countries (Casey 2011). The dominant political and cultural norms continue to value the independence of private voluntary endeavors, and both the US government and nonprofits seem to be somewhat wary of entering into such agreements. The dependence of the nonprofit sector on private philanthropy means that nonprofits spend more organizational effort cultivating relationships with the for-profit sector than with government. Various structural realities also make such agreements difficult to achieve, as the federal architecture of US public administration devolves much of the oversight of nonprofits and the regulation of program funding to the fifty states. In most states, the governors, who oversee program implementation through the line agencies, and the attorneys general, who regulate nonprofits, are both directly elected and so have separate, and often conflicting, political bases and agendas.

These factors may explain why framework agreements have not emerged; however, they should not be interpreted as evidence that US exceptionalism has provided alternative pathways to resolve the concerns that have emerged in other countries. On the contrary, the Aspen Institute (2002) noted that "the relationship between government and the nonprofit sector has grown without a great deal of attention or focus" (4). They also noted that ambiguity exists about how that relationship should best evolve. Kirstin Grønbjerg and Lester Salamon (2012) decried the poor state of relations between the sectors and recommended a new paradigm of government-nonprofit interaction in which nonprofits acknowledge the legitimate performance requirements of the government, and the government acknowledges the advocacy responsibilities of nonprofits and its own obligation to provide greater stability in public funding for nonprofits.

Numerous efforts have been made by advocates for closer ties between the sectors in the United States to create more deliberate relations at a national level. In the 1970s, the Filer Commission recommended that Congress create a permanent commission on nonprofits (Filer Commission 1975). Although the hopes of the advocates for this new commission were thwarted in the transition to the administration of President Jimmy Carter, the push for new coordination structures has never left the policy agenda. The Filer Commission's recommendation has resurfaced periodically, often in the form of calls to create a federal agency for nonprofits that would match the work done by the Small Business Administration created in 1953 to aid and protect the interests of small business.

On the campaign trail, then senator Barack Obama proposed creating the Social Entrepreneurship Agency, which he envisaged as residing in the Corporation for National and Community Service. After his victory, he created a new White House Office on Social Innovation and Civic Participation to identify and scale up successful nonprofit initiatives by developing partnerships between the government and nonprofits, businesses, and philanthropists and by promoting greater civic participation and national service. Meanwhile, in November 2009, the Congressional Research Service issued a report, *An Overview of the Nonprofit and Charitable Sector* (Sherlock and Gravelle 2009), which canvassed the need to increase funding to nonprofits and again broached the possibility of creating a federal agency along the line of the Small Business Administration. In 2010, a bill was introduced to create the Nonprofit Sector and Community Solutions Act (H.R. 5533). The legislation, which died in committee at the end of the congressional session, called for a new cross-sector council and federal cross-agency working group (McCollum 2010). Even though these initiatives to strengthen deliberate relations appear to have widespread support in the nonprofit sector, some commentators scorn the "fawning" between the government and nonprofit sectors and question whether the relationship is becoming too close for comfort (Hudson Institute 2010; Paletta 2010).

Comparing Compacts

The emergence of more deliberate relations in different countries has been the result of both independent development processes and policy convergence. The origins of most compacts and other deliberate relations processes can be traced back to the early 1990s, based on a common theme of the need to address tensions arising from the purchaser-provider model and the need to create a new culture of collaboration that can better harness the expanding roles of nonprofits (Casey et al. 2010). At the same time, compacts are symptomatic of international policy transfers and convergence among nonprofit sectors. Almost all post-1998 processes make some reference to the United Kingdom, whose legislation continues to be the benchmark by which other jurisdictions measure their own processes (Johansson and Johansson 2012; Reuter, Wijkström, and von Essen 2012).

So, can one validly consider all of the written agreements and related processes of deliberate relations in different countries as analogous? One always faces the danger of falling under the spell of the "golden hammer maxim" (i.e., when all one has is a hammer, every problem becomes a nail), but parallels are evident between the different evolutionary paths of these relations across the world. Table 5.1 provides examples of these deliberate relations and quotes the guiding principles contained in the preambles, forewords, or introductions of the key compact-related documents in each country.

The quotes in Table 5.1 clearly demonstrate a common goal of strengthening intersector relations and service outcomes but also highlight the considerable variations between countries. Ultimately, however, the similarities in processes appear to be greater than the differences in outcomes. The diversity between countries highlighted in the previous chapter cannot be minimized, but what clearly emerges from the commonalities is the search for new forms of coordination and liaison between governments and nonprofits.

Table 5.1 Deliberate Relations Around the World

Country	Compact Development	Outcomes	Guiding Principles
United Kingdom	1998 English compact, followed by regional and local compacts. Compacts complemented by specific codes and supported by a range of administrative structures.	Continued support for the compact through the transition from Labour to Conservative coalition governments.	From compact: "The voluntary and community sector has a vital role in society as the nation's 'third sector'. . . . This Compact is aimed at creating a new approach to partnership between Government and the voluntary and community sector."
Canada	2001 national accord; Quebec Government Policy on Community Action 2001; other provincial compacts.	The national accord in effect was abandoned when the government changed. Provincial accords continue to be developed and supported.	From accord: "The Government of Canada and the voluntary sector have long worked side-by-side. Now the Accord marks the launch of a new era of cooperation and respect."
Australia	State-level compacts since 2001; federal compact in 2011.	State-level compacts were adopted with considerable variations in form and outcomes. Federal government launched national compact in 2011.	From national compact: "The Australian Government believes a strong, vibrant, independent and innovative not-for-profit sector is essential to underpin a productive and inclusive Australia. . . . The national compact outlines how the Government and not-for-profit organizations will work together in new ways based on partnership and respect."

continues

Table 5.1 continued

Country	Compact Development	Outcomes	Guiding Principles
United States	No national compacts, but in 2010 a bill would have created the Nonprofit Sector and Community Solutions Act (H.R. 5533). Increasing number of state-level initiatives.	Since the Filer Commission, multiple efforts have been made to create stronger national coordinating structures, but these have not yet been successful. H.R. 5533 died in committee. Numerous state-level contracting reform task forces and cabinet-level liaison officials.	From Representative Betty McCollum, sponsor of H.R. 5533: "The aim is to improve the relationship between the federal government and nonprofits . . . by making the federal government a more productive partner with nonprofit organizations."
France	2001 charter.	A symbolic statement that appears not to have any ongoing impact.	From charter: "This Charter, enacted on the basis of mutual commitments, recognizes and reinforces the partnership relations based on mutual trust and respect for the independence of associations. It clarifies the respective roles and shared commitments of each part."
Estonia	2002 strategy document called the Civil Society Development Concept.	Widespread support for the document and continuing negotiations to strengthen implementation structures.	From the document: "[The Civil Society Development Concept] frames the basis of partnership between nonprofit associations and the public sector, and a framework to promote civic initiative and strengthen democracy in Estonia."

continues

Table 5.1 continued

Country	Development	Outcomes	Guiding Principles
Spain	2006 Strategic Plan for the Social Action Third Sector. Regional plans include both government and nonprofit sector plans in Catalonia.	Strategic plans are not cosigned agreements, but they are jointly developed. Catalonia has parallel government and nonprofit sector development plans.	From the strategic plan: "This [process] has shown that it is possible [for government and nonprofits] to work together constructively despite the different roles and responsibilities and there is a basis for collaborative and complementary action to defend the rights of the most vulnerable in our society."
Sweden	2007 agreement between the Swedish government, national idea-based organizations in the social sphere, and the Swedish associations of local authorities and regions.	Continued implementation of agreement.	From the text of the agreement: "The Government recognizes the important role of the voluntary organizations with respect to democracy and social welfare. Hundreds of thousands of people take part in various voluntary activities every day and make indispensable contributions through their commitment and interest."
United Nations	Various reforms to strengthen the consultative status granted to NGOs in the 1945 UN Charter.	Increase in the number of nonprofits with consultative status and increased civil society participation in UN conferences.	From the secretary-general's response to the 2004 Cardoso Report on UN–Civil Society Relations: "Effective engagement with NGOs increases the likelihood that United Nations decisions will be better understood and supported by a broad and diverse public."

Source: See Casey et al. 2010.

Whereas some argue that these documents are symptomatic of the "best of times" for nonprofits as they have never been so central to service delivery and policymaking, others argue that these processes may represent the "the worst of times," and that the new relations have led only to a loss of nonprofit autonomy and a concentration of power in government hands (Casey and Dalton 2006; Craig, Taylor, and Parkes 2004). The new structures and process are seen as heralding a new era in the evolving relationship between governments and nonprofits and as much-needed coordination mechanisms for interactions potentially beset by fragmentation and inefficiencies. The compacts are peace treaties between sectors that have been at odds due to previous excesses of the contracting and competitive tendering approaches and because of a history of mutual distrust and political rivalry.

Changes in government often derail specific compacts, and their utility is weakened by the increasing incursion of markets into social action (S. R. Smith 2012), but the various forms of deliberate relations and compacts are likely to continue as a central feature of government-nonprofit relations around the world for years to come. On a more cautious note, however, although these compacts may have positive short-term process outcomes and help improve the relationships between those negotiating the documents, the challenge continues to be in embedding longer-term structural impacts. Evidence can be found that many of the new structures and framework agreements have helped create stronger partnerships between governments and nonprofits, but others have simply become empty gestures that have had little enduring impact on relations between the sectors.

Social Enterprise

Arguably the most important redefinition of the work of nonprofits around the world is the concept of social enterprise. Social enterprises and the entrepreneurs who found them are increasingly representing the zeitgeist of the early twenty-first century as they are seen as effectively blending the nonprofit and business sectors and, in doing so, potentially reconciling political, economic, and social objectives. Academic interest in their dynamics is dwarfed by popular media representations of social entrepreneurs as the "new heroes," who personify the best hope for addressing entrenched social ills and global inequalities.

However, social enterprise and entrepreneurship remain fuzzy concepts, interpreted through the particular lens of those who invoke the terms. A gap can be found between the heroization rhetoric around social entrepreneurs, particularly younger ones, and the reality of the challenges they face in creating sustainable enterprises and achieving their organizational and social goals.

Academic Discourses on Social Enterprise

The core concept of the academic definitions of social enterprise is the creation of social value through the entrepreneurial activities of existing or newly created organizations. The definitions of social enterprise often highlight either the process of entrepreneurship or the characteristics of the entrepreneurs, and sometimes both. David Bornstein and Susan Davis (2010) and Georgia Keohane (2013) focused on the processes by which citizens build or transform organizations to advance social change; conversely, J. Gregory Dees and Peter Economy (2001) noted that social entrepreneurs are typically innovative, resourceful, value creating, and change oriented, and Roger Martin and Sally Osberg (2007) saw them as inspired, creative, possessing fortitude, and prone to direct action.

The relationship between social enterprise and the for-profit and nonprofit sectors is somewhat ambiguous. The various academic definitions tend to avoid specifying organizational forms and mainly speak in general terms about the application of business practices in the social sector (Nash 2010) or about commercial imperatives (Dees and Economy 2001). Some authors seek to differentiate between social businesses and social enterprises (Gidron 2010), but to most commentators social enterprise has come to mean both commercial business activities with social purposes and the revenue-generating activities of nonprofits. Dees and Economy (2001) talked about a spectrum of options that range from purely philanthropic to purely commercial. Keohane (2013) maintained that social enterprises can be commercial businesses, nonprofit organizations, or even public-sector organizations.

A key concept is some form of blending, mixing, or hybridity of for-profit and nonprofit discourses and practices (Aiken 2010; Barraket 2008; Dees 2001). A for-profit business renounces a purely monetary profit-only imperative and instead works on a "not-for-personal profit" or "not-only-for-profit" basis, with greater priority given to the creation of social value. Alternatively, a nonprofit organization operates in a more entrepreneurial, businesslike fashion and pursues more earned income activities, without losing sight of its traditional mission.

Hybridity is not only about these blended discourses, in which a single hybrid organization has a mixed personality or culture, but also refers to the combined use of separate and different organizational forms. Existing corporate regulatory structures in most countries generally force social enterprises to choose between either nonprofit or for-profit corporations, so social entrepreneurs often create multiple legal structures for their operations: they may establish both a for-profit company to raise capital and commercialize revenue-generating activities and a nonprofit to receive grants and donations and to provide revenue-neutral social goods. The exact organizational forms of the hybridity depend on the legal-regulatory environments for business and nonprofits in each jurisdiction. Some offer nonprofits more scope for earned income, whereas others have hybrid forms of incorporation that allow for-profit entities to also focus on social goals and to receive donations or compete for other funding normally only available to nonprofits. The UK Community Interest Company and the US Low-profit, Limited Liability Company and B Corporations are relatively new hybrid forms of incorporation that reduce some of the imperatives for multiple legal identities by allowing the better integration of a profit motive and social outcomes. Some of the hybridity may even be manifested through corporate social responsibility structures and company foundations (Gidron 2010), particularly when they take a more active operational role instead of restricting themselves to grant making.

Also contested is the novelty of social enterprise and the nature of "newness" in entrepreneurial activities. Various scholars note the long history of entrepreneurial activities, even if they were not labeled as such, pointing to the development of settlement houses and thrift stores in the late 1800s (see, for example, Gaudiani and Burnett 2011). The modern application of the enterprise concept to the social sector dates from the international work of entities such as Ashoka in the 1980s and was introduced into academia in the 1990s through the research and teaching of business school professors. But significant differences are evident in how the idea of newness is incorporated into contemporary definitions of entrepreneurship. Can *entrepreneurship* as a word apply to any new activity (i.e., new to the person or the organization)? Does the activity have to be innovative (i.e., change the way something is done) or unique (i.e., a whole new way of operating)?

Attempts have been made to capture these various strands of meaning. J. Gregory Dees (2001) noted that social entrepreneurship "means different things to different people" (1), and some authors see broad inclusive definitions as the best path. Jane Wei-Skillern and colleagues (2007) defined social entrepreneurship as "an innovative, social value–creating activity that can occur within or across the nonprofit, business, or government sector" (4), whereas Keohane (2013) suggested adopting the oft-quoted definition of pornography: "It's hard to define, but you know it when you see it" (9). But others argue for a more rigorous definition. Martin and Osberg (2007) maintained that "the social entrepreneur should be understood as someone who targets an unfortunate but stable equilibrium . . . and . . . effects the establishment of a new stable equilibrium that secures permanent benefit for the targeted group and society at large" (39). Simon Teasdale (2010) offered a two-dimensional plotting of discourses and organizational forms that superimposes dimensions of hierarchy versus collectivity and social versus economic outcomes to differentiate social enterprise into four categories: social business, earned income by nonprofits, community enterprises, and co-ops.

Social enterprise has become a universal paradigm invoked in industrialized and nonindustrialized countries alike, but at the same time, significant national-cultural differences are apparent in how it is conceptualized (Barraket 2008; Defourny and Nyssens 2010; Gidron 2010). In the more individualist ideological milieu of the United States, the emphasis has been on the individual entrepreneur, who creates a new organization, or on the "intrapreneur," who transforms an existing organization. In the UK and Continental European context, more rooted in social economy ideologies, a somewhat more collectivist discourse is taking place, with a greater emphasis on the strengthening of local participatory processes and on the creation of social value through the renewed economic activities of collectives and cooperatives. In the developing world, the focus is on creating small-scale businesses that have the potential to lift the entrepreneurs out of poverty and on establishing social services in previously underserved areas or working with underserved populations.

Also important to acknowledge is that emerging social enterprise discourses must be analyzed in the wider context of the growing salience of nonprofits in the delivery of public goods and services and in policymaking, a context that has been analyzed throughout this book. Even when the words *enterprise* and *entrepreneurship* are not invoked, a significant trend has developed toward promoting the more managerialist and businesslike approaches to the governance of nonprofits. Moreover, until 2008, enterprise discourses also benefited from the economic bubble and a dominance of market ideologies moving into the sector through concepts such as social venture capital and philanthrocapitalism (G. Jenkins 2011). The instruments that were creating economic wealth were also seen as more efficiently and effectively generating social goods. Social enterprise was a perfect fit to the normative discourses of the boom and to a correlated shift from political patronage to economic entrepreneurship as a key to nonprofit organizational sustainability. The post-2008 global financial crisis may have taken some of the gloss off social enterprise, but conversely the crisis may have reinforced the notion that the business world should be giving more priority to social outcomes. As the economies of industrialized countries are seen to recover, market-based funding instruments such as social venture capital and social impact bonds will likely again become the drivers of social enterprise discourses around the world (Keohane 2013). In the fields of international development, market-based enterprise approaches such as microloans and marketing to the poor continue to gain momentum as the discourse shifts from aid to investment.

Public Discourses on Social Enterprise

This discussion of the definitions has so far focused primarily on the academic realm, but social enterprise has also caught the imagination of the wider public. Through popular literature such as Greg Mortenson's (2006) *Three Cups of Tea* (now discredited, see Box 7.9), mass-market policy books such as David Bornstein's (2007) *How to Change the World*, and the numerous media articles dedicated to the subject, social enterprise has now become firmly entrenched in the popular vernacular. Social entrepreneurs have even been nominated by the US Public Broadcasting Service (PBS) as "the new heroes" (PBS 2005a). The political activists of the past have been replaced by the new entrepreneurs as the perceived drivers of social change.

The popular discourses somewhat mirror academic definitions and so demonstrate similar confusion and uncertainty. The focus is on the newness, on the use of business strategies, and on the contrast with traditional notions of the nonprofit sector and with the increasingly maligned notion of "charity," but considerable variations exist. However, two clear tendencies in popular discourses can be identified.

"Hard" discourses. In the hard version of the social enterprise discourse, the focus is both on the game-changing nature of social enterprise and on the businesslike imperative. The web page for the PBS series *The New Heroes* (PBS 2005b) stated, "Just as business entrepreneurs create and transform whole industries, social entrepreneurs act as the change agents for society, seizing opportunities others miss in order to improve systems, invent and disseminate new approaches and advance sustainable solutions that create social value."

A more populist definition is expressed by Cheryl Kernot, a former senator in the Australian Parliament and later director of social business at the Centre for Social Impact at the University of New South Wales, who in a newspaper opinion article described social enterprise in the following terms:

> Some charities give people food. Some teach farmers to grow food. Social entrepreneurs teach the farmer to grow food, how to make money, turn it back over to the farm and hire 10 more people. They're not satisfied until they have transformed the entire food industry. In essence, a social business is any business venture created for a social purpose—mitigating/reducing a social problem or a market failure and to generate social value while operating with the financial discipline, innovation and determination of a private sector business. (Kernot 2010, 1)

Kernot uses a food industry analogy that is more commonly used in a version that refers to "giving fish, teaching to fish, and transforming the fishing industry." Its use directly contrasts the supposed transformational dimensions of social enterprise with earlier generations of community development and international aid workers who used the shift from giving to teaching as a leitmotif for their work (see Box 7.4).

Other authors take an even more direct shot at more traditional nonprofits and at the concept of charity as they promote the virtues of market-based social enterprise. In the blurb for *The End of Charity* (Frances 2008) on the back cover, the author is described as a social entrepreneur who once worked for charity, and potential readers are informed that "he came to understand that charity can never deliver a just and sustainable world. It is only through a value-centered market economy that we will ever see real social change."

Even those who rise in defense of traditional nonprofits often reinforce the contrast with for-profits and between old and new. On the Change.org website, a commentator noted:

> These days, nonprofits get far less airtime in the social innovation movement than their for-profit, social entrepreneur counterparts. Perhaps that's because the for-profit form of social change is new, so it seems more interesting, sexier—more apt to create change. . . . There's great danger in dismissing the [nonprofit] sector. Sure, it's inefficient, dysfunctional and broken. Yet it has tremendous potential for innovation. (Edgington 2011, 1)

"Soft" discourses. The soft version focuses only on the entrepreneurial spirit of those involved and on the creation of new organizations. A *New York Times* article on young social entrepreneurs expressed this version in the following terms:

> Social entrepreneurs . . . fill a societal need by starting their own organizations. These men and women have sought to remake the world around them. "Our generation is replacing signs and protests with individual actions," says Kyle Taylor, 23, an advocate for the social-entrepreneur movement who started his own mentoring organization. "This is our civil rights movement and what will define our generation." (*New York Times* 2008, 1)

In its soft version, entrepreneurship is often seen as a movement driven largely by generational change—it is the young philanthroteens who are generating new approaches to social action (Kreinin Souccar 2011). The use of the term *social enterprise* can also be seen simply as an exercise in rebranding, as it is increasingly becoming the term of choice for communicating a more favorable image of the sector or an organization.

In these confusing, and at times seemingly contradictory, academic and popular approaches to social enterprise and entrepreneurship, two key dimensions of the discourse emerge: (1) The nonprofit versus for-profit dimension:

Social enterprise is viewed primarily as market driven, either through businesses that produce social value or new business ventures of nonprofits. When organizational forms are mentioned, they are rarely identified as nonprofit and readers are often left with the default supposition that social enterprise operates primarily in the for-profit business sector. (2) The "old school" versus "new school" dimension: Social enterprise is presented as a new, more effective approach that is supplanting a staid, largely ineffective, traditional nonprofit charity sector. At times, such as in *The End of Charity: Time for Social Enterprise* (Frances 2008), this discourse is explicit; at other times, it is more of a subtext.

The foundational stories of new-school, for-profit social businesses usually involve a "go-getter" entrepreneur often experienced in business (often a dot-com billionaire who has had a midlife epiphany) who parachutes in to apply her or his skills to solving social problems. At the other extreme, the old-school traditional nonprofits usually have foundational stories about local activists or missionaries who seek to do good (even if they plod along because they do not have the know-how for managing entrepreneurial activities). In between are various forms of hybridity: traditional charities have for many years run entrepreneurial activities such as thrift shops and sheltered workshops, and many for-profit social enterprises establish nonprofit affiliates to tap into government funds and foundation grants.

Analyzing the Rhetoric

Given the confusion of what exactly constitutes social enterprise and the rhetoric it has engendered about its potential for driving social change, documenting how social enterprise operates in practice has become increasingly important. For example, a quick review of the projects posted on the website of the emblematic organization Ashoka, which funds social enterprise "fellows" around the world, suggests that the focus is on entrepreneurship primarily in the sense of those who start their own organizations or creatively adapt existing strategies. The strategies implemented by the Ashoka fellows in Box 5.4 have been part of the toolkit of nonprofits in many countries for a number of years, so one has to assume that the entrepreneurship label comes from the fact that they are being implemented in new contexts, often in adverse circumstances, and, in some cases, in the face of considerable personal risk.

Another possible avenue for exploring the complexities of this rhetoric and reality is to analyze how specific social enterprise projects evolve, in order to understand the life cycles of the organizational structures created by social entrepreneurs. Such longitudinal case studies can document the organizational choices made by the entrepreneurs and evaluate the out-

---

Box 5.4 Ashoka Projects

Among the projects highlighted on the Ashoka website are those of the following individuals. Their names and other identifiers have been changed.

Fatima is developing a team of skilled child-nutrition professionals to support mothers in the first two years of their children's lives, a critical age for cognitive and physical development. Fatima is developing a new profession, called "child nutritional workers," to provide valuable information and skills to mothers around the clock through new support centers in hospitals and in homes.

Jane is creating a new link between successful college graduates and youth from disadvantaged backgrounds who need support in the final years of high school. The goal is to help disadvantaged youth to access tertiary education opportunities with an objective of improving their chances of securing meaningful and dignified employment.

Deepak is developing a holistic, integrated approach to the management of a large national park, in which local communities are integral to park management.

Kizuko is revolutionizing the field of medical care by transforming the way nurses are utilized and medical care is received. Rather than being bound to conventional norms of the nursing profession, Kizuko has created a new career path for nurses, one in which nurses can work outside of the traditional construct of a hospital in a network of self-check medical stations where patients can easily understand and access their health care needs.

Source: See Ashoka Innovators for the Public, https://www.ashoka.org/fellows.

---

comes and impact of their efforts, as well as counter the tendency of popular and academic discourse to use transversal, snapshot case studies that show a person or organization at the moment of success.

A recent study examined the continuing work of four entrepreneurs profiled by the *Sunday Magazine* section of a major national newspaper as the young rock stars of social enterprise in the United States (Casey 2013). The profiles consisted of full-page studio celebrity photographs of each of the four entrepreneurs and accompanying biographies that lauded their groundbreaking work and suggested that their organizations had already achieved significant social impact. The follow-up research found that at the time the profiles were published, the extent of the entrepreneurs' organizations had been somewhat more modest than the accompanying texts had suggested. Two years later, two of the four organizations no longer existed, one was in the hands of other managers after the original entrepreneur had been pushed out and accused of mismanagement, and one continued to operate as a time-limited research project at a university. Two of the entrepreneurs had recast themselves as private consultants, and the other two had largely put their careers on hold while they completed their education. Each of these entrepreneurs did at one time create their own new projects and organizations, but they were not necessarily groundbreaking and at best could be said to have extended existing strategies and organizational forms into new areas (Casey 2013). In Box 5.5 one of the case studies is summarized.

Despite the seemingly poor results of the projects profiled, some possible positive outcomes can be inferred from the work of such entrepreneurs in terms of potential agenda setting and through the creation of social and personal capital. Even when their organizations prove to be unsustainable, the work of the entrepreneurs may have shifted paradigms and reframed

---

Box 5.5 A Young Social Entrepreneur

The *Sunday Magazine* profiled twenty-five-year-old Frank Solis, founder of Opportunity Streets. According to the profile, Solis was seventeen when he opened his family's home as a makeshift drop-in center for drifting young people in his New York City neighborhood. He mobilized a group of young neighbors to raise money to rent their own community center and started Opportunity Streets. According to the profile, Opportunity Streets was thriving as a youth-led after-school program aimed primarily at thirteen- to twenty-three-year-olds and had made an impact on the lives of over 500 participants since its inception, with no signs of slowing.

The follow-up research two years later found that Opportunity Streets had been registered as a 501(c)(3) charity and the last tax return on the public records was from the year before the magazine profile. The follow-up indicated that at that time the organization had revenues of only $44,000 and negative assets ($1,000 in the red), which made it unlikely that it was operating the "numerous programs" claimed in the profile. Since the profile, the organization had not filed any further tax returns. The website and domain name previously used by the organization were no longer active and the storefront drop-in center that appeared in a number of press articles about Opportunity Street had closed.

Although the organization no longer appeared to be operational, Solis himself continued to have an active online presence. He described himself on social media sites as the Opportunity Guru, a motivational speaker and team trainer, and he had established a for-profit consultancy. In his blog, he stated that "my new company START NOW is having a nationwide speaking tour." The website had an online store that sold T-shirts and other collectibles that carried the START NOW logo.

Source: Casey 2013.

agendas in their areas of interest. They may have focused attention on the lack of services, created precedents for the provision of new services, reframed expectations, and demonstrated the possibilities of extending services to where they had not been previously provided. The four entrepreneurs profiled in the research above were still relatively young, so the lessons learned from these experiences may contribute to the growth of their personal capital through the strengthening of their management and leadership capacities. Although their early ventures certainly do not seem to have had any lasting successes, chances are that their later ones will have more solid outcomes and that they will eventually become experienced leaders who know how to avoid organizational pitfalls. Equally, while working with others in these projects, they most likely increased broader social capital by strengthening the capacities of those around them.

Other benchmarks can also be used for evaluating such case studies of social enterprises. First, one needs to examine the nature of the entrepreneurial spirit and the transformational leadership of entrepreneurs. Some commentators argue that entrepreneurs should have both the drive to create new organizations or projects and the skills to follow through on them (Dees and Economy 2001), and they should display an "inner locus of control" (Bornstein and Davis 2010). However, others counter that the experience of trying and failing is what drives innovation. An extensive literature can be found on risk in entrepreneurship (Light 2008), the high failure rate of new for-profit businesses (Shane 2008), and vulnerability and organizational demise (Hager 2001). One could argue that a high failure rate in social enterprise is to be expected and even encouraged. A New York foundation that specializes in providing venture capital to social entrepreneurs acclaims on its web page those who "fall and get up again" and notes that it only funds start-up ventures and never existing organizations because its mission is to drive innovation in the social sector by underwriting the creation of new organizations that "break molds."

Second, one needs to consider the contribution of the research that examines the internal and external ecologies of organizations and their sustainability. The creation of sustainable organizations can be conceived as an ascending flight of steps that represent the stages of creating, building, and sustaining an organization (Bloom and Smith 2010; Light 2008). Many entrepreneurs are successful in imagining and inventing their projects but then have problems in launching and sustaining them. The capacity to climb the staircase to sustainable organizations depends on the skills and knowledge of the entrepreneurs and on the external ecology of supporters and stakeholders. If funders are always moving on to the next big thing, or entrepreneurs find that other essential external supports fail them, then outcomes are unsurprisingly disappointing.

Third, the role of the media and other boosters of social enterprise along with the lure of fame need to be explored. The hyperbole in the press articles and websites may simply reflect the dynamics of the media industry hungry to sell new ideas, or it may be social enterprise organizations marketing their approach and seeking to boost their fund-raising potential. The youthful subjects of the lavish praise being heaped on social entrepreneurs in articles such as the *Sunday Magazine* profile perhaps cannot be blamed for being carried away by their moment of fame. They are flattered by the attention, or they let hubris get the better of them, and they allow unsustainable claims to be made about their careers and organizations.

However, undoubtedly, the rhetoric of social enterprise and entrepreneurship far outstrips the reality of what they can deliver (Andersson 2012; Edwards 2010a). The rhetoric tends to be about new forms of self-sustaining organization that generate novel strategies for addressing social problems, but the reality tends to be more prosaic. The business plans of the majority of social enterprises involve the creation of nonprofits that generally follow traditional forms and the re-creation of tried-and-true social and organizational responses.

Blurring of the Sectors

Perhaps the inescapable force of isomorphism simply pushes initiatives that aspire to break the old rules back to existing routines and organizational structures. Some suggest that social entrepreneurs around the world are creating new forms of organizations and new strategies for social action and development, but more often they seem to be re-creating existing templates and perhaps just rebranding them with the newer, sexier packaging of enterprise. As Ruth McCambridge (2011) noted, "entrepreneurialism is entrepreneurialism"—ultimately more concerned about packaging and promotion than about a new or inherently good idea.

The mystique surrounding social enterprise may have made it the "dream catcher," as Fredrik Andersson (2012) suggested, for our aspirations to be bold and innovative in solving seemingly intractable problems, and so it could be understood not as a new mode of operation but as a shift in mind-set that integrates the entrepreneurial rhetoric into the social action objectives of the nonprofit sector. At the same time, not all market-oriented approaches to addressing social issues use the language of social enterprise. The Omidyar Network, established by the founder of eBay, describes itself as a philanthropic investment firm dedicated to harnessing the power of markets to help scale up innovative organizations and to catalyze economic, social, and political change (Omidyar Network 2013). Although the focus is on a market-based approach, the Omidyar Network appears to studiously avoid the term *social enterprise*, which does not appear in its documentation. And despite its emphasis on a market orientation, the structure of the organization and focus of its funding suggest limits to the impact of the market: the Omidyar Network is a US-registered nonprofit organization and its international portfolio of funded organizations shows that some 70 percent are nonprofits.

The rise of social enterprise rhetoric is symptomatic of the increased blurring of the boundaries between the three sectors around the world, particularly between for-profits and nonprofits. Even though the general assumption is that the business sector is teaching nonprofits to be more efficient and effective, the reverse flow also occurs, with nonprofits offering lessons on creating socially responsible and environmentally sustainable businesses and how to achieve more with "zilch" resources (Lublin 2010). In addition to this practical cross-fertilization, a symbolic dimension has developed with businesses wanting to appear more socially responsible and nonprofits more businesslike. This blurring even extends to online identities. As noted above, the Omidyar Network is a nonprofit organization, yet its website uses a *.com* domain extension, a designation more often associated with for-profits. Many other organizations make seemingly incongruous choices in their online personas (see Box 5.6).

Box 5.6 Internet Domain Extensions: *.org, .com,* or *.ngo?*

The Internet domain extension *.org* was designed to be used by noncommercial entities and is the preferred extension for most nonprofit organizations. However, no formal restrictions or qualifications exist for its use as a top-level domain even though some national top-level domains restrict their second-level *.org* domains to registered noncommercial organizations (e.g., in Australia, *.org.au* can only be used by registered nonprofits).

Perhaps a marker of the growing cachet of the nonprofit sector is that certain for-profit organizations choose to use *.org,* particularly if they want to create an organizational persona based on a mission, community, or socially oriented outcomes. The for-profit online marketplace Craigslist.org is one of the more high-profile examples (although affiliates in some countries and cities use *.com,* and the parent company has an affiliated nonprofit foundation). Other examples include InterNations.org, a for-profit social network for expatriates. Change.org, a for-profit company that provides a platform for online petitions, expresses its choice to use *.org* in the following manner: "Unlike many companies, our business is social good. Change.org

continues

Box 5.6 continued

is focused entirely on our mission of empowerment, and we are re-investing all our revenue into our service to users. This focus on mission instead of profit is why our name ends with *.org* instead of *.com*."

Another option is the use of the *.net* domain. Although *.net* was originally designed for technology infrastructure networks such as Internet service providers, the implied association with "network" has also made it an option for nonprofits seeking to avoid the charity stigma and for private companies seeking a more socially conscious persona. The Pangora Group, at panagoragroup.net, is a private company working in health-related development programs.

At the same time, many nonprofits choose to use *.com* as their online domain to demonstrate a more businesslike and entrepreneurial approach or to otherwise increase their identification with the private sector. The Indian nonprofit Janaagraha.org runs an antibribary site targeting the private sector, which they title Ipaidabribe.com. Compassion International, a charity that tackles child poverty in twenty-six of the world's poorest countries, uses the address compassion.com.

A push has been made for cooperatives to use the *.coop* top-level domain, and some countries have specific second-level domains for different types of nonprofits, such as *.asn.au* for associations in Australia, but use does not appear to be widespread for any of these domains.

Since October 2014, a new domain, *.ngo* (*.ong* is the acronym in romance languages such as French and Spanish), has been available. It will be managed by the same Public Interest Registry that oversees *.org,* but it will be available only to validated organizations that can demonstrate that they are nonprofit and independent and act in the public interest.

The choice of which domain to use can also be somewhat serendipitous or the result of competition for the domain name. One Australian start-up nonprofit reported using a *.com.au* domain simply because the website was set up by a board member who did not know *.org.au* existed. The US health charity March of Dimes uses a *.com* domain, marchofdimes.com, apparently because the *.org* version is controlled by the Canadian affiliate.

Source: See Change.org, Business Model, http://www.change.org/about/business -model.

6

The Internationalization of the Nonprofit Sector

The first part of this book was focused on the expansion and evolution of domestic nonprofit sectors around the world. The focus now shifts to the international and global arenas. Just as nonprofits have become increasingly influential at national levels, the activities of the international dimensions of a nonprofit sector that operates between the expanding intergovernmental structures and the global marketplace for transnational and multinational businesses have correspondingly escalated (Anheier 2014; Batliwala and Brown 2006; Boli 2006; Schechter 2010). The current wave of globalization and deterritorialization has engendered denser networks of cross-border connections in almost every sphere of modern life, and the nonprofit sector is no exception.

The international work of the nonprofit sector addressed in this book encompasses all aspects of the operations and impact of nonprofit organizations that transcend national borders. Formerly domestic, nonprofits are "going international" at the same time as increasing numbers of deliberately international nonprofits are being established (Anheier 2014; Boli 2006; Lewis 2007). The following discussion is focused on organizations that are autonomous, nongovernmental entities that comply with the structural-functional definition of nonprofits cited in Chapter 2. Excluded are the purely intergovernmental international organizations—the bilateral or multilateral institutions created through treaties or other agreements that have national governments as their primary membership, including global organizations such as the United Nations, the World Bank, and the World Trade Organization and regional institutions such as the European Union and the African Union.

Many hybrid organizations straddle definitions, either in themselves or through their affiliated organizations. The UN Children's Fund (UNICEF) is a UN agency with an executive board comprising representatives of member nations, and as such it is clearly an intergovernmental organization. To support its work, UNICEF has fostered the creation of a network of UNICEF national committees, which are incorporated as independent local nonprofit organizations in their countries of operations. Currently thirty-seven such nonprofit UNICEF national committees are in operation, all in industrialized wealthy countries, which raise funds on behalf of UNICEF and advocate in support of its programs. The United Nations itself has also adopted the same strategy of creating numerous "friends of" nonprofits, including the UN Foundation, created in 1998 as a US 501(c)(3) nonprofit with a donation from the media baron Ted Turner, who sought to bolster support for UN programs and the reform efforts of then Secretary-General Kofi Annan. The current headquarters of the foundation is in Washington, DC, and it operates on an annual budget of $137 million.

Some commentators consider such hybrid organizations to be a third category of international organizations (often designated as transnational hybrid organizations [THOs]), separate from both intergovernmental organizations and nonprofits (Missoni and Alesani 2013; Willetts 2011), but they are included in this book because they are deliberately constituted with nonprofit legal personalities. Given the considerable national variations in political regimes and service delivery models, the nonprofit legal structure has become a "flag of convenience" for international dialogues in a wide range of fields. The nonprofit form sidesteps many of the constraints imposed on intergovernmental structures by sovereignty and geopolitical tensions. How an international cultural nonprofit straddles the sectors is illustrated in Box 6.1.

Box 6.1 The International Council of Museums

The International Council of Museums (ICOM) was established in 1946 as an international nonprofit under French law as a global forum for national museum associations. Most delegates are civil servants or directly appointed by their respective governments, but some are representatives of nongovernmental national museum associations. The general secretariat is housed at the UN Educational, Scientific and Cultural Organization (UNESCO) headquarters in Paris (UNESCO is an intergovernmental organization), and much of the work of ICOM is focused on international intergovernmental agreements about the preservation and display of national patrimonies. Its web page describes ICOM as a "diplomatic forum" made up of experts from 137 countries and territories to respond to the challenges museums face worldwide.

A significant number of nonprofit international professional and trade associations exist with either individual members from around the world or member national associations. Like their domestic counterparts, they function as autonomous nonprofits that foster the commercial interests of members by providing a range of services, including acting as clearinghouses for information and research on good practice and doing advocacy work to promote policies and practices favorable to members (see Box 6.2).

Box 6.2 International Window Film Association

Window film is the thin plastic sheeting applied to windows to control light, save energy, or provide privacy. The International Window Film Association (IWFA) is an industry association of window film manufacturers and distributors that facilitates the growth of the window film industry by publishing research, influencing policy, and promoting awareness of window film. Registered in the United States as a 501(c)(6) (business association), it is located in Martinsville, Virginia. It has members on all continents, although most of its legislative work has been in the United States and Canada. The IWFA's current annual income is $1.1 million.

Source: See International Window Film Association, http://www.iwfa.com.

The Rise of the International Nonprofit Sector

Since 1907, the Union of International Associations has documented the growth of intergovernmental and international nongovernmental organizations. The union was established in Brussels, Belgium, which at the beginning of the twentieth century was host to one-third of the then existing 150 international organizations (primarily intergovernmental organizations dominated by the European powers of that era). The union was an outgrowth of the International Institute of Bibliography, founded in 1895, which had developed the Universal Decimal Classification system for libraries (see Box 6.3 further on in this chapter).

The database of the union includes only "prominent" organizations and so does not count the thousands of smaller international nonprofits or the primarily domestic nonprofits around the world that also have an international dimension to their work. In the database, international nonprofits now outnumber intergovernmental organizations by a factor of 10, and their growth rate since the 1970s has been significantly larger. Figure 6.1 shows the growth of both intergovernmental organizations and international nongovernmental organizations since 1909 as documented in the union's yearbook (Union of International Associations 2012).

The organizations that from a contemporary lens would now be considered international nonprofits have a long history. Faith-based institutions have long fomented contact and exchange between the far-flung corners of their influence and have actively proselytized and fought wars to extend their range. The colonial structures of the European powers in the sixteenth to twentieth centuries often went accompanied by philanthropic outreach to indigenous populations and indigent colonialists (generally through faith-based organizations).

In the database of the union is recorded the years of founding for international nongovernmental organizations. The first entry is for the Sovereign Constantinian Order, a monastic order founded in 312; the second is the Order of Saint Basil in 358. A steady trickle of organizations were founded in the fourth to eighteenth centuries, almost exclusively religious, including Muslim Sufi tariqas after the ninth century. Early fraternal organizations, universities, scientific and academic associations, mercantile organizations, and performing arts groups were also founded around this time, but not until the mid-1800s did secular international nonprofits—advocacy, social welfare, professional, and sports—begin to appear in greater numbers than faith-based organizations.

Figure 6.1 Growth in International Organizations

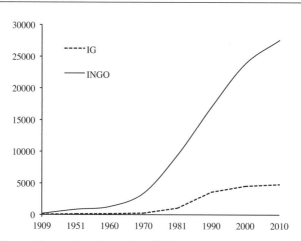

Source: Union of International Associations 2012.

Notes: This figure does not include inactive or proposed organizations registered in the database. IG stands for "intergovernmental" and INGO stands for "international nongovernmental organization."

As noted in Chapter 2, the secular independent international nonprofit sector began to emerge in significant numbers through social movements focused on humanitarianism and human rights, including antislavery and women's suffrage. Although avowedly secular, many of these new organizations had identifiably faith-related roots, particularly in Quaker communities. A number of now emblematic international nonprofits appeared in the mid-1800s, albeit in original forms that do not necessarily correspond with their current focus—the Young Men's Christian Association (YMCA) was founded in London in 1844 as an evangelical organization, and the Red Cross was formed in Geneva in 1863 to minister to soldiers wounded on European battlefields.

The globalization of the labor movement and radical left also date from this period—the Universal League for the Material Elevation of the Industrious Classes was an English political organization established in 1863 primarily to agitate for the right to assembly, labor rights, and suffrage of English workers, but its founding mandate also sought to increase recreational and educational opportunities and to promote international fraternity. It was the progenitor of the International Workingmen's Association (1864–1876), also known as the First International. This workers' movement, best known as the ideological battleground that pitted socialism against anarchism, championed many of the human and labor rights agendas currently associated with the nonprofit sector.

The emergence of these organizations can be seen as part of a nascent internationalization of idealism that coincided with the establishment of the first modern international institutions during a mid-nineteenth-century wave of globalization (see Box 6.3).

Even though some of the earliest organizations continued to exist, the early 1900s saw the first surge of truly modern international nonprofits, instantly identifiable as such to contemporary observers. Save the Children was founded in the United Kingdom in early 1919 by two Quaker social activist sisters, Eglantyne Jebb and Dorothy Buxton, in response to the aftermath of World War I and the Russian Revolution. The organization was controversial, as it sought to aid children in Germany and Austria, the enemies in the war. However, the concept of children's rights quickly found support around the world, particularly from women who were also campaigning for their own suffrage. The Australian feminist and pacifist Cecilia Annie John had been in London when Save the Children was launched and returned to Melbourne soon afterwards, setting up a branch there by the end of 1919. The International Save the Children Union was founded in Geneva in 1920.

Also established in the first decades of the twentieth century were the US service clubs such as the Rotary (1905), the Kiwanis (1915), the Lions (1917), and Toastmasters (1924), as well as the large foundations associated with the US barons of industry, the Carnegie Corporation of New York

Box 6.3 When Did the World Globalize?

The tendency is to think of globalization as a late twentieth-century phenomenon, driven by the new information technologies and cheaper travel, but a long series of significant events and disruptive technologies has provided the historical markers of global integration and an emerging internationalism.

Various ancient empires in Europe, Asia, the Americas, and Africa, established primarily through military conquests, created vast regions of political and cultural interconnections.

Iconic journeys, such as Marco Polo's twenty-four-year adventure in Asia starting in 1271 and Ferdinand Magellan's first circumnavigation of the globe from 1519 to 1522, are often cited as landmarks of globalization. Most significantly, Christopher Columbus's voyage of 1492 and subsequent European colonization of the Americas, and later of Asia, Africa, and Australasia, established new political and economic spheres and new global transport routes. The colonial world was highly connected, with a handful of European powers ruling empires that spanned the globe.

In the mid-1800s, a series of new technologies greatly expanded the scope of human contact. The development in the 1840s of the telegraph revolutionized communications, and the large-scale development of railways beginning in the 1840s, and of propeller-driven steamships after the 1870s, made long-distance travel more viable for larger segments of the population. In 1865, the year before the first telegraph line between America and Europe was inaugurated, the International Telegraph Union (now the International Telecommunications Union) was established. It is now recognized as the first modern international organization created with the consent of the majority of sovereign governments.

As the telegraph, railways, and steamships created quicker commercial links, the formerly ad hoc nature of timekeeping based on local calculations was no longer sufficient. In 1884, representatives from twenty-six nations (including the Austro-Hungarian and Ottoman empires) met for the International Meridian Conference in Washington, DC, to negotiate the choice of a common zero of longitude and a standard for the reckoning of time around the globe. The delegates agreed to establish the Greenwich Meridian as the international standard against which all time zones were calibrated.

The global dissemination of knowledge was facilitated by the development of two international library classification systems: the Dewey Decimal Classification System in 1876 and the Universal Decimal Classification in 1905.

The introduction of large, standardized metal shipping containers in the late 1950s radically altered global trade. Until then, all goods had been loaded in their individual boxes, crates, or barrels. Loading and unloading ships was laborious and expensive, and pilfering was rife. With the widespread adoption of the containers by the early 1960s, the cost of shipping fell by up to 90 percent, creating new international markets for goods that had previously only been economically viable in local markets.

(1911) and the Rockefeller Foundation (1913) (the foundations were originally chartered by legislation but later converted to nonprofits).

The importance of the work of international nonprofits was acknowledged in the 1945 Charter of the United Nations. The term *nongovernmental organization* (NGO) is commonly regarded as having come into widespread use through its inclusion in Article 71 of Chapter 10 of the Charter, which established a formal consultative status for organizations that were not agencies of member states (see the section on the United Nations in Chapter 8). In the first years of the United Nations, only some fifty NGOs had consultative status (there are currently 3,800). The earliest NGOs with this status reflected both the primarily European, UK, and US origins of the first international nonprofits and the diversity of what constitutes the nongovernmental sector: they included the Howard League for Penal Reform, the oldest penal reform charity in the United Kingdom, established in 1866; the International Air Traffic Association, founded in The Hague in 1919; the International Association of Schools of Social Work, founded at the First International Conference of Social Work in Paris in 1928; Pax Romana, the international Catholic movement for intellectual cultural affairs, first founded as a student lay Catholic association in Switzerland in 1921; and the International Bar Association, founded at an international meeting of jurists in New York in 1947.

As Figure 6.1 illustrates, a considerable uptick can be seen in the international sector since the 1970s as part of the same associational revolution evident at domestic levels. The combination of the comparative advantage of the nonprofit sector in service delivery and policymaking, along with the globalization of professional and epistemic communities, has resulted in an explosion of the international nonprofit sector in numbers and salience. The expansion of the sector has been both a consequence and driver of globalization. It is a key part of the humanitarian aid industry but also of the environmental, peace, and justice movements. It also includes academic, professional, and cultural exchanges in areas as diverse as sport, gourmet cooking, and a range of commercial interests. In the past the focus of the work of international nonprofits had primarily been on issues of "low politics" of the environment, development assistance, human rights, and disaster relief, and on "Track II" international relations between professionals and civil servants. International nonprofits now increasingly also work directly with the "high politics" of international affairs and security and help manage "Track I" state-level relations (Ahmed and Potter 2006; Carey 2012; Schechter 2010).

Religious faith continues to be an important impetus in international nonprofits. The modern nonprofit sector may be more secular and universalist than earlier iterations, but religion is still a key part of the sector. Large historic faith-based entities, such as the Salvation Army, Islamic Relief, and American Jewish World Service, as well as networks such as the Association of World Council of Churches Related Development Organisations in Europe (APRODEV), continue to be major players in the international nonprofit scene, and the foundation story of a significant percentage of contemporary organizations includes narratives of faith-based inspirations. The YMCA evolved its focus and mission from the "aggressive evangelism" of its origins to its current focus on "social responsibility for human beings" (Muukkonen 2002), and a similar description could be applied to many of the historic nonprofits.

Currently, no figures have been consolidated on the broader international nonprofit sector beyond the some 30,000 active organizations identified in the Union of International Associations database (see Figure 6.1). A Basic Registry of Identified Global Entities (BRIDGE) is currently under development by four partners, GuideStar USA, GlobalGiving, the Foundation Center, and TechSoup Global, which will assign a new unique global identification number to the some 3 million nonprofits with international reach that are in their databases (TechSoup Global 2013).

The number of international nonprofits is hard to estimate due to varying opinions on what qualifies an organization to be included in the count. Where national statistics formally identify international nonprofits as a separate category from domestic organizations, they appear to be around only 1 percent to 2 percent of the total number of nonprofits in any country (Anheier 2014), and within that figure, only a minority are large enough to be included in international databases. However, many more organizations, although not formally classified as international, are still doing international work. In the United States, for example, of the 1.6 million nonprofits registered with the IRS, only around 20,000 (1.3 percent) register under the National Taxonomy of Exempt Entities (NTEE) Category Q, "international, foreign affairs, and national security" (the NTEE classification is self-designated by the organizations, and it allows for multiple classifications). Of these 20,000 organizations, 75 percent have an income of less than $100,000 per annum or do not report their income, and only 2.5 percent have an income of more than $5 million (National Center for Charitable Statistics 2012). However, any count based only on NTEE Category Q does not include the many organizations that clearly do international work but do not use that designation when registering. Teach for All, the international arm of the US domestic nonprofit Teach for America, states that its mission is "responding to educational needs in countries around the world" and operates with annual revenues of $10 million but classifies itself in the NTEE category of B99, "education not elsewhere classified." Compassion International, which "tackles global poverty one child at a time, serving more than 1 million children in 26 of the world's poorest countries" and has annual revenues of $520 million, uses the category X20, "Christian religious organization." Finally, Olympic sports organizations, including the US Olympic Committee (with revenues of $140 million), are in a separate code, N71, "Olympics." While international nonprofits are only a small minority of the sector in the United States, they are well represented among the largest nonprofits in the country (see Chapter 7).

In contrast to the small number of organizations classified as Category Q in the NTEE database, a keyword search of the some 1.8 million US organizations in the database of GuideStar, the nonprofit transparency website, identifies 163,000 organizations (9 percent) that use the word *international* as part of their name, mission statement, or program description. In the United Kingdom, a similar keyword search of the 180,000 charities registered with the Charity Commission identifies only some 6,800 organizations (3.7 percent) that use the descriptor *international*. The US and UK figures are not directly comparable given differences in their criteria for registration and in the classifications systems, but they confirm that international activities are only a minor part of the work of the formal nonprofit sector in industrialized countries.

In addition, an extensive network of international nonprofit activity is not formally constituted or is operating under the legal and fiscal sponsorship of other organizations. These informal organizations and the smaller formal organizations appear to be part of a rising number of "boutique" international nonprofits, which include numerous immigrant hometown associations (see the discussion of diaspora development in Chapter 7). Many all-volunteer efforts are created to support specific foreign institutions (most often schools, orphanages, or medical clinics) or localities with which the principals have a particular bond, either because their ancestral roots are there or because they feel some particular affinity after traveling, volunteering, or working in that area.

In this book, I also address the increasing international contacts between nonprofits in different countries that continue to describe their work in primarily domestic terms. As globalization drives fundamental changes in economic, political, and social relations, organizations in the public and for-profit sectors are becoming more international and complex, and the nonprofit sector is keeping pace, driven by the same imperatives to scale-up in response to global concerns and facilitated by innovations in communications technology and the reduced transaction costs of the movement of information, capital, and personnel. The nonprofit sector has been able to act akin to the for-profit sector, without the sovereignty constraints that limit collaborations between governments. Nonprofits can construct multinational identities and operations, and parallels are evident between international nonprofits and multinational corporations in their search for new markets, brand promotion at the worldwide level, the internationalization of personnel, and the deterritorialization of the organizations (Siméant 2005). The growth of Oxfam, for example, exhibits many of the processes of partnerships and mergers more commonly associated with the for-profit sector (see Box 6.4).

Box 6.4 Oxfam

Oxfam was founded in Britain in 1942 by a group of Quakers, social activists, and Oxford academics as the Oxford Committee for Famine Relief. The group campaigned for food supplies to be sent through an Allied naval blockade to starving women and children in enemy-occupied Greece during World War II. At the end of the war, the campaign shifted to lobby to allow Britons to send food parcels to occupied Europe, including to Germany. In 1948, Oxfam opened the first permanent charity thrift shop in the United Kingdom. In 1951, the organization began its transformation from a local lobby for hunger relief into an aid agency, with its first emergency effort in response to a famine in Bihar, India. The first branch of Oxfam outside the United Kingdom was established in Canada in 1963, and in 1968 Oxfam extended its reach even further by opening an affiliate in Peru.

Oxfam International was formed in 1994 as a federation of independent nongovernmental aid organizations in Australia, Belgium, Canada, Hong Kong, Holland, New Zealand, and the United States, which had already been collaborating for a number of years. Their aim was to work together for greater impact. Some of the organizations had already been affiliated with Oxfam, whereas others such as Community Aid Abroad in Australia and Novib in Holland had operated with different identities. Some of the affiliates continued with their previous identities even after joining the federation. Community Aid Abroad became Oxfam Community Aid Abroad in 1995 and then Oxfam Australia in 2005; however, Novib changed its name to Oxfam Novib only in 2006.

Oxfam now describes itself as an international confederation of seventeen organizations working in approximately ninety countries worldwide with a total budget of $1.5 billion. The secretariat is in London, but the organization is legally registered in Holland as a nonprofit foundation, Stichting Oxfam International. It is currently implementing a new single management system to improve coordination between the international secretariat and field operations. As part of the strategy, only one Oxfam affiliate will be tasked to lead the organization's efforts in any particular country.

Sources: See Oxfam, https://www.oxfam.org.uk, https://www.oxfam.org.au, and http://www.oxfam.org/en/about/annual-reports.

In the following sections, I look at three forms, or degrees, of the internationalization of nonprofits: international cooperation between primarily domestic nonprofits, the increasing international reach of the work of formerly domestic nonprofits, and purposely created international nonprofits. They can be considered stages of internationalization (Anheier 2014), but they can also be seen as a series of coexisting ecologies of international connectivity. Overlaps and transitions can be found as existing domestic organizations become increasingly internationalized and new organizations are created with specific international intent, sometimes as the direct consequences of the increased connections between domestic nonprofits.

The Drivers of International Growth

The growth of the sector has been bolstered at the international level by the same debates unfolding at the domestic level about the inefficiencies of governmental institutions and the need to engage a wider range of partners in policymaking and service delivery. The growth in intergovernmental cooperation has helped drive a parallel expansion of "bottom-up multilateralism," as Michael Schechter (2010) called it, built on the connections between stronger activity "nodes" created by the expanding domestic nonprofit sectors (Florini 2000). The international versions of new public management, governance, and third-party agency approaches are the justifications for reducing government footprints and working with organizations that are seen as more flexible and innovative than public bureaucracies. Just as nonprofits have been seen as the answer to domestic service delivery and policymaking conundrums, they also became an international "magic bullet" (Edwards and Hulme 1996; Lindenberg and Dobel 1999). As state capacity wanes around the world in the face of economic constraints and eroding trust, the international nonprofit sector plays an ever-escalating role in delivering and regulating transnational public goods. The nonprofits' work is embraced by a wide range of ideologies and commercial interests. In 2012, the United Nations designated September 5, the anniversary of the death of Mother Teresa, as the International Day of Charity, recognizing "the role of charity in alleviating humanitarian crises and human suffering within and among nations and in the promotion of dialogue among people from different civilizations, cultures and religions" (United Nations 2013).

Perhaps the most visible and most commonly identified driving force for the globalization of the nonprofit sector is the impact of new communication technologies. The Internet, social media, and other elements of new communication technologies have immeasurably reduced the transaction costs of managerial tasks, long-distance operations, and cross-border collaborations. Technology has also facilitated the creation of a new class of digital nonprofits that operate almost entirely in the ether of the Internet. The online encyclopedia Wikipedia is perhaps the most prominent example of a digital nonprofit (see Box 6.5). Notably, the founder, Jimmy Wales, chose to create a nonprofit although other online portals and social media sites such as Facebook, Yahoo, Huffington Post, and Twitter are all for-profit organizations that have achieved considerable commercial value.

More specific drivers can be identified for the growth of international humanitarian aid and advocacy organizations. Decolonization and national-ist liberation movements in the 1950s and 1960s created new sovereign countries, many of which were underdeveloped and fertile ground for the expansion of the activities of humanitarian nonprofits. Development assis-tance to these new countries was at first primarily channeled through offi-cial government-to-government aid, particularly as part of the client rela-tionships of the Cold War superpowers, but the international nonprofits that had previously focused their work on war relief in Europe then began to take on a wider developmental role around the globe.

During the Cold War, the battle of the two superpowers was the pri-mary global backdrop for conflicts between and within nations. The end of the Cold War has opened up new political and programmatic space for a wider range of nonstate actors (Florini 2000; Götz 2010). It has shifted the focus of international aid from client states to an even broader development agenda by shining a harsh light on previous official aid projects in which the funds ended up in the pockets of corrupt elites. The broader agenda, as exemplified by the adoption by the United Nations of the Millennium Development Goals (see Chapter 7), has facilitated the emergence of the new interventionist principles such as the "Responsibility to Protect" (often referred to as R2P), which argues that the international community has the responsibility to intervene to protect threatened populations.

Box 6.5 Wikipedia

Wikipedia is managed by the US nonprofit Wikimedia Foundation and a network of over forty affiliated national chapters around the world. Users of the site often see the following plea for donations: "*Dear Wikipedia readers:* We are the small non-profit that runs the #5 website in the world. We have only 150 staff but serve 450 million users, and have costs like any other top site: servers, power, rent, programs, staff and legal help. To protect our independence, we'll never run ads. We take no gov-ernment funds. We run on donations averaging about $30. If everyone reading this gave $5, our fundraiser would be done within an hour. If Wikipedia is useful to you, take one minute to keep it online another year by donating whatever you can today. Please help us forget fundraising and get back to Wikipedia. *Thank you, from the Wikimedia Foundation.*"

Sources: See Wikipedia, https://wikimediafoundation.org/wiki/Local_chapters, and http://wikimediafoundation.org/wiki/Tax_Deductibility/en.

The opening of political spaces, the reconceptualization of the obligations of the international community, the growing demands of the more educated and prosperous citizens in the developing world, and the increasing availability of resources have all contributed to the expansion of the international activities of nonprofits. Those who may have been hesitant to act under previous nonintervention doctrines have left such reluctance behind, and many regimes that in the past resisted the work of nonprofits have come to accept that they can play a useful role.

More prosaically, nonprofit approaches to service delivery are also disseminated globally by the increasing numbers of people from around the world who have studied or worked in the United States and other industrialized countries with strong nonprofit sectors. The focus of this book is on organizations, but nonprofit globalization also has a substantial individual dimension. International workers, expatriates, students, and volunteers are circulating more freely around the globe and becoming key carriers of nonprofit mind-sets and the agents of cross-border linkages. The flow of individuals and ideas is facilitated by a number of key international networks (see Box 6.6).

Box 6.6 The Worldwide Initiatives for Grantmaker Support

The Worldwide Initiatives for Grantmaker Support (WINGS) is a global network of eighty-six philanthropy support organizations in thirty-five countries that represent 15,000 foundations, grant makers, and social investors worldwide. Created as a result of the International Meeting of Associations Serving Grantmakers in Oaxaca, Mexico, in 1998, for the first ten years, it operated as a semiformal network with a temporary secretariat that rotated between members in the United States, Canada, Belgium, and the Philippines. In 2011, it was incorporated as a nonprofit public charity in the United States, and the secretariat was moved to a new permanent home in São Paulo, Brazil. The current executive director, Helena Monteiro, has extensive experience in international development and the nonprofit sector, having worked for the Canadian Public Health Association, the Pan American Health Organization, and the Organization of American States. In Brazil, she worked as program director at the Instituto para o Desenvolvimento do Investimento Social (Institute for the Development of Social Investment), a support organization serving corporate and family philanthropy. She has a master's degree in social work from the University of Toronto and was a senior fellow at the City University of New York's Center on Philanthropy and Civil Society.

Source: See the Worldwide Initiatives for Grantmaker Support, http://www.wings web.org/?page=Staff.

The evolving dynamics that have driven the expansion of the international nonprofit sector have also led to its greater politicization. As international nonprofits take on more responsibility for providing disaster relief, delivering aid, and managing international cultural and professional exchanges, some inevitably become more embroiled in the policymaking process and political conflicts. As a result, these organizations increasingly find themselves the target of ideological critiques, as well as of physical attacks by armed groups (Ronalds 2010).

The history of the internationalization of the nonprofit sector is a narrative recounted primarily from the perspective of the economic North and in the context of the vastly different political geography of the era from which early international nonprofits emerged. The capital cities of the European colonial powers that ruled most of the globe until after World War II were the hubs of the first waves of emerging international nonprofits in the mid-nineteenth century and through the early twentieth century. After World War II, even as new sovereign countries emerged through decolonization, the establishment, headquartering, and membership of international structures continued to have a distinct Northern and Western bias. The bias was as much structural as ideological, a function of where the means, experience, and resources could be found to create the infrastructures needed for the sustainability of organizations, as well as the political regimes that encouraged or allowed the creation of independent, nonstate organizations. Independent organizations were banned in the Soviet Bloc and in other authoritarian regimes, although state-sponsored aid programs, solidarity brigades, and a range of cultural and educational exchange programs performed many similar functions within the Soviet sphere of influence.

The Northern bias has generally continued during the uptick in the sector in the past decades, although recently the trend has been shifting somewhat as more diverse ownership of international structures is promoted, and information technologies open up new possibilities for situating organizational hubs. The bias is reflected in the working languages, with almost half of all international nonprofit organizations using English as an official language, followed a distant second by French and then other European languages (Boli 2006). Table 6.1 demonstrates how North America and Europe are overrepresented among NGOs that have consultative status with the United Nations.

An important feature of the recent growth of the sector has been the increasing numbers of indigenous, South-based organizations that are emerging as a consequence of a growing skill base and the greater availability of funds in developing countries. These new organizations often work in partnership with nonprofits from the North, but they are increasingly forming their own regional networks. Although resources and know-how have in the past flowed primarily from the North to the South, increas-

Table 6.1 Population and Consultative Status by Continent

Continent	Population, 2010 (percentage of world total)	NGOs with Consultative Status, 2007 (percentage of total)
Africa	14.95	11
Asia	60.31	16
Europe	10.61	37
Latin America/Caribbean	8.52	6
North America	5.09	29
Oceania	0.52	1

Source: Global Policy Forum 2012.

ingly South-South collaborations and knowledge networks are forming. A nascent "reverse imperialism" can be identified. Many Northern international aid nonprofits now also operate "at home," working to address domestic social justice issues using strategies they have learned in the developing world (Lewis 2014), and organizations from the South are setting up branches in the North. In Box 6.7 is documented the process by which the Bangladeshi organization BRAC (once known as the Bangladesh Rural Advancement Committee) has established itself in countries around the world, including the United States.

International Nomenclature

Although the language used to describe the international nonprofit sector generally draws on the same potpourri of terms documented in Chapter 2, the two most commonly used terms at the international level are *NGO* (the acronym is more widely used than the original long form—*nongovernmental organization*) and *civil society*. These two terms appear most often in the discourses and publications on international organizations.

As the list of the original NGOs given consultative status with the United Nations cited earlier in this chapter attests, the term can be used to refer to the full range of organizations discussed in this book. However, it is used by many commentators to refer only to those international nonprofits that work with humanitarian aid and development. David Lewis (2007) stated that NGOs are "not-for-profit or 'third sector' organizations concerned with addressing problems of poverty and social justice, and working primarily in the developing world" (1).

Other authors distinguish between NGOs and other nonprofits using a more directly structural definition. Afef Benessaieh (2011) stated:

NGO is used to refer to a local civil-society actor that acts as a primary intermediary between foreign aid donors and other local [non-NGO] actors (among them formal and informal grassroots organizations, cooperatives, peasant federations, and agricultural workers' unions, the Catholic Church and related actors, evangelical religious groups and churches, academic institutions, social movements and coalitions, and left-wing or right-wing civilian armed groups). (70)

Box 6.7 The Expansion of BRAC

The Bangladesh Rehabilitation Assistance Committee was founded as a small-scale relief and rehabilitation project to help returning war refugees after the Bangladesh Liberation War of 1971. At the end of 1972, after the initial emergency subsided, the organization turned to addressing long-term development needs and reorganized itself to focus on the empowerment of the poor and landless, particularly women and children. As it expanded, it changed its name to the Bangladesh Rural Advancement Committee and later simply became BRAC.

In 1974, BRAC began microcredit programs and focused on community development through village development programs that included agriculture, fisheries, cooperatives, rural crafts, adult literacy, health and family planning, vocational training for women, and construction of community centers. In 1977, it shifted from community development and took on a more targeted approach by organizing village groups called village organizations. It also began to open a number of related for-profit enterprises to support its work.

In the 2000s, BRAC began an international expansion program, by creating its own affiliates and by partnering with a range of international and local development organizations. BRAC registered in Afghanistan in 2002, in Sri Lanka in 2005, in Tanzania in 2006, and in Pakistan in 2007. Microfinance is its signature program, but it also provides a range of income-generation activities, as well as education and health programs. In 2006, BRAC established affiliates in the United Kingdom and the United States to promote its work and raise funds in those markets. It now maintains offices in fourteen countries.

BRAC is now a conglomerate of related nonprofit and for-profit organizations, including BRAC Bank, its private financial institution; BRAC University, with a campus for 9,000 students in Dhaka, Bangladesh; and BRACNet Limited, a technology services company. BRAC is reputedly one of the largest international nonprofits in the world, employing over 100,000 people, roughly 70 percent of whom are women, and claims to reach more than 126 million people. It is the largest development agency in some of the countries in which it operates.

Source: See BRAC, http://www.brac.net.

Yet, as discussed in Chapter 2, most of the parenthetical organizations in this quote could be considered nonprofits within the broader definition used in this book. The quote also demonstrates that although the term *NGO* could equally be applied to domestic organizations, in the lexicon of many commentators it is used to refer only to international nonprofits.

Civil society (particularly when rendered as the more specific *civil society organizations*) is the more generic term that perhaps better embraces the broad range of organizations addressed in this book. CIVICUS (2012), for example, described civil society as "the arena, outside of the family, the State and the market, which is created by individual and collective actions, organizations and institutions to advance shared interests. Civil society therefore encompasses civil society organizations and the actions of less formalized groups and individuals" (8).

The preference for the terms *NGO* and *civil society* in discourses about international nonprofits appears to be based on the fact that they more specifically differentiate nongovernmental forms of international exchange from actions on behalf of states. They are also relatively neutral terms that can be used comfortably to describe both international and domestic activities under a range of regimes, without the baggage inherent in terms such as *nonprofit*, *voluntary*, *community*, or *charity*.

At the same time, some commentators assert that because the term *NGO* deliberately purports to be apolitical, attaching that label and its associated logics to organizations that have sprung from grassroots or oppositional movements depoliticizes them and decouples them from their roots (Banks and Hulme 2012). In this framework, NGOs are seen as the domain of educated professionals and are driven by the agendas of foreign or local elite donors. Organizations that seek to maintain a more grassroots identity instead prefer labels such as *social movement*, *civil society*, *community based*, or *right-holder*. Progressive feminists decry the "NGOization" of the women's movement (Bernal and Grewal 2014; Jad 2007; Lang 2013), which they claim has eviscerated it by reframing the struggle of women as a technical process instead of a political movement. Their concerns are primarily about the impact of professionalization and the role played by international sponsors of the movement, but the critique also focuses on the label *NGO* itself and the impact it has on the discourse around the movement.

The use of the concept of civil society in the international context goes beyond the mere identification of organizational forms as it raises the question of whether or not speaking of an emerging international, transnational, cosmopolitan, or global civil society (all of these descriptors have been used by different authors) is legitimate. International civil society transcends the aggregation of the work of individual organizations and so projects to the international polis the role that civil society is said to play in national contexts.

International Nonprofits and Global Civil Society

No global government or executive body legislates and regulates affairs or exercises the coercive powers equivalent to states. Yet public and private affairs are increasingly global, so regulation is effected through international governance "regimes" (Abbott and Snidal 2009; Karns and Mingst 2004), "systems" (Willetts 2011), "webs" (Zadek 2011), or "triangles" (Abbott and Snidal 2009) constructed by a patchwork of processes and institutions that include intergovernmental institutions, for-profit industry self-regulation, and international nonprofits. The treaties and conventions that emerge from the United Nations and the dozens of other multilateral and regional agreements, combined with the protocols and agreements from global summit meetings and conferences, constitute the dense networks of regulation and oversight that are the basis of international law. But the powers of these various instruments fall far short of those exercised by sovereign states within their own borders, particularly in matters of enforcement. The global governance organizations that develop and administer the patchwork are continually negotiating their legitimacy and authority (Koppell 2008), and in doing so, they are potentially conferring considerable political space to nonstate actors.

Scholars continue to debate whether globalization is leaving nation-states behind as the highest legitimate level of democratic power, a position they have held since the modern concepts of national sovereignty emerged from the Westphalia peace treaties of the 1640s (Chandhoke 2005; Clark 2008; Kaldor 2000; Keane 2003; Sparke 2013; Walzer 1998). For much of the twentieth century, the debates focused largely on interstate relations and the possible emergence and merits of a global government. More recently, however, the focus has broadened to include analyses of the multilayered and multifaceted governance of international rule making and the processes of global governmentality. Nonprofits are seen as an integral element of the construction of global governance "from below," as intergovernmental and multilateral institutions increasingly incorporate a broader range of nonstate actors into the processes for policy development and legitimation (Jonsson and Tallberg 2010; Karns and Mingst 2004; Sparke 2013; Willetts 2011).

Are international nonprofits part of an emerging global civil society that constitutes a truly new institutional realm with an increasingly autonomous role in global governance, as the "authentic" voice of world public opinion? Or are they unrepresentative artifacts, bound to the donor elites, narrow interests, or national governments that created them and facilitated their growth? John Keane (2003) argued that a global civil society is emerging, and it is a new "society of societies," but it is still evolving, and its salience will depend on its ability to become more democratic, better integrated into governance institutions, and more invested with universal values. However, others argue that international nonprofits continue to primarily represent the interests of their donors and sponsor states over those of their putative constituencies or beneficiaries.

In fact, their authority to represent anyone is often called into question. The mandate of international nonprofits is ambiguous at best given that their combined claimed membership is less than the population of a small state, and the internal governance processes of most organizations are less than democratic (Archibugi 2008). After the mass demonstrations at the meetings of the World Trade Organization and the World Bank in 1999 and 2000, an editorial in *The Economist* (2000) acknowledged the effectiveness of the protests and conceded that they raised important issues, but the author of the article also questioned the legitimacy of the most prominent organizer of the protests by posing the question, "Who elected Oxfam?"

The debates around the existence of an autonomous global civil society focus particularly on the role of nonprofits as opinion makers and as rule makers through their work in promoting, developing, and supervising international norms, standards, and regulations. They perform in these roles in fields as diverse as environmental issues, human rights, the empowerment of women, corporate social responsibility, election monitoring, prison reform, and posttransitional justice. Even though they have limited formal legal standing in the international arena (Lindblom 2013), nonprofits can be advocates for new standards and watchdogs for their implementation and oversight. L. David Brown and colleagues (2000) noted that nonprofits help shape international events by identifying problems that might otherwise be ignored, articulating new values and norms to guide international practice, building transnational alliances, disseminating social innovations, helping negotiate resolutions to transnational disagreements, and mobilizing resources to intervene directly to address problems.

Steven Charnovitz (1997) argued that nonprofits had previously played this role during the emergence of international institutions in the nineteenth century when a clear distinction could not be made between intergovernmental organizations and nonprofits. Notably, at that time such organizations were drawing from the same relatively small pool of educated elites. England, a hub of many early intergovernmental organizations and international nonprofits, had a population of 9 million in the early 1800s (it is currently 53 million), of which some 40 percent were illiterate, and only a small minority had graduated from high school or earned higher degrees (it was not until the higher education boom after World War II that the percentage of the adult population in industrialized countries with university degrees rose above 3 percent).

Governments sometimes took the lead, but Charnovitz (1997) noted that "in most aspects of nineteenth century internationalism they followed reluctantly and hesitantly a trail blazed by others" (212). He documented the role of religious institutions and the emerging secular peace societies, temperance groups, scientific organizations, and labor movements in pushing for international conventions regarding rules of war, intellectual property, prostitution, narcotics, workers' rights, and nature protection. Two International Criminal Police Congresses in 1914 and 1923, organized by an international association of police officers, led to the creation of the International Criminal Police Commission at the end of the second congress. The commission, headquartered in Vienna, ceased functions during World War II, when it was taken over by the Nazi regime, but was reestablished in France after the war and received consultative status as an NGO by the newly established United Nations. In 1956, the commission adopted its telegraph name, Interpol, as its new official name, and in 1971 its status was upgraded to that of an intergovernmental organization. The police of every country except North Korea are now members of Interpol.

After the post–World War II period, in which nonprofits "underachieved" (Charnovitz 1997), the policy role of international nonprofits reemerged post–Cold War in the late twentieth century with high-profile campaigns such as the International Campaign to Ban Landmines and the continuing advocacy of the numerous environmental organizations. Perhaps the most durable contributions to global governance structures are the oversight and accreditation functions of dozens of international nonprofit professional and trade associations. At national levels, professional associations and advocacy groups may operate in effect as "private authorities" (Green 2014), regulating individuals and organizations that must, or voluntarily agree to, meet their standards. Some are chartered by their governments to steward the third-party accreditation or certification needed to exercise professions or to meet production standards, whereas others simply adopt this role through entrepreneurial accreditation or "seal of approval" schemes (Evetts 1995; Green 2014). Their international equivalents play similar roles in filling the voids of global regulation. The International Air Transport Association (IATA) is the successor organization to the International Air Traffic Association, which was cited earlier as one of the original NGOs given consultative status by the United Nations. It is the trade association for the world's airlines and is a key player in formulating industry policy on aviation issues and representing the industry in negotiations with the International Civil Aviation Organization, an agency established by the United Nations in 1947 to codify international air navigation. IATA regulations and seals cover all aspects of air travel from the transport of dangerous goods to the conduct of travel agents. Both IATA and the International Civil Aviation Organization have their headquarters in Montreal, Canada.

Arguably, the international regulatory nonprofit that has the greatest impact on the everyday lives of the global population is the International Organization for Standardization (see Box 6.8).

Box 6.8   The International Organization for Standardization

The International Organization for Standardization (commonly known as ISO, which is a short name adopted to avoid confusion between the acronyms in different languages) is the most widely accepted international standard-setting body. ISO describes itself as an independent NGO made up of members from the national standards bodies of 164 countries. Member associations reflect the political administrative arrangements of their nations: some are government agencies, some are quasi-governmental administrative bodies, and others are voluntary associations.

ISO began in 1926 as the International Federation of the National Standardizing Associations, with a focus on mechanical engineering, but was disbanded during World War II. It was reorganized in 1946 under its current name when delegates from twenty-five countries met in London, and the restructured organization began operations in February 1947. The central secretariat, now in Geneva, Switzerland, coordinates the system, which comprises some 20,000 ISO standards in areas as diverse as the pictograms used to mark "This Way Up" on packages, freight container dimensions, international standard book numbers (ISBNs) on publications, and the sizes for screw threads. The ISO 9000 series is widely accepted as the standard for quality management in private, public, and nonprofit organizations.

The ISO is an NGO, so it has no enforcement powers. The adoption of its standards is voluntary. However, many standards, particularly those concerned with health, safety, or the environment, have been incorporated into the legislation and regulatory frameworks of many countries. Other standards, such as the sizes of connectors for electronic devices, have become so universal that they in effect become gatekeepers for market entry.

Source: See the International Organization for Standardization, http://www.iso.org.

The question of whether true global "governing without government" is built on the relationships between multilateral institutions, nonprofits, and other nonstate actors, and how sustainable it can be, is an increasing preoccupation of international relations discourses (Karns and Mingst 2004; Reinicke 1998). International nonprofits are often not "at the table" when final rule making takes place, as that is generally the preserve of international civil servants and diplomats designated by their governments, but they may have been instrumental in shaping public perceptions and in pressuring for changes, and they are likely to help ensure that new rules are implemented and adhered to.

Within the international nonprofit sector, relationships are often strained between the various factions that lay claim to the title of the "true" civil society, given the chasm between those that have the resources to organize and project their voice, and the grassroots movements that see themselves as the authentic disenfranchised (Bond 2008). A civil society debate that focuses primarily on the role of larger, more established international non-profits is regarded by some critics as a top-down institutional version divorced from its roots and should be contrasted, or contested, by a more bottom-up version. Certain factions reject the institutionalization of social movements, whether the antiglobalization (or alter-globalization) movement that gained international attention with the protests against the World Trade Organization meeting in Seattle in 1999, or the different iterations of the more contemporary Occupy and Indignados movements that have emerged in industrialized countries in response to the 2008 fiscal crisis. These tensions are exemplified in the Wikipedia page for the World Social Forums, which talks about the relationship between what the authors consider to be "civil society" and "NGOs" (see Box 6.9).

Box 6.9 World Social Forums, Civil Society, and NGOs

The first World Social Forum was held in Porto Alegre, Brazil, in 2001 with some 12,000 participants. In 2013, the World Social Forum took place in Tunis, Tunisia, with 50,000 participants representing more than 4,000 organizations and groups. Wikipedia describes the World Social Forum as "an annual meeting of civil society organizations, which offers a self-conscious effort to develop an alternative future through the championing of counter-hegemonic globalization. Some consider the World Social Forum to be a physical manifestation of global civil society as it brings together nongovernmental organization advocacy campaigns as well as formal and informal social movements seeking international solidarity."

In the section on criticism of the forum, the narrative of the relationship between civil society, social movements, and NGOs becomes a little confused: "The World Social Forum has, especially in recent years, been strongly criticized for replacing popular movements of the poor with NGOs. Movements of the poor in poorer parts of the world, like Africa, have argued that they are almost completely excluded from the forum and . . . they have protested against donor funded NGOs that, they argue, determine and dominate representation at the forum. It has also been argued that NGOs sometimes compete with popular grassroots movements for access to the forum and for influence there. The 2007 World Social Forum in Nairobi, Kenya, in particular was criticized as an 'NGO fair' because of how many NGOs attended, crowding out less formal groups of activists."

Source: See Wikipedia, http://en.wikipedia.org/wiki/World_Social_Forum.

Classifying International Nonprofits

International nonprofits are most commonly classified by their subject or field of work. The Union of International Associations (2012) has a complex classification system, with categories based on a typology of world problems, human values, and human development concepts originally developed for its publication *The Encyclopedia of World Problems and Human Potential*. The US NTEE Category Q subcodes present a more typical field-based taxonomy:

- Q01: Alliances and Advocacy
- Q02: Management and Technical Assistance
- Q03: Professional Societies and Associations
- Q05: Research Institutes and Public Policy Analysis
- Q11: Single Organization Support
- Q12: Fund-raising and Fund Distribution
- Q19: Support Not Elsewhere Classified
- Q20: Promotion of International Understanding
- Q21: International Cultural Exchange
- Q22: International Academic Exchange
- Q23: International Exchange Not Elsewhere Classified
- Q30: International Development
- Q31: International Agricultural Development
- Q32: International Economic Development
- Q33: International Relief
- Q35: Democracy and Civil Society Development
- Q40: International Peace and Security
- Q41: Arms Control and Peace
- Q42: United Nations Associations
- Q43: National Security
- Q50: International Affairs, Foreign Policy, and Globalization
- Q51: International Economic and Trade Policy
- Q70: International Human Rights
- Q71: International Migration and Refugee Issues
- Q99: International, Foreign Affairs, and National Security Not Elsewhere Classified

In addition, many faith-based international organizations use the subcodes from NTEE code X, Religion, Spiritual Development; international education development organizations use B, Educational Institutions; sports organizations use N71, Olympics Committees and Related International Competitions; human rights organizations use V26, Law, International Law, and Jurisprudence; and research institutes use V35, International Studies.

Other taxonomies of international nonprofits focus on key structural markers such as the geographic reach of organizations, the nature of the membership, and the relationship between the various international units. The Union of International Associations (2012) distinguishes between internationally oriented national organizations and international organizations that are regional, intercontinental, and universal. It also differentiates between membership organizations and federations of membership organizations. Helmut Anheier and Nuno Themudo (2004) distinguished between member-owned organizations, in which members (individual and institutional) are a key part of bottom-up governance, and member-supported organizations, in which the majority of members, most of whom are small donors, support the goal of the organization but have little influence on governance and decisionmaking.

International nonprofits generally have multilevel structures with international, national, and local elements. The articulation between headquarters and the units scattered around the world varies considerably according to how each organization manages the centrifugal-centripetal dynamics that push it toward decentralization or centralization. David Lewis (2007) distinguished between ethnocentric structures, in which central hubs exert tight control over subsidiary offices, and polycentric or nodal organizations with a high degree of distributed local control. What the public identifies as a single organization may in fact be a conglomerate of linked international and national organizations. The structure of the Red Cross is detailed in Box 6.10.

In contrast, Toastmasters International, the leadership and public-speaking club, is in effect a unitary organization with some 13,500 clubs worldwide, all of which are under the oversight of the headquarters near Los Angeles, California. At the same time, local clubs may need a separate local legal identity to operate. In the United States, over 8,500 Toastmasters clubs are registered with the IRS, but the vast majority declare zero income. The global organization is structured into districts and regions that generally do not coincide with national boundaries or traditional regions based on the continents (e.g., Region 11 includes most of Europe, the Middle East, and Africa). Each region sends representatives to the international board of directors.

Researchers (L. D. Brown, Ebrahim, and Batliwala 2012; Lindenberg and Bryant 2001; Young et al. 1999) who focus on such intraorganizational relationships have identified clusters along a continuum of the centralization-decentralization of governance structures and accountabilities that typically include the following:

• Networks: Are created by fully independent organizations that form loose connections to exchange information about strategies and advocacy campaigns.
• Weak umbrellas: Seek to coordinate strategies and collaborate on advocacy campaigns through stable coalitions but do not delegate any powers to

Box 6.10 The Red Cross

The Red Cross consists of numerous organizations that are united through common basic principles, objectives, and symbols but are legally independent from each other. In its own literature, the Red Cross refers to itself as a "movement" and a "network" that encompasses the following organizations.

The International Committee of the Red Cross (ICRC), an international humanitarian organization founded in 1863, is headquartered in Geneva, Switzerland. Its twenty-five-member committee has a unique authority under international humanitarian law to protect the life and dignity of the victims of international and internal armed conflicts. A private association formed under the Swiss Civil Code, ICRC is nongovernmental and non-profit, but because of its role in administering the Geneva Conventions, it has an international legal personality with privileges and immunities comparable to intergovernmental organizations. The ICRC has been awarded the Nobel Peace Prize on three occasions (in 1917, 1944, and 1963).

The International Federation of Red Cross and Red Crescent Societies (IFRC), founded in 1919, coordinates the activities of the national Red Cross and Red Crescent Societies around the world. On an international level, the federation leads and organizes, in close cooperation with the individual Red Cross and Red Crescent national societies, relief assistance missions responding to large-scale emergencies. The international federation secretariat is also based in Geneva (some two kilometers from the ICRC headquarters). In 1963, the federation (then known as the League of Red Cross Societies) was awarded the Nobel Peace Prize jointly with the ICRC.

Currently, 187 national Red Cross and Red Crescent societies function under the laws and regulations of their home countries. In some countries they are independent nonprofits, whereas in others they are quasi-governmental entities, and their functions and activities vary greatly in humanitarian aid, social service, civil defense, and emergency management.

Although most people are familiar with the cross symbol, the crescent and other red symbols have been used throughout the history of the organization and have been a constant source of tension in the international body. The Red Crescent was first used by Turkey in 1876 as the cross was seen as an affront to Muslim soldiers, but its use was highly restricted until the 1980s. Continued agitation over the possible use of other symbols, including the Red Star of David, finally led to the adoption in 2006 of the Red Crystal (a square standing upright on one corner) as an additional official symbol devoid of any national, political, or religious connotation.

Source: See International Federation of the Red Cross, https://www.ifrc.org/en/who -we-are/the-movement/.

a central secretariat (which may be rotating or housed in the offices of a wealthier member).

• Confederations: Delegate a central office or secretariat with limited responsibilities for coordination and standard setting, but leave significant powers with affiliates. Larger and wealthier affiliates often dominate the confederation dynamics.

• Federations: Have strong centralized powers for standard setting and resource acquisition. Members retain separate boards and some operational independence, but the federation structure requires joint decisions for core operating principles and strategies.

• Unitary organizations: Have a single, central board and strong hierarchy. Local structures are branch offices, controlled directly from headquarters, with only limited distributed powers of independent action (although field operations may require some form of local registration).

This continuum is a bit misleading as the extremes generally describe different sets of organizations that in all likelihood cannot, or will not, migrate too far along the spectrum. Independent organizations in a network may seek to deepen their coordination and to harmonize their activities, and occasionally two or more may even choose to merge, but as a network they are unlikely to move beyond the federation stage (although some federations such as Oxfam have built such a strong brand identity that many outsiders assume they are a unitary organization—see Box 6.4). Equally, a unitary organization is unlikely to devolve to the point that its former units become independent organizations, although the increasingly common practice of Northern organizations partnering with existing local Southern organizations, or sponsoring the establishment of new affiliates, is in effect the process of a unitary organization creating its own federation that may spin off increasingly independent organizations.

Any analysis of the tensions between centralization and decentralization is contingent on whether it focuses on a single organization or on the relationships between multiple organizations. Also pertinent is whether the focus is on bottom-up network building by like-minded organizations seeking to coordinate their activities or on top-down outreach by organizations seeking partnerships or fostering the creation of local affiliates. The international "franchising" of organizational models such as Teach for America (corps of young teachers working in poverty zones) and the Repair Cafés (clubs of volunteer retirees, primarily men, who run community repair shops) generally create linkages that are somewhere between federations and confederations (the Repair Cafés also have a parallel in the Men's Sheds, popular in Ireland and Australia).

The structures of international nonprofits and their networks are inherently unstable (Foreman 1999; Lindenberg and Bryant 2001). Organizations that form part of a weak umbrella structure find that competition for resources, duplication of efforts, and donor confusion create pressures to strengthen the linkages between members; confederations face the challenge of noncompliant members so they often seek to strengthen the mechanisms of centralized control; and strong federations and unitary organizations must deal with demands for increased local autonomy. Different aspects of the work of an organization may operate in different structural modes. James Crowley and Morgana Ryan (2013) noted that the nature of the product determines the structure of commercial firms (selling alcoholic beverages around the world requires different organizational structures and supply chains from those needed to deliver software or consulting services). They suggested that nonprofits have the same imperatives to develop the best structural fit and processes for delivering their programs. L. David Brown, Alnoor Ebrahim, and Srilatha Batliwala (2012) linked the structural and governance configurations of transnational advocacy nonprofits to their issues, missions, strategies, and accountabilities. Some choose to configure their structure to focus on their relations to constituents and beneficiaries, others to donors and members, and yet others to affiliate organizations. Wendy Wong (2012) suggested that human rights advocacy nonprofits that centralize agenda setting and decentralize the implementation of that agenda will be more successful in influencing public policy.

Continued tension can be found over the trade-off when balancing centralized coordination and efficiency in decisionmaking and resource allocation against decentralized local autonomy and buy-in by disparate units (Young et al. 1999). Unitary organizations decentralize to strengthen local ownership, at the same time as alliances, networks, and confederations move to greater centralization to improve harmonization while retaining the diversity and independence of members (Johnston 2012). Organizations are continually seeking the holy grail of the optimal equilibrium point in the intricate interactions and power relationships between affiliates and the central office. Some commentators suggest that the optimal configuration is a "bumblebee" federation of interdependent organizations that can flexibly adapt to the flurries of activity (Foreman 1999; Lindenberg and Bryant 2001; Lindenberg and Dobel 1999).

Marc Lindenberg and Coralie Bryant (2001) documented how the prominent international nonprofits Médecins Sans Frontières (Doctors Without Borders), Save the Children, and Plan International have moved through different structural configurations in response to changing organizational and political pressures. Many international organizations, including World Vision International and Habitat for Humanity, have adapted their international governance structure to allow for a range of relationships with the central office, based on the level of stability and strength of local affiliates. Some are branch offices, whereas others are federated independent organizations.

The Largest International Nonprofits

Which are the largest international nonprofit organizations? The question is difficult to answer given the different conceptualizations of the category and the ambiguities of what constitutes an organization for such calculations. Does the term *international nonprofit organization* refer to only a single legal entity, or does it also include all affiliates of conglomerates, federations, subsidiaries, and brands? Separating the eleemosynary activities of organizations from their faith-based or commercial work or separating their international work from domestic activities can also be difficult. The YMCA, for example, is a global federation operating in 119 countries, including China, Cuba, and Egypt, but no consolidated accounting of the worldwide revenues of all the affiliates is undertaken. The US YMCA is at the top of the list of the largest US nonprofit organizations, with an annual income of over $6 billion. It provides a broad range of social services nationally and internationally, but most of its income is derived from, and expended on, fitness facilities, residential accommodations, and summer camps at the 2,600 YMCA centers around the country. The associated women's organization, the Young Women's Christian Association (YWCA), is generally independent of the men's organization, although some chapters around the United States and the world have amalgamated to create YM/YWCAs.

Added to the definitional and jurisdictional complications are differences in transparency regulations and in the enforcement of accounting standards between countries, as well as idiosyncrasies in accounting practices regarding contributions. Regulators in the United States have recently alleged that some international nonprofits are overvaluing noncash contributions (supplies, logistic support, etc.) to raise their profile and to inflate perceptions of their effectiveness. In 2012, a prominent international aid organization, World Help, which had previously reported a $239 million annual income, reduced the figure by $135 million after the value of some of the noncash donations were questioned (Donovan and Preston 2012).

Notwithstanding these challenges in documenting income and assets, the organizations below can still be identified as among the largest international nonprofits. Almost all of the organizations have some type of federated structure with semiautonomous affiliates around the world. Only a few provide consolidated worldwide income figures for all their federated affiliates, and even fewer include in their accounting any subsidiary or related organizations operating under different brands. Even though the figures quoted below are from the organizations' own annual reports or tax returns, they are not necessarily definitive appraisals of their full wealth or reach.

Arguably, at the top of the list of the largest international nonprofits should be the *faith-based organizations* that also have a social service and aid mission, including the Salvation Army, St. Vincent de Paul, the Anglican Mission societies, Jewish Communal Fund, and Islamic Relief. The structures of these organizations vary, and they generally do not provide worldwide accounts or fully separate their international activities from domestic service and pastoral work.

Operating as international nonprofits (see discussion later in this chapter), the largest *sports associations* move billions of dollars through multiple legal entities. The International Olympic Committee (IOC) and the Fédération Internationale de Football Association (FIFA, the governing body for football-soccer) are Switzerland-based nonprofits, but both are also registered in the United States as 501(c)(4) organizations. In 2012, the IOC declared to the US tax authorities an annual income of $3.4 billion and FIFA $1.1 billion. Both have substantial additional income through numerous affiliated nonprofit and for-profit legal entities, and their national associations move many billions more.

Given that the United States is by far the largest contributor to both official development aid and global philanthropy, international aid organizations headquartered (or with a substantial presence) in the United States dominate the list of the largest *aid and relief organizations*. Seventeen international aid and relief organizations are among the fifty largest nonprofits in the United States (see Table 6.2).

The incomes reported in Table 6.2 are for the US branches only, but organizations such as Habitat for Humanity, World Vision, Save the Children, and the US Fund for UNICEF have dozens of federated affiliates around the world. The US affiliates generally contribute 30 percent to 50 percent of the worldwide income of their organizations or federations. World Vision, for example, reported a worldwide income of $2.67 billion, some 2.5 times its US income. Other large aid organizations and federations include the following (the incomes quoted are worldwide figures from annual reports):

- BRAC: $4.2 billion (see Box 6.7)
- International Committee of the Red Cross: $1.2 billion (see Box 6.10)
- Oxfam: $1.1 billion (see Box 6.4)
- Plan International: $960 million (see Box 7.3)
- Médecins Sans Frontières: $568 million
- Danish Refugee Council (officially an umbrella organization of over thirty Danish refugee organizations): $300 million

Calculations of the size of *foundations* are based on their endowments and do not necessarily reflect their disbursements or their impact. Some of the foundations listed below (see Table 6.3) have recently come under criticism for providing comparatively few grants relative to their size.

Table 6.2 Largest US International Aid and Relief Organizations

Name	Activities (summary from the organization's website)	Income, 2012 (US$ millions)
American Red Cross	Providing humanitarian aid and social services	$3,154.5
Habitat for Humanity International	Providing affordable housing	$1,492.3
World Vision	Providing relief, development, and advocacy organization (Christian nonprofit)	$1,009.7
Food for the Poor	Providing food, medicine, and shelter (ecumenical Christian nonprofit)	$900.1
Catholic Relief Services	Providing humanitarian aid (international Catholic nonprofit)	$699.5
Feed the Children	Providing food, clothing, educational supplies, medical equipment, and other necessities to needy individuals (international Christian nonprofit)	$617.8
Compassion International	Providing for the development of children living in poverty around the world (Christian child sponsorship organization)	$598.8
Save the Children USA	Promoting of children's rights, providing relief and support for children in developing countries	$576.5
CARE (Cooperative for Assistance and Relief Everywhere)	Fighting global poverty, with a special focus on empowering women and girls	$557.5
AmeriCares	Providing disaster relief and humanitarian medical aid	$526.1
US Fund for UNICEF	Supporting UNICEF work	$501.8
International Rescue Committee	Supporting refugees and displaced persons	$386.5
Samaritan's Purse	Providing medical aid (Christian nonprofit)	$376.1
Kingsway Charities	Providing medical aid	$331.4
American Jewish Joint Distribution Committee	Providing humanitarian assistance (Jewish nonprofit organization)	$315.8
Direct Relief	Improving the health and lives of people affected by poverty, disaster, and civil unrest	$299.7
Good360/ Gifts in Kind International	Fostering corporate donations to nonprofits	$298.4

Source: "America's Top 50 Charities in 2013 Ranked by Total Income," *Christian Science Monitor,* http://www.csmonitor.com/Business/Guide-to-Giving/America-s-Top-50-charities-in-2013-ranked-by -total-income.

Notes: These figures are from the *Christian Science Monitor* annual review of US nonprofits. A similar review by *Forbes* gives a somewhat different ranking, even though both indicate that they are based on Form 990 tax returns. Neither of the two rankings includes Family Health International (now known as FHI360) or Partnership for Supply Chain Management, two nonprofits that appear on the list of the largest USAID vendors (see Table 7.2) and appear to have incomes that qualify them for this list.

Table 6.3 Foundations with Endowments of More Than $7 Billion, 2012

Organization	Country	Headquarters	Endowment (US$ billions)
Bill and Melinda Gates Foundation	US	Seattle, WA	$37.1
Stichting INGKA Foundation (associated with IKEA)	Netherlands	Leiden	$36.0
Wellcome Trust	UK	London	$22.1
Howard Hughes Medical Institute	US	Chevy Chase, MD	$16.1
Ford Foundation	US	New York City	$11.2
J. Paul Getty Trust	US	Los Angeles	$10.5
Mohammed bin Rashid Al Maktoum Foundation	United Arab Emirates	Dubai	$10.0
Robert Wood Johnson Foundation	US	Princeton, NJ	$9.0
Li Ka Shing Foundation	China	Hong Kong	$8.3
W. K. Kellogg Foundation	US	Battle Creek, MI	$8.2
Church Commissioners, Church of England	UK	London	$8.1
William and Flora Hewlett Foundation	US	Menlo Park, CA	$7.4
Kamehameha Schools	US	Honolulu, HI	$7.3
Lilly Endowment	US	Indianapolis, IN	$7.28

Sources: "Top Funders," Foundation Center, http://foundationcenter.org/findfunders/topfunders/top100assets .html; "List of Wealthiest Charitable Foundations," Wikipedia, http://en.wikipedia.org/wiki/List_of_wealthiest _charitable_foundations.

The Rotary, Lions, Kiwanis, and other *service clubs* each have hundreds of affiliates around the world, which raise funds for local and international projects. Rotary claims a worldwide membership of 1.22 million in over 34,000 clubs; Rotary organizations registered in the United States include Rotary Foundation of Rotary International, a 501(c)(3) that has a declared annual income of $233 million, Rotary International, a 501(c)(4) with an income of $90 million, and some 9,000 local clubs. The service clubs generally do not provide consolidated global accounts.

The Boy Scouts and Girl Scouts, the YMCA and YWCA, and the *youth groups* of religious organizations and service clubs (e.g., Rotaract, the youth program of Rotary) have hundreds of affiliates around the world. They generally do not have consolidated global accounts.

Only two *environmental organizations* appear among the largest international nonprofits: the World Wildlife Fund ($720 million) and Greenpeace ($320 million).

A grab bag of dozens of *other large entities with nonprofit legal status* also exists. They include organizations as diverse as the ISO (see Box 6.8), which has a core funding of $36 million for the Swiss secretariat and estimates that some $140 million is spent by member organizations to support the individual standards secretariats, and the British Council, the UK cultural relations and development organization created by royal charter in 1934, which is now, according to its website, "a public corporation, a charity and an executive non-departmental public body with operational independence from the U.K. government." The British Council reports an income of $1.2 billion and has over 100 federated councils around the world, many of which operate under the nonprofit legislation of their host countries.

The "Top 100" Nonprofits

Another dimension of "internationalness" is the global reputation a nonprofit garners regardless of the scope of its activities. In 2012, the *Global Journal*, a Swiss magazine focusing on global governance, published its first ranking of the global top 100 NGOs and now publishes an annual list. The rankings are based on reputation surveys that ask key informants to rate nonprofits based on their perceived impact, innovation, and sustainability. Reputation surveys have their evident limits: the lists are heavily weighted to a newer generation of "popular" organizations. However, the lists provide a noteworthy snapshot of nonprofits around the world. The NGOs that head the ranking are, according to the *Global Journal* (2013),

- BRAC (Bangladesh, international development)
- Wikimedia Foundation (United States, parent organization of Wikipedia)
- Acumen (United States, fund for social innovation)
- Danish Refugee Council (Denmark, international humanitarian work)
- Partners in Health (United States, international health)
- Ceres (United States, corporate social responsibility)
- CARE International (Switzerland, poverty reduction)
- Médecins Sans Frontières (Switzerland, medical assistance)
- Cure Violence (United States, community-based antiviolence)
- Mercy Corps (United States, international relief and recovery)

The remainder of the top 100 demonstrates the diversity of origins and of fields of interests. Although most are among the largest international nonprofits, a number of small organizations are also represented, such as Krousar Thmey, a Cambodian foundation for children. Many are nominally domestic organizations, but they almost all have an international dimension, either because they receive a substantial portion of their funding from outside the country and work closely with international partners or because they have extended their domestic work globally. Common Ground, a US organization on the list, works with the homeless in New York City and through its affiliated organization, Community Solutions, is replicating the model nationally and internationally. The ranking also demonstrates the dominance of the United States in the nonprofit sector, with one-third of the organizations headquartered there.

The Internationalization of Domestic Nonprofits

The primary focus of the literature on the international dimensions of the nonprofit sector is on those organizations created deliberately to work in the international arena. The current globalization dynamics are having an equally significant impact through the international contacts and collaborations between domestic nonprofits in different countries and the phenomena of previously domestic nonprofits expanding their operations to other countries. All these dynamics are interconnected. Contact between organizations often leads to international outreach work, domestic nonprofits often create a separate international affiliate to extend their work abroad, and many international organizations foster the creation of new domestic organizations around the world to promote local ownership.

International Contact and Cooperation
Between Domestic Nonprofits

Almost endless iterations can be identified of the increasing incidence of international contact and collaborative relations between organizations that continue to maintain a primarily domestic focus. In a globalizing world, with its ease of Internet communications and the relative low cost of travel, few nonprofits anywhere in the world have not entered into some exchange with counterparts in other countries, even if it as modest as entertaining foreign professionals on fact-finding tours, visiting foreign counterparts while traveling, touring internationally for the first time with a performing arts group, or participating in international forums of organizations working in the same field. While individually each of these contacts may appear to have little transcendence, their cumulative effect is a greatly enhanced international dialogue on nonprofit policy and practice.

For domestic nonprofits from industrialized democratic countries, their international contact may be primarily for professional development and understanding of international good practice. It may also stem from a desire to create international solidarity networks to facilitate advocacy work in global arenas. Such contact is even touted as the future of international development of civil society. Box 6.11 summarizes one commentator's arguments in favor of strengthening cross-border contact between nonprofits.

Box 6.11 The Way Forward: Civil Society, Not Civil Service

David Holdridge, on the *Stanford Social Innovation Review: Civil Society Blog,* argued that "for the cost of placing one federal aid worker overseas, America could, for example, fund a women's empowerment group in Flatbush, Brooklyn, or any other community, to link, advocate, and support a women's rights group in [developing countries]. In the 50 years since the 1961 Foreign Assistance Act was created, emerging civil society organizations overseas have become ubiquitous and capable, and more importantly, they have become owners of their own national development. They are universally enthusiastic about connecting and uniting with their likenesses in the US."

The same commentator went on to say, "Over the last 20 years, new technologies have taken root across the developing world. [The partner in the developing country] could now, at little cost, communicate by phone, email, or webcam with the group in Flatbush, and form a lasting union around their shared concerns. The group in Flatbush might also choose to send money through a payment portal to support local needs, as defined by the members of the local group. Transparency and compliance with local and US law could be assured by other civil society organizations that have offices on the ground. This same model could work for the Chamber of Commerce in Boise, the Persons with Disability Rights Group in Jacksonville, or the Youth Civic Participation Group in Des Moines. America has a mighty asset: a well-established civil society that we can use to project American interests and values overseas effectively. It would be counterproductive to do otherwise."

Source: See Holdridge 2011.

Nonprofits in developing and authoritarian countries have additional incentives for international outreach as they face the challenge of few domestic sources of funding, and their activities may be proscribed by the authorities. Many nonprofits in aid-recipient nations receive the majority of their funds from external sources, and often they look to external supporters to help ensure a certain measure of protection for their work. To survive and thrive they must have the capacity to plug into international networks. Casa Amiga, a one-facility nonprofit that supports victims of gender violence in Ciudad Juárez, Mexico, lists on its contributors page the governments of Canada, the United States, Germany, Spain, and Holland and multilateral institutions such as the European Union and the Inter-American Development Bank, as well as numerous philanthropic foundations and multinational corporations from Europe and the Americas (Casa Amiga 2013). But external support is not without peril, and in recent years a number of governments have moved to restrict external funding of nonprofits, branding it as foreign interference in internal affairs (see Box 8.5).

Networks, Movements, Coalitions, and Collaborations

Casual or sporadic international contacts are often the precursors to more stable relationships between nonprofits in different countries. A continuum of growing stability can be identified that moves from loose, informal networks with fluid membership and participation to stable alliances, often coalescing around an anchor organization (see Box 6.6 and Box 6.12 below). Some of these alliances are formally constituted organizations created specifically to manage relations between collaborators in different countries and to lobby on their behalf, so in effect should be categorized as international nonprofit membership organizations, but many others are more informal. A network secretariat may be housed in one of the more active promoters, or the network may operate without a fixed central coordinating body.

Some global political and social movements generally eschew traditional organizational structures. The antiglobalization/alter-globalization movement, in the form of the solidarity campaigns that support indigenous

---

Box 6.12   The International
Rehabilitation Council for Torture Victims

The International Rehabilitation Council for Torture Victims (IRCT), based in Copenhagen, Denmark, is the umbrella organization for 144 independent organizations in over seventy countries that work on the rehabilitation of torture victims and the prevention of torture. It began as the outreach and professional exchange programs of the Danish Rehabilitation Council for Torture Victims (RCT), established in 1973, which had become a world leader in treating torture victims.

The IRCT was founded in 1985, initially as the international arm of the RCT. In 1997, it became an independent international membership organization. In addition to the income from membership dues, the IRCT raises its own funds to promote the work of its members and lobby on their behalf. It maintains offices in Brussels and Geneva to facilitate access to the European Union and the United Nations.

In 2012, the Danish RCT rebranded itself as DIGNITY (Danish Institute Against Torture). DIGNITY maintains an active international research and development program. It continues as a member of IRCT.

Source: See International Rehabilitation Council for Torture Victims, http://www .irct.org/.

struggles or nationalist movements such as Zapatistas in Chiapas, Mexico, and the contemporary Occupy movements, often operates at the margins of the more formal nonprofit sector. These campaigns generally have a looser structure, both within the individual member entities and in the networks they create, and some may deliberately shun any attempt to define them as part of the nonprofit sector (see Box 6.9 about the debate within the World Social Forum). Nevertheless, they are often supported by entities formally constituted in their own countries as nonprofit organizations.

The North-South dimensions of networks present particular challenges with the richer, more powerful Northern elements often accused of speaking on behalf of the South. Increasingly, Northern domination is being tempered by more independent ownership in the South through the emergence of stronger indigenous nonprofits. The conduct of North-South collaborations continues to be controversial, with claims that they do little more than whitewash ongoing power differentials and that they are often used to shift blame for failures to Southern partners that cannot meet the terms imposed by Northern partners (Abrahamsen 2004). The challenges can also be more prosaic: the founding statute of a network or federation may state that each member pays its own way to the international general meetings, a reasonable provision when all members were from the economic North, but a provision that becomes less viable when organizations from poorer nations join. Power imbalances and cultural differences can also lead to inequities in participation. An observer at the nonprofit forums that ran parallel to the 1992 UN Earth Summit conference remarked, "The Africans were watching, the Asians listening, the Latin Americans talking, while the North Americans and Europeans were doing business" (Colás 2002, 154).

Domestic Nonprofits Internationalize

This section is focused on formerly domestic organizations that have chosen to go global, by extending membership across borders, seeking to replicate abroad the work they do domestically, or merging with similar organizations in other countries. These efforts transcend the networks addressed in the previous section, as they go beyond international contacts meant primarily to strengthen existing domestic activities. Instead, a deliberate choice is being made to internationalize the work of an organization.

The size and economic power of US nonprofits often mean that a nominally domestic organization from that country becomes in effect the international organization for its field. The Muscular Dystrophy Association, based in Tucson, Arizona, which focuses on supporting research on neuromuscular diseases around the world, was founded in the 1950s as the Muscular Dystrophy Association of America. It evolved into its current international identity in the 1970s as it increased its work with other countries. Catholic Relief Services, which is widely identified as the international humanitarian arm of the Catholic Church and is one of the largest humanitarian organizations in the world, was founded in 1943 by the US Conference of Catholic Bishops in order to serve World War II survivors in Europe. It continues to be under the sponsorship of the US Catholic community. However, at the same time it is a member of the Caritas Internationalis confederation of Catholic humanitarian organizations headquartered in the Vatican.

Numerous US nonprofits are now going through similar processes. The National Association of Schools of Public Affairs and Administration (NASPAA), the US accrediting body for university public administration programs, changed its name in 2013 to the Network of Schools of Public Policy, Affairs, and Administration, though it still goes by the acronym NASPAA, and adopted a new tagline, "The Global Standard in Public Service Education," after receiving a growing number of requests for accreditation from non-US programs. Such dynamics may lead to possible demarcation disputes with existing international associations or other large national associations that are operating internationally. In the case of NASPAA and public administration education, they face competition from the Brussels-based International Association of Schools and Institutes of Administration (IASIA—tagline "Improving Public Administration Worldwide"), which brings together universities and other public sector training institutions and professional associations from around the world (NASPAA is a member of IASIA, along with the American Society for Public Administration and a number of US universities). In 2012, IASIA created its own accreditation system, enforced by the International Commission on Accreditation of Public Administration Education and Training Programs.

Internationalization requires the adjustment of a range of organizational procedures and practices. The internationalization strategy of GrantCraft, a joint project of the US and European Foundation Centers, is described in Box 6.13.

More common than a large organization from one country acting as the de facto international organization are the various iterations of the establishment of global brands and franchises such as the Teach for America and Repair Cafés examples cited earlier. Historic organizations, such as the Anglican Mission societies and the Red Cross, and the service clubs, such as the Lions, Rotary, and Kiwanis, are early exemplars of global brands, but the period since the 1990s has witnessed an explosion of these dynamics as the transaction costs of the cross-border pollination of brands has decreased.

A global brand might be created simply by using the coda "without borders." Inspired by the objectives and evocative name of Médecins Sans Frontières (Doctors Without Borders), currently more than fifty organizations and networks use those words in their name (or close variants such as "without frontiers"). They include Librarians Without Borders, Bikes Without Borders, and Geeks Without Frontiers. Some are single international organizations, whereas others are global networks of national organizations

---

Box 6.13 GrantCraft—Going Global

GrantCraft is a project of the US and European Foundation Centers, through which the Foundation Centers seek to improve funding and evaluation processes in the nonprofit sector through training programs and the publication of how-to manuals and case studies. Traditionally, the focus has been on foundations in developing countries, but recently the project has committed to "going global," focusing on three key strategies: developing new resources that consciously target either global or regional audiences; contextualizing existing resources to suit new, broader audiences; and continuing to promote and translate existing materials. GrantCraft describes the challenges of their new direction in the following terms: "Our vision is to have a diverse community of grantmakers that draws on the practical wisdom embodied in diverse, global experiences. But catering to a diverse audience of practitioners has its challenges. Practices from diverse realities may inspire but they can also confuse. Is it fundamentally different for a program officer at a Russian foundation to say 'no' to a local grantee, compared to how staff at a foundation in Baltimore rejects an application from a community organization, or can they draw on similar wisdom? Are insights based on the experience with collaboration with the private sector in Germany and the UK—undoubtedly different among them—relevant and stimulating for foundations in Italy? And, while philanthropy in China and Egypt may be profoundly different compared to the Netherlands, are not the basic aspects of a project assessment pretty much the same in both countries?"

They go on to ask, "And what about the guides themselves? Will existing GrantCraft materials fit the needs of these audiences? Can you actually make a GrantCraft guide for a global audience? We think our GrantCraft guides will go a long way because they are not prescriptive. But in some cases we will need to add (different) context, and some guides may require an addendum or new examples. All the same, there will be guides that can be used and translated as they are."

The US and European Foundation Centers have also encouraged the establishment of similar and affiliate organizations around the world, such as the China Foundation Center, which opened in 2010 and has translated the GrantCraft material into Chinese.

Source: See GrantCraft, http://blog.grantcraft.org/2011/09/globalizing-grantcraft/.

---

that share that name. Similar replications of brands are a combination of the spontaneous adoption of approaches by those who have heard about the work being done in other countries and a direct strategy of expansion by some organizations. The expansion of the mental health community Fountain House typifies such internationalization (see Box 6.14).

The globalization of nonprofit brands can also be driven by the global aspirations of their commercial sponsors. The Australian clothing brand Cotton On, through its affiliated Cotton On Foundation, has established

---

Box 6.14 Expansion of the Clubhouse Model of Fountain House

Fountain House opened in New York City in 1948 as a community for people who suffered from mental illness, in the belief that these people could lead productive and normal lives in both their work and their socialization. The model went against the then current medical model of treatment for people who suffered from psychiatric disorders, in which such people were treated as patients.

In 1977, Fountain House received a multiyear grant from the National Institute of Mental Health to develop a training program nationally based on their "clubhouse model." By 1987, 220 clubhouses had been established in the United States, along with clubhouses in Canada, Denmark, Germany, Holland, Pakistan, Sweden, and South Africa. Because the clubhouse model was based on "universal human values," it cut across national, ethnic, and cultural differences and could be implemented virtually anywhere.

In 1987, Fountain House received funding from the Robert Wood Johnson Foundation, the Public Welfare Foundation, and the Pew Charitable Trust for their National Clubhouse Expansion Project. As part of this project, a group of experts, the Faculty for Clubhouse Development, was cultivated to oversee the establishment of new clubhouses, and a set of international standards was put in place at the end of 1989.

Although the National Clubhouse Expansion Program ceased being funded in the fall of 1992, those directing the organization clearly saw that the work needed to continue, and an international organization was necessary to that effort. In 1993, at the annual meeting of the Faculty for Clubhouse Development, the group appointed a committee from among its members, staff, and board members to develop a plan for the international organization. In 1994, the International Center for Clubhouse Development came into being, supported financially by dues from member clubhouses and two nonprofits, the Public Welfare Foundation and the Van Ameringen Foundation.

Finally, in a transformation that took nearly sixty-five years, in January 2013, the international organization created a new "doing business as" name, Clubhouse International, to more succinctly and accurately communicate its dreams and aspirations for the organization.

Source: See International Center for Clubhouse Development, http://www.iccd .org/history.html.

charitable projects around the world. It is the lead sponsor of the New York–based Global Citizen project, which runs online antipoverty campaigns and has organized solidarity concerts in New York's Central Park.

At the same time, the globalization of brands is highly dependent on how the model can be transferred to different cultures and administrative environments. GuideStar International is a project that seeks to replicate the GuideStar model of nonprofit transparency programs around the world. In both the United States and the United Kingdom, the main feature of GuideStar is an online database that provides easy access to the legal, financial, and operational aspects of all registered nonprofits. In the United States, the database relies on the information submitted to the IRS as part of 501(c) registration, and in the United Kingdom, it is based on reporting to the UK Charity Commission. But the GuideStar model seems to have been fully replicated so far only in Israel, although other countries have programs that partially duplicate the model under other names, usually through their regulating agencies. Most countries do not provide such comprehensive and easily accessible GuideStar-style information, and no equivalent to GuideStar can be found on an international level, given the variations in definitions of nonprofits, in the regulating authorities, and in the privacy status of their financial information.

In contrast, the scouting movement, the service clubs, such as the Lions and Zonta, and the philanthropy organization United Way have demonstrated that many seemingly culture-bound models can be successfully adopted around the world. In the past, the spread of such organizations was fostered by colonial structures and the deliberate expansion strategies of a few organizations. Now, expatriates and "returnees" who have lived or worked abroad colonize new territories with familiar nonprofit brands.

The International Reach of Foundations

As noted in Chapter 2, the term *foundation* refers to a nonprofit organization established through an individual or institutional endowment. The endowment is usually held in perpetual trust, and the foundation uses the income generated by that trust for its activities, although in some cases the foundation has the mission to spend down the endowment and disband when it is expended. Foundations can be either grant-making or operational organizations. In civil law countries (generally Continental European and the former colonies of those countries), foundations are often operational and function similarly to other service delivery nonprofits; in common law countries (generally the English-speaking democracies), they tend to be primarily grant making.

Foundations are generally headquartered in, and identified with, the country of origin of their founders. Although most have a domestic focus for their activities, a few have had an avowedly international vocation. In the past decades, cross-border collaborations and grant making by foundations have seen a marked increase, and a growing subset of internationally focused foundations have established regional offices abroad to oversee their activities.

The factors identified as driving the rise of domestic and international nonprofits have had their echo in the foundation sector. Retrenchment in governments around the world has driven the growth of the complementary and supplementary role of foundations in providing quasi-public goods; the end of the Cold War freed foundations from the constraints imposed by their relations to the superpower blocs and has opened new arenas for international work; and increasing numbers of corporate social responsibility programs by global corporations have injected considerable new funds into the sector (Hewa and Stapleton 2005). In the United States, international grants as a portion of foundation giving have risen from around 5 percent in the early 1980s to nearly 25 percent currently (Spero 2010). Four major types of foundations extend their work internationally.

Individual and family foundations. The Gilded Age in the United States resulted in the early twentieth-century wave of foundations such as the Carnegie Corporation of New York (1911) and the Rockefeller Foundation (1913), followed by the W. K. Kellogg Foundation (1930) and the Ford Foundation (1936), which were seen as key to bolstering US hegemony (Krige and Rausch 2012). The current era may one day be regarded as a new "Global Gilded Age," with the wealthiest people in many countries establishing new family foundations, including Bill Gates (Microsoft) in the United States, Amancio Ortega Gaona (Inditex/Zara) in Spain, and Stefan Persson (H&M) in Sweden. Billionaires around the world are endorsing the Giving Pledge (see Box 6.15). However, not all family foundations come from the wealthiest individuals: in the United States, more than 40,000 family foundations are currently in operation, half of which grant less than $50,000 annually (Foundation Center 2014).

Global corporate foundations. Almost all global corporations now have foundations as part of their corporate social responsibility programs. Some seek to extend the work of the corporations into social and humanitarian areas (see Thompson Reuters Foundation in Box 3.4), whereas others support professional and cultural exchanges (e.g., the Volkswagen Foundation) or economic development (e.g., the Walmart Foundation).

Government foundations. Governments charter national foundations to pursue a range of domestic and foreign policy goals. The Fondation de France, the Qatar Foundation, and dozens of other national foundations support a wide range of international programs.

Foundations established by nonprofits. Many domestic nonprofits create foundations to support their international work (e.g., the Rotary Foundation in the United States), and international nonprofits may use a foundation legal structure as part of their international corporate architecture (see Oxfam in Box 6.4).

Given that the wealthiest foundations have considerable assets, they are counted among the largest nonprofits in the world (see Chapter 7), and the activities of megafoundations, such as the Gates family foundation and the Stichting INGKA Foundation, have considerable international projection.

Box 6.15 The Giving Pledge

The Giving Pledge is a campaign started in 2010 by Bill Gates and Warren Buffett to encourage billionaires to commit to donating most of their wealth to philanthropic causes while they are still alive. Gates and Buffett are actively promoting the pledge and have held meetings with billionaires in a number of countries urging them to commit. By early 2014, some 120 of the estimated 1,600 billionaires in the world had signed the Giving Pledge. The majority of the pledgers are from the United States, reflecting its US origins, the US culture of philanthropy, and the fact that 25 percent of the world's billionaires are from there. The non-US pledgers include Mohamed Ibrahim, a Sudanese-British mobile communications entrepreneur, who in 2007 initiated the Mo Ibrahim Prize for Achievement in African Leadership, which awards a $5 million prize and a lifetime pension to African heads of state who deliver security and economic development to their constituents and democratically transfer power to their successors.

Even though the Giving Pledge has generally received accolades, some pushback has occurred, including from billionaires who have been asked to sign. Criticism of the pledge reflects many of the cultural differences and policy debates in philanthropy. The pledge has been criticized as too ostentatious, designed to give publicity to self-serving people who should be supporting causes more anonymously. It has also been criticized as a smoke screen to help the wealthy use their charitable efforts to obscure the dishonest means of obtaining their wealth and to justify avoiding their tax obligations. Celebrating philanthropy through the Giving Pledge is seen as transferring the legitimacy for the allocation of the public funds away from the democratically elected governments and putting it in the hands of the wealthy. The pledge does not specify how funds should be spent, and critics have noted that the additional philanthropic funds are likely to mirror existing giving, which tends to flow to elite educational, cultural, and health services that do not necessarily serve the most disadvantaged. Billionaires who have refused to sign have noted that their obligations are to operate ethically and to pay their taxes.

Source: See the Giving Pledge, http://www.givingpledge.org.

7

International Nonprofits at Work

The overwhelming majority of international nonprofits have emerged from the industrialized democracies of the North, and that is where most continue to be headquartered. In the North, organizations have found the most favorable political and legal enabling environments, where they can more easily mobilize the inputs needed to sustain themselves (i.e., funding, infrastructure, and skilled staff), and where they are most visible to the major intergovernmental organizations and corporations they collaborate with. However, the sector is now diversifying as more nonprofits are founded in the South and some formerly Northern-based organizations transfer headquarters there.

Some organizations have such a quintessentially international or global identity that they could be considered "stateless." Although they have their origins in a specific locality and must incorporate as a legal entity in a national jurisdiction (or have multiple registrations in different jurisdictions—see the Chapter 8 commentary on incorporation), these stateless nonprofits are in effect not identified with any one nation or region. Examples include prominent international organizations that by the nature of their activities are considered global, such as the large aid organizations the Red Cross and Oxfam and the advocacy organizations Amnesty International and Transparency International. A new generation of Internet organizations also has a global virtual identity. WikiLeaks, the online whistleblower site, is perhaps the most notorious example. It has no fixed headquarters; it operates with secure Internet servers housed in countries with strong privacy laws, such as Sweden and Iceland; its funds are administered through a Dutch foundation; and it is operated by online volunteers dispersed around the world, with a very small core staff whose names are not publicized in order to protect them from possible harassment or prosecution. Its Australian-born leader, Julian Assange, sought the protection of the Ecuadorian Consulate in London to avoid deportation to Sweden to answer charges of sexual assault, from where he feared he would be sent to the United States to face trial on charges of espionage.

Texts on international nonprofits tend to focus only on a small subset of large, high-profile humanitarian and advocacy organizations, but in this chapter, I seek to provide an outline of the wider parameters of the sector. In any field of nonprofit endeavors, large, renowned players often get the most attention, while others work at the margins and struggle to survive. In Box 7.1 are traced the fortunes of two organizations founded in the aftermath of the collapse of the Soviet Union with seemingly similar missions focused on the development of civil society organizations around the world.

In this chapter, the work of three key categories of international nonprofits is examined: humanitarian aid, relief, and development organizations; advocacy organizations; and organizations that seek to promote global communities of common interests.

Humanitarian Aid, Relief, and Development

The most high-profile international nonprofit organizations are those that work in humanitarian aid and emergency relief in developing countries. In addition to responding to immediate emergency needs caused by natural disasters and armed conflicts, they work on a wide range of social and economic justice and civil rights issues, including poverty reduction, medical services, education, gender equality, political rights, environmental conservation, and small-business development. These organizations are the ones that most people conjure up when hearing the terms *international nonprofit* or *NGO*. Some of these organizations are among the largest international nonprofits, and much of the discussion below is focused most directly on the work of these mega–aid organizations.

At the same time, hundreds of smaller but still substantial organizations have budgets in the millions of dollars, and there are countless "micro–aid organizations" that may be little more than "kitchen table" or "boutique" entities. The number of small aid nonprofits is increasing, through which individuals or small groups in industrialized countries work directly on projects in developing countries. The projects are most often connected to schools, health clinics, or orphanages, and their foundation stories are usually about a person who lived or traveled in a developing country and felt a special affinity for that country and its people. On returning home, this person started a project to support an existing institution or build a new facility. Many of these organizations never become large enough to hire full-

---

Box 7.1 Promoting Civil Society

Civil Society International was founded in 1992 in Seattle, Washington, "to assist independent organizations working for democracy and civil society in countries closed, or inhospitable, to these principles." Its goal was to "bring together in one place information about projects worldwide committed to the keystones of civil society: limited government, popular elections, and the rule of law; free association and expression; regulated, but open and market-oriented economies; aid to the poor, orphaned, elderly, sick, or disabled; and civic cultures that value pluralism and individual liberty." In 2001, the organization had a declared income of $10,000, but by 2011, its nonprofit exemption had been revoked by the IRS because it had not submitted tax returns for three years. The organization had two web pages, civilsocietyinternational.org and www.civilsoc.org, both of which have expired. The founding executive director indicates in an online profile on another site that his employment with Civil Society International ended in 2013, and the organization appears to be no longer active.

CIVICUS was founded in 1993 at a meeting of civil society leaders in Barcelona, Spain, as "an international alliance dedicated to strengthening citizen action and civil society around the world." Originally based in Washington, DC, CIVICUS shifted its global headquarters in 2002 to Johannesburg, South Africa. CIVICUS is "based on the belief that the health of societies exists in direct proportion to the degree of balance between the State, the private sector and civil society." It provides a focal point for knowledge sharing, common interest representation, global institution building, and engagement among these disparate sectors. CIVICUS is the curator of the Civil Society Index (CSI) and the Enabling Environment Index (see Chapter 4) and currently functions with an annual budget of $3 million.

Source: See CIVICUS, https://www.civicus.org/.

---

time staff, but they continue to raise funds and may provide other support, including sending volunteers to work on-site (see Box 7.2).

The recognizably modern international aid nonprofits that were established in the mid-nineteenth and the first half of the twentieth century were focused primarily on alleviating the consequences of war. The provision of relief to war survivors, particularly of World War I and II in Europe, is the common founding narrative of many of the large, historic Northern aid nonprofits. Plan International, now one of the largest international nonprofits (which claims to have devised the child sponsorship strategy), is emblematic of these origins and of the later evolution of the organizations (see Box 7.3).

Box 7.2 The Liberian Assistance Program

The Liberian Assistance Program (LAP) operates with the motto "Building schools and hope for Liberians." It began in 2007 after two friends, Judy Reed and Jane Scharer, visited Liberia to reconnect with people Judy had taught from 1964 to 1966 when she was a Peace Corps volunteer in the small village of Gbonkonimah. In Liberia, they found the infrastructure destroyed by war: no electricity or running water, poor roads, limited housing, few operating schools, and understaffed hospitals. And yet they also found people struggling to put their lives back together, people who were hopeful that the future would be better. They met with more than fifteen of Reed's former students and even her former principal. The former students told how their children had not been able to go to school for years, how they had fled during the war, and how they had barely survived.

When Reed and Scharer got back to the United States, they gave a presentation on their trip for about seventy-five family and friends, serving the same Liberian meal they had in Gbonkonimah. They decided the best way to help was to form a nonprofit organization, LAP, and develop specific projects focused on strengthening the local schools.

LAP is a very small operation, with a small board of directors and advisory council and a current annual budget of $30,000. LAP has no paid employees. LAP directors state that they have no interest in competing with the large nonprofits. Instead, the organization "seeks to work in an intimate way with very poor people who just want a chance to help their children go to school, to grow their own food and to have a safe and healthy life."

Source: See the Liberian Assistance Program, http://www.liberianassistanceprogram
.org/aboutus.html.

After World War II, these organizations, along with an emerging generation of new nonprofits, continued to be primarily service oriented, focused on short-term poverty and disaster relief and medical aid that complemented the efforts of the newly established United Nations and other emerging intergovernmental organizations. Their field of operations expanded to include a wider range of regions in need and to work with the newly established postcolonial nations, with the provision of emergency food and building of health clinics and schools typically at the vanguard of such programs. Gradually aid expanded to include agriculture, water supply programs, and economic development programs. These first postwar nonprofits generally con-

Box 7.3 Plan International

Plan International (now commonly known as simply Plan) is a global child sponsorship organization that works in fifty developing countries to promote the rights of children and to lift them out of poverty. The following timeline traces its history.

- 1937: The organization was founded in Britain by journalist John Langdon-Davies and refugee worker Eric Muggeridge to provide food, accommodation, and education to children whose lives had been disrupted by the Spanish Civil War. Langdon-Davies conceived the idea of a personal relationship between child and sponsor. The original name was Foster Parents Plan for Children in Spain.
- 1940s: During World War II, the organization became known as Foster Parents Plan for War Children and worked in England, helping displaced children from all over Europe. After the war, the organization extended aid to children in France, Belgium, Italy, the Netherlands, Germany, Greece, and briefly in Poland, Czechoslovakia, and China (until they become part of the Communist Bloc).
- 1950s: As Europe recovered, Plan gradually moved out of these countries and opened new programs in less developed countries. The organization removed the reference to war children and became Foster Parents Plan to reflect the goal of working with children in need, whatever their circumstances.
- 1960s: Plan expanded its work in Asia and to countries in South America. In 1962, US first lady Jacqueline Kennedy was honorary chairwoman during Plan's Silver Jubilee.
- 1970s: The global name became Plan International as programs now spanned Latin America and the Caribbean, Asia, and Africa.
- 1980s: Belgium, Germany, Japan, and the United Kingdom joined Canada, the United States, Australia, and the Netherlands as donor countries. Plan achieved consultative status to the UN Economic and Social Council.
- 1990s: Plan marked its sixtieth anniversary of helping children. Offices opened in France, Norway, Finland, Denmark, Sweden, and South Korea.
- 2000s: Plan's donor countries increased to twenty as offices opened in Colombia, India, Ireland, Hong Kong, Spain, and Switzerland. The name Plan International evolved to simply Plan and a unified global identity was created to help make the organization more easily recognized around the world.

Source: See Plan International, http://plan-international.org/about-plan/history.

sidered the policy arena to be beyond their mandate, particularly in the orbits of influence of the United States and Soviet Union power blocs. Although there was a substantial group of nominally "nonaligned" countries, many of them still openly courted the two superpowers. The nascent international humanitarian organizations knew to tread carefully.

A new more structural and political approach began to emerge in the early 1970s as some international nonprofits adopted strategies that went beyond direct relief in response to what they perceived as the failure of traditional approaches to address the root causes of global inequalities. Their analysis was fueled by the radical ideologies of the youth and student movements in the industrialized North and the liberation movements in the South. They sought to address not only the direct ravages of poverty, famine, and war but also their causes through more openly political advocacy, as well as through education and "consciousness raising." The new goal was to generate structural changes in the aid process and in the relationships between donors and recipient nations.

The 1970s and 1980s were a coming-of-age of the international nonprofit sector, which echoed their domestic-focused evolution and expansion in industrialized countries. Faith-based missionary work ceded ground to more secular humanitarian efforts and political agitation. Government and private donors turned to them as an alternative to what was perceived as problematic government-to-government institutionalized aid programs. The burgeoning strength of the larger international aid organization coincided with the broader international implementation of the outsourcing agendas of the Washington Consensus, which led to a significant flow of new contract funds to nonprofits. The 1980s were perhaps a fleeting golden age of international nonprofit action with a considerable stock of goodwill (Tvedt 2006). The emblematic event was the 1985 Live Aid concerts and simulcasts, which were watched by an estimated audience of 1.9 million worldwide and raised an estimated $250 million toward famine relief, helped kick-start much of the current aid industry, and cemented celebrity support for international aid.

By the late 1990s, however, the comparative advantage of nonprofits in the delivery of more effective aid and poverty-relief strategies began to be called into question, and the end of the Cold War shifted previous political alignments. "Politics" were still central, but they became increasingly redefined in terms of strategies and capacity to manage large, professionalized programs. A notable feature of the new landscape was the theme of pragmatism and partnerships driven by the quest for legitimacy and efficiency. The number of international nonprofits in the North multiplied, while in the South new local organizations were emerging (some sponsored by Northern nonprofits whereas others were local initiatives). A key dynamic of the post-1990s era has been the decentralization of responsibilities and practice through partnership with local nonprofits. Large international nonprofits have increasingly found that public and private donors prefer to channel funds to smaller local organizations (Agg 2006), and the advent of online giving has provided individual donors the means to deal directly with non-profits in far-flung countries.

In response to criticism of the inefficient use of money, organizations began to adopt business strategies driven by corporate rhetoric. Nonprofits also began to collaborate more with previously unacceptable bedfellows such as governments, intergovernmental organizations, and businesses through participation in consultative mechanisms, as well as the coproduction and implementation of intervention strategies. Partnerships that would have previously been viewed with suspicion and derision began to be recognized as potentially beneficial.

Relations between the nonprofits and for-profit businesses had been somewhat fraught, but increasingly more pragmatic relations emerged, and many nonprofits began to seek collaborative relations with businesses they may have boycotted in the past: for example, medical nonprofits began working with drug companies, and environmental organizations began working with mining companies and heavy industries. Through these new relationships, the two sectors sought to create mutual advantages, with the nonprofits accessing new resources and increasing their influence from within while corporations sought to strengthen their brand by building goodwill. Although such relationships have now become commonplace, nonprofits who are exploring new partnerships can face a difficult balancing act while seeking to maintain their integrity (see the section on relations with the other sectors in Chapter 8).

Defining the Generations

The dates cited above are in no way precise, but clearly the prevailing paradigms of international humanitarian intervention have continued to evolve. By the late 1980s, David Korten (1987, 1990) had already identified four generations of nonprofits. A first generation focused on relief and medical care, defining problems in terms of responses to immediate shortages facing individuals or families. Nonprofits acted primarily alone and focused their efforts on the logistics of distribution. A second generation focused on small-scale development projects that would equip a locality or community with the means for addressing economic and social concerns. Northern nonprofits worked with extant and emerging local structures to build community-level capacity for independent action. A third generation focused on the development of more sustainable economic and political structures by seeking to influence the policy and practices of national government, intergovernmental organizations, and multinational corporations. A fourth generation focused on building sustainable people's movements focused on empowerment and participation that would work with loosely defined networks to agitate for continuing social change. One should note that Korten was writing at the end of the Cold War, and much of the agitation was in the context of the political alignments of the superpowers.

Three central themes emerge from the narratives of the generational changes. First, the sector has had to continually confront the entrenched challenges of combating poverty. Aid organizations have developed newer, more multifaceted strategies, which have shifted from addressing symptoms to attacking root causes and have increasingly included political and structural work. Second, centralized, top-down, and unitary approaches have neither enfranchised local populations nor succeeded in marshaling the best resources. They have been largely replaced by partnerships and networks that include a range of nonprofit actors from the North and South, as well as governments, intergovernmental organizations, and for-profit corporations, as well as by the devolution of policymaking and service delivery to more local levels. Third, organizations have grown and professionalized in order to better steward the increased responsibilities they are assuming.

The generations represent both the evolution of the strategies of existing organizations and the rise of new organizations (among which are the international advocacy organizations described in the following sections). The narrative of empowerment, change, and professionalization does not apply to all organizations: some still maintain a purely service orientation and eschew any hint of political work. Furthermore, with the constant expansion of the sector, new, small, "amateur" organizations are never in short supply.

Although the concept of generations suggests that the new strategies displaced the earlier ones, or that new organizations replaced the older ones, the generations instead continue to coexist as competing or complementary approaches to development. Many organizations combine elements of all four generations in their operational toolkits. The generations, therefore, can also be analyzed from the perspective of the ongoing ideological and operational debates about development paradigms. First-generation strategies are disparaged by some analysts as anachronistic, paternalistic charity or as Band-Aid solutions that only superficially address entrenched structural concerns. Third- and fourth-generation strategies are dismissed by others as illegitimate political interference, concealing ideological agendas behind spurious constituencies. Although few would argue that direct aid and relief are not necessary in response to the humanitarian crises generated by natural disasters and armed conflicts, their use as a continuing development strategy has been increasingly branded as anachronistic and analogous to domestic charity. At the same time, the political activities of the third and fourth generation have been redefined in the post–Cold War and professionalized era as technical-structural changes (as opposed to political-structural): what were formerly grassroots political struggles against exploitative regimes are now often the purview of professional watchdog and capacity-building organizations focusing on eliminating corruption and strengthening good governance.

Differences in approaches are also driven by the dominant domestic nonprofit sector models of the home countries of the international nonprofits. The United States and the United Kingdom have been the historic homes of the large nonprofits; however, now such organizations are resident in all Western industrialized democracies and also increasingly in the emerging economies such as those of BRICS, South Korea, and Turkey, as well as of Gulf states such as Qatar and Kuwait. Kees Biekart (2008), in his analysis of the largest European nonprofits operating in Latin America, listed eighteen organizations from nine European countries, covering the liberal, social democratic, and corporatist frames. Organizations accustomed to operating under different home models tend to replicate those approaches in their international work, and organizations from the world superpowers have different agendas than organizations based in the middle or lesser powers. Countries from the European Union have emphasized since the mid-1990s the importance of coproduction development strategies based on migration flows, remittances, and immigrant associations in countries of settlement (see the section below on diaspora development), and northern European countries have garnered a reputation of being "benevolent imperialists" more willing to dialogue with a broader range of local entities (Tvedt 1998).

Moreover, with the growing presence of China in Africa, its state-centric neoauthoritarian approach is increasingly becoming a model for economic growth referenced by developing countries. The higher profile of China is part of the growing phenomena of South-South cooperation. As the BRICS and other emerging countries from the South acquire growing confidence, a recalibration of their relationship with institutional and private donors from the North and with Northern nonprofits will take place. Despite much of the focus being on government-to-government cooperation, international nonprofits with origins in countries such as South Korea (see Box 4.9) and Bangladesh (see Box 6.7) can establish relationships that are perceived as free of the taint of the imperialism of the North.

The generational shifts in strategies and theories of change reflect the evolution of official development approaches. Nonprofits have had to play catch-up to adjust programs to the new directions favored by governments, intergovernmental organizations, and the private sector. The geopolitical maneuvers of powerful nations, the economic interests of multinational corporations, the mandates of the Bretton Woods financial institutions, and the development polices of the United Nations and other intergovernmental bodies have led the way in development policies and practices. International nonprofits have been, at best, influential stakeholders, often only invoked as representatives of an amorphous civil society whenever other players want to establish credentials for local consultation and ownership. In his 2011 annual report to the United Nations on progress toward the Millennium Development Goals, Secretary-General Ban Ki-moon indicated that the process of developing the new goals would be "an inclusive, open and transparent process with multi-stakeholder participation" (United Nations 2013, 19). The International Monetary Fund and the World Bank have, since 1999, required low-income country governments to develop poverty reduction strategy papers, linked to the Millennium Development Goals, before they receive aid from major donors or are considered for debt relief. The first principle of the papers is that they should be "country-driven," defined as "promoting national ownership of strategies through broad-based participation of civil society" (International Monetary Fund 2014).

The latest generation has developed its own jargon. *Upstreaming* has become the technical term for strategies that seek more structural changes and country-level approaches as opposed to *downstream* project-based work. The shift from "charity" to "rights" is identified as a key axis of the ideological and operational debates on humanitarian aid and development, and the emergence of a "rights-based approach" summarizes many of the evolutionary trends. David Lewis (2007) cited the following implications of the rights-based approach:

- Increasing transparency that makes organizations more accountable and responsive.
- Shifting from beneficiaries to partners to transform voiceless recipients into active citizens.
- Building new skills in political analysis and diplomacy.
- Emphasizing aid for the poorest.
- Engaging more fully with legal systems.
- Encouraging better accountability between governments and citizens.

All the technical jargon has been distilled in Box 7.4 into two common aphorisms often heard in development circles.

The shifts in the zeitgeist are also evident in the general political and societal environment in which humanitarian aid operates. The 2005 version of the Live Aid concerts (i.e., the twentieth anniversary of the original) was called Live 8 to signal its support of the eight Millennium Development Goals. Bono, the rock god of African aid, now promotes business opportunities on that continent, following a new credo echoed by many political and business leaders. It is typified by the exhortation, usually attributed to UN Secretary-General Ban Ki-moon, that "Africa does not need charity; it needs investments and partnership."

Box 7.4   Development Aphorisms: Fish and Babies

The allegedly ancient Chinese proverb, "Give a man a fish and he will eat for a day; teach a man to fish and his family will eat for a lifetime," is often used as an allegory for the debate between charity aid and development. As noted in Chapter 5, recently, a third part has been added to the above aphorism, along the lines of "restructure the fishing industry and a community will be transformed." This addition is used to distinguish new social enterprise strategies from earlier charity and development approaches.

Various versions of the following metaphor appear in development texts and at workshops: "If you see a baby drowning, you jump in to save it. If you see a second and a third, you do the same. Soon you are so busy saving drowning babies, you no longer have time to ask why someone is throwing these babies in the river."

The Next Generation?

The disappointment at past results of aid and development work and the post–Cold War realignments have meant that an ongoing search for new strategies continues to be the driving force. The new millennium has spawned a newer generation of more market-driven strategies and organizations. This marketization of development theory and strategies is the international echo of the social entrepreneurship dynamics analyzed in Chapter 5. It includes the notions both that extant organizations should embrace key aspects of market discipline and that market forces are central to lifting populations out of poverty.

Perhaps the most potent symbols of the market approach are various iterations of financial services for the poor. A range of services, backed by both nonprofit and for-profit entities, exists to provide basic financial products such as savings accounts, money transfers, and various forms of insurance. The most emblematic are the microcredit or microloan programs that provide small loans to start or support business initiatives. Mutual associations and revolving credit clubs have a long history of providing start-up funds to members, but the contemporary version of third-party microloans targeting the poor was popularized in Latin America and South Asia in the 1970s and 1980s. It has since become a staple for economic development throughout the developing world, and it is also used for the poor in the industrialized world. In 2006, Muhammad Yunus, the founder of the Grameen Bank, one of the first and the most widely known microlending institutions, was awarded the Nobel Peace Prize. However, like all development strategies, microfinance has its critics (see Box 7.5).

Box 7.5 Microfinance Debate

Although microfinance institutions continue to have strong support from across the political spectrum, critical voices are casting doubt on their developmental impact and warning of predatory microlending practices and of a microfinance "bubble" that is likely to burst. The back cover blurb of *Confessions of a Microfinance Heretic: How Microlending Lost Its Way and Betrayed the Poor* reads in part: "[The author] worked with several microfinance institutions and funds as he traveled from Mexico to Mongolia, with Nigeria, Holland, and Mozambique in between. He could not help but notice that even with a booming $70 billion industry on their side, the poor did not seem any better off in practice. Exorbitant interest rates led borrowers into never-ending debt spirals, and aggressive collection practices resulted in cases of forced prostitution, child labor, suicide, and nationwide revolts against the microfinance community."

Source: Sinclair 2012.

A general push is being made for market-based development, expressed as an "aid versus investment" debate (Hudson Institute 2012; M. Martin 2011). Although much of the market-based rhetoric features the theory of trickle-down economics that simply assumes market-based economies will be engines of growth that benefit all, some approaches also focus on the market economics of the poor. In 2004, the Commission on the Private Sector and Development, formed by the UN Development Programme, published the report *Unleashing Entrepreneurship: Making Business Work for the Poor* (UN Development Programme 2004), which focuses on how businesses can create domestic employment and wealth, free local entrepreneurial energies, and help achieve the Millennium Development Goals. This approach argues that aid and charity strategies see the poor only as victims in need of a handout, whereas business empowers them by treating them as entrepreneurs, employees, or customers. The market-based approaches that focus on the poor are symbolized by two commonly cited iterations: (1) bottom-of-the-pyramid marketing, popularized by Coimbatore Prahalad (2006), which focuses on encouraging businesses to work with the poor, whom they have not traditionally seen as consumers, and (2) the movement to make markets work for the poor, which focuses somewhat more directly on creating stronger market economies within the poorer strata of society (M4P Hub 2013).

Another key factor is the post–September 11, 2001, war on terror and the range of security issues it has engendered. *Securitization* is the catchall term that covers a number of dynamics, including closer alignment of development work with the priorities of defense and diplomacy (since 9/11 Iraq and Afghanistan have been among the largest recipients of aid flows). The war on terror has also resulted in a greater scrutiny of the operations of any organization that might possibly be accused of aiding or abetting terrorist groups, which has inhibited the work of many legitimate organizations working in conflict zones or with populations considered under suspicion (Rutzen 2015; Sidel 2010). This instrumentalization of aid work in general and of the work of international nonprofits has contributed to the deteriorating security conditions for aid workers in conflict zones.

The most significant dynamic of the emerging context is the increasing pressure to justify the work of international aid organizations to the public and donors in the face of the criticism of their work. Questions are constantly raised about how important nonprofits are in the wider scheme of international development and how successful their strategies have been. As Sarah Michael (2002) noted, "[to] some observers they are the universal panacea to underdevelopment, to others the torch-bearers of civil society, and to still others the David to the Goliaths of oppressive government regimes, globalization and poverty" (12). Undoubtedly, hubris is present in the nonprofit aid and development community along with a tendency for organizations to overstate the outcomes of their programs and their importance in the wider scheme of international politics and economics. However, fund-raising and other resource development are predicated on convincing donors and contracting entities of the worth of the sector and individual organizations. Michael (2002) warned that an uncritical view of nonprofits is unhelpful as they suffer from the same inefficiencies, corruption, and self-interest as organizations in the other sectors. Alan Fowler (2012) also spoke of a "false promise" and the inflated expectations that international nonprofits could supplant many aspects of the work of governments and intergovernmental organizations.

Twenty-first-century aid organizations must continually demonstrate that they are legitimate and effective in the shifting development landscape in which private organizations and the favored causes of "celanthropists" play an increasing role. Donors, large and small, can now circumvent the previous networks of aid distributions and deal directly with recipients in any part of the world.

The Relative Size of Nonprofit Aid

The role of nonprofits in humanitarian aid, relief, and development has expanded since the 1980s. However, they continue to be minor partners when measured in terms of their contribution to the financial flows from developed to developing countries. Table 7.1 indicates the relative magnitude of official development aid, private investment, grants by nonprofits, and remittances by migrants.

Table 7.1 Net Financial Flows to Developing Countries, 2011

Type of Flow	US$ Billions	Percentage
Official development assistance: from donor governments to developing countries and multilateral institutions[a]	$134.4	15
Other official flows: other payments not primarily aimed at development[a]	$8.6	1
Private flows at market terms: private investments, bank lending, bonds, export credits, etc.[a]	$326.5	37
Grants by nonprofits[a]	$31.9	4
Remittances by migrants to developing countries[b]	$373.0	43
Total net flows	$874.4	100

Sources: a. From the twenty-seven members of the Development Aid Committee, formed from industrialized countries of the OECD. OECD, "Statistics on Resource Flows to Developing Countries," Table 3: Total Net Flows by DAC Country, http://www.oecd.org/dac/stats/statisticson resourceflowstodevelopingcountries.htm.
b. World Bank 2013. Source includes some countries that are not members of the Development Aid Committee.

These figures are at best indicative of the relatively little clout of the work of nonprofits and international philanthropy. However, the figures do not capture many of the flows from smaller donors, they also do not include data from OECD countries that are not part of the Development Aid Committee or from non-OECD countries, and one can assume that part of the official and private flows as well as of remittances by migrants are channeled to nonprofits through donations, grants, and contracts for program delivery. The portion of official development aid that goes to nonprofits varies between source countries as a reflection of their cultural frames. Liberal and social democratic countries commit a significant part of their aid to nonprofit delivery, whereas corporatist countries such as France and Japan deliver aid almost exclusively to recipient governments (Buthe and Cheng 2014). Globally, the best estimates appear to be that about 6 percent of official development aid is channeled through nonprofits (Agg 2006; OECD 2013a, 2013b), and no accurate corresponding figures can be found for private flows. Whichever estimates are used, nonprofits would appear to account for less than 10 percent of financial flows to developing countries.

Given that less than 1 percent of official development aid was channeled through nonprofits until the mid-1980s, there has without doubt been a substantial expansion in their activities (Agg 2006). Even so, a significant discrepancy exists between the low level of activity and financial stake of nonprofits in development and their high visibility. Perhaps this discrepancy appears because giving the industry a nongovernment, nonprofit gloss in the face of concerns about the ineffectiveness of government and multilateral institutions and about the motives of commercial firms suits all parties (Agg 2006). At the same time, many analyses of the future of development continue to give relatively little attention to the role or operations of nonprofits. Instead the focus is on geopolitical shifts, technological changes, and demographic shifts such as aging populations and immigration, as well as the impact of multinational corporations and even of organized crime. Development, however defined, is hostage to macrogeopolitical and macroeconomic forces beyond the control of the nonprofit sector. In these narratives, nonprofits occasionally appear at best as bit players, as third-party agents of the governments and intergovernmental organizations that contract with them, or as part of an amorphous civil society that is mostly cited in passing and with the qualifier that it needs to be strengthened.

Although in this book I focus on nonprofit organizations, I need to emphasize that for-profit companies also play a significant role in development. For-profit development companies appear to receive a considerably larger share of development aid than nonprofit organizations. Of the top twenty-five contracts awarded by the UK Department for International Development between 1998 and 2003 and completed by 2004, twenty went to for-profit companies and five to nonprofits, with the for-profits receiving 82.5 percent of the funds awarded (Huysentruyt 2011). Table 7.2 shows the ten top recipients of contracts from USAID in 2012.

For-profit companies appear to receive two to four times more official development aid than nonprofits, even in countries with large nonprofit sec-

Table 7.2 Top Vendors for USAID Development Programs, Fiscal Year 2012

Vendor Name	Type	Total Amount Received in US$
World Bank	Intergovernmental	$2,262,021,806
UN World Food Programme	Intergovernmental	$909,326,833
Chemonics	For-profit	$681,759,506
John Snow, Inc.	For-profit	$482,863,181
Government of Pakistan	Government	$460,982,618
Partnership for Supply Chain Management	Nonprofit	$431,746,164
Development Alternatives Inc.	For-profit	$324,519,705
Abt Associates	For-profit	$319,199,514
Family Health International	Nonprofit	$292,092,608
Government of Jordan	Government	$284,229,683

Source: USAID 2013.

tors. Some of the explanation for the disparity may be that for-profits are awarded the bulk of contracts that involve capital-intensive projects such as infrastructure development and emergency response logistics, but many of the contracts are for health services, economic development, and capacity-building activities that are similar to those also provided by nonprofit organizations. Chemonics, the third-ranked vendor in Table 7.2, is an employee-owned for-profit development company that focuses on social and economic change around the world through projects that include improving health services, promoting sound environmental practices, and encouraging local staff development.

For-profit development companies are often the prime contractors for government-funded aid programs and may subcontract implementation to nonprofits or individual private consultants. For-profit companies generally cannot directly receive philanthropic donations but may have a nonprofit subsidiary or partner organization that enables donor support for projects. The size and scope of the for-profit development sector is difficult to quantify, and tracking the revenues of individual companies can be all but impossible. For-profit development companies function in the same manner as other multinational corporations, with frequent mergers and acquisitions. In November 2013, the Australian international development company GRM announced that it was acquiring theIDLgroup, a development consultancy based in the United Kingdom. GRM had earlier acquired another Australian development company, Effective Development Group, and had merged with the US-based Futures Group, whereas theIDLgroup had merged with the UK company FRR Ltd in 2007. The new conglomerate, operating as GRM Futures Group, will have over $400 million in annual revenues.

GRM Futures Group and Chemonics are both members of the Council of International Development Companies (CIDC), a subcommittee of the Professional Services Council, the industry association that represents private vendors to the US government (the Professional Services Council itself, like other industry associations, is a registered nonprofit). On its web page, CIDC extols the virtues of for-profit development, claiming that it offers superior accountability and transparency, and states that "we believe the debate over who should implement more of our foreign aid programs— nonprofits or development companies—misses the point. The better question is what type of implementation instrument, what type of funding vehicle, will be most effective for a given program" (CIDC 2014).

Incidences are growing of collaborative efforts between nonprofits and for-profit companies that have not previously worked in development. Multinational corporations from a wide range of fields are becoming in effect co-deliverers of aid through their corporate social responsibility and citizenship programs (see Box 7.6).

Box 7.6 Corporations Lend Expertise to Aid Groups

Major corporations are lending their expertise on issues such as logistics and security to help relief organizations deliver food aid in the drought-stricken Horn of Africa. The United Parcel Service (UPS) is helping the World Food Programme institute bar codes and other electronic tools to track deliveries. Furthermore, Walmart is providing a lockdown system for controlling food supplies, technologies that could otherwise cost the UN agency hundreds of millions of dollars. In Haiti, the pharmaceuticals giant Abbott Laboratories is teaming with medical charity Partners in Health to produce a high-calorie peanut paste to combat malnutrition. The company and the charity worked together on everything from choosing equipment to determining which vitamins would be mixed into the paste.

Source: See the Chronicle of Philanthropy, http://philanthropy.com/blogs/philanthropy today/big-companies-lend-expertise-to-aid-groups-in-africa-and-haiti/39158.

Critiques of Humanitarian and Development Organizations

Since the 1960s, realist theorists have argued that aid serves primarily to advance the political and economic self-interests of powerful nations (Morgenthau 1962), whereas neoliberals have claimed that aid is a disincentive to reform (Bauer 1969). Currently, a genre of mass-market denunciation books with attention-grabbing titles is burgeoning. Some take aim at aid in general whereas others focus on philanthropy and the work of international NGOs (see Box 7.7).

Aid and aid organizations are disparagingly dubbed the "white savior industrial complex" (Cole 2012). The debates in the books in Box 7.7 and in other related academic and popular literature largely mirror the domestic wrangles about welfare in general. Conservative critics claim that no evidence can be given that aid or the work of international nonprofits has helped countries or communities move out of poverty, and they further contend that aid traps recipient nations and their populations in cycles of dependency that rob them of initiatives to reform or wean themselves from handouts (Bauer 1969; Deaton 2013; Moyo 2009). Conservatives argue for a scaling back or an end to aid and the termination of contracts to NGOs. They wield arguments that favor more market-based macrosolutions to stimulate economic growth. The way forward is couched in the classical neoliberal discourse of small government, free-market development, deregulation and trickle-down economics. In the current context of competing aid strategies, some free-market critics of traditional aid interventions end

Box 7.7 The Critics of Aid and NGOs

Some of the recent books that seek to raise public consciousness about the failure and ills of international aid and nonprofits include:

- Giles Bolton, *Aid and Other Dirty Business*, 2008.
- William Easterly, *The White Man's Burden: Why the West's Efforts to Aid the Rest Have Done So Much Ill and So Little Good*, 2007.
- Tori Hogan, *Beyond Good Intentions: A Journey into the Realities of International Aid*, 2012.
- Hans Holmén, *Snakes in Paradise: NGOs and the Aid Industry in Africa*, 2009.
- David Kennedy, *The Dark Sides of Virtue: Reassessing International Humanitarianism*, 2005.
- Robert D. Lupton, *Toxic Charity: How Churches and Charities Hurt Those They Help*, 2012.
- Michael Maren, *The Road to Hell: The Ravaging Effects of Foreign Aid and International Charity*, 2002.
- Dambisa Moyo, *Dead Aid*, 2009.
- Linda Polman, *The Crisis Caravan: What's Wrong with Humanitarian Aid?* 2011.
- David Rieff, *A Bed for the Night: Humanitarianism in Crisis*, 2003.
- Mark Schuller and Paul Farmer, *Killing with Kindness: Haiti, International Aid, and NGOs*, 2012.

up, somewhat incongruously, touting China's more transactional approach, which focuses on infrastructure and trade (Moyo 2012).

Progressive critics argue that aid and international nonprofits have not made a significant impact because they have not effectively represented marginalized groups or succeeded in leveraging efforts to address power imbalances (Edwards 2010b; Suleiman 2013; T. Wallace, Bornstein, and Chapman 2007). A common trope of progressive critics is that international nonprofits have assumed the roles formerly attributed to colonial masters and missionaries in entrenching corrupt elites and embedding neoliberal agendas (Sankore 2005; Shivji 2007). Condemned as agents of new colonialism, or neocolonialism, international nonprofits are seen as the Trojan horses of neoliberal capitalism, quashing autochthonous forms of organizing and development and disrupting revolutionary movements by co-opting leaders into ameliorative projects (Abzug and Webb 1996; Banks and Hulme 2012; Jad 2007; Roelofs 2006; Shivji 2007; T. Wallace 2003). Others argue that aid projects have become commodities that international nonprofits sell to funders and that the pressure to demonstrate success means that many projects do not reach those most in need (Krause 2014). Marketization, competitive tendering, and the scramble for funding have generated incentives that produce perverse outcomes and discourage contestation (Cooley and Ron 2002).

Analyses from across the political spectrum also focus on the ambiguities inherent in working in developing countries and intervening in conflict zones. They contend that humanitarian aid, although trying to do good, often also causes harm. In the worst instances, services provided by humanitarian aid can help prolong wars and enable atrocities. Warring factions often factor in the "support" of aid organizations as part of their belligerent strategies, and if a faction can exert control over a territory, members of that faction often extract tributes from organizations operating in those areas (Jackson and Aynte 2013; T. G. Weiss 2013). Aid dollars often end up in the pockets of corrupt elites, perpetuating their extractive kleptocracies by allowing them to govern without the consent of the population. UN Secretary-General Ban Ki-moon has conceded that some 30 percent of aid does not reach its intended destination (United Nations 2012).

Proponents of increasing aid point to countries such as Botswana, Brazil, Mauritius, Mexico, Morocco, Peru, and Thailand that in the past received significant aid but now have reached middle-income status. Moreover, a wide range of human development metrics in many other countries are showing an upward trend, including those related to the Millennium Development Goals for infant mortality and educational attainment (United Nations 2011), as well as those involving civil and political rights (Freedom House 2011). Program evaluations by donors and individual organizations regularly trumpet their successes despite the difficulties in linking such outcomes to broader developmental goals. These seeming contradictions are described as the difference between "effectiveness" and "impact" (an organization can effectively implement its planned program in terms of the outputs achieved, but that may not have the desired impact in terms of outcomes) and as the "micro-macro paradox," in which localized successes can coexist with more global failures (Arndt, Jones, and Tarp 2010).

Channing Arndt, Sam Jones, and Finn Tarp (2010) argued that, in aggregate, aid improves the development prospects of poor nations, but they conceded that the pendulum has swung to skepticism. A dilemma for progressive critics of aid and the work of international nonprofits is how to not simply add fuel to the fire of conservative critics. Tina Wallace, Lisa Bornstein, and Jennifer Chapman (2007) dedicated almost all of the 177 pages in their book *The Aid Chain* to a trenchant criticism of the current processes of international aid and the role of nonprofits. Then, on the second to last page, at the beginning of the final conclusion, they stated, "This book is not calling for an end of aid or the end of NGOs" (176), and offered recommendations based on more effective downward accountability to end users, more equitable North-South partnerships, and better information dissemination. Alexander Cooley and James Ron (2002) urged nonprofits to resist the competitive scramble and reject contracts that encourage fragmentation and create disincentives for contestation. Progressive critics argue that aid is flawed but generally express the hope that those flaws can be addressed. Apparently, the only thing worse than bad aid would be no aid at all. Moreover, many progressive critiques contain a fundamental paradox. The current ideological alternatives to neoliberalism (e.g., *chavismo*, the populist left-wing centralism associated with the former president of Venezuela, Hugo Chávez) are generally more state-centric and authoritarian and so concede less political and operating space to independent organizing and nonprofit organizations.

Can Northern nonprofits work in the South without being neocolonialists? How can the work of international nonprofits from the North contribute to emancipatory development and reform in the South without imposing "external values" (a term usually used as code for neoliberalism)? Some commentators cite as examples of appropriate development the use of autochthonous concepts such as South Africa's *ubuntu*, a humanist concept of collective responsibility ("Ubuntu in Evaluation" 2013), and Rwanda's *imihigo*, an accountability mechanism based on a precolonial practice in which tribal chiefs and elders would publicly vow to achieve certain goals (Scher and MacAulay 2010). The labels may be indigenous, but what they name may in effect replicate many of the practices that are supposedly being inappropriately imposed—*imihigo*, in particular, seems to mirror the planning, monitoring, and oversight programs of the North. Other examples of alternative approaches appear to be simply semantic shifts. One international capacity-building organization stopped referring in its training materials to "models" from the North that could be adapted to the South and instead spoke only of "examples" that could be part of a global dialogue on effective practice.

In additional to these ideological debates, operational concerns can be found regarding the legitimacy, accountability, and effectiveness of nonprofits. These issues are explored in more depth in Chapter 8 in the context of the stewardship of organizations, but a broader discussion is also taking place among donor countries and multilateral institutions about improving aid outcomes and the search for "better, smarter" aid. Despite criticisms from some quarters about the performance of nonprofits, a series of UN-sponsored High Level Forums on Aid Effectiveness has increasingly stressed the importance of their growing role. The third forum in the series in Accra, Ghana, in 2008 was the first to formally recognize nonprofits as development partners and the final statement of the fourth forum in Busan, South Korea, provided an even clearer sentiment (see Box 7.8).

Box 7.8 Busan Forum on Aid Effectiveness

In November 2011, the UN-sponsored Fourth High Level Forum on Aid Effectiveness was held in Busan, South Korea. Earlier forums had included only representatives of member states and focused primarily on aid funding. By the fourth forum, representation was wider.

The final statement of the first forum began, "We the heads of State and Government, gathered in Monterrey, Mexico [in March 2002] have resolved to address the challenges of financing for development around the world, particularly in developing countries." In contrast, the final statement at Busan began, "We, Heads of State, Ministers and representatives of developing and developed countries, heads of multilateral and bilateral institutions, representatives of different types of public, civil society, private, parliamentary, local and regional organizations recognize that we are united by a new partnership that is broader and more inclusive than ever before, founded on shared principles, common goals and differential commitments for effective international development."

The final Busan document, titled Partnership for Effective Development Cooperation, included the following statements: "We also have a more complex architecture for development cooperation, characterized by a greater number of State and non-State actors, as well as cooperation among countries at different stages in their development, many of them middle-income countries. South-South and triangular cooperation, new forms of public-private partnership, and other modalities and vehicles for development have become more prominent, complementing North-South forms of cooperation."

The document continued, "Civil society organizations (CSOs) play a vital role in enabling people to claim their rights, in promoting rights-based approaches, in shaping development policies and partnerships, and in overseeing their implementation. They also provide services in areas that are complementary to those provided by States. Recognizing this, we will:

- Implement fully our respective commitments to enable CSOs to exercise their roles as independent development actors, with a particular focus on an enabling environment, consistent with agreed international rights, that maximizes the contributions of CSOs to development.
- Encourage CSOs to implement practices that strengthen their accountability and their contribution to development effectiveness, guided by the Istanbul Principles and the International Framework for CSO Development Effectiveness."

continues

Box 7.8 continued

The post-Busan process is now administered by the Global Partnership for Effective Development Cooperation secretariat supported by the UN Development Programme and the OECD. The steering committee is composed primarily of government ministers but also includes civil society and business representation, and the agreement document has been endorsed by more than fifty organizations including international nonprofits and intergovernmental organizations.

Sources: See United Nations, http://www.un.org/esa/ffd/monterrey/MonterreyConsensus .pdf; Organisation for Economic Co-operation and Development; http://www.oecd.org /dac/effectiveness/busanpartnership.htm; Global Partnership for Effective Development Cooperation, http://effectivecooperation.org/.

Scandals and Failures

The critiques of development outlined in the previous section focused primarily on the structural, macrolevel impact, but more microlevel concerns have also been voiced about the work of aid organizations and their workers. Humanitarian aid and relief attract their share of charlatans, opportunists, felons, and incompetents, so as the sector grows, the tales of failure and scandal are becoming all too common. Corruption in the recipient countries, which diverts aid to local elites or criminal gangs, is a constant concern, but one can also find a constant stream of exposés of the miscalculations, ineptitude, and mendacity of the rich North in its attempts to help the poor South.

One of the more high-profile scandals of the past few years in the English-speaking world is that of Greg Mortenson (see Box 7.9).

Even well-intentioned strategies can have unintended consequences. Financial support for orphanages is a popular cause for foreign donors, but it is often in conflict with prevailing trends toward deinstitutionalization and foster care and may even lead to the poor surrendering their children on the hope they will be better fed in orphanages or get access to a better life through adoption by foreigners (see the example in Alexander 2013). The provision of accessible clean water is another prominent strategy, yet a common anecdote (so often repeated in the development literature without identifying its source that it has become somewhat apocryphal) tells of an African village in which an international nonprofit installed a well so the women would not have to walk for miles each day to fetch water from a distant river. The well was initially greeted with celebration, but it soon fell into disuse because the women refused to renounce their daily walks to the river. It was the only social time they had together away from the grind of their family responsibilities.

Box 7.9 Three Cups of Tea

Greg Mortenson is a US mountain climber who claimed that after an accident in Pakistan in 1993, he was sheltered by poor villagers, and that after he recovered, he decided to dedicate his life to building schools in the area and championing the cause of girls' education. He created a nonprofit, the Central Asia Institute, and chronicled his aid work and adventures in two best-selling books *Three Cups of Tea* (2006) and *Stones into Schools* (2009). Bolstered by the popularity of the books, the Central Asia Institute reached an annual income of some $20 million by 2010 and was commonly cited in the academic and popular literature as a paragon of social entrepreneurship and meaningful aid.

In 2011, the current affairs television program *60 Minutes* aired an exposé that claimed that many of the incidents in the book, including the foundation story of the accident and recovery, were false or highly exaggerated; that many of the schools that the Central Asia Institute claimed to assist either did not exist or had not received any meaningful aid; and that a large part of the income of the institute was spent in the United States to pay for publicity for the books and speaking tours, even though Mortenson kept the income from the books and appearances.

A subsequent investigation by the Montana attorney general Steve Bullock had found that Mortenson had misspent over $6 million, although Mortenson's actions were not considered criminal. Mortenson was required to repay $1 million to the institute and resign as executive director, although he was permitted to stay on as an ex officio board member.

Sources: See Social Capital Blog, http://socialcapital.wordpress.com/2008/10/01/three-cups-of-tea/; CBS News (Online), http://www.cbsnews.com/stories/2011/04/15/60minutes/main20054397.shtm.

A better-documented failure of a strategy to create new water sources is the PlayPump fiasco (see Box 7.10).

Unintended consequences also include the creation of "disaster economies." Expatriate aid workers in developing countries are usually paid considerably higher salaries than locals, and local staff, even administrative and support staff, earn salaries that are often significantly higher than local professionals. When international nonprofits (along with other aid agencies, consultants, military personnel, and the media) become a significant presence in a region, they distort the equilibriums of the local economy and organizational structures: they can drive up the prices of housing and basic goods, and they tempt local professionals to abandon their current employment to work in semiskilled positions in nonprofits. Moreover, those deemed eligible to receive aid, such as refugees from a nearby conflict, often end up in seem-

Box 7.10 PlayPump

In the early 1990s, a billboard advertising executive in South Africa had an innovative idea—by spinning on a merry-go-round connected to a water pump, children could generate plentiful, clean water without the time-consuming work of traditional hand pumps. The pumps would have the supposed advantages that children got a place to play, their communities got free drinking water, and girls and women, who bear much of the burden of collecting water for their families, got time to attend school or pursue other activities. Billboards on the raised water tanks that were an integral part of the system would bring in advertising revenue to fund maintenance and spread public health messages. A nonprofit organization, PlayPump, was established to disseminate the concept and install the pumps.

In 2000, the idea won the World Bank's Development Marketplace Award. In 2006, Laura Bush, wife of then US president George W. Bush, announced $16 million in funding from USAID and private foundations, with the goal of raising $45 million more to install 4,000 pumps in Africa by 2010. The singer Jay-Z pitched in with concerts and hosted an MTV documentary. PlayPumps announced plans to extend across Africa and launched a social networking campaign, successfully raising money for "100 Pumps in 100 Days" on World Water Day in 2007 and 2008.

Unfortunately, PlayPumps soon stopped being a smart homegrown idea and became a donor-pleasing, top-down solution that simply did not fit many of the target communities. Flush with funds and with installation targets that had to be met, PlayPump went into many locations, ripped out existing simple hand pumps and replaced them with Play-Pumps that the locals did not want to use and that were difficult to maintain. PlayPumps cost four times as much as traditional pump systems, the mechanism required specialized skills to repair and so could not be fixed with local labor, and spare parts were hard to find and expensive. Advertising revenue that was supposed to fund the maintenance never materialized. The PlayPumps quickly fell into disuse, and some villages that previously had access to water were left without. Critics decried the reliance on child labor, especially as children would have to "play" for twenty-seven hours every day to meet PlayPumps' stated targets of providing 2,500 liters of water.

PlayPump folded in 2010 and gifted its inventory to another water charity. Although the large-scale rollout of the concept is seen as a failure, a number of water charities continue to install a small number of modified versions within strict sustainability guidelines.

Sources: See Aid Watch, http://aidwatchers.com/2010/02/some-ngos-can-adjust-to -failure-the-playpumps-story/; PBS, *Frontline,* http://www.pbs.org/frontlineworld/stories /southernafrica904/video_index.html; Water for People, http://www.waterforpeople.org.

ingly more favorable circumstances than their impoverished neighbors, which may exacerbate ethnic or religious rivalries.

As a result of the scandals and failure, the acronym *NGO* has become fodder for satire and derision. In earlier chapters the terms *GONGO* (*government-organized nongovernment organization*) and *QUANGO* (*quasi-nongovernment organization*) were introduced, and one can add the following, mostly pejorative, versions of the acronyms (for longer lists, see Lewis 2007 and Najam 1996):

- BINGO (business interest) or BONGO (business organized): created by, and often as fronts for, commercial interests.
- BRINGO (briefcase): little more than a briefcase carrying a well-written proposal.
- CONGO (commercial): set up by businesses in order to participate in bids, help win contracts, and reduce taxation.
- DONGO (donor organized): created to implement policies designed by donor organizations.
- FLAMINGO (flashy minded): ostentatious with their equipment, accommodation, and uniforms.
- GINGO (government inspired) or GRINGO (government run and initiated): variations on the GONGO theme of creation by governments or having a too-close relationship with them.
- MANGO (mafia): a criminal organization using an NGO as a front for money laundering or extortion activities.
- MANGO (market advocacy): organized by or in support of businesses or related market-based activities.
- MONGO (my own): small nonprofits that are the personal projects of the founders.
- NGO (next government officials): a reference to the future employment prospects of NGO workers.
- NGO (pronounced as en-j-oy): alludes to special privileges enjoyed by NGO staff.
- PANGO (party affiliated) or PONGO (political): created by political parties.
- RONGO (retired officials): created by former civil servants to take advantage of new outsourcing opportunities (which they may have initiated).

International aid workers have also been lampooned as being either "missionaries" (in the religious sense, but also the secular "saving the world" sense), "mercenaries" (attracted by the high salaries paid to some expatriates and consultants), or "misfits" (those who do not fit in at home so find solace abroad) (Lentfer 2011). Another common characterization is that of the "humanitarian widows and widowers" who spent their idealist youth committed to causes but now stay in the field because they have nowhere else to go. Although some expatriate aid workers work under difficult and dangerous conditions in regions with few services and poor infrastructure, most find that they end up living as local elites. Their accommodations are in the best neighborhoods, they employ domestic help and drivers, and they frequent local upmarket restaurants and entertainment venues. The life of an expatriate aid worker can be both disorienting and seductive, and many find it difficult to readjust to life back home. Two Canadian former aid workers who found that indeed they could not settle back home (self-described as "burnt-out misfits") founded Satori Worldwide, a healing center for aid workers in Bali that offers retreats that seek to restore "balance and resilience" to their lives (Lentfer 2011).

A nascent genre of anthropological interest in the lives, motivations, and personalities of development professionals is developing. The more academic analyses *Adventures in Aidland* (Mosse 2011) and *Inside the Everyday Lives of Development Workers: The Challenges and Futures of Aidland* (Fechter and Hindman 2011) are joined by semisatirical, mass-market chronicles, such as *Emergency Sex and Other Desperate Measures: A True Story from Hell on Earth* (Cain, Postlewait, and Thomson 2004) and *Chasing Chaos: My Decade In and Out of Humanitarian Aid* (Alexander 2013). The website Stuff Expatriate Aid Workers Like (stuffexpataidworkerslike.com) lampoons their foibles, and a Kenyan production company has produced a "mockumentary" series called *The Samaritans*, about the fictional NGO Aid for Aid (aidforaid.org). A common theme of these chronicles is the evolution from naïve idealists to hardened or burnt-out cynics, generally in the decade from their midtwenties graduation from college to their midthirties search for a more stable life back home.

Diaspora Development and Immigrant Hometown Associations

An increasingly key element of the development dynamic is "diaspora development": the contribution of the emigrants and refugees from developing countries. Emigrants send back remittances to their home countries in sums that exceed official development aid (see Table 7.1); they create new transnational businesses and other economic ties between their countries of settlement and origin; and they create intellectual and political capital that can significantly influence the political landscape and policymaking back home (Agunias and Newland 2012; Orozco 2008).

The bulk of immigration-related economic transfers from countries of settlement to countries of origin is in the form of family remittances. At the same time, many collective remittance programs and nonprofit organizations have been organized for and by immigrants. In the countries of settlement, networks of hometown associations (organizations of immigrants from a particular country, region, or town) are established to focus on development back home. A few well-funded flagship associations represent transnational social, political, and business elites, which tend to function under the auspices of the home government. More often, however, the hometown associations are small independent organizations, stymied by the limited economic situation of their working-class immigrant members and their lack of experience in managing such organizations (Orozco 2008).

Even though individual organizations may be small, collectively the hometown associations generate significant transfers of financial and intellectual capital, and they are increasingly being drawn into more mainstream development efforts by both sending and receiving nations (Agunias and Newland 2012; Asian Philanthropy Advisory Network 2012; Orozco 2008). The "3x1" program of the Mexican government augments collective remittances by matching every $1 in funds raised in the United States with $3 in public funds to support public and social infrastructure projects of hometown associations.

The hometown associations are becoming more prominent, but they have limitations within development strategies. Better relations between the associations and home governments can build important links with diaspora communities, but the projects that are chosen by the emigrants do not always respond to the most urgent development needs. Those who emigrate to foreign countries do not necessarily come from the regions most in need or from the poorest strata of their home societies, so remittances may serve to entrench economic stratification. Hometown associations also tend to prefer symbolic or recreational projects, such as refurbishing a plaza or building a sports facility, over social or economic development (Agunias and Newland 2012).

Global Advocacy

Many international nonprofits focus primarily on the expressive and voice aspects of economic justice, human rights, health, and environmental issues. Despite the frequent characterization of advocacy as separate from aid and relief organizations, the evolution of the humanitarian strategies described earlier demonstrate evident overlaps. Campaigns such as debt cancellation and Make Poverty History are directly related to humanitarian aid; the International Campaign to Ban Landmines and human rights monitoring campaigns seek to establish the safety and security conditions essential for development; women's rights organizations often offer education programs and grants to support emerging female leaders and entrepreneurs; and many of the environmental organizations pressing for legislative and regulatory changes also manage local preservation and recovery projects.

Notwithstanding the crossover role of many organizations, a core group of international nonprofits is identified by policymakers and the public as more overtly policy oriented or "political," and a conceptual separation continues between the service-dominant and expressive-dominant organizations. The expressive-dominant organizations are often those most directly associated with playing active roles in global governance and rule making, an activity that was addressed in Chapter 6.

The expressive functions focused on policymaking and politics are generally labeled as advocacy. The advocacy activities of nonprofits working in more global realms are most commonly conceptualized as forming part of transnational advocacy networks or international policy communities operating in new global agoras (Bob 2012; DeMars 2005; Keck and Sikkink 1999). These networks and communities encompass a wide range of institutional and individual policy actors, including government and intergovernmental instrumentalities, business sector lobbies, research institutes, individual experts, and the media. But nonprofits often constitute the core of the network and give institutional form to transnational social movements (see the discussion on epistemic communities later in this chapter). Prominent organizations working in this arena include Amnesty International, Greenpeace, Human Rights Watch, and Transparency International, but thousands of other organizations also focus primarily on advocacy work for both progressive and conservative causes.

Transnational advocacy networks have gone through their own evolution and generations. The epicenter is moving South as more organizations emerge from transitional and developing countries (Lewis 2014; Stares, Deel, and Timms 2012). A professionalization of advocacy work has taken place, with expanded use of collaborative dialogue through institutionalized advisory and consultation structures, but also, and somewhat contradictorily, more confrontational alter- and antiglobalization movements have emerged.

Communications technologies are fostering an emerging digital civil society with new forms of organizing and policy dialogue (Bernholz, Cordelli, and Reich 2013a). Online organizers such as MoveOn.org choose issues and lead advocacy campaigns, whereas other platforms such as Change.org simply offer the opportunity for anyone to create petitions and generate their own campaigns. (Note that while Change.org uses the nonprofit extension for its website, it is a private for-profit built on a business model of revenues through advertising and linking petitioners to nonprofits and businesses that can cultivate them as donors or consumers—see Box 5.6.)

Moreover, the advocacy work of international nonprofits is moving deeper into almost all political arenas. Peace and security has traditionally been seen as "high politics," the exclusive domain of sovereign nations and their intergovernmental organizations, but the key role played by the International Campaign to Ban Landmines in the development and adoption of the Mine Ban Treaty in 1997 (for which it was awarded the Nobel Peace Prize) set new precedents. International nonprofits such as the Centre for Humanitarian Dialogue, the International Crisis Group, and the International Center for Transitional Justice are increasingly working at the center of peace negotiations and postconflict transitions. Significantly, these organizations have a strong presence, on their boards and in executive positions, of former senior legislators and government officials (including prime ministers, foreign affairs ministers, and ambassadors), which reflects both their growing legitimacy and their increasing integration into dialogues formerly the preserve of states.

Advocacy Activities

The term *advocacy* can be defined in the broadest possible sense as the catchall term for the work of international nonprofits seeking to change minds and mobilize the public in order to influence the decisions of institutional elites (Casey and Dalton 2006; GrantCraft 2005; C. J. Jenkins 2006; Salamon 2002b). Although advocacy is primarily seen as seeking to influence governments and intergovernmental organizations, it can also focus on promoting changes in the private sector and monitoring the work of multinational corporations.

Advocacy is a deliberate activity undertaken by an organization to enhance its political capital and capacity to influence other actors in the deliberative process. A number of related terms also define this work, including *activism, advising, campaigning, commenting, consulting, engagement, giving voice, lobbying, negotiating, organizing, political action, providing input*, and *social action*, which are all used to describe attempts to directly influence policymaking. Terms such as *educating, disseminating information, innovating*, and *modeling* are used to describe more indirect attempts to influence. Differences in meanings between these terms are evident, and some countries have specific legal definitions of terms such as *campaigning* and *lobbying*. Nonetheless, considerable variations in their use can be found, and they are often used interchangeably. The term chosen to describe the advocacy work of a nonprofit is more likely to be the result of which label sits comfortably with the participants involved than of any strict academic or legal definition.

An extensive repertoire has developed of possible advocacy strategies and activities that can be utilized to attempt to influence decisionmakers (see Table 7.3).

Table 7.3 Advocacy Activities

Category	Examples of Advocacy Initiatives
Legal	• Initiate or support public interest litigation. • Provide expert evidence for public interest litigation.
Representative, legislative, and administrative	• Encourage national legislators or international representatives to support or oppose propositions, legislation, or regulations (direct lobbying). • Encourage members of the public to express support for, or opposition to, specific propositions, legislation, or regulations through phone calls, letters, e-mails, and so on (indirect or grassroots lobbying). • Encourage people to support or oppose specific candidates/parties for national or international positions (campaigning). • Inform public about candidates' platforms/policies. • Organize forum/discussions about specific candidates or proposals. • Contact elected or appointed officials, staffers, and advisers to promote changes in regulations, guidelines, and other administrative practices.
Research and policy analysis	• Prepare and disseminate research reports, policy briefs, and so on. • Evaluate effectiveness and outcomes of existing programs. • Provide data/access to external researchers.
Coalition building and capacity development	• Create and sustain new organizations. • Create and sustain coalitions of organizations.
Education and mobilization	• Prepare and distribute print or online materials to educate about an issue. • Organize or promote educational, art, cultural, and community activities. • Organize or promote campaigns, including petitions or boycotts, to express concerns to governments, multilateral institutions, and multinational corporations. • Organize or promote demonstrations, rallies, street actions, or civil disobedience. • Become activist shareholders in for-profit corporations.
Communication and media outreach	• Write opinion articles, letters to editors, and press releases. • Post blog entries, tweets, and comments on online forums. • Express opinions during media interviews.
Institutional relations and oversight	• Participate in ongoing formal consultation or advisory processes with governments and multilateral institutions. • Participate in ad hoc consultation or advisory processes such as hearings, high-level meetings, or conferences, or respond to requests for advice. • Prepare submissions for commissions and hearings. • Engage in independent "watchdog" activities to monitor and evaluate activities of governments, multilateral institutions, and multinational corporations.
Service delivery modeling	• Implement and disseminate new models of service delivery.

Many of these activities can be mapped along a continuum from confrontation to cooperation. Demonstrations, boycotts, and critical reports or media coverage put nonprofits in direct conflict with decisionmakers, whereas participation in advisory committees, responding to requests for information, or participating in the development of new service delivery models involve partnership and coproduction with governments, multilateral institutions, and multinational corporations. Decisions about which advocacy strategies to pursue are based on the political and administrative context of the issue, as well as on an organization's own theory of change and its convictions about the best strategies for accessing the levers of power and influencing decisions.

Some nonprofits choose to be "outsiders" (Grant 1995), or "polarizers" (Elkington and Beloe 2010), employing more militant and confrontational activities. Others are "insiders" or "integrators," who choose to collaborate with governments, multilateral organizations, and multinational corporations and to work within the parameters of the roles allotted to them. Organizational leaders make deliberate choices on strategies. The founder of the ecological direct action organization Sea Shepherd Conservation Society split from Greenpeace in disagreement with its commitment to nonviolence and negotiation; the founders of Médecins du Monde split with Médecins Sans Frontières because they felt that by adopting a policy of neutrality, the latter had abandoned its founding principle of *témoignage* (witnessing) through which it publicized atrocities its workers observed.

Any nonprofit that wishes to maintain a more confrontational relationship with governments, multilateral institutions, corporations, and other nonprofits must assume the inherent consequences and costs for the organization. Direct political work by nonprofits is an activity legally restricted in many countries, and in some it is violently repressed. Many nonprofits work on the razor's edge, conducting their relations with multiple layers of stakeholders in a constant to and fro that allows them to maintain a confrontational stance without crossing the line and incurring the wrath of the government or other elites. Collaborative organizations must also calculate potential political costs as they weigh the balance between meaningful influence through their close relationships with other sectors and possible co-optation that would render them all but irrelevant as policy actors (see the Chapter 8 section on nonprofit relations with other sectors).

The dynamics created by the interplay between nonprofits that favor collaboration and those that tend to be more confrontational are open to differing interpretations. Collaborative arrangements can reinforce the marginalization of those that maintain a more combative position. However, the presence of combative radicals can reinforce the negotiating position of the moderate insiders. The "radical flank" threat strengthens the bargaining position of more mainstream organizations (Minkoff 1994), and the "good cop, bad cop" strategy is a time-honored tactic (Lyon 2010).

Even in the most favorable of circumstance, attitudes toward advocacy work vary greatly. Advocacy is generally promoted if seen as strengthening democratic society, giving voice to marginalized communities, providing oversight of public institutions, and promoting innovation in public policy. It is generally rejected if it is considered too openly partisan or as promoting private or narrow interests, particularly if those interests are seen as impinging on the rights of others. Some advocacy activities, particularly lobbying on specific legislation or campaigning for candidates for office, are restricted if using public funds or tax-deductible private donations. The regulations for registration, tax codes, and caveats on public funding generally limit the use of certain funds for advocacy activities.

International nonprofits will embrace advocacy if it is considered to be core to their mission and as helping to gain legitimacy with their constituency. However, they will avoid advocacy if it is seen as compromising funding (public or private) by being too controversial, as biting the hand that feeds, or as violating the conditions of funding or registration in their countries of operation. A minority of nonprofits, such as public interest and issue-based organizations, as well as associations and umbrella groups that represent the sector, focus the bulk of their work on advocacy. Most nonprofits, however, studiously maintain an appearance of being apolitical and prefer not to identify advocacy as a core activity of the organization.

In the United States, for example, where advocacy is a protected activity under the Constitution (but is restricted for nonprofits that receive tax-deductible donations), only 67 of the 18,267 nonprofits (i.e., 0.4 percent) registered under the NTEE Category Q, "international, foreign affairs, and national security," identify advocacy as a primary activity (National Center for Charitable Statistics 2012). At the same time, in other types of research and reporting, considerably more nonprofits identify advocacy as a purpose or activity of the organization. In a nationwide survey by the Johns Hopkins Listening Post Project, 73 percent of nonprofits in all domestic and international categories reported conducting some type of policy advocacy or lobbying activity (Salamon and Geller 2008), although an earlier Johns Hopkins research report found that only 16 percent of nonprofits indicated expenditures on advocacy (Salamon 2002b).

The wide discrepancies between the NTEE self-reports and the various survey results are due to different sampling frames (differences in sizes and types of the organizations surveyed), differences in responses to macrolevel questions (e.g., Is advocacy a purpose or activity of the organization?) and microlevel questions (e.g., Have you contacted a legislator about a policy issue?), and differences in the definitions of advocacy (protests versus participation in advisory committees). Organizations are also reluctant to label their activities as advocacy when reporting to US authorities, as restrictions on advocacy are in place for nonprofits receiving tax-deductible donations.

Other survey and ethnographic research also confirms that whereas only a very small minority of nonprofits are openly political advocacy organizations, a significant majority of nonprofits engage in some form of advocacy either directly or through intermediary organizations, although it tends to be a minor part of their activities (see the research cited in Casey 2004). In democratic countries, advocacy activities may imperil some funding, but in authoritarian countries, advocacy can mean harassment, imprisonment, and physical attacks on staff.

The advocacy strategies chosen by organizations may also be a product of the political and cultural contexts of their countries of origin. Sandra Moog (2009) documented the work of US and German environmental organizations in the Amazon Basin. The US organizations, the product of a larger, wealthier, and more pluralistic nonprofit sector, adopted a wide range of tactics including encouraging the founding of new local organizations and developing strategic alliances with for-profit corporations but, at the same time, tended to create a fragmented dialogue. The German organizations, the product of a smaller, corporatist nonprofit sector, worked more closely with existing local organizations and existing government structures and were more committed to collaborating among themselves to work on joint campaigns.

Measuring the Impact of Advocacy

Defining the desired outcomes and measuring the effectiveness of advocacy can be problematic. The goal of advocacy is to effect change, which can signify anything from profound structural shifts to simply leaving a "residue of reform" (Tarrow 1994). How does one distinguish between short-term success (e.g., having forced a commitment to change) and possible long-term failure (e.g., that commitment is later reneged on or not implemented due to lack of funding)? Even when a court ruling is favorable to nonprofit advocates, no guarantees can be given that the judgment will be properly implemented or that the remedies will have the desired impact. As the old adage goes, one can win many battles but still lose the war. Table 7.4 identifies six possible levels of policy outcomes of advocacy work.

Ultimately, long-term success should be measured in terms of achieving the intended impact and structural changes, but any movement to the next level of outcome can also be an important affirmation of advocacy work. Although the desired end result of advocacy may take years to achieve, significant contributions to the goal of effecting change can be achieved along the way.

Table 7.4 Levels of Advocacy Outcomes

Levels of Outcome	Impact on Policy
Access	The voices of previously excluded stakeholders are now heard.
Agenda	Desired policy change is supported by powerful decisionmakers.
Policy	Desired change is translated into new legislation or regulations.
Output	New policy is implemented as proposed.
Impact	New policy has intended consequence.
Structural	The policy change is now widely accepted as the new norm.

Source: See Burstein, Einwohner, and Hollander 1995.

Even when one can identify what has been achieved, evaluating how it was achieved can be difficult. William DeMars (2005) called nonprofits the "wild cards" of transnational advocacy networks and stated that their influence is greater than either their boosters or their detractors claim, as much through inadvertent consequences as anything else. But to establish the causality between advocacy by nonprofits and policy outcomes, one must attempt to peer inside a "black box" of power relationships and of legislative and administrative decisionmaking processes. The difficulty of understanding the motivations of those involved in decisionmaking, combined with a tendency of all actors to overstate their role, makes unequivocally evaluating the outcomes and impact of nonprofit advocacy almost impossible.

One of the most emblematic international advocacy cases is the Brent Spar incident, which was widely acknowledged as a "victory" for Greenpeace and a watershed moment for environmental activism (G. Jordan 2001), but it was also mired in controversy about the nature and impact of the outcome (see Box 7.11).

Despite the challenges of judging the effectiveness of advocacy, a range of monitoring and evaluation techniques have been developed based on logical frameworks, theory of change, and stakeholder analysis (see, for example, Bolder Advocacy 2014 and Wilson-Grau and Britt 2013). These techniques adapt those used in other areas of policy and social change research to measure key indicators of success in terms of the processes, outputs, and outcomes of advocacy (see the discussion on accountability in Chapter 8).

Advocacy Networks

International nonprofit organizations operate within transnational advocacy networks as policy entrepreneurs, as catalysts for change, and as evaluators and monitors of other actors. A number of recent texts have provided in-depth case studies of progressive networks working on women's rights, human rights, foreign aid, urban development, security, and environment (Ahmed and Potter 2006; DeMars 2005; Keck and Sikkink 1999; Lang

Box 7.11 Brent Spar

Brent Spar, or Brent E, was a loading platform for oil storage tankers in the North Sea operated by the UK division of Shell. With the completion of a new pipeline, it was considered to be obsolete, and Shell received approval from the British government to dump it in the deep Atlantic some 200 miles west of Scotland, at a depth of around two miles. Greenpeace organized a worldwide, high-profile media campaign against that plan, and its activists occupied the Brent Spar for more than three weeks. In the face of public and political opposition, including a widespread boycott, Shell abandoned its plans to dispose of the Brent Spar at sea (but continued to stand by its claim that this option was the safest, both from an environmental and an industrial health and safety perspective).

Despite achieving its goals, Greenpeace saw its reputation suffer during the campaign, when it had to acknowledge that its assessment of the oil remaining in Brent Spar's storage tanks had been grossly overestimated. Furthermore, during the dismantling of the Brent Spar, colonies of an endangered cold-water coral, *Lophelia pertusa,* were found growing on the legs of the platform. At the time, this phenomenon was considered unusual, although later studies indicated that such growths were a common occurrence, with thirteen of fourteen North Sea oil rigs examined having colonies of the coral. The authors of the original work suggested that it may have been better to leave the lower parts of such structures in place—a suggestion opposed by Greenpeace, which compared such a move to dumping a car in a forest, noting that moss would likely grow on it, and a bird may even nest in it, but that was not a justification for filling forests with disused cars.

2013), as well as on conservative networks pushing back against gun control and the extension of gay rights (Bob 2012). But given the size and fluidity of such networks, they present a considerable challenge to document and analyze. A small subset of more prominent players appears in case study narratives, but the full extent of any particular network and the relative power and influence of the various actors are all but impossible to assess. Sally Stares, Sean Deel, and Jill Timms (2012) reviewed the various attempts at such network analysis and concluded that, despite some strong efforts at mapping the landscape, understanding of exactly how they operate is still bordering on the unknown.

Some international advocacy nonprofits are so prominent in their network that they appear to own their issue. Amnesty International dominates the discourse on "prisoners of conscience," a term coined by its founder, Peter Benenson, in the early 1960s. At the same time, Amnesty International is embedded in an extensive policy network of human rights organizations working to assist those persecuted because of their political views, race, or religion. Such organizations include other international nonprofit advocacy groups that work globally (e.g., Freedom Now), others that focus on a single country (e.g., US Campaign for Burma) or a single profession (e.g., Reporters Sans Frontières), and the many national nonprofits that monitor human rights in their own countries. The more overtly expressive advocacy organizations collaborate with others that take a more service orientation, including the Prisoners of Conscience Appeal Fund, an organization founded by Amnesty as its relief arm to provide monetary support to prisoners and their families during their ordeal and rehabilitation. The policy network also includes a broad range of other actors, including the human rights agencies of national governments and multilateral institutions as well as organizational and individual allies in academia, the arts, media, labor movements, and judiciaries.

Global Communities

The literature on international nonprofits tends to focus primarily on the work of high-profile, hot-button humanitarian aid and advocacy organizations. However, the genus international nonprofits also includes thousands of other organizations that focus on professional, intellectual, educational, cultural, and sporting exchanges (Iriye 2002). They construct world cultures by promoting a global, cosmopolitan imagining of their field and creating international communities of interest (Boli and Thomas 1999). These world cultures may cover common interests as esoteric as folk arts or as popular as global sports. The International Quilt Association and the football federation FIFA, despite the huge gulf between them in terms of size and global reach, are both international nonprofits.

Numerically, these other less visible organizations constitute the bulk of the international nonprofits, but they receive less attention, primarily because of the normative and heuristic content of the concept nonprofit. The difference in logics between organizations that strive to improve the conditions of others (public-serving organizations) and those that are considered as more self-serving (member-serving organizations) is a common theme in classifications of nonprofits. In the international realm the focus is squarely on the former, as though the latter in some way violates the spirit of the sector. The nonprofits that promote global communities, however, often have the specific intention of benefiting members as well. Their membership may include civil servants (e.g., the various international associations of police officers), for-profit employees (e.g., trade associations such as the International Window Film Association—see Box 6.2), government agencies (e.g., the International Council of Museums—see Box 6.1), or even governments themselves (e.g., the Commonwealth Secretariat, the association of countries that are part of the British Commonwealth).

These organizations adopt nonprofit legal identities and deliberately identify themselves and their operations using nonprofit code words such as *nongovernmental*, *civil society*, and *voluntary*. Equally importantly, the lines between member serving and public serving are more blurred than some commentators suggest. The logics of the International Olympic Committee (IOC) may include, as its many critics contend, self-serving delegates making high-stakes deals that funnel even more money to already-wealthy athletic elites. However, the IOC also claims its place in the pantheon of nonprofit organizations working, in its own words, "to create a better world through sport" and to promote the Olympic values of friendship, nondiscrimination, and global citizenship. In the introduction to their study of the football federation FIFA, John Sugden and Alan Tomlinson (1998) had no qualms about conceptually equating that organization to Greenpeace, the Council for a Parliament of the World Religions, and the International Sociology Association. Similarly, Steven Charnovitz (1997) specifically identified the International Association of Athletics Federations as an NGO and noted that it has a broader membership than most intergovernmental organizations.

Similarly, most international professional and business organizations combine both the private interests of members and their public interests in advocacy. They may have been established primarily to respond to members' interest in international networking, disseminating good practice, coordination of research, or protecting a brand, but their activities often also include offering expertise to transnational advocacy networks and directly lobbying to push causes. The activities of the International Association of Youth and Family Judges and Magistrates are examples of the multiple logics of many such organizations (see Box 7.12).

These organizations are active globalizers and avowedly cosmopolitan, with the specific goal of creating cross-border dialogues in their field. Although many are part of the global governance and advocacy processes described earlier, they also have a broader role in facilitating intellectual exchanges and creating global mind-sets. The Global Civics Academy, a project established in 2013 by the US Brookings Institution and the German foundation Stiftung Mercator, purposely seeks to educate the public on the dynamics of increasing global interdependences, but most internationally oriented nonprofits regard their cross-border reach as simply a logical consequence of their interest in fostering broader dialogues about their work. The following sections highlight the work of three important subgroups of the nonprofits that nurture global communities.

Box 7.12 The International Association of Youth and Family Judges and Magistrates

The International Association of Youth and Family Judges and Magistrates was founded in 1928 and registered in Brussels, Belgium. An NGO with consultative status with the United Nations and the Council of Europe, it operates with the motto "Supporting youth and family judges and magistrates in maintaining the rule of law." The objectives of the association are:

1. To establish links among judges, magistrates, and specialists all over the world who are attached to judicial authority concerned with the protection of youth or with the family.
2. To study all problems raised by the functioning of judicial authorities and organizations for the protection of youth and the family.
3. To ensure the continuance of the national and international principles governing those authorities and to make them more widely known.
4. To examine legislation designed for the protection of youth and the family and the various systems existing for the protection of the youth at risk with a view to improving such systems both nationally and internationally.
5. To promote the awareness and application of children's rights.
6. To assist collaboration between nations and competent authorities with regard to foreign minors and their families.
7. To encourage research into the causes of the criminal behavior or maladjustment of youth, to combat their effects, and to seek a permanent prevention and rehabilitation program, and to concern itself with the moral and material improvement of youth's destiny and, in particular, with the future of children and young people at risk.
8. To collaborate with international associations concerned with the protection of youth and with the family.

Source: The International Association of Youth and Family Judges and Magistrates, http://www.aimjf.org/en/about/?about-aims.

Sports Associations

Organized sports and their formal institutions are pioneers of both modern voluntary nonprofit activity and globalization dynamics. The origins of the international federations that regulate the major sports worldwide largely coincided with the late nineteenth-century wave of globalization and international institution building. The transformation from ad hoc local games to organized sports with national and international associations occurred as industrialization brought increased leisure time and was achieved primarily through nonprofit structures and philanthropic means.

Many of the now most popular international sports were first systematically organized in Britain and were transported around the world by the British colonialists, military, and migrants. In 1863, formal rules and an association for football (soccer) were established in London, and the first official international match was played in 1872 between England and Scotland. Because the new football rules did not allow carrying the ball, clubs that played the rugby style of the precursor games withdrew from the original meeting and instead in 1871 formed the Rugby Football Union.

The modern Olympic movement was established at a congress in Paris in 1894, attended by fifty-eight French delegates representing twenty-four sports organizations and another twenty delegates from Belgium, Great Britain, Greece, Italy, Russia, Spain, Sweden, and the United States. The first modern games were held in 1896 in Athens, largely funded through a trust created by Evangelos Zappas, a wealthy Greek-Romanian philanthropist. The resurgence of the Olympics was soon followed by the formation of a broad range of international sports federations:

- Union Cycliste Internationale (International Cycling Union), founded in 1900 in Paris, current headquarters in Switzerland.
- Fédération Internationale de Football Association (FIFA, International Football Federation), founded in 1904 in Paris, current headquarters in Switzerland.
- Fédération Internationale de Natation (International Swimming Federation), founded in 1908 in London, current headquarters in Switzerland.
- International Association of Athletics Federations, founded in 1912 in Stockholm, current headquarters in Monaco.
- International Tennis Federation, founded as the International Lawn Tennis Federation in 1913 in Paris, current headquarters in England.

All these organizations reflect the historic Northern bias of the international nonprofit sector. The founding meetings were held in Europe, and almost all the delegates were from European and US sports associations. Although now national federations and regional structures have been developed for each of the sports covering all continents, the international headquarters generally remain in Europe. Switzerland hosts the largest number of headquarters because of its favorable legal environment, political neutrality, and ease of access to the other international organizations clustered there.

Although the superstars of the major sports earn stratospheric salaries, their governing bodies—international, national, and local—generally operate as nonprofits. In democratic countries, they are usually independent organizations, whereas in authoritarian countries they fall under the more direct control of the regime. High-profile professional teams generally function as private for-profit businesses, but some are still technically nonprofit organizations. These include FC Barcelona in Spain, governed by its members who vote for the club president, and the Green Bay Packers in the United States, which operates as a community-owned nonprofit organization. Almost all teams below the professional tier operate as nonprofits, and the countless formal and informal sporting clubs around the world are often key components of local civic and charitable life.

Organized sport replicates many of the pathologies of modern societies: it is dominated by wealthy elites who seek to exploit it for their commercial purposes, it is tainted by corruption and illegal activities, and it can reinforce exclusionary tribalism and male domination (Goldblatt 2007). At the same time, sport is also utilized by governments and nonprofits as a tool of policies and programs to promote cross-cultural understanding and global citizenship, and it is a key strategy in providing integration and rehabilitation activities for groups such as the disabled and returned veterans. David Goldblatt (2007) documented these contradictions in the context of global football, which juxtaposes its exploitative and exclusionary dimensions with a commitment to development and community building. Many international development programs have football-related components, and numerous football tournaments are held to promote global harmony, including the Homeless World Cup, the Anti-Racist World Cup, and the Unrepresented Nations and Peoples Organization Football Cup.

Sport is becoming increasingly integrated into international aid and development programs (Levermore and Beacom 2009; Tiessen 2011). International sports corporations, particularly the global sportswear and footwear brands, are collaborating with the outreach efforts of international sports federations, multilateral organizations, and a new crop of sport-based nonprofits on issues such as health promotion, gender equity, social integration, peace building, disaster relief, economic development, and social mobilization.

Nonprofit Epistemic Communities

Epistemic communities are networks of individuals who share knowledge based on their common interests, understandings, or backgrounds. In international relations theory, the label *epistemic community* is applied primarily to cross-sectoral networks of professionals with defined policy objectives (Haas 1992; Iriye 2002). It overlaps with related concepts such as "Track II" international relations (i.e., policy and program negotiations between civil servants and professionals in different countries), transnational advocacy networks, and policy communities.

The term *epistemic communities* is used here in a somewhat narrower sense to refer to strictly nongovernmental, nonprofit networks, but also in a broader sense to refer to any nonprofit common interest network, not just those deemed to be professional or policy related. This broad definition encompasses organizations as diverse as academic, professional, and business associations, think tanks, hobby groups, alumni associations, international artistic exchanges, and just about any organization that gives itself the name or descriptor "The International Association of" or its cognates. Epistemic communities include the International Council of Museums (see Box 6.1), the International Window Film Association (see Box 6.2), the International Association of Youth and Family Judges and Magistrates (see Box 7.12), and Urban Sketchers (see Box 7.13).

Box 7.13 Urban Sketchers

Urban Sketchers describes itself as a "nonprofit organization dedicated to raising the artistic, storytelling, and educational value of location drawing, promoting its practice and connecting people around the world who draw on location where they live and travel." It runs a blog site featuring the work of 100 invited artists in more than thirty countries around the world and has a broader online community of artists through its Flickr and Facebook pages. Volunteers also manage more than thirty regional blogs in cities and countries around the world, and many of those also have their own sister Flickr groups and Facebook pages to help sketchers showcase their work and connect with each other.

Urban Sketchers was created by Seattle-based, Spanish-born illustrator and journalist Gabriel Campanario, a staff artist and blogger at the *Seattle Times*. After seeing an increasing number of people sharing their location drawings in the blogosphere, Campanario started a Flickr group (an online photo sharing site) in November 2007 as a showcase of urban sketches. A year later, he decided to expand the Flickr initiative with a by-invitation group blog where correspondents would commit to posting on a regular basis and also sharing the stories behind the sketches. Campanario and other blog correspondents established Urban Sketchers as a nonprofit organization to help better serve the rapidly growing online community by organizing educational workshops and raising funds for grants and scholarships.

Urban Sketchers became a US 501(c)(3) tax-exempt organization in 2011. It currently has some 1,100 member sketchers from all around the globe and is governed by a twenty-seven-member board and advisory group with members from Canada, the Dominican Republic, Germany, Hong Kong, Italy, Portugal, Sweden, Singapore, and the United States. It organizes an annual International Urban Sketching Symposium. The 2010 symposium was held in Portland, Oregon, in the United States, the 2011 symposium in Lisbon, Portugal, and the 2012 symposium in Santo Domingo, Dominican Republic.

Source: See Urban Sketchers, http://www.urbansketchers.org.

An Internet search using the keywords *international association of* reveals the many thousands of such English-language associations, formal and informal, around the world. Clicking through to the "Contact Us" pages of a random selection also demonstrates that the United States is the home of the majority of such organizations, particularly those in the commercial and hobby fields. The size of the US population, its culture of civic engagement and philanthropy, the relative wealth of US-based anchors, and the relatively low transaction costs of creating and maintaining nonprofits in the United States, all combine to ensure that the United States dominates as the hub of such organizations (Box 7.13).

Youth Exchange Programs and Voluntourism

Academic scholarships, semesters abroad, and youth exchanges through service clubs such as the Rotary have a long history, but such programs have increased significantly since the 1990s and have been expanded through new international volunteering and temporary work programs. An earlier generation of young people from industrialized countries may have spent time backpacking around the world or working on an Israeli kibbutz, but the current generation also participates in the growing field of nonprofit international youth exchanges and volunteering programs.

Historic organizations such as the International Association for the Exchange of Students for Technical Experience founded in 1948 in London as an association for the exchange of work experiences for technical students within Europe has expanded to include eighty countries across the world, and a new generation of programs provides work experiences not necessarily directly related to education, including jobs such as camp counselors and au pairs and a range of internships in private companies. Although most of the organizations provide meaningful cultural exchanges, abuses are also found (see Box 7.14).

As the market for volunteering has grown, such programs have seen significant commodification, and they now even have their own guidebook, *Lonely Planet Volunteer: A Traveller's Guide to Making a Difference Around the World* (Lonely Planet 2010). Participants can pay significant fees to nonprofit or for-profit brokers to volunteer overseas in environmental programs, construction brigades, and pastoral programs in schools, orphanages, and hospitals. The placements are usually short term, lasting only a few days or weeks. The experience is often described by the volunteers themselves as "life changing," and for many nonprofits, both in sending countries of the North and in the destinations in the South, this sort of voluntourism can be a significant source of income. However, controversy has arisen about their impact, particularly when the volunteering involves unskilled labor and contact with children (L. M. Richter and Norman 2010;

Box 7.14 Exchange Students Picket Factory

A group of 200 international exchange students waving placards and chanting union slogans got the attention of the US State Department when the students walked out of the US confectionary factory where they had been sent for work experience. The sponsor for the protesting students had placed nearly 400 foreigners from eighteen countries (many of them graduate students in medicine, engineering, and economics) into physically arduous jobs at the factory. The protests exposed serious lapses by some of the almost seventy nonprofit sponsors contracted by the State Department to organize the students' trips to the United States and find jobs and housing for them.

The sponsor in this case was a nonprofit educational and cultural exchange organization, CETUSA, based in California with an annual income of $7 million. It is the US nonprofit subsidiary of an international for-profit labor management and language education corporation, CET Management Group, that has offices and schools in Great Britain, Canada, and Germany. As a result of an investigation into the situation at the confectionary factory, the sponsor was banned from participating in the State Department contracted program for at least two years.

Source: See *New York Times* (Online), http://www.nytimes.com/2012/02/02/us /company-firm-banned-in-effort-to-protect-foreign-students.html.

Wearing and McGehee 2013). The most common criticisms are that educated Northerners perform work that they know little about, such as construction, when the organization could instead have provided employment to local tradesmen and unskilled laborers. When the activities involve children, particularly those in orphanages and hospitals, the revolving door of volunteer teachers or caregivers can have a negative emotional impact and exacerbate children's sense of abandonment. Critics of voluntourism claim that potential participants would make a better contribution to the organizations by simply donating the cost of their journey.

Accusations have also been made that in order to generate donations from short-term volunteers and "poverty tourists," false institutions are created and existing institutions are deliberately kept squalid, and children are exploited as exhibitions for gawking tourists. Critics point to the contradiction that Northerners often treat orphanages or slums in developing countries as tourist attractions but would be horrified if similar places in their home countries were exploited so cavalierly (L. M. Richter and Norman 2010). The Lonely Planet (2010) guidebook dedicates a short section to ethical volunteering—recommending, for example, that potential volunteers ask themselves if and how their presence will help the host community—and refers readers to a code of conduct developed by the Irish Association of Development Workers (see the section on accountability in Chapter 8 for more discussion of codes of conduct).

8

Stewarding International Nonprofits

To create sustainable and resilient international nonprofits, executives must successfully negotiate the diverse languages, cultures, political-economic environments, and organizational norms of the countries in which they operate. In this chapter, the concept of stewardship is used to emphasize the caretaking dimensions of international nonprofits. Effective stewardship seeks to harmonize seven interrelated dimensions of leadership, management, and governance (see Figure 8.1).

Figure 8.1 Interrelated Dimensions of NGO Stewardship

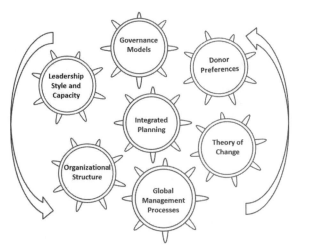

Source: See Crowley and Ryan 2013, 190.

Cristina Balboa (2014) separated stewardship capacities into three categories—political, administrative, and technical—and identified how they differ in the global, domestic, and local spheres of influence. The resultant nine-cell table maps the broad range of possible knowledge areas in which nonprofits must develop their capacities in order to steward international projects (see Table 8.1). Organizations must work effectively in all three spheres and build productive bridges between them.

The stewardship of international nonprofits is evolving through similar reform processes that have driven the changes in national sectors. Paul

Table 8.1 Sphere-Specific Capacities for International Nonprofits

Global	National	Local
Political		
• Fund-raising from multilaterals, bilaterals, foundations. • International and inter-governmental legal processes. • Anticorruption and ethical norms. • International treaties and conventions. • Foreign aid processes. • UN languages. • Global media networks.	• National political actors and coalitions. • National political and policy culture. • National languages. • National history of interactions with international NGOs. • National bureaucratic requirements (e.g., work permits, driver's licenses).	• Local views on partnership, accountability, leadership, and legitimacy. • Partnerships with local organizations. • Local conflict resolution processes. • Local governance and tenure systems (chiefdoms, clans, etc.). • Communication processes. • Local languages.
Administrative		
• Vision, mission, and strategy of global organizations. • Reporting requirements and processes. • Contractual norms. • Global accounting norms and laws. • Leadership and governance approaches.	• National nonprofit laws and regulations. • National accounting and tax laws.	• View of obligation/contracts. • Capacity building and adaptation for change. • Audience analysis to create appropriate reporting requirements. • Local approaches to work.
Technical		
• Field-specific knowledge base. • International policy processes. • Global norms of technical practice.	• Legal frameworks, national biodiversity plans. • National information and data networks.	• Local resource status and use. • Local monitoring for data. • Cultural ideas about nature, philanthropy, leadership, and business practices.

Source: See Balboa 2014.

Light (2000) talked of tides of reform that involved bringing more focus on the science of management, focusing on the vision and mission, reducing waste by increasing efficiency and effectiveness, and battling fraud. Such reforms are almost invariably couched in terms of bringing more businesslike practices into international organizations, echoing the shifts to corporatization and managerialism in domestic nonprofit sectors (Roberts, Jones, and Fröhling 2005).

Skeptics point out the perils of some of these reforms, as tension continues within the sector between a more business-based, hierarchical approach to stewardship and a collectivist, nonhierarchical, mission-driven approach. As Michael Edwards (2010a) noted,

> there were organizations that couldn't get support because their work didn't generate a "social return on investment", community groups forced to compete with each other for resources instead of collaborating in common cause ... and activists who felt passed over by a new generation of Samaritans who stopped to calculate how much they would make before deciding to help. (vii)

Despite any pushback against the introduction of business values, the shift to professionalization and corporatization has had a major impact in strengthening the stewardship of international nonprofits. However, large swathes of the sector are still characterized as "unprofessional," and many commentators frame the choice facing organizations as either remaining inept amateurs or becoming uncaring bureaucracies. Others analyze such dynamics from the organizational life cycle perspective, focusing on the inevitable isomorphism and standardization that emerge as organizations grow, and the concomitant struggle against the possible loss of the original core values that were the impetus for the creation of the organization in the first place (Anheier 2014; DiMaggio and Powell 1983).

Historically, religious faith has been a primary driver for the creation of international nonprofits, and it continues to be a major factor in humanitarian organizations (R. James 2010). At the same time, religion is now also accompanied by more secular variants of faith, expressed most often as the founders' "calling" or "commitment." The organizational mythmaking and zeal created by such a mission-driven focus often cloud many of the other organizational imperatives and can sustain international nonprofits through crises that might be the death knell of other organizations. Faith is a value in itself, but equally importantly it can also directly translate into an income flow: a committed base of donors, or even a single large donor, wedded to the cause provides guaranteed resources for an organization and may make the organization resilient and sustainable even in the face of evidence about its limited impact. A case study currently used in many graduate school nonprofit management programs is based on the organizational and existential crisis in the early 1990s of a midsized international nonprofit that sought to combat world hunger. In analyzing what appears to be a significant crisis for the organization, most students predict a significant organizational restructuring and a radical rethinking of its mission and activities or perhaps even its dissolution or merger. Students are surprised to find that twenty years later the structure, mission, and activities of the organization have continued much the same and that it has grown three-fold, nurtured by the network of churches that sponsors it.

How-to manuals on the stewardship of international nonprofits are becoming increasingly available (see, for example, Crowley and Ryan 2013; Fowler and Malunga 2010; Lewis 2007; Shah 2012), and training and resources are offered by many colleges, industry associations, multilateral organizations, and private and nonprofit technical assistance and consulting companies (see Box 8.1).

Box 8.1 Online Resources

Numerous organizations offer online resources on the stewardship of international nonprofits.
• The NGO Management Association is a Swiss consulting organization run by former international aid workers. It also has a training academy, the NGO Management School (http://ngomanager.org/).
• Mango is a UK consulting nonprofit group (http://www.mango.org.uk).
• Network Learning is a Dutch resource site (http://www.networklearning.org/).
• The Hauser Institute for Civil Society at Harvard University has an extensive publications library (http://www.hks.harvard.edu/centers/hauser/publications).
• People in Aid is an international membership-based association of aid and development NGOs that provides training and resources, as well as the Quality Mark certification program (http://www.peopleinaid.org/).

In this chapter, I do not attempt to cover the same ground as these practice manuals. Instead, I focus on a few key aspects of stewardship, particularly those that distinguish domestic leadership and management from that at the international level. This question of how organizational concepts and challenges translate in the shift from the national to the international arenas is the constant backdrop to the discussion on the stewardship of international nonprofits.

Cosmopolitan Leadership

For nonprofit sector leaders, the increasingly international dimensions of their work require a much greater understanding of global contexts and international collaborative structures, as well as advanced skills in working in a range of cultural and linguistic settings. Successful international nonprofits are built on the basis of the cosmopolitan leadership of executives who can work both locally and globally (Kanter 2006), effectively translating concepts from one culture to another and integrating enterprises across borders. The use of the descriptor *cosmopolitan* shifts the focus from the institutional dimensions of international work to the mind-set needed to work in more global realms.

Opposing discourses about leadership are debated in the international arena. One perspective is that "leadership is leadership" and that expansion into the international arena is simply an extension of the same challenges facing all organizations as they grow, become more complex, and diversify. Conversely, others argue that the transnational challenges in the international arena are unique and require a distinctive form and style of global, cosmopolitan leadership (Kanter 2006; Osland 2008). Both perspectives tend to focus on nonprofits and their leaders in the global North, the industrialized democracies that dominate the international sector. These leadership models are primarily based on the individualistic, but increasingly nonhierarchical, approach promoted as the most desirable and effective in contemporary Northern leadership literature and education (although not always practiced in organizations!).

Parallel to this debate over whether leadership in international arenas is a unique realm, research on leadership styles across countries either emphasizes cultural differences or seeks to minimize them. Building on work such as Geert Hofstede's (2001) analysis of cultural differences in the conceptualization of individualism, power distance, uncertainty avoidance, and masculinity, many writers document national variations in interpersonal relations and analyze the impact on the leaders and the led. However, other authors, although accepting that cultural differences have some impact, maintain that certain leadership practices or competencies are universal. James Kouzes and Barry Posner (2007) noted that appreciating differences in how people behave as a result of their cultural differences can be key to effective organizational relations, but that these differences do not necessarily have more impact than those resulting from differences in age, gender, and background. Although Kouzes and Posner acknowledged the need to understand and be sensitive to these differences, they identified five practices of exemplary leaders—model the way, inspire a shared vision, challenge the process, enable others to act, and encourage the heart—which they claim will be effective in different national settings (Kouzes and Posner 2007; Posner 2011). Again, a Northern bias is evident, and one can question how relevant this research is to countries where leadership of nonprofits is based more on the charismatic leadership of the founding "Great Man" or "Big Man" (they are usually men, although increasingly there may be a "Great Woman"), on family dynasties, or on traditional kinship and community collective structures.

Notwithstanding such debates, the reality appears to be that many current leaders in the nonprofit sector may not have the preparation, experience, or positive orientation needed for their new international responsibilities. To work effectively across borders, nonprofit leaders must successfully negotiate the cultural, economic, and political environment and the organizational norms of the countries in which they operate and of their institutional partners. The current lacunas include a lack of knowledge about the different legal systems and institutional support structures for nonprofits in other countries and in the global arena, a lack of sensitivity to the cultural implications of working in other countries and with foreign colleagues, and a lack of language skills.

Leadership theories focus variously on the traits or styles of leaders, on the contingencies of applying leadership approaches, and on the transformative orientation of leaders. At the same time, much of the contemporary literature focuses primarily on the skills, knowledge, and attributes of effective leaders, summarized as their "capabilities" or "competencies" (Kouzes and Posner 2007; Lombardo and Eichinger 2001).

Many of the same competencies and strategies used to address diversity at the domestic level can also be part of building organizational capacity to work at an international level. Nonprofits can build on approaches such as diversity management, cultural competence, and productive diversity, which are already being used in the domestic context, to also strengthen competencies for working in broader cross-cultural and international contexts. A range of strategic managerial processes are available to understand, value, and work with diversity in order to respond more productively to operational challenges. Training materials to help build such organizational capacities are widely available at a domestic level (see, for example, the Denver Foundation 2010), but now the challenge is to translate them into a global mindset (Turley 2010).

The need for new skills, and the commitment to developing them, start at the top of agencies. Marshall Goldsmith and Cathy Walt (1999) maintained that all future leaders will need to think globally, appreciate cultural diversity, and build partnerships across cultural divides. However, these skills are needed not only by senior leadership; staff at all levels will need to develop a cosmopolitan approach to international work, building on competencies such as the following:

- Openness: Enjoy working internationally and being exposed to ideas and approaches with which they are unfamiliar; are not threatened by, or intolerant of, working practices that conflict with their own sense of best practice; and can question assumptions and modify stereotypes about how people from different cultures operate.
- Cultural knowledge: Take time to learn about unfamiliar cultures; are motivated to learn and use foreign languages, or to draw on key expressions and words from other languages, to build trust and show respect; and are sensitive to how their own patterns of communication and behavior are interpreted and choose verbal and nonverbal behaviors that are comfortable for international counterparts.
- Emotional strength: Can deal with change and high levels of pressure even in unfamiliar situations and deal effectively with the stress from culture shock.
- Transparency: Can build and maintain trust in international contexts by openly indicating intentions and putting needs into a clear and explicit context.
- Synergy: Are sensitive to the need for a careful and systematic approach to facilitating group- and teamwork to ensure that different cultural perspectives are used in the problem-solving process (World-Work Ltd 2010).

Cultural knowledge will need to include both the "big things" and "small things" (Goldsmith and Walt 1999), so education and training programs focusing on building cosmopolitan leadership must help participants navigate the myriad differences that they will encounter in international work and reduce the chance of making a cultural faux pas. Cultural knowledge includes self-awareness about one's own cultural influences as well as an understanding of the cultures of foreign colleagues and the local populations that staff will work with on international collaborations. At the same time, a need is present to develop a critical approach to understanding that the behavior and beliefs of individuals within each culture vary considerably and that cultural norms are transforming as a result of globalization, migration, and the influence of diasporas on home countries.

Staff who regularly work on international projects will undoubtedly become more adept at forming strong multinational teams by addressing the friction that often arises because of differences in cultural expectations and behaviors (Adler 2008). These differences can include emphasizing ritual and process, not just outcomes. Some cultures put considerable emphasis on formal rituals and hierarchies, as well as on showing respect for those of higher rank. The notion of "let's break some rules to get the job done" may be anathema to team members who have an interest in preserving status and "keeping face." Another difference is the use of socializing as a basis for group bonding. Some cultures expect that participants in work teams will also spend considerable time socializing, which may be in places such as bars that are uncomfortable or unacceptable for some team members. Working with different notions of time and deadlines can cause friction. Some cultures use, with a mixture of both pride and despair, variations on the expression "we operate on 'island time'" to explain why schedules, timetables, and punctuality are not always sacrosanct. And, finally, giving answers that reflect politeness instead of accuracy is a cultural norm for some people. In some cultures, giving a positive answer is considered more polite than saying, "I don't know," or providing a contradictory alternative. The answer to the question "Will it be ready next week?" may be always "yes," even if it will not be.

Although such differences can make collaborations challenging for novices, those with international experience can usually negotiate work dynamics acceptable to the whole team. However, international projects must ultimately address more profound and thorny cultural issues, such as the role of women, the use of child labor, and loyalty to an ethnic group or clan. Unless these issues are handled with skill and sensitivity, they can have serious consequences for any international project. If the collaboration involves the implementation of programs in developing countries, volatile politics, poor infrastructure, and a scarcity of skilled labor may present themselves as issues. And when the project involves emergency aid and relief, organizations by definition will be operating in areas of deprivation and chaos, where they are likely to be faced with corruption and heightened rent seeking. They must ensure the safety of their local and expatriate staff and deal with the difficult ethical dilemmas and trade-offs of working with belligerent factions.

Also important are crucial cross-cultural communication skills, which are based partly on cultural awareness but also on the more prosaic skills of knowing how to communicate effectively with people who do not speak your own language fluently. Anyone who has been brought up monolingual with only limited exposure to other languages may have difficulty in communicating across languages. Monolingual English speakers from industrialized countries have the particular reputation of practicing linguistic imperialism and assuming that everyone should speak English fluently. Modifying speaking style and using "international English" or "Euringlish" (see Box 8.2) to facilitate communication, as well as learning to work effectively with interpreters and translators, are essential skills for working in international domains (Adler 2008).

Governance and Management

The "demos" of international nonprofits is particularly hard to define, given the large distances, literal and conceptual, between their members, donors, recipients, and the people they claim to represent. Whether they are work-

---

Box 8.2 Euringlish

When collaborating in Europe, "Euringlish" tends to be used as the working language. It sounds like English, but it isn't. The possible confusion between English and Euringlish is a major risk factor and occasionally a source of frustration in working together. Three main risks are involved in collaborations among people with different mother tongues and with the use of Euringlish: first is that people are hesitant to speak up because they lack confidence in their English; second is that people actually do not understand what is said because their English is not good enough or they do not know the words that are being used; and third, people make up words—creating confusion and talking nonsense. Both native English speakers and nonnative speakers have a role to play. Key steps in managing the issue and reducing confusion are to be aware of these risks, to avoid jargon and fancy words when speaking, and to ask for explanations or clarification if what is being said is not clear.

Source: See GrantCraft Blog, http://www.grantcraft.org/blog/euringlish-fried-air-and-confusion.

---

ing in direct service, advocacy, professional exchanges, or humanitarian aid, international nonprofits seek to develop effective stewardship processes that can overcome the challenges of working on a global scale and accommodate the profound cultural differences and power imbalances they invariably face (Anheier and Themudo 2004).

Incorporation

International nonprofits generally first incorporate in the home country of the founders or the network's lead member. Some subsequently move to a more favorable jurisdiction or incorporate in more than one jurisdiction. Many international nonprofits choose Holland as the place to establish their legal headquarters because of its particularly favorable corporate laws and tax environment. Greenpeace was founded in Canada but now bases its international secretariat in Amsterdam, where it is formally registered as Stichting Greenpeace Council (see also Box 6.4 for Oxfam).

Wherever they incorporate, international nonprofits must operate within the regulatory environment and organizational ecologies of that country (Bloodgood, Tremblay-Boire, and Prakash 2014; Stroup 2008, 2012). With the increasing globalization of the marketplace for nonprofits and the new logistical possibilities offered by communications technologies, some organizations are moving headquarters to the South in an attempt to promote a better North-South equilibrium and help overcome the taints of imperialism and colonialism. ActionAid and CIVICUS have both recently moved their world secretariats to South Africa, one of the countries emerging as the new centers of international nonprofit work. Other organizations, although not moving headquarters, are establishing stronger regional offices that are assuming many of the responsibilities that were previously administered directly from the North. Establishing offices in the South requires finding locations that can provide the stability, infrastructure, and access to skilled staff needed to effectively operate international headquarters or regional offices. One international membership nonprofit that moved headquarters to a middle-income country found that, because of the inadequate electrical grid and Internet network infrastructures, no single provider could guarantee continuity of Internet service, so it had to contract with two separate vendors to maintain its online communications, resulting in both increased costs and greater vulnerability.

International nonprofits generally have some form of legal status or registration in multiple countries. Most governments require local legal status for any organization operating in their territory, and tax deductibility for donations is generally only available for locally incorporated organizations. Multiple incorporation is achieved either through affiliates (whose independence from headquarters depends on the organizational models discussed in Chapter 6), or the headquarters may simply incorporate or register the same organization in a number of countries or jurisdictions. Many large international nonprofits headquartered outside the United States, such as the IOC, FIFA, and the Nobel Foundation, are also registered with the IRS and submit tax returns there.

Boards

While a few international nonprofits draw their board membership almost exclusively from the home country of the headquarters, the majority seek to incorporate board members from across the reach of the organization. Complex logistics, transportation, and communication costs conspire to limit the number of times international boards meet and so complicate the processes of building trust and a strong esprit de corps among board members. International board meetings also face myriad linguistic and cultural conundrums, from seeking to ensure that native speakers of the working language do not dominate unduly, to deciding whether to allow smoking, timing meals to fit in with the habits of all members, and accommodating different participation styles (Pearson 2004).

International boards are also faced with particularly difficult nuances regarding the question of whom they represent. Do board members give priority to their role as trustees of the donors' funds or to their role as advocates for the end users and recipients? Do board members participate in order to represent their region or individual affiliates or to advance the collective needs of the organization? Should voting rights be apportioned according to size of affiliates or based on their financial contribution? Keith Johnston (2012) spoke of "sensemaking" as the process by which international boards move from balancing members' competing interests to cocreating a larger communal interest.

Staffing

International nonprofit organizations are undergoing shifts in their staffing structures and personnel practices that reflect both international labor dynamics and the evolving management processes of nonprofits around the world. Outsourcing, part-time consultants, and performance-based employment contracts figure prominently.

Perhaps the biggest shift in large international nonprofits has been the increasing use of national staff instead of expatriates. A combination of the growing pool of skilled professionals around the world and an interest in building local capacity and ownership have entrenched the idea that international organizations should hire local staff instead of sending expatriates. Humanitarian organizations are sending fewer Northern workers into the field, and a wide range of international nonprofits are hiring local professionals when they shift head offices, set up branch offices, or create foreign affiliates. The past use of expatriates has always resulted in a certain mismatch, particularly in aid organizations, with younger staff more willing to work overseas but often lacking the experience needed to be fully effective in their positions. Those who wanted the expatriate jobs were not always fully qualified, and those who were more qualified no longer wanted to be separated from their homeland and endure the dislocation of expatriate life or the rigors of working in developing countries or conflict zones. International nonprofits are offering fewer long-term overseas assignments, so staff stay closer to home but may travel more for oversight functions such as monitoring and evaluation.

These shifts have been at times traumatic for organizations, and international nonprofits have not been immune to labor strife. In 2012, the London offices of Amnesty International, which houses both Amnesty UK and the international secretariat, was the subject of a union picket by staff protesting the restructuring of the international secretariat. It was being downsized to free the resources needed to strengthen regional offices, and the striking staff alleged management incompetence and unfair treatment during the restructuring process (*Independent* 2012).

The use of more locally employed staff also raises a number of equity and safety issues. In developing countries, local employees are paid at rates that reflect the national labor market, so usually receive considerably less than expatriates working in the same organization who are generally paid at rates based on their home labor market. When danger or disaster hits, expatriate staff are easily evacuated (they are often living without their families, have valid passports, and have somewhere to go as legal citizens of their home country), whereas local staff are often left behind because of personal and administrative constraints on their movements (they have their families locally, they may not have travel documents, and if they leave their home country, they become refugees). Expatriates rotate through placements and have an international labor market in which they can move on to a new position elsewhere. For local staff—administrators, direct service providers, drivers, cleaners, or security guards—the labor market created by the activities of international nonprofits may be the only job opportunity they have.

For aid organizations, security has become a growing issue. In 2011, 308 aid workers from governments, multilateral organizations, and nonprofits were killed, kidnapped, or wounded, the highest annual number recorded and part of a rising trend in both the number of incidents and the number of victims (Stoddard, Harmer, and Hughes 2012). The violence has an impact on both expatriate and local staff and is concentrated in regions of active armed conflict and unstable states. In response, many international nonprofits have developed increasingly sophisticated protocols for security—CARE published the first edition of its "Safety and Security Handbook" in 2004 (CARE International 2004)—and various attempts have been made to focus attention on the dangers faced by humanitarian workers and to advise organizations on how to respond to threats and incidents. In 2009, the United Nations designated August 19 as World Humanitarian Day to commemorate humanitarian workers killed in the field. It marks the day on which the UN special representative to Iraq, Sérgio Vieira de Mello, and twenty-one of his colleagues were killed in the bombing of the UN headquarters in Baghdad.

Sustainability

Despite the changing paradigms of international work and any uncertainties about funding, the international nonprofit sector, particularly at the high end, is remarkably stable. Even though international nonprofits can act like multinational corporations in creating global brands and extending the reach of their work unencumbered by sovereignty considerations, they are not subject to the same market volatility or competitive pressures as commercial organizations. The large international nonprofits of the 1970s and 1980s are generally still operating under the same organizational identity, whereas most of the prominent multinational commercial firms of that period have disappeared or have been transformed almost beyond recognition through buyouts and mergers. But even seemingly substantial organizations can fail as circumstances change (see Box 8.3).

Box 8.3 Liquidation of Global Hearts

In 2012, Global Hearts for Children, an eighteen-year-old UK international aid charity, went into liquidation, indicating that its income no longer covered operating costs after it had suffered a 45 percent drop in donations over two years. The organization had reached a peak annual income of $7 million only a few years earlier, which it used to send aid packages to countries in long-term need or hit by famine or disaster. The organization had been the UK affiliate of a large US-based international nonprofit but had rebranded itself only a few months previously. Public statements about the rebranding and subsequent closure made no reference to the break with the US organization, which had gone through its own recent controversy over the resignation of its CEO. Global Hearts donated its remaining inventory to other international aid organizations.

Source: See Third Sector, http://www.thirdsector.co.uk/bulletin/third_sector_daily
_bulletin/article/1145362/international-development-charity-global-hearts-children
-goes-liquidation.

Organizational sustainability and growth require capable stewardship of the full range of elements in Figure 8.1 and Table 8.1, but income is unmistakably the key to reducing risks. In state-centric countries and in those where nonprofits have not developed fully independently from political parties or labor unions, political connections pave the way to stable incomes. In other countries, nonprofits must rely on business connections. One of the fastest-growing international nonprofits is the US-based Room to Read, which since its founding in 2000 has grown to an annual income of $40 million and appears on the list of the world's 100 best nonprofits (see Chapter 6). The organization promotes education in the developing world by building schools and libraries, publishing local-language children's books, training teachers, and supporting girls' completion of secondary school. It works on the principle of challenge grants to communities, which are required to also make a contribution to the project. These goals and strategies are common to many development and education nonprofits, but Room to Read has been particularly successful in this somewhat crowded field. Part of the story of its success is that the founder, John Wood, was a former Microsoft executive who seeded the start-up and has been able to attract an elite board with CEOs and chief financial officers from blue-chip technology and finance companies. He has also skillfully managed public relations, including authoring two mass-market books: *Leaving Microsoft to Change the World: An Entrepreneur's Odyssey to Educate the World's Children* (Wood 2007) and *Creating Room to Read: A Story of Hope in the Battle for Global Literacy* (Wood 2013).

Accountability

The procedures linked to accountability—including balanced scorecards, benchmarking, evaluation, monitoring, performance measurement, return on investment, social accounting, and transparency—are conceptually and operationally somewhat distinct, but all share a common framework of using organizational analysis to drive internal change and improvement. They all require organizations to better understand the processes and standards they must use to engender trust and ensure their continued legal, political, operational, and moral legitimacy (L. D. Brown and Moore 2001).

Many systems used by domestic nonprofits to achieve these ends are difficult to sustain at international levels. Significant national differences in laws, cultural practices, and capacities to implement oversight processes can lead to considerable accountability deficits, whether the issue is the personal liability of board members, the transparency of organizational accounts, governance structures for ensuring ethnic and gender representation, or the mechanisms for collecting and reporting data. The challenge is ensuring responsive representation, professional management, and robust oversight across borders and between cultures (Anheier and Themudo 2004; Lewis 2007).

The literature on accountability emphasizes the "directions" or "dimensions" needed to respond to the full range of stakeholders. The varying descriptions of these include:

- Upward (to donors, sponsors, and regulators), outward (to collaborators and peers), inward (to staff and members), or downward (to recipients and communities) (Ebrahim 2003).
- Representative (to members), principal-agent (to donors and contractors), or mutual (to allies and peers) (L. D. Brown and Jagadananda 2010).
- Constituency based (to the interests of the beneficiaries), movement based (to the values of a movement), or mission based (to the expectations of affiliates and members) (L. D. Brown, Ebrahim, and Batliwala 2012).
- Functional (short-term accounting for resource use and outputs) or strategic (accounting for ongoing impact and relations) (Edwards and Hulme 1996).
- Full (financial accounting of use of resource), explanatory (provision of information and explanations for action), or responsive (maintaining trust and faith) (Lewis 2007).

Accountability implies that if an organization proves itself unaccountable, the consequences are sanctions and redress. Donors can withdraw funding and decisionmakers can refuse a place at the negotiation table, but the multidirectionality of international accountability, coupled with the distances—physical, political, and cultural—between many of the stakeholders and the ground-level outcomes introduces multiple asymmetries in information and perception and reduces the probabilities of sanctions. Donors in the North, particularly small donors, may have little true understanding of the impact of the aid programs they support in the South, far-flung members are often not in a position to verify the claimed outcomes of an international professional association, and committed supporters may continue to have faith in ineffective or counterproductive political strategies of advocacy organizations. Even in those countries with accreditation and rating agencies for the nonprofit sector, those processes can only in effect address the domestic dimensions of their operations, such as governance and accounting structures, and have a restricted capacity to monitor and evaluate foreign outputs or outcomes.

The impact and effectiveness of international nonprofits, as well as of their legitimacy and credibility, are constantly in question. Within the sector, internecine clashes arise over strategies and ideologies, and discrediting rival nonprofits is a common tool of the battles between different ideologies. NGO Watch, a project of the conservative American Enterprise Institute, denounced the "unelected few" progressive advocacy organizations (note that the American Enterprise Institute is itself a nonprofit funded by a select group of wealthy donors); NGO Monitor (2015) declares that its mission is to "end the practice used by certain self-declared 'humanitarian NGOs' of exploiting the label 'universal human rights values' to promote politically and ideologically motivated agendas," but its primary focus is on organizations that criticize certain aspects of Israeli policies on Palestine. Instead of arguing specific political points, both organizations tend to attack the legitimacy of other organizations, with Amnesty International and Human Rights Watch as particular targets of their ire.

Transparency. Transparency has emerged as the key element of accountability. Prominent international nonprofits have understood the imperatives of the higher stakes presented by the growth of a sector whose very identity is wrapped in the flags of empowerment, opportunity, and participation, and one that seeks to demonstrate it is above the rot that has weakened governments and businesses. There is growing clamor for greater transparency in the allocation by governments of official development aid (e.g., the International Aid Transparency Initiative), and nonprofits have had to respond in kind.

The new century has seen a proliferation of accountability charters and codes of conduct generated as part of self-regulation efforts by the sector. In a response to questioning of their legitimacy, international nonprofits have banded together to develop common operating principles and standards to assure stakeholders of the integrity and effectiveness of organizations. This process can be one of "club accountability" and an adaptation of the concept of conditionality (Gugerty and Prakash 2010). Such oversight and accountability mechanisms foster compliance through the standards and rules agreed to by "member," "signatory," or "accredited" organizations. Some of the charters are little more than general statements of principles, but others provide detailed processes, tools, and benchmarks that seek to bolster the credentials of organizations that sign on to them. Creating the charters and ensuring signatories' compliance implies complex negotiations between organizations from around the globe working in diverse cultural contexts and having differing access to resources. Compliance relies heavily on trust as the information asymmetries inherent in international work make verification by peer organizations and external principals all but impossible.

In 2006, a group of the largest international aid and advocacy nonprofits launched the International Non-Governmental Organisations (INGO) Accountability Charter, whose signatories are required to submit a detailed report annually to prove compliance in the following areas: (1) respect for human rights, (2) independence, (3) responsible advocacy, (4) diversity and inclusion, (5) transparency, (6) good governance, (7) ethical fund-raising, (8) professional management, (9) environmental responsibility, and (10) participation (INGO Accountability Charter 2014).

The charter was created as part of a series of International Advocacy Non-Governmental Organisations Workshops sponsored by CIVICUS starting in 2003. After its launch, the charter secretariat was registered first as the International NGO Charter of Accountability Company, a UK nonprofit, operating from the Amnesty International offices in London, but later the secretariat relocated to the International Civil Society Centre in Berlin.

Similarly, in September 2010 in Istanbul, Turkey, representatives from major development nonprofits endorsed the Principles for CSO (Civil Society Organization) Development Effectiveness (also known as the Istanbul Principles). These principles were the foundation for a subsequent meeting in Siem Reap, Cambodia, that endorsed the International Framework for CSO Development Effectiveness (also known as the Siem Reap Consensus). This framework was later incorporated into the broader aid effectiveness processes adopted by the UN conference in Busan, South Korea (see Chapter 7). The key elements of the principles and framework are to respect and promote human rights and social justice; embody gender equality and equity while promoting women and girls' rights; focus on people's empowerment, democratic ownership, and participation; promote environmental sustainability; practice transparency and accountability; pursue equitable partnerships and solidarity; create and share knowledge and commit to mutual learning; and commit to realizing positive sustainable change (Open Forum for CSO Development Effectiveness 2013).

The elements of both the accountability charter and the principles for effectiveness have essentially become implementation handbooks that provide specific benchmarks for compliance. They are two of the more prominent examples of the many local, regional, and international self-regulation initiatives, including the Code of Conduct for Arab Civil Society Organizations (European-Arab Project 2008). The UK nonprofit One World Trust has developed a comprehensive database that provides full-text access to the hundreds of such initiatives worldwide that define common standards and promote good practice through codes of conduct, certification schemes, reporting frameworks, directories, and awards (see http://www.oneworld trust.org/csoproject).

Evaluation. In addition to these general charters, widespread development of specific methods and tools has occurred for all of the processes related to accountability, with a particular emphasis on strengthening evaluative capacity. Many practitioners in international aid use variants of Logical Framework (commonly referred to as a LogFrame) as a general approach to planning, monitoring, and evaluation, and they use the LogFrame Matrix as the basis for identifying specific evaluation processes. In its most basic form, the LogFrame is used to encourage a systematic approach to understanding the relationships among design, implementation, and evaluation of projects and assists in identifying indicators and tools to measure them. Table 8.2 demonstrates the basic structure of a LogFrame Matrix.

The emphases on businesslike practices and on entrepreneurship are driving more extensive evaluation of impact, with no shortage of techniques

Table 8.2 Simplified LogFrame Matrix

Project Description	Indicators	Verification	Assumptions
Goals: Statement of impact toward which the project is targeted	Evidence that the goals are meaningful, respond to stakeholder input, and are based on solid theory of change	Methods of verification of inputs	Assumptions that determined the framing of the goals
Outputs: List of tangible services and products of the activity	Indicators used to demonstrate achievement of the outputs (quantity, quality, time frames)	Methods of verification of the outputs	Assumptions that are likely to have an impact on outputs
Outcomes: List of medium- and long-term benefits to target group	Indicators used to demonstrate achievement of the outcomes (quantity, quality, time frames)	Methods of verification of the outcomes	Assumptions that are likely to have an impact on outcomes

and tools. Perhaps the biggest challenge for many organizations is to decide which tools are best suited to their purposes. An initiative by a group of research and development organizations in Australia, the United Kingdom, the United States, and Italy has brought about the Better Evaluation Framework, which focuses on seven stewardship clusters (manage, define, frame, describe, understand causes, synthesize, and report) using the following evaluative approaches, as listed by BetterEvaluation.org (2013):

- Appreciative inquiry
- Case study
- Collaborative-outcomes reporting
- Contribution analysis
- Critical-system heuristics
- Developmental evaluation
- Empowerment evaluation
- Horizontal evaluation
- Innovation history
- Institutional histories
- Most significant change
- Outcome mapping
- Participatory evaluation
- Participatory rural appraisal
- Positive deviance
- Randomized controlled trials
- Realist evaluation
- Social return on investment
- Utilization-focused evaluation

Independent ratings organizations, such as Charity Navigator and the Wise Giving Alliance in the United States, can be found. However, these ratings generally only address the administrative conduct of an organization and the activities associated with its registration in the country of the ratings organizations. Other ratings organizations seek to more directly assist donors in making better choices by evaluating the impact of international nonprofits (see Box 8.4).

Although the rhetoric of accountability maintains that codes of conduct and evaluation processes are increasingly necessary to secure and continue funding and to reassure the broader community, the complexities and resources required for their implementation put them beyond the reach of all but the largest and most professionalized organizations. Although they may be "necessary," they are also burdensome, expensive, and often exclusionary: currently INGO Accountability Charter has only twenty-five members, the requirements of such membership serving to maintain the privileges of the

---

Box 8.4 Evaluation for Donors

Various organizations in the United Kingdom and the United States seek to advise donors on the work of international nonprofits. Here, the stated aims of two such evaluation organizations, Giving What We Can in the United Kingdom and GiveWell in the United States, are presented.

Giving What We Can states, "We want to help you support those charities that are able to do the most good with your donations. We take charity evaluation very seriously. Choosing where to give is important: it can be a far more important decision than how much you choose to give. Some aid programs are many times more effective than others: amongst aid programs focusing on poverty in the developing world, a factor of more than 1,000 separates the most from the least cost-effective."

GiveWell describes itself as "a nonprofit dedicated to finding outstanding giving opportunities and publishing the full details of our analysis to help donors decide where to give. Unlike charity evaluators that focus solely on financials, assessing administrative or fundraising costs, we conduct in-depth research aiming to determine how much good a given program accomplishes (in terms of lives saved, lives improved, etc.) per dollar spent. Rather than try to rate as many charities as possible, we focus on the few charities that stand out most in order to find and confidently recommend the best giving opportunities possible."

Given the difficulties of demonstrating the development impact of specific nonprofits, the evaluation narratives on such websites can be somewhat sobering, with conclusions similar to "there is little evidence of their effectiveness" appearing all too often.

Sources: See Giving What We Can, http://www.givingwhatwecan.org; GiveWell, http://www.givewell.org.

---

large elite organizations (Sparke 2013). Evaluation processes tend to focus on upward accountability to donors and other public- and private-sector patrons and too often neglect the downward accountability to end users and recipients (T. Wallace, Bornstein, and Chapman 2007). Although various forms of "participatory accountability" seek to strengthen input by recipients, the economic hold of the donors and the nature of expertise result in priority being given to top-down accountability (L. Jordan 2005; T. Wallace 2003).

The emphasis on measurement and accountability and on their relationship to continued donor support inevitably places more burden on organizations to report only successes, a situation that often precludes honest reflections on outcomes. Another approach is to disseminate stories of well-intentioned miscalculations by international nonprofits. The website Admitting Failure (admittingfailure.com), a joint project of the Canadian chapter of Engineers Without Borders and the private consulting firm Fail Forward, documents case studies in failure, and training is provided, using the case studies as organizational development tools to drive innovation. It is part of an "embrace failure" line of argument that urges organizations and donors to accept the fact that failure is a natural part of doing business and of organizational learning. A number of organizations, including the UN agency International Fund for Agricultural Development, have organized "Fail Faires," workshops at which people highlight failures and "celebrate" them.

Fund-raising for international humanitarian aid and development is a particularly vexing area of accountability. Although ethical fund-raising is one of the compliance areas of the INGO Accountability Charter, the reality is that what "sells" to donors and attracts funds is not necessarily the most effective development strategies or the most honest assessments of the possible outcomes, so organizations have to manage the potential conflict between aggressive, successful marketing and ethical, accountable practices. Fund-raising often becomes a "reverse beauty contest," given that aid nonprofits have an interest in emphasizing the poverty, dysfunction, and crises of the areas in which they work, and the competition for funding tends to foster hyperbole in the claims of the impact of the organizations' work. Such concerns about the images and messages being propagated are becoming more acute as the new generation of peer-to-peer crowdfunding and aggregator sites, both nonprofit and commercial, are creating even more tenuous connections between fund-raising and outcomes. The Internet has made global fund-raising accessible for even the smallest organizations, by directly linking donors and recipients. But it has also reduced oversight and is making fund-raising a game of viral videos and social media "likes."

The economics and business imperatives of fund-raising can also lead to poor practices. Particular concern has arisen over the aggressive practices and high overheads charged by commercial fund-raising firms, particularly those that provide street solicitation services to international nonprofits. In the United Kingdom, street solicitors have been dubbed *chuggers*, a portmanteau of *charity* and *muggers*. Various investigative exposés have accused them of intimidatory and unlawful tactics and indicate that in many cases up to 80 percent of the donations are kept by the solicitors and the organizations that employ them.

Nonprofit Relations with Other Sectors

As noted in the discussion of global governance in Chapter 6, the field of international relations in the mid-twentieth century largely neglected nonprofits. The focus has been on relations between nations, and the primary theoretical frameworks in the fields have generally been couched in terms of the dialectics between national sovereignty and intergovernmental interests and structures (Götz 2008; Karns and Mingst 2004). The emergence of non-state actors and their expanding potential to set agendas and deliver services through cross-sectoral collaborations in fields as diverse as protection of the environment, poverty reduction, and security are identified as a major new development in international relations in the second half of the twentieth century (L. D. Brown et al. 2000; T. G. Weiss, Carayannis, and Jolly 2009). Nonprofits cannot draw on the legal, political, or military powers of states, and they have tenuous political mandates and limited economic resources, but the new policy arenas created by sovereignty vacuums and multilateralism provide openings for contestation. Nonprofits must rely primarily on their soft power potential through their expertise and their capacity to engage and mobilize publics across borders. In certain policy arenas they have increased the reach and decibel level of their voices (DeMars 2005; T. G. Weiss, Carayannis, and Jolly 2009), and in doing so, they have become the "proxy public" (Lang 2013).

Nonprofits are seen as a force for ethical globalization (Clark 2008; Willetts 2011), helping to create and mobilize global networks to pressure governments, multilateral organizations, and multinational corporations. The normative discourse on international nonprofits emphasizes the progressive and rights-based dimensions of such work, but racist and religious fundamentalist organizations also operate in the same arenas (Willetts 2011).

Nonprofits are key sources of expertise that seek to educate policymakers, help expand policy options, and provide neutral spaces for dialogues on policy issues. They are increasingly prominent at a range of international policy conferences, either working with the delegates of their national governments prior to the conference or directly lobbying during the conferences. They enhance public participation before and during conferences and monitor implementation. The emphasis is on nongovernment, independent organizations, but BONGOs (business-organized NGOs), GONGOs (government-organized NGOs), and THOs (transnational hybrid organizations)—nonprofits that have in effect been created by the other two sectors—are common, complicating even more the complex and multifaceted relationships with nations, intergovernmental organizations, and for-profit multinational corporations. The term *public-private partnership* is now used to describe almost any combination of collaborations between the three sectors.

Governments

At the same time that most national governments are faced with the proliferation of domestic nonstate actors within their borders, international nonprofit activity is also increasingly intruding in domestic matters. In developing countries many national nonprofits are sustained by external funding, and almost all governments now must contend with "boomerang advocacy," in which local nonprofits work in global arenas to involve multilateral institutions or international nonprofit networks in campaigns on domestic issues (Keck and Sikkink 1999).

The relations between international nonprofits and national governments, in their home country and in others where they seek to work, continue to be central to their operations. Nonprofits generally do not have an international legal personality (the few exceptions include the International Red Cross—see Box 6.10) (Lindblom 2013), so only at national levels do they have their legal basis and are bestowed regulatory legitimacy. Relations with national governments are based on a combination of the cultural frames addressed in earlier chapters and on different modes of relationships. As noted in Chapter 5, Dennis Young (2006) identified three dominant modes of relationships between governments and nonprofits: (1) adversarial (opponents), (2) supplementary (substitutes), and (3) complementary (collaborators). The modes are not mutually exclusive, and the cultural frames determine how they mix and match in the ongoing dynamics between any particular national government and the domestic and international nonprofit sectors to which that national government relates.

In the adversarial mode, nonprofits challenge the state through collective action from below or by invoking moral authority from above (DeMars 2005). The international dimensions of adversarial relationships are often manifested by governments attempting to resist or control "foreign influences." Almost all countries have rules that limit foreign funding to local nonprofits and require registration by foreign nonprofits seeking to operate in their territory (Moore and Rutzen 2011). In developing countries, where the majority of nonprofit funding may be from external sources, contentious relationships often develop between the government and any nonprofits that are seen as straying from the strict confines of humanitarian aid (Carothers and Brechenmacher 2014). Although these dynamics are particularly in the forefront in developing countries, industrialized countries have similar restrictions and concerns about foreign support of domestic nonprofits: witness the discomfort in any country when it is revealed that a local cultural or community center or an advocacy organization is receiving funding from "hostile" governments or private donors from those countries. The parameters of the debates over possible restrictions on foreign funding to Israeli nonprofits are illustrated in Box 8.5.

The supplementary dimension is also most evident in poorer or weaker states where the government relies on multilateral organizations and nonprofits to provide even the most basic of public services. Two oft-cited examples of countries in which nonprofits act as shadow or quasi-states are Haiti and Bangladesh. However, as perceived by the population and international commentators, the outcomes in these countries appear to be com-

Box 8.5 Israeli Government Backs Limits on Financing for Nonprofit Groups

In 2011, a committee of Israeli cabinet ministers voted to back two bills aimed at curtailing the support of left-wing nonprofit groups from foreign governments. The eleven-to-five vote threw the support of Prime Minister Benjamin Netanyahu's government behind the bills, which human rights groups denounced as violations of free expression and an effort by the government to silence its critics.

One proposed bill limited to $5,000 per year the amount that a foreign government, government-supported foundation, or group of governments such as the European Union could give to Israeli groups considered "political." The other imposed a heavy tax on such contributions. The bills were largely aimed at groups that focus on Palestinian rights, civil liberties, and other causes advocated by the Israeli left, many of which rely on European government support. An official in Netanyahu's office said the prime minister backed efforts to limit foreign government donations to the groups because they amounted, in his view, to interference in Israeli politics. However, he wanted the bills amended so their impact would be narrowed.

Legal experts said that the bills would probably be altered before reaching the Knesset (Israeli parliament) and could ultimately be struck down by the Israeli Supreme Court. Lawyers said defining which groups were political ones was a task that would not pass legal scrutiny. Sari Bashi, director of Gisha, which is an Israeli group devoted to promoting free movement for Palestinians in Gaza and one that would be affected by the new bills, said that "while it seems likely that some of the most antidemocratic aspects of the bills will be softened, that actually could make the situation worse, because it would define political speech in such a way as to silence some but not others and possibly allow the bills to become law." Gisha receives half its annual budget in contributions from European governments and foreign foundations that rely partly on government support.

Source: See *New York Times* (Online), http://www.nytimes.com/2011/11/14/world/middleeast/israeli-government-backs-financing-limits-for-nonprofit-groups.html.

Note: At the time of publication of this book, versions of such legislation were still being considered by the Israeli parliament, but none had become law.

plete opposites (see Box 8.6). Such contrasting experiences are at the heart of the debates over whether nonprofit activity is a result of failing state institutions, or the state is failing because of nonprofit activity. In his analysis of the role of development NGOs in Tanzania, Issa Shivji (2007) asserted that international donors "took a fancy to NGOs, thus undermining the state and its institutions" (56).

Examples of complementarity, in which governments and nonprofits partner on, collaborate on, or coproduce policymaking and service delivery are numerous and varied and have been profiled throughout this book. Gov-

---

Box 8.6 Government by NGOs

Haiti is commonly derided as a "Republic of NGOs." Concerns about the role of NGOs in Haiti's development had been present for decades but gained increasing prominence following the January 2010 earthquake that destroyed much of the capital, Port-au-Prince. Historically, funneling aid through NGOs has perpetuated a situation of limited government capacity and weak institutions, and so Haitians look to NGOs rather than their government for basic public services. As one commentator asked, "How can you have 10,000 NGOs working in Haiti, and yet in the fifty years that that country has been receiving humanitarian aid it has gotten poorer every year?" He also described the wariness and even animosity toward NGOs felt by many Haitians and how, even as they yearn for help, they often wish that most of the current crop of self-appointed helpers would just leave them alone.

Bangladesh has a number of large indigenous NGOs, including the Association for Social Advancement, BRAC (see Box 6.7), Grameen, and Proshika. BRAC and Grameen are among the largest and most-respected international nonprofits. As *The Economist* recently noted, "Bangladesh has dysfunctional politics and a stunted private sector, yet it has been surprisingly good at improving the lives of its poor. It is the things that NGOs do that make Bangladesh's way of fighting poverty unique." Microfinance has played an important role, but the key was the work of NGOs more generally. The government of Bangladesh has been unusually friendly to them perhaps because, to begin with, it realized it needed all the help it could get. An NGO such as BRAC does practically everything: in the 1980s, it sent out volunteers to every household in the country showing mothers how to mix salt, sugar, and water in the right proportions to rehydrate a child suffering from diarrhea. BRAC and the government jointly ran a program to inoculate every Bangladeshi against tuberculosis. BRAC's primary schools are a safety net for children who drop out of government schools. BRAC even has the world's largest legal-aid program: Bangladesh has more BRAC legal centers than police stations. A certain consensus has arisen that NGOs have had a positive impact in Bangladesh; however, concerns have been voiced that the large NGOs marginalize and weaken government and diminish public accountability.

Sources: See *The Economist* 2012; Haque 2002; *New Yorker* (Online), http://www
.newyorker.com/online/blogs/newsdesk/2010/11/the-moral-hazards-of-humanitarian
-aid-what-is-to-be-done.html; US Institute of Peace, Peace Watch, http://www.usip.org
/sites/default/files/PB%2023%20Haiti%20a%20Republic%20of%20NGOs.pdf.

ernments and nonprofits are inextricably linked in aid systems (Tvedt 2006), and they work together on a range of activities associated with the emerging system of international governmentality (Lewis 2007). As Matthew Bolton and Thomas Nash (2010) noted, the funding of nonprofits by the governments of medium-sized states has helped these "middle powers" gain greater clout in shaping global public policy on issues such as land mines, international criminal justice, child soldiers, disability rights, and conflict diamonds.

GONGOs are a particular form of complementarity commonly used by more authoritarian governments to confer legitimacy through their appearance at international forums as representatives of their national civil society. As noted in Chapter 4, national women's organizations are often led by the wife of the leader of the regime, and many other nonprofits are headed by the inner circle of the regime (see Box 9.1). At the same time, democratic governments also establish or fund nonprofits to promote their agendas at home and abroad (see Box 8.7).

Box 8.7 State-Sponsored Nonprofits

In December 2011, Egyptian prosecutors and police raided the offices of ten foreign-based, prodemocracy NGOs operating in the country. As a result of the raids, forty-three people, including sixteen US citizens, were accused of failing to register with the government and of financing protest movements with illicit funds in violation of Egyptian sovereignty. The forty-three defendants worked for five organizations: Freedom House, the National Democratic Institute, the International Republican Institute, the International Center for Journalists (ICFJ), and the Konrad Adenauer Foundation.

The National Democratic Institute, chaired by former US secretary of state Madeline Albright, and the International Republican Institute, chaired by Senator John McCain, represent the US Democratic and Republican political parties. These two, together with the Center for International Private Enterprise, which represents the US Chamber of Commerce, and the Solidarity Center, which represents the American Federation of Labor and Congress of Industrial Organizations (AFL-CIO), make up the four core institutions of the National Endowment for Democracy. The last is a nonprofit, grant-making institution that receives more than 90 percent of its annual budget from the US government.

The Konrad Adenauer Foundation is a nonprofit associated with the German Christian Democratic Union. It receives over 90 percent of its funding from the German government.

Source: See http://www.globalpolicy.org/ngos/introduction/credibility-and-legitimacy/51688-qngoq-the-guise-of-innocence.html.

Intergovernmental Organizations

The interplay between intergovernmental and international nonprofit organizations has been an integral dynamic in the modern history of the globalization of politics and policy (see Box 8.8).

As noted in Chapter 6, in the nineteenth century, a clear distinction had not yet been made between intergovernmental organizations and nongovernmental organizations (Charnovitz 1997), and the emerging international structures of that era often included representatives of both. At the First International Congress on the Prevention and Repression of Crime held in London in 1872 (also known as the International Penitentiary Congress), the participants included representatives from governments, nongovernmental societies advocating prison reform, and societies of jurists.

Box 8.8 The Congress of Vienna

The Congress of Vienna, held from September 1814 to June 1815, sought to establish a lasting peace in Europe after the French Revolution and the Napoleonic Wars. It is considered by many commentators to be the first multilateral face-to-face meeting of national envoys seeking to broker an international agreement. Until then such relations were generally bilateral and handled through emissaries and letters. Even in Vienna no plenary sessions were held, only a rolling series of smaller meetings.

Because the focus was on peace on the Continent, the most prominent delegates represented the five great European continental powers of the time: the Austrian Empire, Great Britain, France, Prussia, and Russia. At the same time, over 200 representatives of smaller states and royal houses were included. Almost all the governments were highly centralized or absolute monarchies (Austria was ruled by the Emperor Franz I, Russia by Tsar Alexander I, and Prussia by King Wilhelm III), and most of the delegates were nobles, high-rank military officers, and other prominent members of the traditional elites.

Also present in Vienna were representatives from religious organizations and interest groups, including German publishers demanding a copyright law and freedom of the press and numerous antislavery and peace societies. The antislavery advocates worked with the delegates from Britain to pressure the congress to support abolition. They were successful, so the final declaration of the congress condemned the slave trade as inconsistent with civilization and proclaimed that it should be abolished, although it left the actual effective date of abolition to negotiation among the various nations.

Source: Reinalda 2011.

However, by the early part of the twentieth century, a clearer separation of the roles of each could be found. The covenant of the League of Nations, formed at the end of World War I, made no formal provisions for the participation of NGOs. Nevertheless, the League worked closely with them, publishing a regular bulletin detailing their activities and policy recommendations. The League sent representatives to attend major nongovernmental conferences, and many NGOs established offices in Geneva to facilitate contact with the League (Davies 2012).

The demise of the League and the outbreak of World War II greatly reduced the activities of NGOs. However, after World War II, the framers of the 1945 UN Charter sought to include them more formally in the new organization, both in recognition of the role they had played in the League of Nations and to gain their support for the new Charter. Article 71 of the Charter states that the Economic and Social Council (ECOSOC) "may make suitable arrangements for consultation with non-governmental organizations which are concerned with matters within its competence." These "arrangements" became a series of rosters of accredited organizations that have attained consultative status through a formal application process. This consultative status in effect embedded the designation *NGO* into the postwar lexicon and consciousness (Charnovitz 1997; Lang 2013).

Despite this recognition of nonprofits, international relations for much of the twentieth century were dominated by the interests of states and intergovernmental organizations, as world wars, colonial liberation struggles, and the Cold War clashes of the superpowers and their proxies entrenched the sacrosanctity of national sovereignty. Nonstate actors were relegated to a more peripheral role, even as the post–World War II period was marked by the unrelenting rise in the number of international nonprofits. As the Union of International Associations figures attest, the late twentieth century witnessed a steady growth in intergovernmental organizations and an exponential growth of nonprofits.

What is the relationship between the growth of the two sectors? Have the intergovernmental and multilateral institutions, such as the United Nations and the World Bank, created the conditions for the rise of international nonprofits by promoting values such as technical rationality, independence from the state, and voluntarism, or has the rise of international nonprofits (and other private and commercial nonstate actors) driven the growth and extended reach of intergovernmental organizations? A dynamic of mutual legitimation is evident. Intergovernmental organizations are the institutional patrons of many international nonprofits, and nonprofits assist intergovernmental organizations to cover democratic deficits and to garner the de facto consent of broad swathes of stakeholders. The representativeness of both intergovernmental organizations and international nonprofits are often questioned, so they seek legitimacy, and perhaps solace, in each other.

This symbiosis also builds operational capacities less constrained by sovereignty. Nonprofits work with intergovernmental organizations to reach the global stage for their agendas. The nonprofits can identify transnational challenges and subsequently implement operational responses in ways that skirt the restriction on intergovernmental entities. As the salience of nonprofits increases, they become more integral to the work on intergovernmental organizations. Some observers note that there are now in effect three United Nations: the forum of states and the secretariat of international public servants are now increasingly seen also as conveners of civil society. This "third UN" (Weiss, Carayannis, and Jolly 2009) creates a supplementary forum for generating and legitimating policy, and UN grants and contracts to nonprofits allow for field testing and evaluation of policy.

Despite any seemingly collaborative approaches, evident power differentials remain between intergovernmental organizations and nonprofits. L. David Brown and Jonathan Fox (2000) characterized the relationship between the World Bank and nonprofits as a "David and Goliath" series of battles that have been playing out not only in the corridors of global conferences but also in the streets. This insider-outsider theme seems to underlie much of the analysis of the current interactions between the sectors and is one of the ways some commentators draw distinctions within the nonprofit sector, labeling those inside as NGOs and those outside as civil society or social movements (see the contributions in Lyon 2010). Certainly, differences can be identified in institutional and operational logics between the more professionalized, hierarchical nonprofits as they dialogue inside with accredited delegates and the more loosely structured mobilization of those outside chanting their demands (and perhaps keeping at bay the actions of a violent radical fringe). However, as the analysis of advocacy in Chapter 7 indicated, considerable overlap can be found in people, structures, and methods.

Whichever interpretation is favored, consensus has arisen that nonstate and noncommercial organizations, whether they are labeled *nongovernment, nonprofit, social movement,* or *civil society,* are playing a more integral part in policy development and implementation processes of intergovernmental organizations through their direct actions and their capacity to mobilize public opinion and to generate media interest. Much of the analysis is focused on whether the expansion of the nonprofit sector has resulted in a shift in the role, from that of observers and critics who are consulted, to that of active participants and coproducers (Popovski 2010).

The United Nations. As noted earlier, the UN Charter established a consultative status for NGOs. The Charter specified that consultation was to be with international organizations and, where appropriate, with national organizations after agreement with the UN member nation concerned. NGOs with consultative status often have the words *international* or *world* in their names (e.g., International Federation of Women Lawyers and the World Muslim Congress), but many national organizations also have consultative status (e.g., Presbyterian Women of Aotearoa New Zealand).

The United Nations has three categories of consultative status: general, special, and roster. Organizations in the "general" category must be "concerned with most of the activities of the Economic and Social Council of the UN (ECOSOC) and its subsidiary bodies"; the "special" category is for NGOs that "have a special competence in, and are concerned specifically with, only a few of the fields of activity covered by the ECOSOC"; and "roster" is for organizations that "can make occasional and useful contributions to the work of ECOSOC or its subsidiary bodies." The NGO Branch of the Department of Economic and Social Affairs maintains a database of NGOs with consultative status and other civil society organizations, including trade unions, employer associations, and universities that have some association with UN agencies and programs. The database currently includes some 3,800 NGOs with consultative status and an additional 20,000 civil society organizations accredited by the ECOSOC subsidiary, the Commission on Sustainable Development, or by UN agencies such as the Food and Agriculture Organization, UNESCO, and the World Health Organization (UN Department of Economic and Social Affairs 2014).

Over 500 NGOs with consultative status are members of the Conference of NGOs in Consultative Relationship with the United Nations (CONGO), an international nonprofit membership association that facilitates the participation of NGOs in UN debates and decisionmaking. CONGO seeks to ensure that NGOs are present when issues of global concern are discussed, by fostering a range of NGO participation processes. Founded in 1948, CONGO has gone through three distinct "generations" (Bloem, Agazzi Ben Attia, and Dam 2008). The first coincided with the Cold War when the relatively few international NGOs with consultative status were all but frozen out of intergovernmental policy deliberations by the realities of the clash between the United States and the Soviet Union and their client states. Some attempts were made at North-South dialogues and at standard setting on human rights, but generally NGO dialogues were held separately from UN intergovernmental deliberations and had little impact on them. During that period, the unwritten convention was that the board of CONGO would be split evenly between Western and Soviet Bloc countries.

The second generation emerged after the end of the Cold War. In 1996, the United Nations opened consultative status to a broader range of organizations, including national and regional NGOs, and encouraged the participation of NGOs from the South and the former Soviet Bloc, and in 1997, the first meeting of NGOs with the UN Security Council took place. The third generation is marked by closer NGO-UN relations, with more stable collaborative arrangements and joint strategic work on issues such as the Millennium Development Goals, the International Criminal Court, and the Global Compact, an agreement on corporate social responsibility.

The United Nations also expanded its strategy of world summit conferences, covering issues such as the status of women, the environment, human health, and urban development. These UN-sponsored summits opened the UN deliberation process to a much broader range of NGOs, given that the formal UN rules on consultative status do not apply to the summits, and each one can establish its own accreditation system. Moreover, some nonprofits have ended up organizing parallel events and protests that attract an even wider range of organizations. Despite criticism of the conduct and outcomes of these summits, nonprofits continue to have high hopes for their impact and attend in large numbers, even if only to protest against the proceedings and express their antipathy for global elites. Many commentators cite the 1992 UN Conference on Environment and Development in Rio de Janeiro (known as the Earth Summit) as the inflection point for extensive civil society participation in UN summits (Charnovitz 1997), but women's civil society organizations were already involved in significant numbers in the First World Conference on Women in Mexico City in 1975. At that conference, some 2,000 delegates from government and 6,000 from NGOs came together, and by the Fourth World Conference on Women in Beijing in 1995, 6,000 government delegates and 40,000 representatives from NGOs were present (Krut 1997). At the 2012 Conference on Sustainable Development in Rio de Janeiro, (known as Rio+20, as it was considered to be a successor conference to the 1992 Earth Summit), some 850 registered nonprofits attended the official conference along with the official delegations from UN member nations, which included fifty-seven heads of state and thirty-one heads of government. Some 50,000 people were said to have participated in the parallel events that included NGOs and the international business community.

The 2004 *Report of the Panel of Eminent Persons on United Nations– Civil Society Relations* (known as the Cardoso Report) (United Nations 2004) noted the need to increase the participation of NGOs in intergovernmental bodies and enhance their country-level engagement. In addition to the database of organizations associated with the United Nations, the NGO Branch of the Department of Economic and Social Affairs has developed CSO Net, a web portal that promotes good practices in economic and social development (UN Department of Economic and Social Affairs 2014), and the NGO Section of the Department of Public Information holds weekly briefings for NGOs and organizes an annual conference (United Nations 2014). The governance project of the UN Economic Commission for Africa has developed the African CSO Network Portal, a clearinghouse that includes a directory of African civil society organizations and a library of resource materials. The commission hopes the portal will promote dialogue and cooperation among civil society organizations and institutions based on the understanding that "an active, informed and viable civil society is essential to the consolidation of pluralistic democracy and promotion of sustainable development" (African CSO Network Portal 2014).

Although all these dynamics are indicative of the growing role and influence of NGOs in the United Nations, as policy partners and service deliverers, caution and pushback still can be sensed in some circles. The recommendations from the Cardoso Report were not universally supported. Some UN member nations do not embrace the activities of nonprofits within their own borders and so are wary of their influence in international arenas, and many national delegations, even those from countries more open to nonprofit activities, express misgivings over the representativeness of some of the nonprofits that seek to work with the United Nations.

The Council of Europe. The Council of Europe, headquartered in Strasbourg, France, is an intergovernmental organization that fosters dialogue between European countries, including those beyond the boundaries of the European Union (although with the continued expansion of the European Union, overlap is increasing). The Council has relatively weak decision-making powers and acts more in an advisory and oversight capacity, but it is still lobbied by numerous nongovernmental and business groups.

The Council of Europe has offered consultative status to international nonprofits since 1952 (it uses the designation *international NGOs* in its official literature). In 2003 the Council, "convinced that initiatives, ideas and suggestions emanating from civil society can be considered a true expression of European citizens," adopted a resolution that upgraded "consultation" with international NGOs to "participation" (Council of Europe 2003). The resolution institutionalized the status of nonprofits as one of the four pillars of a deliberative process identified as a "quadrilogue" that consisted of the Committee of Ministers and its subsidiary bodies, the Parliamentary Assembly, the Congress of Local and Regional Authorities of Europe, and international NGOs. In return for this new participatory status, international NGOs were required to make a greater commitment to the Council of Europe in terms of the level of their engagement with that body's activities. In exchange for their commitment, they were accorded the following privileges:

• Allowed to address memoranda to the secretary-general for submission to the committees as well as to the commissioner for human rights.

- Invited to provide expert advice on Council of Europe policies, programs, and actions.
- Issued the agenda and public documents of the Parliamentary Assembly in order to facilitate their attendance at public sittings of the Parliamentary Assembly.
- Invited to public sittings of the Congress of Local and Regional Authorities of Europe.
- Invited to activities organized for them by the secretariat.
- Invited to attend seminars, conferences, and colloquies of interest to their work according to the applicable Council of Europe rules (Council of Europe 2003).

International NGOs with participatory status form part of the Conference of International Non-Governmental Organisations, which meets in Strasbourg twice a year during the ordinary sessions of the Parliamentary Assembly. The some 400 international NGOs that currently have participatory status reflect the full range of the broadest definition of an NGO; they include the International Academy of Legal Medicine, Médecins du Monde, Penal Reform International, Rotary International, World Association of Women Entrepreneurs, and the World Veterans Federation.

The Conference of International Non-Governmental Organisations also works with the Council to promote the participation of nonprofits in the policymaking processes of member nations. In 2009, the conference adopted the Code of Good Practice for Civil Participation in the Decision-Making Process in the hope of creating a stronger enabling environment for nonprofits in member states by defining a set of general principles, guidelines, tools, and mechanisms for civil participation in the policy process (Council of Europe 2009). This code is similar to the policy participation codes that have been generated at national levels through the compact processes outlined in Chapter 5.

The World Bank. The Bretton Woods institutions, including the International Monetary Fund and the World Bank Group (including its affiliated development banks and trade organizations), have had a more equivocal relationship with international nonprofits. The World Bank in particular became a bête noir of the progressive nonprofit sector. Many progressives regard the World Bank as the font of the neoliberal globalizing agenda and so hold it responsible for entrenching poverty and indebtedness in the developing world through its structural adjustment and austerity programs (Ebrahim and Herz 2007). Even those who see the World Bank as a necessary multilateral global development actor have been pushing for reform and for the greater participation of civil society organizations in its governance and policy processes.

Since the late 1970s, sustained advocacy campaigns have taken place to hold the World Bank accountable for the perceived negative economic and social impact of its operations. In 1981, the World Bank established the NGO–World Bank Committee, and subsequently some NGO members of this committee, largely from the South, established an autonomous working group to coordinate their advocacy agendas. This collaborative work helped drive the Bank's expanding participation agenda and expanded the role of Southern voices in the shaping of policies and projects. Nonprofit involvement in Bank-funded projects has risen steadily since the establishment of the committee and working group, in both monitoring and evaluation and in the development of policy agendas such as the Bank's poverty reduction strategies.

A broad coalition of critics, led by nonprofit advocacy organizations, rallied around the Fifty Years Is Enough campaigns in 1994, and the subsequent Sixty Years Is Enough campaign in 2004, seeking to curtail the power of the World Bank and to reform or replace it with more democratic institutions. Meetings of the World Bank and other Bretton Woods institutions now regularly attract mass street protests and are subject to more institutionalized forms of oversight such as the UK-based Bretton Woods Project. The critiques of the work of the World Bank continue, but the fact that in 2014 no organized Seventy Years Is Enough campaign appeared seems indicative of a changing advocacy and development landscape. Instead, 2014 was more noteworthy as the year of the founding of the New Development Bank, an alternative international financial institution launched by the BRICS, which seeks to challenge the dominance of the World Bank and the International Monetary Fund in lending and economic policy and to promote greater economic engagement among developing nations.

Multinational Corporations

The evolving relations between international nonprofits and multinational corporations are most commonly characterized as a shift from conflict to cooperation, or as Simon Zadek (2011) termed it, from "poachers and gamekeepers" to "uncomfortable bedfellows." International nonprofits that were former critics and external watchdogs now often work closely with multinationals in a range of collaborations, including sponsorships, cause-related marketing, eco-labeling, and service partnerships. Corporations are sensitive to the vulnerability of their brand and realize the advantages of working with nonprofits to improve stakeholder dialogue and burnish their corporate image, as well as to improve employee morale and strengthen internal governance.

New collaborations between nonprofits and corporations are particularly evident on environmental issues (Lyon 2010), but they also encompass human and labor rights, aid logistics, and fair trade, as well as the endorsement of products and services by professional, academic, and sports nonprofits (including third-party certification by organizations such as the ISO—see Box 6.8). As noted in Chapter 3, the increasing use of corporate foundations and variants of corporate social responsibility has been an integral part of the growth of the nonprofit sector, and multinational corporations have reflected this trend and are a major source of funding for nonprofits. In developing countries, the local subsidiaries of multinational corporations are often among the largest contributors to local nonprofits. Relationships between the sectors have also been entrenched by an increasingly fluid flow of personnel between nonprofit, governmental, and corporate roles.

Nonprofits are often portrayed as a key element in civilizing the economic globalization of multinational corporations through their involvement in processes that monitor the impact of market forces and push for global regulatory standards, particularly regarding historical concerns such as the exploitation of child labor, the dumping of tainted or expired foods and pharmaceuticals, or degradation of the environment.

Morton Winston (2002) identified a range of strategies similar to the insider-outsider approaches noted in the earlier section on advocacy that range from engagement to confrontation, with eight typical strategies along this continuum: (1) dialogue aimed at promoting the adoption of voluntary codes of conduct; (2) social accounting and independent verification schemes; (3) shareholder resolutions; (4) documentation of abuses and moral shaming; (5) boycotts of company products or divestment; (6) advocacy of selective purchasing laws; (7) government-imposed standards; and (8) litigation seeking punitive damages.

Zadek (2011) focused on three levels of intended impact of nonprofit advocacy with corporations: tactical (e.g., a campaign against a single corporation), strategic (changing practices, industries, and mind-sets), and systemic (e.g., changing the underlying conditions that foster the abuses). As with the effects identified in Table 7.4, lower-level impact is easier to achieve and measure: multiple examples can be found of companies modifying strategies and adopting new operating principles as the result of pressure by advocacy networks. Systemic effects are harder to define and evaluate.

In the environmental field, for-profit corporations have created their own nonprofit organization, the Global Environmental Management Initiative (GEMI), which is seeking to highlight how partnerships between nonprofits and corporations can meet advocacy goals (see Box 8.9).

Such partnerships are potential minefields for both parties. A recent sting operation mounted by a journalist seeking to expose the seemingly cozy relationship between an environmental organization and a multinational corporation demonstrates some of the risks involved (see Box 8.10).

**Box 8.9 Corporations Create
Their Own Environmental Nonprofit**

The Global Environmental Management Initiative (GEMI) is a nonprofit organization founded in 1990 by leading multinational corporations, including 3M, Coca-Cola, DuPont, and Pfizer, which according to its mission statement is "dedicated to fostering environmental, health and safety and sustainability excellence worldwide through the sharing of tools and information in order for business to help business achieve environmental sustainability excellence." Based in Washington, DC, GEMI has an annual budget of $500,000.

GEMI collaborated with the New York–based Environmental Defense Fund, one of the world's largest environmental advocacy organizations, to publish the *Guide to Successful Corporate-NGO Partnerships,* which highlights case studies of successful partnerships and touts their advantages in the following terms: "Compared to other approaches, such as advocating for legislative or regulatory change, measurable results can often be achieved faster through business-NGO partnerships, as long as they are designed and executed properly. Companies and NGOs have discovered a number of reasons to partner: creating business value and environmental benefits; raising the bar on environmental performance; leveraging skills and perspectives not available in the organization; building respect and credibility; providing independent validation; and helping achieve a long-term vision."

Source: Global Environmental Management Initiative, www.gemi.org.

Intergovernmental organizations have been the key brokers of the engagement between international nonprofits and multinational corporations. Since 2000, the UN Global Compact on corporate social responsibility has been a high-profile component of the oversight of the actions of multinational corporations. The signatories of the Global Compact seek to bolster socially responsible practices by encouraging corporations to voluntarily align their operations and strategies with the ten core principles on human rights, labor, the environment, and anticorruption (UN Global Compact 2013). Its complex, multilayered governance is a good example of the parameters of the cross-sectoral networks working on major global issues. At the core, UN level, the implementation of the Global Compact is overseen by a UN-appointed board that includes business and labor organizations as well as international nonprofits such as Transparency International and the International Union for Conservation of Nature. In addition, the United Nations has sponsored the creation of the Foundation for the Global

Compact, a US-registered nonprofit that raised $13 million in 2012 from a broad range of corporate contributors to support implementation, and it has fostered the creation of over 100 regional and national Global Compact local networks, some of which are semiformal networks whereas others have established new local nonprofit organizations. At each level, boards and working parties comprise representatives from all three sectors.

Box 8.10 Conservation International

In 2011, the British magazine *Don't Panic* sent reporters posing as executives from the defense contractor Lockheed Martin to meet with representatives from Conservation International, an environmental protection nonprofit based in the United States that has an annual income of $120 million. The hoax executives were supposedly seeking the help of the nonprofit in "greenwashing" the company's presumably eco-unfriendly public image. Video and audio recordings from the sting appear to offer a damning portrait of a Conservation International representative who seems all too willing to accommodate the phony executives' needs and even suggests that the company adopt an endangered vulture as a mascot. Critics of the organization claim the recordings demonstrate that it is hopelessly compromised and that it typifies an environmental movement that has become wealthy and addicted to the largesse of polluting corporate donors.

The cofounder and CEO of Conservation International hit back in a series of opinion articles. He claimed that the reporting by *Don't Panic* neglected to mention key elements of the multiple exchanges that took place during the hoax and used other parts out of context to paint a highly inaccurate, biased, and incomplete picture of the organization's work. Specifically, he claimed the recordings omitted discussions of the due diligence process and of the organization's insistence on the need to focus on real, technical work that benefits nature as the core of any corporate partnership. He pointed out that Conservation International has actively and transparently engaged with corporations for more than twenty years for the purpose of improving environmental practices. He stated, "We believe that the most effective way to find solutions is to work with other organizations, including corporations, governments and other NGOs. It is simply not sufficient to throw stones from the sidelines; we must work together to address the needs of a rapidly growing global population that is dependent on a fragile and already overstressed environment."

Sources: See *Huffington Post*, http://www.huffingtonpost.com/2011/05/17/conservation-international-lockheed-martin-video_n_863205.html, and http://www.huffingtonpost.com/peter-seligmann/conservation-international-lockheed-martin_b_863876.html.

The Global Compact has over 10,000 signatories, but none of the affiliated institutional structures have enforcement powers. Consequently, external watchdogs continue to play a role, including those that focus on the compact itself, such as the Global Compact Critics project of the Amsterdam-based Centre for Research on Multinational Corporations, as well as others that continue with the general work of overseeing multinational corporations, such as the International Corporate Accountability Roundtable, a project of the US nonprofit Tides. The roundtable acts as the secretariat of a coalition of human rights, environmental, labor, and development organizations that creates, promotes, and defends legal frameworks to ensure that corporations respect human rights in their global operations. The United Nations has also published the *Guiding Principles on Business and Human Rights* (UN Office of the High Commissioner for Human Rights 2011), which outlines the responsibilities of states to monitor human rights abuses in their business sectors.

A few corporations, such as The Body Shop and Google, are regularly cited as exemplars of social activism and sustainable practices, and they generally work in close partnership with local and international nonprofits. However, the most high-profile aspect of the evolving relationship between business and international nonprofits is the emergence of a new generation of global plutocrats. The renowned philanthropists such as George Soros, Bill Gates, and Richard Branson immediately come to mind, but hundreds of other wealthy individuals combine business skills and charitable instincts. Many acquired their wealth fairly young in Internet ventures and now seek to apply their money and skills to social issues. They provide funding, start their own new organizations, or seek to build closer relationships between their businesses and international nonprofits.

9

Emerging Trends

The late Peter Drucker (1994) predicted that voluntary organiza-
tions and nonprofits would increasingly drive the knowledge economy, and
one can find no shortage of opinion makers from public service, academe,
and the media who have declared the twenty-first century to be the "Nonprofit Century" (Eberly 2008; Lang 2013; D. H. Smith 2010). Even those
commentators who do not use such hyperbole point to the expanding social,
political, and economic spaces for nonprofits (see, in particular, the multiple works of Lester Salamon and Helmut Anheier), or they foretell the rise
of concomitant concepts such as social responsibility, social economy, and
collaborative commons, which tend to find their institutional homes in the
nonprofit sector (Cheema and Popovski 2010; Nicholls and Murdock 2012;
Rifkin 2014). The nonprofit organizational form and its associated logics
are even touted as a sustainable future option for industries such as the print
media, where traditional business models have been undermined by new
economic and technological realities.

For perhaps the first time since the emergence of modern nonprofit
organizations some two centuries ago, a broad consensus has developed that
they are beneficial—however defined ideologically and operationally—and
that their growth should be encouraged. Why wouldn't nonprofits be popular? They potentially offer the building of social capital, citizen engagement,
volunteerism, service innovation, and effective service delivery while at the
same time assuring the loyalties of important constituencies. In international
realms, nonprofits drive the expansion of cosmopolitan communities of
exchange and dialogue and promote global citizenship. To many scholars and
practitioners, nonprofits are the embodiment of modernity.

In Chapters 1 through 4, I traced the rise of the nonprofit sector in different countries around the world and emphasized its great diversity. The sector covers a huge range of interests and is populated by organizations of all sizes and capabilities. Although the nonprofit sector often overlaps with the public and for-profit sectors, nonprofits are distinguished by their independence from government, their lack of a direct profit motive, and their essential mission of serving the interests of their members and the public at large. Through the analysis in this book, I have explored the parameters of the growing domestic and international nonprofit sectors and examined many of the policy and operational dilemmas they currently face.

Given the huge diversity of organizations that fall within the scope of the nonprofit sector, no easy or comprehensive conclusions can be offered. However, some key themes have emerged throughout the book: the dramatic growth of the domestic and international nonprofit sectors since the 1970s; the professionalization of the service and expressive functions of nonprofits; the shifting relations with the other two sectors; the introduction of new technologies; and the greater burden of proof needed to justify the work and outcomes of nonprofit organizations.

Although the primary thesis of the book is that the growth of nonprofits is likely to continue in the near future, this thesis is not uncontested. Pushback comes from across the political spectrum: authoritarian governments are wary of nonprofits' independence; conservatives denounce them as instruments of extremist special interests (even though conservatives certainly also have enjoyed the benefits of organizing through nonprofits); progressives accuse them of acting as the handmaidens of exploitative capitalism and imperialism; and organizational theorists of all ideologies fret about the limits of their operational capacities and their lack of accountability. Government crackdowns on the work of nonprofits have become commonplace around the world—whether to curtail political activity, fight corruption, demand more evidence of effective outcomes, or rollback tax concessions.

In the first section of Chapter 5, I explored the possible convergent drift toward a US-inspired model, concluding that the vastly divergent economic, political, social, and administrative contexts will perpetuate differences in nonprofit sectors around the world. When readers in any part of the world see words such as *nonprofit* or *foundation*, they immediately form a conceptual image of how such organizations are governed and operate, based on their own national experiences and contexts. That image is most likely to be wrong if the organizations they are reading about operate in a cultural context different from their own. How a nonprofit foundation operates in a state-centric country is explored in Box 9.1.

The institutional framework that underpins the analysis in this book contends that nonprofits are not merely passive inhabitants of societal spaces conceded to them by other actors. Instead, they actively operate to redefine their roles and relationships with other actors and to reconstruct

Box 9.1 The Hassan II Foundation

In 1990, the Fondation Hassan II pour les Marocains Résidant à l'Etranger (Hassan II Foundation for Moroccans Residing Abroad) was created in Rabat, Morocco. Established by royal decree by the late king Hassan II, it is officially described as a "nonprofit institution with a social vocation, endowed with a moral personality and financial autonomy." It is an operating foundation that seeks to provide social and legal assistance to Moroccans abroad and to help improve economic outcomes for emigrants.

Like many nationally sponsored foundations around the world, it has a very close relationship with government. The current president is Princess Lalla Meryem, daughter of the late king Hassan II and sister of the current king Mohammed VI. At one time the government minister in charge of working with Moroccans abroad also ran the foundation.

A government official noted that a foundation was preferable to a ministry, because when a foundation intervenes on behalf of immigrants, it does not provoke the same sensibilities as a government ministry, and because an NGO has a stronger voice with the governments of the countries where Moroccans have settled.

Source: See the Hassan II Foundation for Moroccans Residing Abroad, http://www.fh2mre.ma/.

the societies in which they operate. However, throughout the book, the limits of the independent agency of nonprofits have been analyzed, and the evidence suggests that they are perhaps more minor actors than many aspire to be, or believe themselves to be. The boundaries and powers of the sector are shaped by forces generally outside the control of the sector and certainly outside the control of individual organizations.

Perspectives on the future of nonprofits are dependent on the observers' worldviews and their interpretation of past and present dynamics. The nexus between the work of nonprofits and societal evolutions appears to be a blank slate onto which different ideologies and disciplinary traditions etch their own perspectives. In industrialized democracies, nonprofits are seen as both the cause of the withering of the welfare state and its savior. In developing countries, nonprofits are seen as actors that have lifted populations out of poverty or condemned them to continued exploitation. These subjective realities are time and place bound, dependent on complex historical conjunctures. In times of transitions to more democratic regimes, the nonprofit sector may be lauded as progressive and emancipatory, whereas in more stable situations it may be scorned as reactionary and entrenching elite privileges. The rise of the nonprofit sector in many industrialized democracies since the 1980s has coincided with a resurgence of inequality and the concentration of wealth in the hands of elites, but also with significant gains in human rights, health, education, and the environment. Have nonprofits been the protectors against even worse economic inequality and enablers of the social gains, or have they merely been spectators to dynamics propelled by other actors?

In Chapters 1 and 7, I noted that nonprofit scholars are often sobered by the realization of how little time and space other commentators less versed in nonprofit debates seem to dedicate to the sector. In many analyses of economic, social, and political futures, nonprofits appear only in general statements about the need to strengthen civil society, and even then they generally are treated as merely agents of other institutions and policies. Books analyzing future trends by the world's most respected pundits often have no index entries for nonprofits, civil society, or any of the other equivalent terms used in this book. Perhaps this issue is simply one of a misidentification of the units of analysis, as a closer examination of the futurist literature reveals that many of the structures cited as key actors in future dynamics are in fact nonprofit organizations, even if they are not identified as such.

Megatrends

Most commentaries on current societal dynamics bode well for the nonprofit sector. It may well be for ideologically opposing reasons and conflicting dynamics, but the upshot is that many current world trends point to conditions that are likely to enable the expansion of the sector. Of the numerous factors driving the growth of the sector that have been identified in this book, the following are arguably the most significant:

- Retrenchment of government under almost all regimes. Industrialized democracies, centralized states, and intergovernmental entities are ceding political and operational space to nonstate actors.
- Shifts to more privatized solutions to public problems and emergence of a wider range of quasi-public goods.
- Expansion of the funding base for nonprofits through government contracting, corporate sponsorship, and private philanthropy.
- A growing middle class in the South that is seeking greater participation and has more disposable income to support philanthropic activities.
- Key demographic and cultural shifts in the North and South, including an increase in the active elderly and a generation of youth schooled in philanthropy. Populations are increasingly educated, empowered, and entrepreneurial.
- New technologies, which reduce transaction costs for starting and operating organizations.
- Global spread of nonprofit mind-sets and toolkits.

The growth of the nonprofit sector in China illustrates many of these trends (see Box 9.2).

Box 9.2 The Nonprofit Sector in China

The People's Republic of China is the most populous country in the world with a population of approximately 1.3 billion. It has had a long history of charitable and mutual welfare organizations. However, since the end of its civil war in 1949, China has been under the single-party rule of the Communist Party, which assumed direct control over all political and social institutions.

Economic and social reforms after the death of Mao Zedong in 1976 allowed the tentative flowering of a more independent civil society. Registration of new organizations required sponsorship by a government entity, and most of the early registered nonprofits were in fact GONGOs set up by governments or ex-officials to help control the sector. After the 1989 Tiananmen Square protests, the government allowed more nonprofits to be established as long as they did not engage in political activism, including human rights work.

Even under these restricted conditions, the number of registered nonprofits has grown dramatically. In 1990 only some 20,000 organizations were officially registered, but by 2011 that number had climbed to close to 500,000. These registered nonprofits work in a range of subsectors, including health, education, poverty relief, culture, sports, and professional exchange, and many are now contracted by the government to deliver services. The government also began to allow foreign nonprofits to operate in China and even encouraged the importation of foreign operational models. In 2002, Lions Clubs International was the first international volunteer service club organization to be officially recognized. The government issued an executive order that was countersigned by the Chinese premier to officially establish two pilot Lions clubs in Shenzhen and Guangdong. Currently there are some 200 Lions Clubs in China.

In addition to the officially registered organizations, many others have been started by individual entrepreneurs operating outside the formal nonprofit legal regime. They are mostly small organizations, often referred to as unregistered social organizations. Estimates of the number of these organizations range from 1.5 million up to 10 million, many of which have registered as businesses.

The Sichuan earthquake of 2008 is often cited as a key turning point in government and popular attitudes toward domestic and foreign nonprofits as they were seen as more effective in responding to the emergency than the government. Government officials now accept that domestic and international nonprofits can help meet a wide range of social demands and that

continues

Box 9.2 continued

the growing middle class is turning to nonprofits for new ways to participate in society and to become more active and philanthropic citizens.
China was one of the first countries that Bill Gates and Warren Buffett
visited to promote their Giving Pledge (see Box 6.15), and online giving
is flourishing despite restrictions on fund-raising.

In 2012, the government announced that nonprofits no longer needed
official sponsorship for registration and eased many of the rules that
mandated direct government supervision of the work of domestic and
international organizations. The registration and oversight system was
decentralized, with the central Ministry of Civil Affairs transferring these
responsibilities to provincial civil affairs authorities.

The nonprofit sector in China is typically characterized with qualifiers
such as "emerging," "young," and "fragile." Even with the recent reforms,
the Chinese government continues to tightly control nonprofits, through
regulations, revenue control, and the shutdown of organizations that dare to
push the boundaries too far. The sector is expanding quickly, but it still
faces the challenges of a tenuous funding base and a lack of managerial
expertise. Although many organizations are genuinely independent, the sector continues to be largely dominated by GONGOs, burdened by red tape,
and bedeviled by corruption. However, commentators concur that the
expanding sector presents a potential challenge to the hegemony of the
regime, and that the 2012 reforms are only one more milestone in the evolving relations between the government and nonprofits in China.

Sources: Guo et al. 2012; J. Richter and Hatch 2013.

Maintaining Legitimacy

The future of the nonprofit sector is dependent on its continuing legitimacy,
yet it is always in some danger of faltering under the weight of its own contradictions. If it cannot continue to demonstrate that it is more effective, efficient, and trustworthy than the other two sectors, it may find itself crowded
out by a resurgent public sector and an increasingly socially responsible for-
profit sector. Of most concern is malfeasance and rent seeking in nonprofits,
but upstanding, well-managed organizations still face considerable challenges in demonstrating their impact and public benefit. Even ardent supporters of the sector decry that many domestic and international nonprofits
have "lost their way," becoming bureaucratic, depoliticized organizations
responding primarily to government and donor agendas rather than being the
autonomous, grassroots-oriented, and innovative organizations that they

once supposedly were. In the section on accountability in Chapter 8, I illustrated many of the key initiatives currently under way in the international arena to strengthen the capacity of nonprofits to demonstrate and communicate their impact.

As the sector grows, its base will become broader, but the peak of the demographic pyramid that represents the incomes of organizations will be higher. The separation between the corporatized heavyweights and the grassroots is being driven by the growth of a small group of super-nonprofits. A "big versus small" debate continues to vex every nonprofit ecosystem. Unease can be sensed regarding not only the emergence of nonprofit oligarchies but also the fragmentation of the sector into small organizations without agency. Larger nonprofits are seen as more professional and more capable of delivering complex services and are, for those reasons, more likely to be treated as equals by powerful stakeholders from government and the for-profit sector. Smaller is seen as more responsive, agile, and able to incorporate diversity. As social innovation becomes the new creed, the focus shifts to celebrating entrepreneurship, and questions of sustainability often recede into the background. The same centrifugal-centripetal tensions between consolidation and decentralization identified in international structures in Chapter 6 have their echo in the debates about the optimal size of organizations.

The Rise of the South

The growth of the nonprofit sector around the world over the past decades has occurred in various waves, some successive and some parallel. Growth has been driven by the implementation of new public management in industrialized English-speaking liberal countries, transitions to more democratic regimes in Eastern Europe and Latin America, the restructuring of the welfare state in social democratic and corporatist countries, and the economic growth of Asia. The current wave appears to be the rising economic and political influence of the global South. In part this overlaps with the aforementioned changes in Latin America, Eastern Europe, and Asia, but it is also a new dynamic created by some of the earlier changes reaching the "critical mass" needed for their global projection, as well as by the economic and political development of sub-Saharan Africa and the recent transitions in Arab countries. More, and more powerful, nonprofits are developing outside the North, including new grassroots and domestic organizations in low- and middle-income countries and new regional and international players from BRICS, the Gulf states, and other emerging economies. The tendency is to focus on the high-profile humanitarian aid and advocacy nonprofits, but as has been illustrated in Chapters 6 and 7, the international dimension of nonprofit work involves a wide range of issues and many modes of cross-border contact. In Box 9.3, how a domestic nonprofit in Turkey that focuses on strengthening corporate governance operates as part of a complex international network of similar organizations is documented.

Optimists argue that this changing geopolitical stage will pave the way for more locally relevant Southern organizations to emerge and to mobilize using indigenous bottom-up approaches with operational philosophies that do not necessarily mirror those of their Northern counterparts. However, the majority of the funding for the nonprofits in the South will continue to flow from the North, and the push for global standards suggests isomorphism toward established international operating norms based largely on the liberal model of nonprofits. At the same time, yet to be seen is what the impact will be on the nonprofit sector of political dynamics influenced as much by Beijing, Ankara (Turkey), and other illiberal regimes as by Washington, DC. Nonprofit sectors around the world may grow, although many

---

Box 9.3 The Corporate Governance Association of Turkey

The Corporate Governance Association of Turkey (Türkiye Kurumsal Yönetim Derneği, TKYD) was established in 2003 as a voluntary NGO with the mission of implementing international standards of corporate governance practices based on transparency, accountability, and responsibility in the private sector, the public sector, the media, regulators, civil society organizations, and the academic world.

Membership of TKYD comprises multinational corporations operating in Turkey, including Coca-Cola and Deloitte, as well as local corporations. TKYD provides resources to organizations from all sectors along with regular training programs, including a 2010 project that focused on the governance of Turkish football clubs.

TKYD is a signatory to the UN Global Compact (see Chapter 8) and is funded by membership fees and sponsorships from intergovernmental organizations such as the OECD and the World Bank Group, as well as from nongovernmental initiatives to improve governance in the public, private, and nonprofit sectors. The nongovernmental sponsors include the Global Reporting Initiative, an organization based in Amsterdam that has developed a framework for measuring and reporting on the economic, environmental, and social dimensions of NGO activities, products, and services.

Sources: See the Corporate Governance Association of Turkey, http://www.tkyd.org/tr/; Global Reporting Initiative, https://www.globalreporting.org/reporting/sector-guidance /sector-guidance/ngo/Pages/default.aspx.

regimes will continue to erect significant institutional barriers to contain and channel the expansion of nonprofits and will occasionally resort to hard power repression. The Carnegie Endowment for International Peace reports a "viral-like spread" of new laws restricting foreign funding for domestic nonprofits and a shrinking of the political space for independent civil society (Carothers and Brechenmacher 2014). Transitional and emerging countries have witnessed a growth in a wide range of nonprofit organizations, but they are also the epicenter of the "associational counterrevolution," as governments tighten restrictions on foreign funding and seek to constrain the operations of nonprofits (Rutzen 2015).

Intersectoral Trends

In Chapter 2, the concept of nonprofits as a separate third sector was defended. However, the emerging social enterprise discourse and the stronger integration with government and for-profit corporations highlighted throughout the book demonstrate an increasing blurring of the former boundaries between the sectors. This determines not only how organizations collaborate together across sectors but also which sector is seen as the best platform for achieving social goals. The offering of certain goods and services in parallel versions by public, private, and nonprofit organizations has had a long history, but the repertoire of what moves between the sectors appears to be expanding. Urban bicycle sharing systems typify the choices that can be made to implement public projects (see Box 9.4).

All three sectors are increasingly entrepreneurial and are colonizing activities that previously have been associated with the other two sectors. "Shapeshifting" can be seen as organizations and projects migrate between sectors, and new hybrid corporate forms are being developed. The challenge for the nonprofit sector is to maintain a comparative advantage as a public actor despite the increasingly porous boundaries between the sectors.

As noted in Chapters 3 and 8, larger nonprofits are adopting corporate principles and strategies, hiring staff with business backgrounds, and using increasingly complex corporate structures and financial instruments, which may include creating for-profit subsidiaries. The greater monetization of their assets and activities and the emergence of the various forms of impact investing are leading nonprofits into new territory that can potentially bring efficiency, scale, and reach to organizations. However, these benefits must be weighed against the danger that a profit motive may lead to the neglect of low-return outcomes, diminish the quality of a good or service, and alienate traditional constituencies. Commercialization may be improving the bottom line for many nonprofits, but it also makes them less distinguishable from the other sectors.

Box 9.4 Urban Bicycle Sharing

Since 2005, public bicycle-sharing systems in cities around the world have been expanding exponentially. Participant fees cover only part of the costs, so they are funded through one of three typical strategies: the public sector, the private sector, and the nonprofit sector.

In Barcelona, Spain, Bicing, considered part of the municipal public transport system, is subsidized through parking-meter revenues. To reduce the cost burden to the city, the right-of-center mayor entered into a sponsorship contract with a prominent mobile phone company, granting them the right to put small advertisements on the bicycle mudguards. The center-left opposition has vowed to tear up the contract if it wins office, alleging that it is part of a move toward the privatization and commercialization of public services.

In New York City, Citi Bike is a for-profit company sponsored by a private bank with a similar name, Citibank. The bicycles are painted in the corporate colors of the bank, and the Citi Bike's logo replicates the fonts and imagery of the bank logo. Advertising for the bank and a credit card company can be seen on the bicycle docks and payment kiosks. When reports emerged in early 2014 that Citi Bike was running a considerable deficit, the newly elected, center-left mayor, Bill de Blasio, declared that not one cent of public money would be spent on the system.

In Seattle the system is managed by Pronto, a 501(c)(3) nonprofit organization. Donors include state and city governments, as well as local foundations and for-profit corporations, including the airline Alaska and the outdoor equipment company REI.

Sources: Bicing, http://www.bicing.cat; Citi Bike, http://www.citibikenyc.com; Puget Sound Bike Share, http://www.pugetsoundbikeshare.org; Pronto http://www.pronto cycleshare.com.

The average person may be bewildered by the distinctions between the sectors or perhaps simply does not know or care about organizational forms as long as their needs are met. Ask any New Yorker about Central Park, and he or she will speak admiringly about its revitalization. Yet few will know that it is managed by a nonprofit, and even fewer will have an opinion about whether that nonprofit, the Central Park Conservancy, should pass part of its substantial philanthropic revenues to poorer parks (see Box 3.1). The blurred boundaries are even more evident in the online environment where for-profits and nonprofits indistinctly create virtual social and political communities, and peer-to-peer crowdfunding sites raise funds equally for both nonprofit charitable activities and commercial start-ups. Facebook has created massive privatized social communities, Kickstarter has redefined all notions of what is a "cause" worthy of contributions, and Change.org has demonstrated the substantial profit in political organizing.

As noted in Chapter 8, the peer-to-peer websites and social media are bypassing the intermediary function of nonprofits, particularly of international organizations, by allowing donors to give more directly to recipients around the world. This ability constitutes a potential threat to larger organizations that previously monopolized fund-raising, but also an opportunity for smaller organizations anywhere in the world to reach global audiences. This potentially disruptive disintermediation effect of new technologies is equally true for the convening functions of nonprofits. Interactive and participatory networking is enabling new forms of associational life and engagement. "Digital civil society" (Bernholz, Cordelli, and Reich 2013a), "organizing without organizations" (Shirky 2008), and "government 2.0" (Newsom and Dickey 2014) are just three of the labels created in an attempt to capture the emerging phenomenon. Cheap computing and mobile technologies are creating a "virtual middle class" that confers political voice to a far wider range of people than the traditional bases of militancy (Friedman 2013). The challenge for nonprofits is to understand whether these technologies and social media organizing modes are generating new autonomous processes that will compete with, and ultimately displace, traditional nonprofit organizing, or whether they are simply tools that existing nonprofits will use to extend their reach and influence.

Despite such challenges, the activities and salience of nonprofits will continue to expand domestically and internationally in the foreseeable future. Seemingly opposing ideologies now concur that they are necessary elements of the institutional frameworks for service delivery and policy-making, albeit with vastly different parameters. The outlook for nonprofits in each country and in the international arena will be defined by the equilibriums between the government, the market, and nonprofits as they vie for political space, resources, and the trust of their publics.

The history of the nonprofit sector around the world clearly documents that the three sectors wax and wane. Gains in one sector may lead to setbacks in another. However, this trend is not necessarily a zero-sum game or a trilemma that pits the sectors against each other. More nonprofits do not necessarily mean less government: a country can have more government and more nonprofits. Growing populations and expanding arenas of operation provide opportunities for entrepreneurs from all three sectors. A global cross-fertilization of institutional logics is taking place, but the repertoires of organizational forms and operational strategies still reflect profound cultural differences and competing ideologies. The cultural frames identified in Chapter 4 represent the contexts in which these equilibriums will evolve at national levels, whereas international nonprofit activities will primarily reflect the structures and processes that emerge from a few influential countries that have sufficient economic, political, and moral weight to shape the contours of the sector around the world.

Bibliography

Abbott, Kenneth W., and Duncan Snidal. 2009. "The Governance Triangle: Regulatory Institutions and the Shadow of the State." In *The Politics of Global Regulation*, edited by Walter Mattli and Ngaire Woods, 44–88. Princeton, NJ: Princeton University Press.

Abrahamsen, Rita. 2004. "The Power of Partnerships in Global Governance." *Third World Quarterly* 25 (8): 1453–1467.

Abzug, Rikki, and Natalie J. Webb. 1996. "Another Role for Nonprofits: The Case of Mop-Ups and Nursemaids Resulting from Privatization in Emerging Economies." *Nonprofit and Voluntary Sector Quarterly* 25 (2): 156–173.

Adler, Nancy J. 2008. *International Dimensions of Organizational Behavior.* 5th ed. Eagan, MN: Thomson/South-Western.

African CSO Network Portal. 2014. "About Us." http://www.africancso.org/web /guest/about-us.

Agg, Catherine. 2006. *Trends in Government Support for Non-Governmental Organizations: Is the "Golden Age" of the NGO Behind Us?* UNRISD/PPC-SSM23/06/2. Civil Society and Social Movements Programme Papers. UN Research Institute for Social Development. http://www.unrisd.org/80256B3C00 5BCCF9/(httpAuxPages)/E8BC05C1E4B8AD6FC12571D1002C4F0B/$file /Agg.pdf.

Agunias, Dovelyn Rannveig, and Kathleen Newland. 2012. *Developing a Road Map for Engaging Diasporas in Development: A Handbook for Policymakers and Practitioners in Home and Host Countries.* Geneva: International Organization for Migration.

Ahmed, Shamima, and David M. Potter. 2006. *NGOs in International Politics.* Bloomfield, CT: Kumarian.

Aiken, Mike. 2010. "Social Enterprise: Challenges from the Field." In *Hybrid Organizations and the Third Sector: Challenges for Practice, Theory and Policy*, edited by David Billis, 153–174. Basingstoke, UK: Palgrave Macmillan.

Ainsworth, David. 2011. "Charities Can Be 'Conservative and Self-Satisfied', Says RNIB Chair." *Third Sector*, no. 12, May. http://www.thirdsector.co.uk/News /DailyBulletin/1069568/Charities-conservative-self-satisfied-says-RNIB-chair.

Al Bawaba. 2011. "Forbes Middle East Supports Charitable Work and Reveals the Top Transparent Charities in the Arab World." *Al Bawaba* (Online). http://www.albawaba.com/forbes-middle-east-supports-charitable-work-and-reveals-top-transparent-charities-arab-world-387193.

Alcock, Pete, and Jeremy Kendall. 2011. "Constituting the Third Sector: Processes of Decontestation and Contention Under the UK Labour Governments in England." *Voluntas* 22 (3): 450–469.

Alexander, Jessica. 2013. *Chasing Chaos: My Decade In and Out of Humanitarian Aid*. New York: Broadway.

Andersson, Fredrik O. 2012. "Social Entrepreneurship as Fetish." *Nonprofit Quarterly* (Online). http://nonprofitquarterly.org/management/20140-social-entrepreneurship-as-fetish.html.

Andrews, Kevin. 2012. "Coalition's Approach to the Charitable Sector." http://kevinandrews.com.au/media/public-speech/coalition-approach-to-the-charitable-sector.

Anheier, Helmut. 1990. "Themes in International Research on the Nonprofit Sector." *Nonprofit and Voluntary Sector Quarterly* 19 (4): 371–391.

———. 2005. *Nonprofit Organizations: Theory, Management, Policy*. London: Routledge.

———. 2014. *Nonprofit Organizations: Theory, Management, Policy*. 2nd ed. London: Routledge.

Anheier, Helmut, and Jeremy Kendall, eds. 2001. *Third Sector Policy at the Crossroads: An International Non-Profit Analysis*. London: Routledge.

Anheier, Helmut, and Nuno Themudo. 2004. "Governance and Management of International Membership Organizations." *Brown Journal of World Affairs* 11 (2): 185–198.

Applbaum, Kalman. 1996. "The Endurance of Neighborhood Associations in a Japanese Commuter City." *Urban Anthropology* 25 (1): 1–37.

Applebaum, Anne. 2012. "The Dead Weight of Past Dictatorships." *New York Times* (Online), November 3. http://www.nytimes.com/2012/11/04/opinion/sunday/the-dead-weight-of-past-dictatorships.html.

Archambault, Edith. 2001. "Historical Roots of the Nonprofit Sector in France." *Nonprofit and Voluntary Sector Quarterly* 30 (2): 204–220.

Archibugi, Daniele. 2008. *The Global Commonwealth of Citizens Toward Cosmopolitan Democracy*. Princeton, NJ: Princeton University Press. http://public.eblib.com/EBLPublic/PublicView.do?ptiID=457744.

Arndt, Channing, Sam Jones, and Finn Tarp. 2010. *Aid, Growth, and Development: Have We Come Full Circle?* Helsinki: World Institute for Development Economics Research. http://hdl.handle.net/10419/54076.

Asian Philanthropy Advisory Network. 2012. "Reports on Diaspora Philanthropy." http://asianphilanthropy.org/?s=diaspora.

Aspen Institute. 2002. *The Nonprofit Sector and Government: Clarifying the Relationship*. Washington, DC: Aspen Institute. http://www.aspeninstitute.org/publications/nonprofit-sector-and-government-clarifying-relationship.

Australian Productivity Commission. 2010. *Contribution of the Not-for-Profit Sector*. Canberra, Australia: Australian Government Productivity Commission.

Baggot, Rob. 1995. *Pressure Groups Today*. Manchester, UK: Manchester University Press.

Balboa, Cristina. 2014. "How Successful Transnational Non-Governmental Organizations Set Themselves Up for Failure on the Ground." *World Development* 54 (February): 273–287.

Baldwin, Peter. 2009. *The Narcissism of Minor Differences: How America and Europe Are Alike*. New York: Oxford University Press.

Banks, Nicola, and David Hulme. 2012. *The Role of NGOs and Civil Society in Development and Poverty Reduction*. Brooks World Poverty Institute Working Paper no. 171. Manchester University. http://papers.ssrn.com/sol3/papers.cfm?abstract_id=2072157.

Barraket, Jo. 2008. "Social Enterprise and Governance: Implications for the Australian Third Sector." In *Strategic Issues for the Not-for-Profit Sector*, edited by Jo Barraket, 126–142. Sydney: UNSW Press.

Batliwala, Srilatha, and L. David Brown. 2006. *Transnational Civil Society: An Introduction*. Bloomfield, CT: Kumarian.

Bauer, Peter T. 1969. "Dissent on Development." *Scottish Journal of Political Economy* 16 (3): 75–94.

Benessaieh, Afef. 2011. "Global Civil Society Speaking in Northern Tongues?" *Latin American Perspectives* 38 (6): 69–90.

Beng-Huat, Chua. 2003. "Non-Transformative Politics: Civil Society in Singapore." In *Civil Society in Asia*, edited by David Schak and Wayne Hudson, 20–39. Burlington, VT: Ashgate.

Bernal, Victoria, and Inderpal Grewal, eds. 2014. *Theorizing NGOs: States, Feminisms, and Neoliberalism*. Next Wave: New Directions in Women's Studies. Durham, NC: Duke University Press.

Bernholz, Lucy, Chiara Cordelli, and Rob Reich. 2013a. *The Emergence of Digital Civil Society*. Stanford, CA: Stanford Center on Philanthropy and Civil Society. http://www.grantcraft.org/index.cfm?fuseaction=Page.ViewPage&pageId=3796.

———. 2013b. *Good Fences: The Importance of Institutional Boundaries in the New Social Economy*. Stanford, CA: Stanford Center on Philanthropy and Civil Society. http://www.grantcraft.org/index.cfm?fuseaction=Page.ViewPage&pageId=3796.

BetterEvaluation.org. 2013. "Approaches." http://betterevaluation.org/approaches.

Biekart, Kees. 2008. "Learning from Latin America: Recent Trends in European NGO Policymaking." In *Can NGOs Make a Difference? The Challenge of Development Alternatives*, edited by Anthony Bebbington, Samuel Hickey, and Diana Mitlin, 71–89. London: Zed.

Birchall, Johnston. 2001. *The New Mutualism in Public Policy*. London: Routledge. http://search.ebscohost.com/login.aspx?direct=true&scope=site&db=nlebk&db=nlabk&AN=71378.

Bislev, Sven. 2004. "Globalization, State Transformation, and Public Security." *International Political Science Review* 25 (3): 281–296.

Blair, Elizabeth. 2011. "World Art Managers Find New Funding Models in D.C.," National Public Radio, August 11. http://www.npr.org/.

Blair, Tony, and Gerhard Schroeder. 1999. "The Blair/Schroeder Manifesto." *Amsterdam Post*, June 11. http://adampost.home.xs4all.nl/Archive/arc000006.html.

Bloem, Renate, Isolda Agazzi Ben Attia, and Phillipe Dam. 2008. "The Conference of NGOs (CONGO): The Story of Strengthening Civil Society Engagement with the United Nations." In *Critical Mass: The Emergence of Global Civil Society,* edited by James W. S. G. Walker and Andrew S. Thompson. Waterloo, Canada: Wilfried Laurier.

Bloodgood, Elizabeth A., Joannie Tremblay-Boire, and Aseem Prakash. 2014. "National Styles of NGO Regulation." *Nonprofit and Voluntary Sector Quarterly* 43 (4): 716–736.

Bloom, Paul, and Brett Smith. 2010. "Identifying the Drivers of Social Entrepreneurial Impact: Theoretical Development and an Exploratory Empirical Test of SCALERS." *Journal of Social Entrepreneurship* 1 (1): 126–145.

Board Source. 2012. "What Is the Nonprofit Sector? (Reprinted from 2009)." In *The Nature of the Nonprofit Sector*, 2nd ed., edited by J. Steven Ott and Lisa A. Dicke, 10–11. Philadelphia: Westview.

Bob, Clifford. 2011. "Civil and Uncivil Society." In *The Oxford Handbook of Civil Society*, edited by Michael Edwards, 209–219. New York: Oxford University Press.

———. 2012. *The Global Right Wing and the Clash of World Politics*. Cambridge Studies in Contentious Politics. New York: Cambridge University Press.

Bolder Advocacy. 2014. *International Advocacy Capacity Tool*. Washington, DC: Alliance for Justice. http://bolderadvocacy.org/tools-for-effective-advocacy/evaluating-advocacy/international-advocacy-capacity-tool.

Boli, John. 1992. "The Ties That Bind: The Nonprofit Sector and the State in Sweden." In *The Nonprofit Sector in the Global Community: Voices from Many Nations*, edited by Kathleen McCarthy, Virginia Ann Hodgkinson, and Russy D. Sumariwalla, 240–253. San Francisco: Jossey-Bass.

———. 2006. "International Nongovernmental Organizations." In *The Nonprofit Sector: A Research Handbook*, 2nd ed., edited by Walter W. Powell and Richard Steinberg, 333–351. New Haven, CT: Yale University Press.

Boli, John, and George M. Thomas, eds. 1999. *Constructing World Culture: International Nongovernmental Organizations Since 1875*. Stanford, CA: Stanford University Press.

Bolton, Matthew, and Thomas Nash. 2010. "The Role of Middle Power–NGO Coalitions in Global Policy: The Case of the Cluster Munitions Ban." *Global Policy* 1 (2): 172–184.

Bond, Patrick. 2008. "Reformist Reforms, Non-Reformist Reforms and Global Justice: Activist, NGO and Intellectual Challenges in the World Social Forum." *Societies Without Borders* 3: 4–19.

Bornstein, David. 2007. *How to Change the World*. Updated ed. New York: Oxford University Press.

Bornstein, David, and Susan Davis. 2010. *Social Entrepreneurship: What Everyone Needs to Know*. New York: Oxford University Press.

Borzaga, Carlo, and Luca Fazzi. 2010. "Processes of Institutionalization and Differentiation in the Italian Third Sector." *Voluntas* 22 (3): 409–427.

Brecher, Charles, and Oliver Wise. 2008. "Looking a Gift Horse in the Mouth: Challenges in Managing Philanthropic Support for Public Services." *Public Administration Review* 68 (S1 [December]): S146–S161.

Brown, Kevin M, and Susan Kenny. 2000. *Rhetorics of Welfare: Uncertainty, Choice and Voluntary Associations*. Basingstoke, UK: Macmillan.

Brown, L. David, Alnoor Ebrahim, and Srilatha Batliwala. 2012. "Governing International Advocacy NGOs." *World Development* 40 (6): 1098–1108.

Brown, L. David, and Jonathan Fox. 2000. *Transnational Civil Society Coalitions and the World Bank: Lessons from Project and Policy Influence Campaigns*. Working Paper no. 3. Cambridge, MA: Hauser Center for Nonprofit Organizations, Kennedy School of Government, Harvard University.

Brown, L. David, and Jagadananda. 2010. "Civil Society Legitimacy and Accountability: Issues and Challenges." In *NGO Management: The Earthscan Companion*, edited by Alan Fowler and Chiku Malunga, 115–135. London: Earthscan.

Brown, L. David, Sanjeev Khagram, Mark H. Moore, and Peter Frumkin. 2000. *Globalization, NGOs and Multi-Sectoral Relations.* Working Paper no. 1. Cambridge, MA: Hauser Center for Nonprofit Organizations, Kennedy School of Government, Harvard University.

Brown, L. David, and Mark H. Moore. 2001. "Accountability, Strategy, and International Nongovernmental Organizations." *Nonprofit and Voluntary Quarterly* 30 (3): 569–587.

Brown, Rajeswary Ampalavanar, and Justin Pierce, eds. 2013. *Charities in the Non-Western World: The Development and Regulation of Indigenous and Islamic Charities.* New York: Routledge.

Buckley, Charles. 2013. "China Takes Aim at Western Ideas." *New York Times* (Online), August 20. http://www.nytimes.com/2013/08/20/world/asia/chinas-new-leadership-takes-hard-line-in-secret-memo.html.

Buffett, Peter. 2013. "The Charitable-Industrial Complex." *New York Times* (Online), July 27. http://www.nytimes.com/2013/07/27/opinion/the-charitable-industrial-complex.html.

Bullain, Nilda, and Radost Toftisova. 2005. "A Comparative Analysis of European Policies and Practices of NGO-Government Cooperation." *International Journal of Not-for-Profit Law* 7 (4): 64–112.

Burstein, Paul, Rachel Einwohner, and Jocelyn A. Hollander. 1995. "The Success of Political Movements: A Bargaining Perspective." In *The Politics of Social Protest*, edited by J. Craig Jenkins and Bert Klandermans, 275–295. Minneapolis: Minnesota University Press.

Buthe, Tim, and Cindy Cheng. 2014. "Private Transnational Governance of Economic Development: International Development Aid." In *Handbook of Global Economic Governance*, edited by Manuela Moschella and Catherine Weaver, 322–342. New York: Routledge. http://www.ssrn.com/abstract=2290424.

Cain, Kenneth, Heidi Postlewait, and Andrew Thomson. 2004. *Emergency Sex and Other Desperate Measures: A True Story from Hell on Earth.* New York: Hyperion.

CARE International. 2004. "Safety and Security Handbook." http://www.coe-dmha.org/care/pdf/EntireBook.pdf.

Carey, Henry F. 2012. *Privatizing the Democratic Peace: Policy Dilemmas of NGO Peacebuilding.* Basingstoke, UK: Palgrave Macmillan.

Carothers, Thomas, and Saskia Brechenmacher. 2014. *Closing Space: Democracy and Human Right Support Under Fire.* Washington, DC: Carnegie Endowment for International Peace.

Carter, Susan, and Paula Speevak Sladowski. 2008. *Deliberate Relationships Between Government and the Nonprofit/Voluntary Sector: An Unfolding Picture.* Ottawa: Wellesley Institute and the Centre for Voluntary Sector Research and Development.

Casa Amiga. 2013. "Financiadores." http://www.casa-amiga.org.mx/index.php/Contenido/financiadores.html.

Casey, John. 2004. "Third Sector Participation in the Policy Process: A Framework for Comparative Analysis." *Policy and Politics* 32 (2): 239–256.

———. 2011. "A New Era of Collaborative Government-Nonprofit Relations in the U.S.?" *Nonprofit Policy Forum* 2 (1). http://www.degruyter.com/view/j/npf.2011.2.1/npf.2011.2.1.1010/npf.2011.2.1.1010.xml.

———. 2013. "Hybrid Discourses on Social Enterprise: Unpacking the Zeitgeist." In *Social Entrepreneurship*, Vol. 1, edited by Thomas Lyons, 71–90. Santa Barbara, CA: Praeger.

Casey, John, and Bronwen Dalton. 2006. "The Best of Times, the Worst of Times: Community-Sector Advocacy in the Age of 'Compacts.'" *Australian Journal of Political Science* 41 (1): 23–38.

Casey, John, Bronwen Dalton, Rose Melville, and Jenny Onyx. 2010. "Strengthening Government-Nonprofit Relations: International Experiences with Compacts." *Voluntary Sector Review* 1 (1): 59–76.

Center on Wealth and Philanthropy. 2010. "Transfer of Wealth." http://www.bc.edu /research/cwp/features/wealthtransfer.html.

Centre for Voluntary Sector Research and Development (CVSRD). 2009. *A Gathering of Counterparts*. Ottawa: CVSRD. http://www.cvsrd.org/eng/connections -communities/cc_counterparts.html.

Chandhoke, Neera. 2005. "How Global Is Global Civil Society?" *Journal of World-Systems Research* 11 (2): 354–371.

Charities Aid Foundation. 2006. *International Comparisons of Charitable Giving*. CAF Briefing Paper. Kent, UK: Charities Aid Foundation.

———. 2010. "World Giving Index 2010." https://www.cafonline.org/navigation /footer/about-caf/publications/2010-publications/world-giving-index.aspx.

———. 2011. "World Giving Index 2011." https://www.cafonline.org/publications /2011-publications/world-giving-index-2011.aspx.

———. 2012. "World Giving Index 2012." https://www.cafonline.org/PDF/World GivingIndex2012WEB.pdf.

———. 2014. *Give Me a Break: Why the UK Should Not Aspire to a "US-Style" Culture of Charitable Giving*. 1. Giving Thought Discussion Paper. Kent, UK: Charities Aid Foundation.

Charnovitz, Steven. 1997. "Two Centuries of Participation: NGOs and International Governance." *Michigan Journal of International Law* 18 (2): 183–286.

Cheema, G. Shabbir. 2010. "Civil Society and Democratic Governance: An Introduction." In *Engaging Civil Society: Emerging Trends in Democratic Governance*, edited by G. Shabbir Cheema and Vesselin Popovski, 1–20. New York: United Nations University.

Cheema, G. Shabbir, and Vesselin Popovski, eds. 2010. *Engaging Civil Society: Emerging Trends in Democratic Governance*. New York: United Nations University.

CIVICUS. 2012. *State of Civil Society 2011*. Johannesburg, South Africa. http://socs .civicus.org/2011/wp-content/uploads/2012/04/State-of-Civil-Society-2011.pdf.

———. 2013a. *State of Civil Society 2013*. Johannesburg, South Africa. http://socs .civicus.org/wp-content/uploads/2013/04/2013StateofCivilSocietyReport_full .pdf.

———. 2013b. *The CIVICUS 2013 Enabling Environment Index*. Johannesburg, South Africa. https://civicus.org/eei/downloads/Civicus_EEI%20REPORT%20 2013_WEB_FINAL.pdf.

Clark, John D. 2008. "The Globalization of Civil Society." In *Critical Mass: The Emergence of Global Civil Society*, edited by James W. St. G. Walker and Andrew S. Thompson. Waterloo, ON: Wilfrid Laurier University Press.

Colás, Alejandro. 2002. *International Civil Society: Social Movements in World Politics*. Cambridge, UK: Polity.

Cole, Teju. 2012. "The White-Savior Industrial Complex." *The Atlantic* (Online), March 21. http://www.theatlantic.com/international/archive/2012/03/the-white -savior-industrial-complex/254843/.

Committee Encouraging Corporate Philanthropy (CECP). 2014a. *Giving in Numbers 2014 Edition*. New York: CECP and the Conference Board.

———. 2014b. *Giving Around the Globe 2014 Edition*. New York: CECP.

Cooley, Alexander, and James Ron. 2002. "The NGO Scramble: Organizational Insecurity and the Political Economy of Transnational Action." *International Security* 27 (1): 5–39.

Corry, Olaf. 2010. "Defining and Theorizing the Third Sector." In *Third Sector Research*, edited by Rupert Taylor, 11–20. New York: Springer.

Council of Europe. 2003. *Participatory Status for International Non-Governmental Organisations with the Council of Europe.* Resolution no. 8 (2003), Council of Europe Committee of Ministers. Strasbourg, France: Council of Europe. https://wcd.coe.int/ViewDoc.jsp?id=88953&Site=CM.

———. 2009. *Code of Good Practice for Civil Participation in the Decision-Making Process.* CONF/PLE(2009)CODE1. Strasbourg, France: Conference of INGOs, Council of Europe. http://www.coe.int/t/ngo/Source/Code_English_final.pdf.

Council of International Development Companies (CIDC). 2014. "Did You Know?" http://www.cidc.us/did-you-know/.

Craig, Gary, Marilyn Taylor, and Tessa Parkes. 2004. "Protest or Partnership? The Voluntary and Community Sectors in the Policy Process." *Social Policy and Administration* 38 (3): 221–239.

Cravens, Jayne, and Susan J. Ellis. 2000. *The Virtual Volunteering Guidebook.* Philadelphia: Energize, Inc.

Crowley, James, and Morgana Ryan. 2013. *Building a Better International NGO: Greater than the Sum of the Parts?* Boulder, CO: Kumarian.

Curry, Bill. 2011. "Ottawa Looks at Rewriting Rules on Charitable Giving." *Globe and Mail* (Online), October 28. http://www.theglobeandmail.com/life/giving /giving-news/ottawa-looks-at-rewriting-rules-on-charitable-giving/article 2216738/.

Dalton, Russell J. 1993. *Citizens, Protest and Democracy.* Newbury Park, CA: Sage.

Dalton, Russell J., and Manfred Keuchler. 1990. *Challenging the Political Order: New Social and Political Movements in Western Democracies.* Cambridge, UK: Polity.

Davies, Thomas. 2012. "A 'Great Experiment' of the League of Nations Era: International Nongovernmental Organizations, Global Governance, and Democracy Beyond the State." *Global Governance* 18 (4): 405–423.

———. 2014. *NGOs: A New History of Transnational Civil Society.* London: C. Hurst.

Deaton, Angus. 2013. *The Great Escape: Health, Wealth, and the Origins of Inequality.* Princeton, NJ: Princeton University Press.

Dees, J. Gregory. 2001. "The Meaning of Social Entrepreneurship." http://www .caseatduke.org/documents/dees_sedef.pdf.

Dees, J. Gregory, and Peter Economy. 2001. "Social Entrepreneurship." In *Enterprising Nonprofits: A Toolkit for Social Entrepreneurs*, edited by J. Gregory Dees, Jed Emerson, and Peter Economy, 1–18. New York: Wiley.

Defourny, Jacques, and Marthe Nyssens. 2010. "Conceptions of Social Enterprise and Social Entrepreneurship in Europe and the United States: Convergences and Differences." *Journal of Social Entrepreneurship* 1 (1): 32–53.

DeMars, William E. 2005. *NGOs and Transnational Networks: Wild Cards in World Politics.* London: Pluto.

Denhardt, Janet Vinzant, and Robert B. Denhardt. 2003. *The New Public Service: Serving, Not Steering.* Armonk, NY: M. E. Sharpe.

Denver Foundation. 2010. "Inclusiveness at Work: How to Build Inclusive Nonprofit Organizations." http://www.nonprofitinclusiveness.org/inclusiveness-work -how-build-inclusive-nonprofit-organizations.

Diani, Mario, and Ron Eyerman, eds. 1992. *Studying Collective Action*. Sage Modern Politics Series, Vol. 30. London: Sage.

DiMaggio, Paul, and Helmut Anheier. 1990. "The Sociology of Nonprofit Organizations and Sectors." *Annual Review of Sociology* 16: 137–159.

DiMaggio, Paul, and Walter W. Powell. 1983. "The Iron Cage Revisited: Institutional Isomorphism and Collective Rationality in Organizational Fields." *American Sociological Review* 48 (2): 147–160.

Donovan, Doug, and Caroline Preston. 2012. "Charity Lowers Revenue Figure by \$135-Million." *Chronicle of Philanthropy*, November 29. http://philanthropy .com/article/Charity-Lowers-Revenue-Figure/135982/.

Douglas, James. 1987. "Political Theories of Nonprofit Organizations." In *The Nonprofit Sector: A Research Handbook*, edited by Walter W. Powell and Richard Steinberg, 43–54. New Haven, CT: Yale University Press.

Douglas, Stephen A., and Paul Pedersen. 1973. *Blood, Believer and Brother: The Development of Voluntary Associations in Malaysia*. Athens: Ohio University Center for International Studies.

Drucker, Peter. 1990. *Managing the Non-Profit Organization*. New York: HarperCollins.

———. 1994. "The Age of Social Transformation." *The Atlantic* 274 (5): 53–80.

Eberly, Don E. 2008. *The Rise of Global Civil Society: Building Communities and Nations from the Bottom Up*. New York: Encounter.

Ebrahim, Alnoor. 2003. "Making Sense of Accountability: Conceptual Perspectives for Northern and Southern Nonprofits." *Nonprofit Management and Leadership* 14 (2): 191–212.

———. 2005. *NGOs and Organizational Change: Discourse, Reporting, and Learning*. Cambridge, UK: Cambridge University Press.

Ebrahim, Alnoor, and Steve Herz. 2007. *Accountability in Complex Organizations: World Bank Responses to Civil Society*. 08-027. Kennedy School of Government Working Papers. Harvard University. http://www.hbs.edu/faculty/Publication%20 Files/08-027_18c99232-358f-456e-b619-3056cb59e915.pdf.

The Economist. 2000. "Angry and Effective." http://www.economist.com/node/374657.

———. 2012. "Bangladesh and Development: The Path Through the Fields." http://www.economist.com/news/briefing/21565617-bangladesh-has-dysfunctional -politics-and-stunted-private-sector-yet-it-has-been-surprisingly.

Edelman Trust Barometer. 2012. "NGOs Most Trusted Institution Globally." http://trust.edelman.com/trusts/trust-in-institutions-2/ngos-remain-most-trusted/.

Edgington, Nell. 2011. "The Danger of Abandoning the Nonprofit Sector." *Change.org News*. http://news.change.org/stories/the-danger-of-abandoning -the-nonprofit-sector.

Edwards, Michael. 2009. *Civil Society*. 2nd ed. Cambridge, UK: Polity.

———. 2010a. *Small Change: Why Business Won't Save the World*. San Francisco: Berrett-Koehler.

———. 2010b. "Have NGOs 'Made a Difference'?" In *NGO Management: The Earthscan Companion*, edited by Alan Fowler and Chiku Malunga, 13–25. London: Earthscan.

———, ed. 2011a. *The Oxford Handbook of Civil Society*. New York: Oxford University Press.

———. 2011b. "Introduction: Civil Society and the Geometry of Human Relations." In *The Oxford Handbook of Civil Society*, edited by Michael Edwards, 3–14. New York: Oxford University Press.

Edwards, Michael, and David Hulme. 1996. *Beyond the Magic Bullet: NGO Performance and Accountability in the Post–Cold War World.* West Hartford, CT: Kumarian.

Eikenberry, Angela M. 2009. "The Hidden Costs of Cause Marketing." *Stanford Social Innovation Review* (Summer): 51–55.

Einolf, Christopher, and Susan M. Chambré. 2011. "Who Volunteers? Constructing a Hybrid Theory." *International Journal of Nonprofit and Voluntary Sector Marketing* 16 (4): 298–310.

Eisenberg, Pablo. 2011. "Nonprofits Need to Put Aside Self-Interest in Tax Debate." *Chronicle of Philanthropy.* http://philanthropy.com/article/Nonprofits-Need-to-Put-Aside/129378.

Elkington, John, and Seb Beloe. 2010. "The Twenty-First-Century NGO." In *Good Cop/Bad Cop: Environmental NGOs and Their Strategies Toward Business,* edited by Thomas P. Lyon, 17–47. Washington, DC: Resources for the Future.

Elson, Peter. 2006. "Tracking the Implementation of Voluntary Sector-Government Policy Agreements: Is the Voluntary and Community Sector in the Frame?" *International Journal of Not-for-Profit Law* 8 (4): 34–49.

Encarnación, Omar Guillermo. 2003. *The Myth of Civil Society: Social Capital and Democratic Consolidation in Spain and Brazil.* New York: Palgrave Macmillan.

Esman, Milton J., and Norman Thomas Uphoff. 1984. *Local Organizations: Intermediaries in Rural Development.* Ithaca, NY: Cornell University Press.

Esping-Andersen, Gøsta. 1990. *The Three Worlds of Welfare Capitalism.* Princeton, NJ: Princeton University Press.

Etzioni, Amatai. 1967. "Mixed Scanning: A 'Third' Approach to Decision Making." *Public Administration Review* 27 (5): 385–392.

———. 1973. "The Third Sector and Domestic Missions." *Public Administration Review* 33 (4): 314–323.

European-Arab Project. 2008. "A Code of Conduct for Arab Civil Society Organizations." European-Arab Project on Freedom of Association in the Arab World, the Friedrich Naumann Foundation. http://archive-org.com/page/1178582/2013-01-17/http://www.oneworldtrust.org/csoproject/cso/initiatives/642/a_code_of_conduct_for_arab_civil_society_organizations.

European Social Survey. 2013. "About the European Social Survey." http://www.europeansocialsurvey.org/.

European Values Study. 2011. "About European Values Study." http://www.europeanvaluesstudy.eu/evs/about-evs/.

Evetts, Julia. 1995. "International Professional Associations: The New Context for Professional Projects." *Work, Employment and Society* 9 (4): 763–772.

Farouk, Azeem Fazwan Ahmad. 2011. "The Limits of Civil Society in Democratising the State: The Malaysian Case." *Kajian Malaysia: Journal of Malaysian Studies* 29 (1): 91–109.

Fechter, Anne-Meike, and Heather Hindman, eds. 2011. *Inside the Everyday Lives of Development Workers: The Challenges and Futures of Aidland.* Sterling, VA: Kumarian.

Filer Commission. 1975. *Giving in America: Toward a Stronger Voluntary Sector: Report of the Commission on Private Philanthropy and Public Needs.* Washington, DC: Commission on Private Philanthropy and Public Needs.

Fisher, Julie. 1998. *Nongovernments: NGOs and the Political Development of the Third World.* West Hartford, CT: Kumarian.

Fishman, James J. 2008. "The Political Use of Private Benevolence: The Statute of Charitable Uses." *Pace Law Faculty Publications* Paper 287. http://digital commons.pace.edu/lawfaculty/487.

Florini, Ann, ed. 2000. *The Third Force: The Rise of Transnational Civil Society.* Washington, DC: Carnegie Endowment for International Peace.

Foley, Michael, and Bob Edwards. 1996. "The Paradox of Civil Society and Democratic Social Change." *Journal of Democracy* 7 (3): 38–52.

Forbes. 2011. "The World's Biggest Companies." http://www.forbes.com/2011/04 /20/biggest-world-business-global-2000-11-intro.html.

Forbes Middle East. 2013. "The Most Transparent Charities in the MENA Region." http://english.forbesmiddleeast.com/view.php?list=35.

Foreman, Karen. 1999. "Evolving Global Structures and the Challenges Facing International Relief and Development Organizations." *Nonprofit and Voluntary Sector Quarterly* 28 (4): 178–197.

Foundation Center. 2014. *Key Facts on U.S. Foundations.* New York: Foundation Center. http://foundationcenter.org/gainknowledge/research/pdf/keyfacts2014.pdf.

Fowler, Alan. 2012. "Measuring Civil Society: Perspectives on Afro-Centrism." *Voluntas* 23 (1): 5–25.

Fowler, Alan, and Chiku Malunga, eds. 2010. *NGO Management: The Earthscan Companion.* London: Earthscan.

Frances, Nic. 2008. *The End of Charity: Time for Social Enterprise.* Crows Nest, NSW: Allen and Unwin.

Freedom House. 2011. "Freedom in the World 2011 Survey Release." http://www .freedomhouse.org/template.cfm?page=594.

Friedman, Thomas L. 2013. "The Virtual Middle Class Rises." *New York Times* (Online), February 2. http://www.nytimes.com/2013/02/03/opinion/sunday /friedman-the-virtual-middle-class-rises.html.

Frumkin, Peter. 2005. *On Being Nonprofit: A Conceptual and Policy Primer.* Cambridge, MA: Harvard University Press.

Fyfe, Nicholas R. 2005. "Making Space for 'Neo-Communitarianism'? The Third Sector, State and Civil Society in the UK." *Antipode* 37 (3): 536–557.

Gaudiani, Claire. 2007. "Let's Put the Word 'Nonprofit' Out of Business." *Chronicle of Philanthropy.* http://philanthropy.com/article/Lets-Put-the-Word-Nonprofit/55354/.

Gaudiani, Claire, and D. Graham Burnett. 2011. *Daughters of the Declaration: How Women Social Entrepreneurs Built the American Dream.* New York: Public Affairs.

Gibelman, Margaret. 2000. "The Nonprofit Sector and Gender Discrimination." *Nonprofit Management and Leadership* 10 (3): 251–269.

Gidron, Benjamin. 2010. "Policy Challenges in Light of the Emerging Phenomenon of Social Businesses." *Nonprofit Policy Forum* 1 (1). http://www.degruyter .com/view/j/npf.2010.1.1/npf.2010.1.1.1003/npf.2010.1.1.1003.xml.

Glasius, Marlies, David Lewis, and Hakan Seckinelgin, eds. 2004. *Exploring Civil Society: Political and Cultural Contexts.* London: Routledge.

Global Journal. 2012. "The Top 100 NGOs 2012," vol. 9. http://theglobaljournal .net/2012/Top100NGOs/.

———. 2013. "The Top 100 NGOs 2013," vol. 15 (special edition). http://www.the globaljournal.net/group/top-100-ngos/.

Global Policy Forum. 2012. "Tables and Charts on NGOs." http://www.global policy.org/ngos/tables-and-charts-on-ngos.html.

Global Volunteer Measurement Project. 2011. "The Global Volunteer Measurement Project." http://volunteermeasurement.org/.

Goldblatt, David. 2007. "The Odd Couple: Football and Global Civil Society." In *Global Civil Society 2006/7*, edited by Helmut Anheier, Mary Kaldor, Marlies Glasius, and Martin Albrow, 160–186. London: Sage. http://site.ebrary.com /id/10218175.

Goldsmith, Marshall, and Cathy Walt. 1999. "The Global Leader of the Future: New Competencies for a New Era." http://www.marshallgoldsmithlibrary.com/cim /articles_display.php?aid=128.

Götz, Norbert. 2008. "Reframing NGOs: The Identity of an International Relations Non-Starter." *European Journal of International Relations* 14 (2): 231–258.

———. 2010. "Civil Society and NGO: Far from Unproblematic Concepts." In *Third Sector Research*, edited by Rupert Taylor, 185–196. New York: Springer.

Government of India. 2009. *Compilation of Accounts for Non-Profit Institutions in India in the Framework of System of National Accounts (Report of Phase-1 of the Survey)*. New Delhi: National Accounts Division Central Statistical Organisation Ministry of Statistics and Programme Implementation.

Government of Liberia. 2008. *National Policy on Non-Governmental Organizations in Liberia*. Monrovia: Minister of Planning and Economic Affairs. www.emansion .gov.lr/doc/NGOPolicguidelines.pdf.

Grant, Wyn. 1995. *Pressure Groups, Politics and Democracy in Britain*. New York: Macmillan.

GrantCraft. 2005. *Advocacy Funding: The Philanthropy of Changing Minds*. New York: GrantCraft, Ford Foundation. http://www.grantcraft.org/index.cfm?fuse action=Page.ViewPage&pageId=1309.

Green, Jessica F. 2014. *Rethinking Private Authority: Agents and Entrepreneurs in Global Environmental Governance*. Princeton, NJ: Princeton University Press.

Grønbjerg, Kirstin A., and Lester M. Salamon. 2012. "Devolution, Marketization, and the Changing Shape of Government-Nonprofit Relations." In *The State of Nonprofit America*, edited by Lester M. Salamon, 447–470. Washington, DC: Brookings Institution Press.

Gugerty, Mary Kay, and Aseem Prakash. 2010. *Voluntary Regulation of NGOs and Nonprofits: An Accountability Club Framework*. Cambridge, UK: Cambridge University Press.

Gundelach, Peter, and Lars Torpe. 1996. *Voluntary Associations, New Types of Involvement and Democracy*. Aalborg, Denmark: Department of Economics, Politics and Public Administration, Aalborg University. http://books.google .com/books?id=mhcYcgAACAAJ&dq=Gundelach+and+Torpe&hl=en&sa=X& ei=cMwzUbS9Lqm20QHPsYGADg&ved=0CDAQ6AEwAA.

Guo, Chao, Jun Xu, David Horton Smith, and Zhibin Zhang. 2012. "Civil Society, Chinese Style: The Rise of the Nonprofit Sector in Post-Mao China." *Nonprofit Quarterly* (Online). https://nonprofitquarterly.org/policysocial-context/21246-civil -society-chinese-stylethe-rise-of-the-nonprofit-sector-in-post-mao-chinaby.html.

Haas, Peter M. 1992. "Epistemic Communities and International Policy Coordination." *International Organization* 46 (1): 1–35.

Hager, M. A. 2001. "Financial Vulnerability Among Arts Organizations: A Test of the Tuckman-Chang Measures." *Nonprofit and Voluntary Sector Quarterly* 30 (2): 376–392.

Hague, Rod, and Martin Harrop. 2010. *Comparative Government and Politics: An Introduction*. New York: Palgrave Macmillan.

Hall, Peter Dobkin. 1992. *Inventing the Nonprofit Sector and Other Essays on Philanthropy, Voluntarism, and Nonprofit Organizations*. Baltimore: Johns Hopkins University Press.

———. 2010. "Historical Perspectives on Nonprofit Organizations in the United States." In *The Jossey-Bass Handbook of Nonprofit Leadership and Management,* 3rd ed., edited by David Renz, 262–298. San Francisco: Jossey-Bass.

Halper, Stefan. 2012. *The Beijing Consensus: Legitimizing Authoritarianism in Our Time*. New York: Basic.

Hamilton, Clive, and Sarah Maddison. 2007. *Silencing Dissent: How the Australian Government Is Controlling Public Opinion and Stifling Debate*. Crows Nest, NSW: Allen and Unwin.

Hammack, David C., and Steven Heydemann, eds. 2009. *Globalization, Philanthropy and Civil Society: Projecting Institutional Logics Abroad*. Philanthropic and Nonprofit Studies. Bloomington: Indiana University Press.

Hansmann, Henry B. 1980. "The Role of Nonprofit Enterprise." *Yale Law Journal* 89 (5): 835–901.

———. 1987. "Economic Theories of Nonprofit Organization." In *The Nonprofit Sector: A Research Handbook*, edited by Walter W. Powell and Richard Steinberg, 27–42. New Haven, CT: Yale University Press.

Haque, M. Shamsul. 2002. "The Changing Balance of Power Between the Government and NGOs in Bangladesh." *International Political Science Review* 23 (4): 411–435.

Hewa, Soma, and Darwin H. Stapleton, eds. 2005. *Globalization, Philanthropy, and Civil Society: Toward a New Political Culture in the Twenty-First Century*. Nonprofit and Civil Society Studies. New York: Springer.

Hodgson, Lesley. 2004. "Manufactured Civil Society: Counting the Cost." *Critical Social Policy* 24 (2): 139–164.

Hofstede, Geert H. 2001. *Culture's Consequences: Comparing Values, Behavior, Institutions and Organizations Across Nations*. Thousand Oaks, CA: Sage.

Holdridge, David. 2011. "Foreign Assistance: Time for a Change." *Stanford Social Innovation Review: Civil Society Blog*. http://www.ssireview.org/blog/entry /foreign_assistance_time_for_a_change.

Home Office. 1998. "Compact on Relations Between the Government and the Voluntary and Community Sector in England." Home Office, Voluntary and Community Unit. http://www.nationalarchives.gov.uk/ERORecords/HO/421/2/P2/ACU /COMPACT.PDF.

Hudson Institute. 2010. "Too Close for Comfort? Obama and the Foundations." http://www.hudson.org/events/749-too-close-for-comfort-obama-and-the -foundations22010.

———. 2012. *Index of Global Philanthropy and Remittances 2012*. Washington, DC: Center for Global Prosperity, Hudson Institute. http://www.hudson.org /content/researchattachments/attachment/1015/2012indexofglobalphilanthropy andremittances.pdf.

———. 2013a. *Index of Global Philanthropy and Remittances 2013*. Washington, DC: Center for Global Prosperity, Hudson Institute. http://www.hudson.org /content/researchattachments/attachment/1229/2013_indexof_global_philanthropy and_remittances.pdf.

———. 2013b. *Philanthropic Freedom: A Pilot Study*. Washington, DC: Center for Global Prosperity, Hudson Institute. http://www.hudson.org/files/documents /FinalOnlineVersionPhilanthropicFreedomAPilotStudy3.pdf.

Hunter, James Davidson, and Joshua Yates. 2002. "The World of American Globalizers." In *Many Globalizations: Cultural Diversity in the Contemporary World*, edited by Peter L. Berger and Samuel P. Huntington, 323–357. New York: Oxford University Press.

Hurrell, Scott A., Chris Warhurst, and Dennis Nickson. 2011. "Giving Miss Marple a Makeover: Graduate Recruitment, Systems Failure, and the Scottish Voluntary Sector." *Nonprofit and Voluntary Sector Quarterly* 40: 336–355.

Huysentruyt, Marieke. 2011. "Development Aid by Contract: Outsourcing and Contractor Identity." London School of Economics (unpublished). http://personal.lse.ac.uk/huysentr/Development%20Aid%20by%20Contract%20%28Full%29.pdf.

Hyden, Goran. 2010. "Civil Society in Africa: Constraints and Opportunities for Democratic Change." In *Engaging Civil Society: Emerging Trends in Democratic Governance*, edited by G. Shabbir Cheema and Vesselin Popovski, 249–264. New York: United Nations University.

Incite. 2007. *The Revolution Will Not Be Funded: Beyond the Non-Profit Industrial Complex.* Cambridge, MA: South End Press.

Independent. 2012. "Animosity International: Staff on Strike in Amnesty Offices Across the Globe," November 15. http://www.independent.co.uk/news/world/politics/animosity-international-staff-on-strike-in-amnesty-offices-across-the-globe-8317303.html.

INGO Accountability Charter. 2014. "Our Accountability Commitments." http://www.ingoaccountabilitycharter.org/home/our-accountability-commitments/.

International Center for Not-for-Profit Law (ICNL). 2011a. "ICNL: Programs by Focus Area." http://www.icnl.org/programs/focus/index.htm.

———. 2011b. "NGO Law Monitor—Saudi Arabia." http://www.icnl.org/knowledge/ngolawmonitor/saudiarabia.htm.

———. 2013. "The Legal and Regulatory Framework for Civil Society." http://www.icnl.org/research/trends/trends4-2.html.

———. 2014. "Assessment Tools for Measuring Civil Society's Enabling Environment." *ICNL: Global Trends in NGO Law* (Online) 5 (1). http://www.icnl.org/research/trends/trends5-1.pdf.

International Monetary Fund. 2014. "Factsheet—Poverty Reduction Strategy Papers (PRSP)." https://www.imf.org/external/np/exr/facts/prsp.htm.

Iriye, Akira. 2002. *Global Community: The Role of International Organizations in the Making of the Contemporary World.* Berkeley: University of California Press. http://hdl.handle.net/2027/heb.90009.

Islamic Development Bank. 2005. *Report of "IDB 1440H Vision": Regional Workshop for Africa.* Jeddah, Saudi Arabia: Islamic Development Bank. http://www.isdb.org/irj/go/km/docs/documents/IDBDevelopments/Internet/English/IDB/CM/About%20IDB/IDB%201440H%20Vision/Africa_Regional_Workshop_Report.pdf.

Jackson, Ashley, and Abdi Aynte. 2013. *Talking to the Other Side: Humanitarian Negotiations with Al-Shabaab in Somalia.* Humanitarian Policy Group Working Paper. London: Overseas Development Institute. http://www.odi.org.uk/sites/odi.org.uk/files/odi-assets/publications-opinion-files/8744.pdf.

Jad, Islah. 2007. "NGOs: Between Buzzwords and Social Movements." *Development in Practice* 17 (4–5): 622–629.

James, Estelle, ed. 1989. *The Nonprofit Sector in International Perspective: Studies in Comparative Culture and Policy.* Yale Studies on Nonprofit Organizations. New York: Oxford University Press.

James, Rick. 2010. "Managing NGOs with Spirit." In *NGO Management: The Earthscan Companion*, edited by Alan Fowler and Chiku Malunga, 255–268. London: Earthscan.

Jenkins, Craig J. 2006. "Nonprofit Organizations and Policy Advocacy." In *The Nonprofit Sector: A Research Handbook*, 2nd ed., edited by Walter W. Powell and Richard Steinberg, 307–332. New Haven, CT: Yale University Press.

Jenkins, Garry. 2011. "Who's Afraid of Philanthrocapitalism?" *Case Western Reserve Law Review* 61 (3): 753–821.

Joassart-Marcelli, Pascuale. 2012. "For Whom and for What? Investigating the Role of Nonprofits as Providers to the Neediest." In *The State of Nonprofit America*, edited by Lester M. Salamon, 657–682. Washington, DC: Brookings Institution Press.

Johansson, Håkan, and Mairon Johansson. 2012. "From a 'Liberal' to a 'Social Democratic' Welfare State: The Translation of the English Compact into a Swedish Context." *Nonprofit Policy Forum* 3 (2). http://www.degruyter.com /view/j/npf.2012.3.issue-2/2154-3348.1057/2154-3348.1057.xml.

Johnston, Keith. 2012. "Acting Globally—Thinking Globally: Stepping Up to Govern an International NGO." Cultivating Leadership. http://www.cultivating leadership.co.nz/wordpress/wp-content/uploads/2012/01/Acting-Globally -Thinking-Globally-January-29-2012-CL.pdf.

Jonsson, Christer, and Jonas Tallberg, eds. 2010. *Transnational Actors in Global Governance: Patterns, Explanations, and Implications.* New York: Palgrave Macmillan.

Jordan, Grant. 2001. *Shell, Greenpeace, and the Brent Spar.* Basingstoke, UK: Palgrave.

Jordan, Lisa. 2005. *Mechanisms for NGO Accountability.* Research Paper no. 3. Global Public Policy Institute. http://www.gppi.net/fileadmin/gppi/Jordan_Lisa _05022005.pdf.

Kaldor, Mary. 2000. "'Civilising' Globalisation? The Implications of the 'Battle in Seattle.'" *Millennium—Journal of International Studies* 29 (1): 105–114.

Kanter, Rosabeth M. 2006. "How Cosmopolitan Leaders Build Confidence: A Profile of the Future." In *The Leader of the Future 2: Visions, Strategies, and Practices for the New Era,* edited by Frances Hesselbein and Marshall Goldsmith, 61–72. San Francisco: Jossey-Bass.

Karns, Margaret P., and Karen A. Mingst. 2004. *International Organizations: The Politics and Processes of Global Governance.* Boulder, CO: Lynne Rienner.

Keane, John. 2003. *Global Civil Society?* Cambridge, UK: Cambridge University Press.

Keck, Margaret E., and Kathryn Sikkink. 1999. "Transnational Advocacy Networks in International and Regional Politics." *International Social Science Journal* 51 (159): 89–101.

Kendall, Jeremy. 2003. *The Voluntary Sector: Comparative Perspectives in the UK.* London: Routledge.

———. 2009. "Beyond the Compact in England: Policy Options in a Post-Compact World." ARNOVA Annual Conference, Philanthropy in Communities: Finding Opportunity in Crisis. November 18–21, Cleveland, OH.

Keohane, Georgia Levenson. 2013. *Social Entrepreneurship for the 21st Century: Innovation Across the Nonprofit, Private, and Public Sectors.* New York: McGraw-Hill.

Kernot, Cheryl. 2010. "Social Entrepreneurs Change Bottom Line." *Newcastle Herald,* October 25. http://csi.edu.au/latest-csi-news/opinion-piece-social-entrepreneurs -change-bottom-line/.

Khagram, Sanjeev, James V. Riker, and Kathryn Sikkink. 2002. *Restructuring World Politics: Transnational Social Movements, Networks, and Norms.* Social Movements, Protest, and Contention, Vol. 14. Minneapolis: University of Minnesota Press.

Kim, Hyuk-Rae. 2003. "Unravelling Civil Society in South Korea: Old Discourses and New Visions." In *Civil Society in Asia,* edited by David Schak and Wayne Hudson, 192–208. Burlington, VT: Ashgate.

Kim, Inchoon, and Changsoon Hwang. 2002. *Defining the Nonprofit Sector: South Korea*. Working Paper no. 41. Baltimore: Center for Civil Society Studies, Johns Hopkins University. http://ccss.jhu.edu/wp-content/uploads/downloads/2011/09/Korea_CNP_WP41_2002.pdf.

Kingdon, John W. 1995. *Agendas, Alternatives, and Public Policies*. 2nd ed. New York: Longman.

Kiran, Ravi, and Anupam Sharma. 2011. "Corporate Social Responsibility: A Corporate Strategy for New Business Opportunities." *Journal of International Business Ethics* 4 (1): 10–17.

Kleiman, Kelly. 2011. "Everything Old Is New Again, and Nonprofits Should Stay That Way." *Stanford Social Innovation Review*, May 3. http://www.ssireview.org/blog/entry/everything_old_is_new_again_and_nonprofits_should_stay_that_way/.

Knoke, David. 1990. *Organizing for Collective Action: The Political Economies of Associations*. New York: Aldine de Gruyter.

Koppell, Jonathan G. S. 2008. "Global Governance Organizations: Legitimacy and Authority in Conflict." *Journal of Public Administration Research and Theory* 18 (2): 177–203.

Korn, Melissa. 2011. "M.B.A.s Choosing Nonprofits over For-Profits." *Wall Street Journal* (Online), December 1. http://online.wsj.com/article/SB10001424052970204397704577070560859827978.html.

Korten, David C. 1987. "Third Generation NGO Strategies: A Key to People-Centered Development." *World Development* 15 (Supplement): 145–159.

———. 1990. *Getting to the 21st Century: Voluntary Action and the Global Agenda*. West Hartford, CT: Kumarian.

Kouzes, James M., and Barry Z. Posner. 2007. *The Leadership Challenge: How to Keep Getting Extraordinary Things Done in Organizations*. San Francisco: Jossey-Bass.

Kramer, Ralph M. 1981. *Voluntary Agencies in the Welfare State*. Los Angeles: University of California Press.

Krause, Monika. 2014. *The Good Project: The Field of Humanitarian Relief NGOs and the Fragmentation of Reason*. Chicago: University of Chicago Press.

Kreinin Souccar, Miriam. 2011. "Philanthro-Teens Delving into Nonprofit World." *Crain's New York Business*, January 30. http://www.crainsnewyork.com/article/20110130/FREE/301309972.

Krige, John, and Helke Rausch, eds. 2012. *American Foundations and the Coproduction of World Order in the Twentieth Century*. Gottingen, Germany: Vandenhoeck and Ruprecht. http://site.ebrary.com/id/10569567.

Krut, Riva. 1997. *Globalization and Civil Society: NGO Influence in International Decision-Making*. Discussion Paper no. 83. UN Research Institute for Social Development. http://www.unrisd.org/unrisd/website/document.nsf/%28http Publications%29/87428A38D3E0403380256B650043B768?OpenDocument.

Kupchan, Charles. 2012. *No One's World: The West, the Rising Rest, and the Coming Global Turn*. New York: Oxford University Press.

Lang, Sabine. 2013. *NGOs, Civil Society, and the Public Sphere*. New York: Cambridge University Press.

Lawrence, Steven, and Christen Dobson. 2013. *Advancing Human Rights: The State of Global Foundation Grantmaking*. New York: Foundation Center. http://foundationcenter.org/gainknowledge/humanrights/.

Layton, Michael. 2009. "A Paradoxical Generosity: Resolving the Puzzle of Community Philanthropy in Mexico." *Giving: Thematic Issues on Philanthropy and Social Innovation* 1 (9): 87–101.

Lentfer, Jennifer. 2011. "Missionaries, Mercenaries & Misfits: How Two Aid Workers Came Full Circle in the Development World." *How Matters*. http://www.how-matters.org/2011/02/11/missionaries-mercenaries-misfits/.

Levermore, Roger, and Aaron Beacom, eds. 2009. *Sport and International Develop-ment*. Global Culture and Sport. Basingstoke, UK: Palgrave Macmillan.

Levi's. 2010. "Levi's Go Forth." http://us.levi.com/shop/index.jsp?categoryId=2843575 &Camp=Brand:GoForth.

Lewis, David. 2007. *The Management of Non-Governmental Development Organi-zations*. 2nd ed. London: Routledge.

———. 2014. "Heading South: Time to Abandon the 'Parallel Worlds' of Interna-tional Non-Governmental Organization (NGO) and Domestic Third Sector Scholarship?" *Voluntas* 25 (5): 1132–1150.

Light, Paul. 2000. *Making Nonprofits Work: A Report on the Tides of Nonprofit Management Reform*. Washington, DC: Brookings Institution Press.

———. 2008. *The Search for Social Entrepreneurship*. Washington, DC: Brookings Institution Press.

Lindblom, Anna-Karin. 2013. *Non-Governmental Organisations in International Law*. Cambridge, UK: Cambridge University Press.

Lindenberg, Marc, and Coralie Bryant. 2001. *Going Global: Transforming Relief and Development NGOs*. Bloomfield, CT: Kumarian.

Lindenberg, Marc, and J. Patrick Dobel. 1999. "The Challenges of Globalization for Northern International Relief and Development NGOs." *Nonprofit and Volun-tary Sector Quarterly* 28 (4): 4–24.

Lohmann, Roger. 1992. *The Commons: New Perspectives on Nonprofit Organiza-tions and Voluntary Action*. San Francisco: Jossey-Bass.

Lombardo, Michael M., and Robert W. Eichinger. 2001. *The Leadership Machine: Architecture to Develop Leaders for Any Future*. Minneapolis, MN: Lominger.

Lonely Planet. 2010. *Lonely Planet Volunteer: A Traveller's Guide to Making a Dif-ference Around the World*. London: Lonely Planet.

Lublin, Nancy. 2010. *Zilch: The Power of Zero in Business*. New York: Portfolio.

Lyon, Thomas P., ed. 2010. *Good Cop/Bad Cop: Environmental NGOs and Their Strategies Toward Business*. Washington, DC: Resources for the Future.

Lyons, Mark. 1993. "The History of Non-Profit Organizations in Australia as a Test of Some Recent Non-Profit Theory." *Voluntas* 4 (3): 301–325.

Lyons, Mark, and Bronwen Dalton. 2011. "Australia—A Continuing Love Affair with the New Public Management." In *Governance and Regulation in the Third Sector*, edited by Steven Rathgeb Smith and Susan D. Phillips, 238–259. New York: Routledge.

M4P Hub. 2013. "What Is M4P?" http://www.m4phub.org/what-is-m4p/introduction.aspx.

Macmillan, Robert, and Heather Buckingham. 2013. *A Strategic Lead for the Third Sector? Some May Lead but Not All Will Ever Follow*. Third Sector Futures Dia-logues: Big Picture Paper 5. Third Sector Research Centre. http://www.birmingham .ac.uk/generic/tsrc/documents/tsrc/news/a-strategic-lead-for-the-third-sector.pdf.

Maloney, William A., and Grant Jordan. 1997. "The Rise of the Protest Business in Britain." In *Private Groups and Public Life: Social Participation, Voluntary Associations and Political Involvement in Representative Democracies*, edited by Jan W. van Deth, 106–126. New York: Routledge.

Management Centre. 2013. "The Management Centre Launches the Big Mac Phi-lanthropy Index." http://www.managementcentre.co.uk/knowledgebase/the -management-centre-seeks-data-for-the-big-mac-philanthropy-index.

Mansfield, Heather. 2012. *Social Media for Social Good: A How-To Guide for Non-profits*. New York: McGraw-Hill.

Martin, Maximilian. 2011. *Four Revolutions in Global Philanthropy*, Vol. 1. Impact Economy Working Papers. Geneva. www.impacteconomy.com/four-revolutions -global-philanthropy.

Martin, Roger L., and Sally Osberg. 2007. "Social Entrepreneurship: The Case for Definition." *Stanford Social Innovation Review* (Spring): 29–39.

McCambridge, Ruth. 2011. "Social Entrepreneurship and Social Innovation: Are They Potentially in Conflict?" *Nonprofit Quarterly* (Online), December 25. http://www.nonprofitquarterly.org/management/18681-social-entrepreneurship -and-social-innovation-are-they-potentially-in-conflict.html.

McCarthy, John D., and Mayer N. Zald. 1977. "Resource Mobilization and Social Movements: A Partial Theory." *American Journal of Sociology* 82 (6): 1212–1241.

McCarthy, Kathleen, Virginia Ann Hodgkinson, and Russy D. Sumariwalla, eds. 1992. *The Nonprofit Sector in the Global Community: Voices from Many Nations*. San Francisco: Jossey-Bass.

McCollum, Betty. 2010. "Giving the US Nonprofit Sector a Seat at the Federal Table." http://thehill.com/blogs/congress-blog/campaign/109795-giving-the-us -nonprofit-sector-a-seat-at-the-federal-table-rep-betty-mccollum.

McGregor-Lowndes, Myles, and Emma Pelling. 2013. *An Examination of Tax Deductible Donations Made by Individual Australian Taxpayers in 2010–2011*. Working Paper No. ACPNS 60. Brisbane: Australian Centre for Philanthropy and Nonprofit Studies, Queensland University of Technology.

McKinsey and Company. 2009. "Valuing Corporate Social Responsibility—McKinsey Global Survey Results." http://www.mckinseyquarterly.com/Valuing_corporate _social_responsibility_McKinsey_Global_Survey_Results_2309.

Mendel, Stuart. 2011. "Book Review: Thomas Adam. Buying Respectability: Philanthropy and Urban Society in Transnational Perspective, 1840s to 1930s." *Nonprofit and Voluntary Sector Quarterly* 40 (March): 404–406.

Meyer, David S., and Douglas R. Imig. 1993. "Political Opportunity and the Rise and Decline of Interest Group Sectors." *Social Science Journal* 30 (3): 253–270.

Michael, Sarah. 2002. *The Role of NGOs in Human Security*. Working Paper No. 12. Cambridge, MA: Hauser Center for Nonprofit Organizations, Kennedy School of Government, Harvard University.

Minkoff, Debra C. 1994. "From Service Provision to Institutional Advocacy: The Shifting Legitimacy of Organizational Forms." *Social Forces* 72 (4): 943–969.

Mirabella, Roseanne M. 2014. "Nonprofit Management Education." http://academic .shu.edu/npo/list.php?sort=degree&type=gconc.

Mirabella, Roseanne M., Giuliana Gemelli, Margy-Jean Malcolm, and Gabriel Berger. 2007. "Nonprofit and Philanthropic Studies: International Overview of the Field in Africa, Canada, Latin America, Asia, the Pacific, and Europe." *Nonprofit and Voluntary Sector Quarterly* 36 (4 Supplement): 110S–135S.

Missoni, Eduardo, and Daniele Alesani. 2013. *Management of International Institutions and NGOs: Frameworks, Practices and Challenges*. Abingdon, UK: Routledge.

Moog, Sandra. 2009. "Exporting Institutional Logics into the Amazon? American and German Efforts to Protect the Ecosystem and Traditional Peoples of the Amazon Basin." In *Globalization, Philanthropy, and Civil Society: Projecting Institutional Logics Abroad*, edited by David C. Hammack and Steven Heydemann, 258–292. Philanthropic and Nonprofit Studies. Bloomington: Indiana University Press.

Moore, David, and Douglas Rutzen. 2011. "Legal Framework for Global Philanthropy: Barriers and Opportunities." *International Journal of Not-for-Profit Law* 13 (1–2): 5–41.

Morgenthau, Hans. 1962. "A Political Theory of Foreign Aid." *American Political Science Review* 56 (2): 301.

Mortenson, Greg. 2006. *Three Cups of Tea: One Man's Mission to Fight Terrorism and Build Nations—One School at a Time.* New York: Viking.

———. 2009. *Stones into Schools: Promoting Peace with Books, Not Bombs, in Afghanistan and Pakistan.* New York: Viking.

Mosse, David. 2011. *Adventures in Aidland: The Anthropology of Professionals in International Development.* Oxford, UK: Berghann.

Moyo, Dambisa. 2009. *Dead Aid: Why Aid Is Not Working and How There Is a Better Way for Africa.* New York: Farrar, Straus, and Giroux.

———. 2012. "Beijing, a Boon for Africa." *New York Times* (Online), June 27. http://www.nytimes.com/2012/06/28/opinion/beijing-a-boon-for-africa.html.

Mozilla Foundation. 2013. "The Mozilla Manifesto." http://www.mozilla.org/en-US/about/manifesto/.

Muukkonen, Martti. 2002. *Ecumenism of the Laity: Continuity and Change in the Mission View of the World's Alliance of Young Men's Christian Associations, 1855–1955.* Joensuun Yliopiston Teologisia Julkaisuja, no. 7. Joensuu, Finland: University of Joensuu.

———. 2009. "Framing the Field: Civil Society and Related Concepts." *Nonprofit and Voluntary Sector Quarterly* 38 (4): 684–700.

Najam, Adil. 1996. "Understanding the Third Sector: Revisiting the Prince, the Merchant, and the Citizen." *Nonprofit Management and Leadership* 7 (2): 203–219.

———. 2000. "The Four C's of Government: Third Sector–Government Relations." *Nonprofit Management and Leadership* 10 (4): 375–396.

Nash, Mathew T. A. 2010. "Social Entrepreneurship and Social Enterprise." In *The Jossey-Bass Handbook of Nonprofit Leadership and Management*, 3rd ed., edited by David Renz, 262–298. San Francisco: Jossey-Bass.

National Center for Charitable Statistics. 2012. "Registered International Nonprofit Organizations by Level of Total Revenue." http://nccsdataweb.urban.org/NCCS/V1Pub/index.php.

———. 2014. "Registered Nonprofit Organizations." http://nccsdataweb.urban.org/tablewiz/tw_bmf.php.

Neal, Alan C. 2008. "Corporate Social Responsibility: Governance Gain or Laissez-Faire Figleaf?" *Comparative Labor Law and Policy* 29 (4): 459–474.

Newsom, Gavin Christopher, and Lisa Dickey. 2014. *Citizenville: How to Take the Town Square Digital and Reinvent Government.* New York: Penguin.

Newton, Kenneth. 1997. "Social Capital and Democracy." *American Behavioral Scientist* 40 (5): 574–585.

New York Times. 2008. "Faces of Social Entrepreneurship." March 9. http://www.nytimes.com/slideshow/2008/03/09/magazine/0309-FACES_index.html.

NGO Monitor. 2015. "About NGO Monitor." http://www.ngo-monitor.org/articles.php?type=about.

Nicholls, Alex, and Alexander Murdock. 2012. "The Nature of Social Innovation." In *Social Innovation: Blurring Boundaries to Reconfigure Markets*, edited by Alex Nicholls and Alexander Murdock, 1–32. Basingstoke, UK: Palgrave Macmillan.

Nickel, Patricia M., and Angela M. Eikenberry. 2009. "A Critique of the Discourse of Marketized Philanthropy." *American Behavioral Scientist* 52 (7): 974–989.

Odendahl, Teresa, and Michael O'Neill, eds. 1994. *Women and Power in the Nonprofit Sector.* San Francisco: Jossey-Bass.

Offe, Claus. 2000. "Civil Society and Social Order: Demarcating and Combining Market, State and Community." *European Journal of Sociology* 41 (1): 71.

Olson, Mancur. 1965. *The Logic of Collective Action.* Cambridge, MA: Harvard University Press.

Omidyar Network. 2013. "Omidyar Network: About Us." http://www.omidyar.com /about_us.

O'Neill, Michael. 2002. *Nonprofit Nation: A New Look at the Third America.* 2nd ed. San Francisco: Jossey-Bass.

Open Forum for CSO Development Effectiveness. 2013. "International Framework— Open Forum for CSO Development Effectiveness." http://cso-effectiveness .org/InternationalFramework.

Organisation for Economic Co-operation and Development (OECD). 2011. "DAC List of ODA Recipients Used for 2008, 2009 and 2010 Flows." http://www.oecd .org/document/45/0,2340,en_2649_34447_2093101_1_1_1_1,00.html.

———. 2013a. "Aid Statistics—Charts, Table and Databases." http://www.oecd .org/dac/stats/data.htm.

———. 2013b. "Aid Statistics—Resource Flows to Developing Countries." http://www .oecd.org/development/stats/statisticsonresourceflowstodevelopingcountries .htm.

Orozco, Manuel. 2008. "Diasporas and Development: Issues and Impediments." In *Diasporas and Development: Exploring the Potential*, edited by Jennifer M. Brinkerhoff, 207–230. Boulder, CO: Lynne Rienner.

Osborne, Stephen, and Kate McLaughlin. 2002. "Trends and Issues in the Implementation of Local 'Voluntary Sector Compacts' in England." *Public Money and Management* 22: 55–64.

Osland, Joyce. 2008. "Overview of the Global Leadership Literature." In *Global Leadership: Research, Practice, and Development*, 40–79. Routledge Global Human Resource Management Series. London: Routledge.

Oster, Sharon. 1996. "Nonprofit Organizations and Their Local Affiliates: A Study in Organizational Forms." *Journal of Economic Behavior and Organization* 30 (1): 83–95.

Page, Susan. 2013. "Poll: Public Service Valued; Politics—Not so Much." *USA Today*, July 22. http://www.usatoday.com/story/news/nation/2013/07/21/public -service-valued-politics—not-so-much/2573743/.

Paletta, Anthony. 2010. "The Fawning of the Foundations as Philanthropists Pledge Allegiance to the Administration's Political Agenda." *Wall Street Journal* (Online), April 30. http://online.wsj.com/news/articles/SB1000142405274870 4471204575210751254846816.

Panel on the Independence of the Voluntary Sector. 2012. *Protecting Independence: The Voluntary Sector in 2012*. http://www.independencepanel.org.uk/wp-content /uploads/2012/01/Protecting-Independence-final.pdf.

Pearson, Kate. 2004. "Creating a Board Without Borders." *Association Management* 56 (1): 87–88.

Pestoff, Victor. 2009. *A Democratic Architecture for the Welfare State*. Routledge Studies in the Management of Voluntary and Non-Profit Organizations No. 11. London: Routledge.

Pestoff, Victor, and Taco Brandsen. 2010. "Public Governance and the Third Sector: Opportunities for Co-Production and Innovation?" In *The New Public Governance? Emerging Perspectives on the Theory and Practice of Public Governance*, edited by Stephen Osborne, 270–300. London: Routledge.

Pfeffer, Jeffrey, and Gerald R. Salancik. 1978. *The External Control of Organizations: A Resource Dependence Perspective*. New York: Harper and Row.

Popovski, Vesselin. 2010. "The Role of Civil Society in Global Governance." In *Engaging Civil Society: Emerging Trends in Democratic Governance*, edited by G. Shabbir Cheema and Vesselin Popovski, 23–43. New York: United Nations University.

Posner, Barry Z. 2011. *The Impact of Leadership Practices Within Cultures.* http://www.leadershipchallenge.com/UserFiles/ATE0212_CrossCulturalMgt Paper.pdf.

Prahalad, Coimbatore K. 2006. *The Fortune at the Bottom of the Pyramid.* Delhi, India: Dorling Kindersley.

Pryor, Frederic L. 2012. "Determinants of the Size of the Nonprofit Sector." *European Journal of Comparative Economics* 9 (3): 337–348.

Public Broadcasting Service (PBS). 2005a. "The New Heroes." http://www.pbs.org /opb/thenewheroes/.

———. 2005b. "The New Heroes. What Is Social Entrepreneurship?" http://www .pbs.org/opb/thenewheroes/whatis/.

Putnam, Robert. 1993. *Making Democracy Work: Civic Tradition in Modern Italy.* Princeton, NJ: Princeton University Press.

Read, Benjamin L. 2012. "State-Linked Associational Life: Illuminating Blind Spots of Existing Paradigms (Reprinted from 2003)." In *The Nature of the Nonprofit Sector*, 2nd ed., edited by J. Steven Ott and Lisa A. Dicke, 385–401. Philadelphia: Westview.

Reinalda, Bob, ed. 2011. *The Ashgate Research Companion to Non-State Actors.* Burlington, VT: Ashgate.

Reinicke, Wolfgang H. 1998. *Global Public Policy: Governing Without Government?* Washington, DC: Brookings Institution Press.

Reuter, Marta, Filip Wijkström, and Johan von Essen. 2012. "Policy Tools or Mirrors of Politics. Government-Voluntary Sector Compacts in the Post-Welfare State Age." *Nonprofit Policy Forum* 3 (2). http://www.degruyter.com/view /j/npf.2012.3.issue-2/2154-3348.1062/2154-3348.1062.xml.

Rey, Marta, and Luis I. Alvarez. 2011. "Foundations and Social Economy: Conceptual Approaches and Socio-Economic Relevance." *Revista de Economía Pública, Social Y Cooperativa*, no. 73: 61–80.

Rich, Richard. 1988. "A Cooperative Approach to the Logic of Collective Action: Voluntary Organizations and the Prisoners' Dilemma." *Journal of Voluntary Action Research* 17 (3–4): 5–18.

Richardson, Jeremy J., ed. 1993. *Pressure Groups.* Oxford: Oxford University Press.

Richter, James, and Walter F. Hatch. 2013. "Organizing Civil Society in Russia and China: A Comparative Approach." *International Journal of Politics, Culture, and Society* 26 (4): 323–347.

Richter, Linda M., and Amy Norman. 2010. "Aids Orphan Tourism: A Threat to Young Children in Residential Care." *Vulnerable Children and Youth Studies* 5 (3): 217–229.

Rifkin, Jeremy. 2014. *The Zero Marginal Cost Society: The Internet of Things, the Collaborative Commons, and the Eclipse of Capitalism.* New York: Palgrave Macmillan.

Roberts, Susan M., John Paul Jones, and Oliver Fröhling. 2005. "NGOs and the Globalization of Managerialism: A Research Framework." *World Development* 33 (11): 1845–1864.

Robertson, D. B., ed. 1966. *Voluntary Associations: A Study of Groups in Free Societies; Essays in Honor of James Luther Adams.* Louisville, KY: John Knox.

Roelofs, Joan. 1987. "Foundations and Public Policy: The Mask of Pluralism." *Insurgent Sociologist* 14 (3): 31–72.

———. 2003. *Foundations and Public Policy: The Mask of Pluralism.* New York: SUNY Press.

———. 2006. "Why They Hate Our Kind Hearts, Too." *CounterPunch*, May 13–14. http://www.counterpunch.org/roelofs05132006.html.

Ronalds, Paul. 2010. *The Change Imperative: Creating the Next Generation NGO.* Boulder, CO: Kumarian.

Rosenman, Mark. 2011. "Calling All Boomers: Don't Start More Nonprofits." *Chronicle of Philanthropy.* http://philanthropy.com/article/Calling-All-Boomers -Don-t/157505.

Rutzen, Douglas. 2015. "Aid Barriers and the Rise of Philanthropic Protectionism." *International Journal of Not-for-Profit Law* 17 (1): 5–44.

Saidel, Janet R. 1991. "Resource Interdependence: The Relationship Between State Agencies and Nonprofit Organizations." *Public Administration Review* 51 (6): 543–553.

———. 2011. "Proxy-Partnership Governance Continuum: Implications for Non-profit Managers." In *The State of Public Administration: Issues, Challenges, and Opportunities*, edited by Donald C. Menzel and Harvey L. White, 156–170. Armonk, NY: M. E. Sharpe.

Salamon, Lester M. 1987. "Of Market Failure, Voluntary Failure, and Third-Party Government: Toward a Theory of Government-Nonprofit Relations in the Modern Welfare State." *Nonprofit and Voluntary Sector Quarterly* 16 (1–2): 29–49.

———. 1994. "The Rise of the Nonprofit Sector." *Foreign Affairs*, no. 1 (July). http://www.foreignaffairs.com/articles/50105/lester-m-salamon/the-rise-of-the -nonprofit-sector.

———. 1995. *Partners in Public Service.* Baltimore: Johns Hopkins University Press.

———, ed. 1999. *Global Civil Society.* Baltimore: Johns Hopkins Center for Civil Society Studies.

———. 2002a. *The Tools of Government: A Guide to the New Governance.* Oxford, UK: Oxford University Press.

———. 2002b. *Explaining Nonprofit Advocacy: An Exploratory Analysis.* Working Paper no. 21. Baltimore: Center for Civil Society Studies, Johns Hopkins University. http://www.jhu.edu/~ccss/publications/ccsswork/workingpaper21.pdf.

———. 2006. "Government-Nonprofit Relations from an International Perspective." In *Nonprofits and Government: Collaboration and Conflict*, 2nd ed., edited by Elizabeth T. Boris and C. Eugene Steuerle, 399–436. Washington, DC: Urban Institute Press.

———. 2010. "Putting the Civil Society Sector on the Economic Map of the World." *Annals of Public and Cooperative Economics* 81 (2): 167–210.

Salamon, Lester M., and Helmut Anheier. 1992a. "In Search of the Non-Profit Sector. I: The Question of Definitions." *Voluntas* 3 (2): 125–151.

———. 1992b. "In Search of the Non-Profit Sector II: The Problem of Classification." *Voluntas* 3 (3): 267–309.

———. 1997. *Defining the Non-Profit Sector: A Cross-National Analysis.* New York: Manchester University Press.

———. 1998. "Social Origins of Civil Society: Explaining the Nonprofit Sector Cross-Nationally." *Voluntas* 9 (3): 213–248.

Salamon, Lester M, Helmut K. Anheier, Regina List, Stefan Toepler, and S. Wojciech Sokolowski. 1999. *Global Civil Society.* The Johns Hopkins Comparative Nonprofit Sector Project. Baltimore: Johns Hopkins Center for Civil Society Studies. http://ccss.jhu.edu/publications-findings?did=47.

Salamon, Lester M., and Stephanie L. Geller. 2008. *Nonprofit America: A Force for Democracy?* Listening Post Project, Communiquè no. 9. Baltimore: Center for Civil Society Studies, Johns Hopkins University. http://www.clpi.org/images /pdf/advocacy%20communique%20final%207-30-08.pdf.

Salamon, Lester M., and S. Wojciech Sokolowski, eds. 2010. *Global Civil Society: Dimensions of the Nonprofit Sector.* 3rd ed. Bloomfield, VT: Kumarian.

Salamon, Lester M., S. Wojciech Sokolowski, and Regina List. 2003. *Global Civil Society: An Overview*. Baltimore: Center for Civil Society Studies, Johns Hopkins University.

Salamon, Lester M., and Stefan Toepler. 1997. *The International Guide to Nonprofit Law*. New York: Wiley.

Sankore, Rotimi. 2005. "What Are the NGOs Doing?" *New African*, no. 443 (September): 12–15.

Schak, David, and Wayne Hudson, eds. 2003. *Civil Society in Asia*. Burlington, VT: Ashgate.

Schechter, Michael G. 2010. *Historical Dictionary of International Organizations*. Lanham, MD: Scarecrow.

Scher, Daniel, and Christine MacAulay. 2010. *The Promise of Imihigo: Decentralized Service Delivery in Rwanda, 2006–2010*. Innovations for Successful Societies. Princeton University. http://www.princeton.edu/successfulsocieties/content /data/policy_note/PN_id133/Policy_Note_ID133.pdf.

Selznick, Philip. 1996. "Institutionalism 'Old' and 'New.'" *Administrative Science Quarterly* 41 (2): 270–277.

Shah, Iqbal. 2012. *A Practical Guide to NGO and Project Management*. Kindle Edition. Amazon Digital Services.

Shane, Scott A. 2008. *The Illusions of Entrepreneurship: The Costly Myths That Entrepreneurs, Investors, and Policy Makers Live By*. New Haven, CT: Yale University Press.

Sherlock, Molly F., and Jane G. Gravelle. 2009. *An Overview of the Nonprofit and Charitable Sector*. RS Report for Congress 7-5700. Washington, DC: Congressional Research Office. www.fas.org/sgp/crs/misc/R40919.pdf.

Shirky, Clay. 2008. *Here Comes Everybody: The Power of Organizing Without Organizations*. New York: Penguin.

Shivji, Issa G. 2007. *Silences in NGO Discourse: The Role and Future of NGOs in Africa*. Nairobi: Fahamu.

Sidel, Mark. 2010. *Regulation of the Voluntary Sector: Freedom and Security in an Era of Uncertainty*. Critical Approaches to Law. New York: Routledge.

Siméant, Johanna. 2005. "What Is Going Global? The Internationalization of French NGOs 'Without Borders.'" *Review of International Political Economy* 12 (5): 851–883.

Sinclair, Hugh. 2012. *Confessions of a Microfinance Heretic: How Microlending Lost Its Way and Betrayed the Poor*. San Francisco: Berrett-Koehler.

Skocpol, Theda. 2011. "Civil Society in the United States." In *The Oxford Handbook of Civil Society*, edited by Michael Edwards, 109–121. New York: Oxford University Press.

Slaughter, Anne-Marie. 2011. "Problems Will Be Global—And Solutions Will Be, Too." *Foreign Policy*, September/October. http://www.foreignpolicy.com/articles /2011/08/15/problems_will_be_global_and_solutions_will_be_too.

Smith, Constance E., and Anne E. Freedman. 1972. *Voluntary Associations: Perspectives on the Literature*. Cambridge, MA: Harvard University Press.

Smith, David Horton. 1981. "Altruism, Volunteers, and Volunteerism." *Nonprofit and Voluntary Sector Quarterly* 10 (1): 21–36.

———. 1997. "The Rest of the Nonprofit Sector: Grassroots Associations as the Dark Matter Ignored in Prevailing 'Flat Earth' Maps of the Sector." *Nonprofit and Voluntary Sector Quarterly* 26 (2): 114–131.

———. 2008. "Accepting and Understanding the 'Dark Side' of the Nonprofit Sector: One Key Part of Building a Healthier Civil Society." http://www.david hortonsmithinternational.com/assets/documents/ARN08.DHSmith.pdf.

————. 2010. "Grassroots Associations." In *International Encyclopedia of Civil Society*, edited by Helmut Anheier and Stephan Toepler, 804–810. New York: Springer.

————. 2012. "The Impact of the Voluntary Sector on Society." In *The Nature of the Nonprofit Sector*, 2nd ed., edited by J. Steven Ott and Lisa A. Dicke, 71–87. Philadelphia: Westview.

————. 2014. "Growth of Research Associations and Journals in the Emerging Discipline of Altruistics." *Nonprofit and Voluntary Sector Quarterly* 43 (4): 638–656.

Smith, Steven Rathgeb. 2012. "Government-Voluntary Sector Compacts Reconsidered." *Nonprofit Policy Forum* 3 (2). http://www.degruyter.com/view/j/npf.2012.3.issue-2/2154-3348.1064/2154-3348.1064.xm.

Smith, Steven Rathgeb, and Kirsten A. Grønbjerg. 2006. "Scope and Theory of Government-Nonprofit Relations." In *The Nonprofit Sector: A Research Handbook*, 2nd ed., edited by Walter W. Powell and Richard Steinberg, 221–242. New Haven, CT: Yale University Press.

Sparke, Matthew. 2013. *Introducing Globalization: Ties, Tension, and Uneven Integration*. Malden, MA: Wiley-Blackwell.

Spero, Joan E. 2010. *The Global Role of U.S. Foundations*. New York: Foundation Center.

Stares, Sally, Sean Deel, and Jill Timms. 2012. "Bordering on the Unknown: Approaches to Global Civil Society Data." In *Global Civil Society 2012: Ten Years of Critical Reflection*, edited by Mary Kaldor, Henrietta L. Moore, and Sabine Selchow, 184–203. London: Sage.

Steinberg, Richard. 2006. "Economic Theories of Nonprofit Organizations." In *The Nonprofit Sector: A Research Handbook*, 2nd ed., edited by Walter W. Powell and Richard Steinberg, 333–351. New Haven, CT: Yale University Press.

Stoddard, Abby, Adele Harmer, and Morgan Hughes. 2012. *Aid Worker Security Report 2012*. The Aid Worker Security Database, Humanitarian Outcomes. http://www.humanitarianoutcomes.org/sites/default/files/resources/AidWorkerSecurityReport20126.pdf.

Streek, Wolfgang, and Philippe C. Schmitter. 1986. "Community, Market, State—and Associations? The Prospective Contribution of Interest Governance to Social Order." In *Private Interest Government: Beyond Market and State*, edited by Wolfgang Streek and Phillipe C. Schmitter, 1–29. London: Sage.

Stroup, Sarah S. 2008. "National Diversity and Global Activism: INGOs, States, and Country of Origin Effects." In *Conference Papers—International Studies Association*, 49th Annual Conference, San Franciso, March 26, 1–44.

————. 2012. *Borders Among Activists: International NGOs in the United States, Britain, and France*. Ithaca, NY: Cornell University Press.

Sugden, John Peter, and Alan Tomlinson. 1998. *FIFA and the Contest for World Football: Who Rules the People's Game?* Cambridge, UK: Polity.

Suleiman, Lina. 2013. "The NGOs and the Grand Illusions of Development and Democracy." *Voluntas* 24 (1): 241–261.

Tanaka, Masako. 2010. "The Changing Roles of NGOs in Nepal: Promoting Emerging Rights-Holder Organizations for Inclusive Aid." *Voluntas*, December. http://www.springerlink.com/index/10.1007/s11266-010-9173-1.

Tarrow, Sidney. 1994. *Power in Movement*. Cambridge, UK: Cambridge University Press.

Taylor, Marilyn. 2010. "Transforming Democracy?" In *Third Sector Research*, edited by Rupert Taylor, 235–252. New York: Springer.

Taylor, Marilyn, Joanna Howard, Vicki Harris, John Lever, Antaoneeta Mateeva, Christopher Miller, Rumen Petrov, and Luis Serra. 2009. "Dilemmas of Engage-

ment: The Experience of Non-Governmental Actors in New Governance Spaces."
Non-Government Public Action Programme, London School of Economics.
http://www2.lse.ac.uk/internationalDevelopment/research/NGPA/publications
/ngpa_wp31.aspx.

Taylor, Rupert, ed. 2010. *Third Sector Research*. New York: Springer.

Teasdale, Simon. 2010. "What's in a Name? The Construction of Social Enterprise."
Third Sector Research Center, Working Paper No. 46. http://www.tsrc.ac.uk
/Research/SocialEnterprise/Whatsinaname/tabid/749/Default.aspx.

TechSoup Global. 2013. "The 'BRIDGE' Project—A New Data Base of 3 Million
NGOs." http://www.techsoupglobal.org/The%20BRIDGE%20Project%20A%
20New%20Data%20Base%20of%203%20Million%20NGOs.

TercerSector.net. 2011. "Temes Clau per Enfortir Les Organitzacions No Lucrati-
ves." http://www.tercersector.net/?p=640&lang=ca.

Themudo, Nuno S. 2013. *Nonprofits in Crisis: Economic Development, Risk, and
the Philanthropic Kuznets Curve*. Philanthropic and Nonprofit Studies. Bloomington: Indiana University Press.

Third Sector. 2013. "Home Page." http://www.thirdsector.co.uk/.

Thomas, Clive S. 1993. *First World Interest Groups: A Comparative Perspective*.
Westport, CT: Greenwood.

Tiessen, Rebecca. 2011. "Global Subjects or Objects of Globalisation? The Promotion of Global Citizenship in Organisations Offering Sport for Development
and/or Peace Programmes." *Third World Quarterly* 32 (3): 571–587.

Turley, James. 2010. "The New Global Mindset." *Bloomberg Businessweek* (Online).
http://www.businessweek.com/managing/content/jan2010/ca20100126_437043
.htm.

Tvedt, Terje. 1998. *Angels of Mercy or Development Diplomats? NGOs and Foreign Aid*. Trenton, NJ: Africa World Press.

————. 2006. "The International Aid System and the Non-Governmental Organisations: A New Research Agenda." *Journal of International Development* 18 (5):
677–690.

"Ubuntu in Evaluation." 2013. *Better Evaluation Blog*. http://betterevaluation.org
/blog/ubuntu_in_evaluation.

Ullman, Claire. 1998. *The Welfare State's Other Crisis: Explaining the New Partnership Between Nonprofit Organizations and the State in France*. Bloomington: Indiana University Press.

UN Department of Economic and Social Affairs. 2014. "United Nations Civil Society Participation (iCSO)." http://esango.un.org/civilsociety/login.do.

UN Development Programme. 2004. *Unleashing Entrepreneurship: Making Business Work for the Poor*. New York: UNDP Commission on the Private Sector
and Development. http://web.undp.org/cpsd/report/index.html.

UN Global Compact. 2013. "The Ten Principles." http://www.unglobalcompact
.org/AboutTheGC/TheTenPrinciples/index.html.

Union of International Associations. 2012. *Yearbook of International Organizations*.
Leiden, Netherlands: Brill.

United Nations. 2003. *Handbook on Non-Profit Institutions in the System of
National Accounts*. ST/ESA/STAT/SER.F/91. New York: UN Department of
Economic and Social Affairs.

————. 2004. *Report of the Panel of Eminent Persons on United Nations–Civil
Society Relations*. A/58/817. New York: UN General Assembly.

————. 2011. *Accelerating Progress Towards the Millennium Development Goals:
Options for Sustained and Inclusive Growth and Issues for Advancing the United
Nations Development Agenda Beyond 2015: Annual Report of the Secretary-
General*. A/66/126. New York: UN General Assembly.

————. 2012. "UN Officials Highlight Costs of Corruption on Societies." http://www.un .org/apps/news/story.asp?NewsID=42430.

————. 2013. *Resolution Adopted by the General Assembly: International Day of Charity*. A/RES/67/105. New York: UN General Assembly.

————. 2014. "Department of Public Information: NGOs." http://outreach.un.org /ngorelations/.

UN Office of the High Commissioner for Human Rights. 2011. *Guiding Principles on Business and Human Rights*. HR/PUB/11/04. United Nations. http://www .ohchr.org/Documents/Publications/GuidingPrinciplesBusinessHR_EN.pdf.

UN Volunteers. 2011. *State of the World's Volunteerism Report, 2011 Universal Values for Global Well-Being*. Bonn, Germany: UN Volunteers. http://www.unv .org/swvr2011.html.

US Agency for International Development (USAID). 2011a. "USAID: Europe and Eurasia: The NGO Sustainability Index." http://www.usaid.gov/locations/europe _eurasia/dem_gov/ngoindex/.

————. 2011b. "USAID: NGO Sustainability Index for Sub-Saharan Africa." http://www.usaid.gov/our_work/democracy_and_governance/technical_areas /civil_society/angosi/.

————. 2013. "Top 40 Vendors." http://www.usaid.gov/results-and-data/budget -spending/top-40-vendors.

Vallory, Eduard. 2012. *World Scouting: Educating for Global Citizenship*. New York: Palgrave Macmillan.

Van Huijstee, Mariette, and Pieter Glasbergen. 2010. "Business-NGO Interactions in a Multi-Stakeholder Context." *Business and Society Review* 115 (3): 249–284.

Van Til, Jon. 2008. *Growing Civil Society: From Nonprofit Sector to Third Space*. Philanthropic and Nonprofit Studies. Bloomington: Indiana University Press.

Walker, James W. St. G., and Andrew S. Thompson, eds. 2008. *Critical Mass: The Emergence of Global Civil Society*. Waterloo, ON: Wilfrid Laurier University Press.

Wallace, Michael, and J. Craig Jenkins. 1995. "The New Class, Postindustrialism, and Neocorporatism: Three Images of Social Protest in Western Democracies." In *The Politics of Social Protest*, edited by J. Craig Jenkins and Bert Klandermans, 96–137. Minneapolis: Minnesota University Press.

Wallace, Tina. 2003. "NGO Dilemmas: Trojan Horses for Global Neoliberalism." In *Socialist Register 2004*, 202–219. London: Merlin.

Wallace, Tina, Lisa Bornstein, and Jennifer Chapman. 2007. *The Aid Chain: Coercion and Commitment in Development NGOs*. Rugby, UK: Practical Action.

Walzer, Michael. 1992. *The Civil Society Argument*. London: Verso.

————. 1998. *Toward a Global Civil Society*. Providence, RI: Berghahn.

Warburton, Jeni, and Jennifer Smith. 2003. "Out of the Generosity of Your Heart: Are We Creating Active Citizens Through Compulsory Volunteer Programmes for Young People in Australia?" *Social Policy and Administration* 37 (7): 772–786.

Washington Post. 2014. "Hungary's Prime Minister a Champion for Illiberalism." August 6. http://www.washingtonpost.com/opinions/harold-meyerson-hungarys -prime-minister-is-a-champion-of-illiberalism/2014/08/06/143a53ae-1d9d -11e4-82f9-2cd6fa8da5c4_story.html.

Wearing, Stephen, and Nancy Gard McGehee. 2013. "Volunteer Tourism: A Review." *Tourism Management* 38: 120–130.

Weisbrod, Burton A. 1977. *The Voluntary Nonprofit Sector: An Economic Analysis*. Lexington, MA: Lexington.

————. 1988. *The Nonprofit Economy*. Cambridge, UK: Harvard University Press.

Wei-Skillern, Jane, James E. Austin, Herman Leonard, and Howard Stevenson. 2007. *Entrepreneurship in the Social Sector*. Los Angeles: Sage.

Weiss, Meredith, and Saliha Hassan. 2003. *Social Movements in Malaysia: From Moral Communities to NGOs*. London: Routledge Curzon.

Weiss, Thomas G. 2013. *Humanitarian Business*. Cambridge, UK: Polity.

Weiss, Thomas G., Tatiana Carayannis, and Richard Jolly. 2009. "The 'Third' United Nations." *Global Governance* 15: 123–142.

Wiggins, Kaye. 2011. "Panel Underestimates Threat to Charities' Independence, Campaign Group Says." *Third Sector* (Online). http://www.thirdsector.co.uk /panel-underestimates-threat-charities-independence-campaign-group -says/infrastructure/article/1097770.

Willetts, Peter. 2011. *Non-Governmental Organizations in World Politics: The Construction of Global Governance*. Routledge Global Institutions Series No. 49. New York: Routledge.

Wilson, Graham K. 1990. *Interest Groups*. Oxford, UK: Basil Blackwell.

Wilson-Grau, Ricardo, and Heather Britt. 2013. *Outcome Harvesting*. Cairo: Ford Foundation's Middle East and North Africa Office. http://www.outcomemapping .ca/download.php?file=/resource/files/wilsongrau_en_OutcomeHarvestingBrief _revisedNov2013.pdf.

Winston, Morton. 2002. "NGO Strategies for Promoting Corporate Social Responsibility." *Ethics and International Affairs* 16 (1): 71–87.

Wolch, Jennifer R. 1990. *The Shadow State: Government and Voluntary Sector in Transition*. New York: Foundation Center.

Wong, Wendy H. 2012. *Internal Affairs: How the Structure of NGOs Transforms Human Rights*. Ithaca, NY: Cornell University Press.

Wood, John. 2007. *Leaving Microsoft to Change the World: An Entrepreneur's Odyssey to Educate the World's Children*. New York: Collins.

———. 2013. *Creating Room to Read: A Story of Hope in the Battle for Global Literacy*. New York: Viking Penguin.

World Bank. 2013. *Migration and Remittance Flows: Recent Trends and Outlook, 2013–2016*. Migration and Development Brief No. 21. http://siteresources .worldbank.org/INTPROSPECTS/Resources/334934-1288990760745/Migration andDevelopmentBrief21.pdf.

World Values Survey. 2011. "The World Values Survey Cultural Map of the World." http://www.worldvaluessurvey.org/wvs/articles/folder_published/article_base_54.

———. 2013. "Word Values Survey—Organization." http://www.worldvaluessurvey .org/index_organization.

WorldWork Ltd. 2010. "International Competency Set." http://www.worldwork.biz /legacy/www/docs3/competencies.html.

Young, Dennis R. 2006. "Complementary, Supplementary, or Adversarial?" In *Nonprofits and Government: Collaboration and Conflict*, 2nd ed., edited by Elizabeth T. Boris and C. Eugene Steuerle, 37–80. Washington, DC: Urban Institute Press.

Young, Dennis R., Bonnie L. Koenig, Adil Najam, and Julie Fisher. 1999. "Strategy and Structure in Managing Global Associations." *Voluntas* 10 (4): 323–343.

Zadek, Simon. 2011. "Civil Society and the Market." In *The Oxford Handbook of Civil Society*, edited by Michael Edwards, 428–440. New York: Oxford University Press.

Zakaria, Fareed. 2009. *The Post-American World*. New York: W. W. Norton.

Index

About the Book

John Casey explores the expanding global reach of nonprofit organizations, examining the increasingly influential role not only of prominent NGOs that work on hot-button global issues, but also of the thousands of smaller, little-known organizations that have an impact on people's daily lives.

What do these nonprofits actually do? How and why have they grown exponentially? How are they managed and funded? What organizational, political, and economic challenges do they face? Casey answers these questions and also, liberally using case studies, situates the evolution of the sector in the broader contexts of differing national environments and global public affairs.

With its broad perspective, *The Nonprofit World* affords readers a thorough understanding of both the place of nonprofits in the global arena and the implications of their growing importance.

John Casey is associate professor in the School of Public Affairs at Baruch College, City University of New York. His previous publications include *Policing the World: The Practice of International and Transnational Policing.*